Allez, viens!®
En route!

HOLT FRENCH

LEVEL 1B

HOLT, RINEHART AND WINSTON

A Harcourt Education Company

Austin • Orlando • Chicago • New York • Toronto • London • San Diego

ASSOCIATE DIRECTOR
Barbara Kristof

EXECUTIVE EDITOR
Priscilla Blanton

SENIOR EDITORS
Marion Bermondy
Jaishree Venkatesan

ASSOCIATE MANAGING EDITOR
Amber P. Martin

EDITORIAL STAFF
Yamilé Dewailly
Virginia Dosher
Ruthie Ford
Serge Laîné
Géraldine Touzeau-Patrick
Mark Eells, *Editorial Coordinator*

EDITORIAL PERMISSIONS
Carrie Jones, *CCP Supervisor*
Nicole Svobodny, *Permissions Editor*
Brigida Donohue, *Interpreter-Translator*

BOOK DESIGN
Marta L. Kimball, *Design Director*
Robin Bouvette, *Senior Designer*
Ed Diaz, *Design Associate*

IMAGE ACQUISITIONS
Curtis Riker, *Director*
Tim Taylor, *Photo Research Supervisor*
Cindy Verheyden, *Senior Photo Researcher*
Elisabeth McCoy, *Photo Researcher*

Michelle Rumpf, *Art Buyer Supervisor*
Coco Weir, *Senior Art Buyer*

DESIGN NEW MEDIA
Edwin Blake, *Design Director*
Kimberly Cammerata, *Design Manager*
Czeslaw Sornat, *Design Manager*
Grant Davidson, *Senior Designer*

COVER DESIGN
Marta L. Kimball, *Design Director*
Robin Bouvette, *Senior Designer*

PRODUCTION
Bill Medellin, *Production Supervisor*
Colette Tichenor, *Production Coordinator*

MANUFACTURING
Jevara Jackson, *Senior Manufacturing Coordinator*
Rhonda Faris, *Inventory Analyst*
Kimberly Harrison, *Media Manufacturing Coordinator*

NEW MEDIA
Liz Kline, *Senior Project Manager*
Lydia Doty, *Senior Project Manager*

VIDEO PRODUCTION
Video materials produced by Edge Productions, Inc., Aiken, S.C.

Requests for permission to make copies of any part of the work should be mailed to the following address: Permissions Department, Holt, Rinehart and Winston, 10801 N. Mopac Expressway, Building 3, Austin, Texas 78759.

FRONT COVER AND TITLE PAGE PHOTOGRAPHY CREDITS: Jardin des Tuileries, © Sime/eStock Photo; gravel, SEBASTIAN BAUSSAIS/Painet Inc.; teens, HRW Photo/Steve Ewert Photography.

BACK COVER PHOTOGRAPHY CREDITS: Ferris wheel, Picture Finders Ltd./eStock Photo; frame, ©1999 Image Farm Inc.

Acknowledgements appear on page R64, which is an extension of the copyright page.

ALLEZ, VIENS! is a trademark licensed to Holt, Rinehart and Winston, registered in the United States of America and/or other jurisdictions.

Printed in the United States of America

ISBN 0-03-0701813

1 2 3 4 5 6 7   48   05 04 03 02

AUTHORS

John DeMado
Washington, CT

Mr. DeMado helped form the general philosophy of the French program and wrote activities to practice basic material, functions, grammar, and vocabulary.

Emmanuel Rongiéras d'Usseau
Le Kremlin-Bicêtre, France

Mr. Rongiéras d'Usseau contributed to the development of the scope and sequence, created the basic material and listening scripts, selected realia, and wrote activities.

CONTRIBUTING WRITERS

Jayne Abrate
The University of Missouri
Rolla Campus
Rolla, MO

Sally Adamson Taylor
Publishers Weekly
San Francisco, CA

Linda Bistodeau
Saint Mary's University
Halifax, Nova Scotia

Betty Peltier
Consultant
Batz-sur-Mer, France

REVIEWERS

Dominique Bach
Rio Linda Senior High School
Rio Linda, CA

Jeannette Caviness
Mount Tabor High School
Winston-Salem, NC

Jennie Bowser Chao
Consultant
Oak Park, IL

Pierre F. Cintas
Penn State University
Abington College
Abington, PA

Donna Clementi
Appleton West High School
Appleton, WI

Cathy Cramer
Homewood High School
Birmingham, AL

Robert H. Didsbury
Consultant
Raleigh, NC

Jennifer Jones
U.S. Peace Corps volunteer
Côte d'Ivoire 1991–1993
Austin, TX

Joan H. Manley
The University of Texas at El Paso
El Paso, TX

Jill Markert
Pflugerville High School
Pflugerville, TX

Inge McCoy
Southwest Texas State University
San Marcos, TX

Gail Montgomery
Foreign Language Program
Administrator
Greenwich, CT Public Schools

Agathe Norman
Consultant
Austin, TX

Audrey O'Keefe
Jordan High School
Los Angeles, CA

Sherry Parker
Selvidge Middle School
Ballwin, MO

Sherron N. Porter
Robert E. Lee High School
Baton Rouge, LA

Marc Prévost
Austin Community College
Austin, TX

Norbert Rouquet
Consultant
La Roche-sur-Yon, France

Michèle Shockey
Gunn High School
Palo Alto, CA

Ashley Shumaker
Central High School West
Tuscaloosa, AL

Antonia Stergiades
Washington High School
Massillon, OH

Frederic L. Toner
Texas Christian University
Fort Worth, TX

Jeannine Waters
Harrisonburg High School
Harrisonburg, VA

Jo Anne S. Wilson
Consultant
Glen Arbor, MI

FIELD TEST PARTICIPANTS

Marie Allison
New Hanover High School
Wilmington, NC

Gabrielle Applequist
Capital High School
Boise, ID

Jana Brinton
Bingham High School
Riverton, UT

Nancy J. Cook
Sam Houston High School
Lake Charles, LA

Rachael Gray
Williams High School
Plano, TX

Katherine Kohler
Nathan Hale Middle School
Norwalk, CT

Nancy Mirsky
Museum Junior High School
Yonkers, NY

Myrna S. Nie
Whetstone High School
Columbus, OH

Jacqueline Reid
Union High School
Tulsa, OK

Judith Ryser
San Marcos High School
San Marcos, TX

Erin Hahn Sass
Lincoln Southeast High School
Lincoln, NE

Linda Sherwin
Sandy Creek High School
Tyrone, GA

Norma Joplin Sivers
Arlington Heights High School
Fort Worth, TX

Lorabeth Stroup
Lovejoy High School
Lovejoy, GA

Robert Vizena
W.W. Lewis Middle School
Sulphur, LA

Gladys Wade
New Hanover High School
Wilmington, NC

Kathy White
Grimsley High School
Greensboro, NC

TO THE STUDENT

*Some people have the opportunity to learn a new language by living in another country.
Most of us, however, begin learning another language and getting acquainted with
a foreign culture in a classroom with the help of a teacher, classmates, and a textbook.
To use your book effectively, you need to know how it works.*

Allez, viens! (*Come along!*) is organized to help you learn French and become familiar with the cultures of people who speak French. The Preliminary Chapter presents basic concepts in French and strategies for learning a new language. This chapter is followed by six Location Openers and twelve chapters.

Location Opener Six four-page photo essays called Location Openers introduce different French-speaking places. You can also see these locations on video, the *CD-ROM Tutor,* and the *DVD Tutor.*

Chapter Opener The Chapter Opener pages tell you the chapter theme and goals.

Mise en train (*Getting started*) This illustrated story, which is also on video, shows you French-speaking people in real-life situations, using the language you'll learn in the chapter.

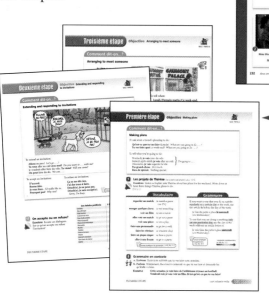

Première, Deuxième, and **Troisième étape** (*First, Second, Third Part*) After the **Mise en train,** the chapter is divided into three sections called **étapes.** Within the **étape,** are **Comment dit-on... ?** (*How do you say . . . ?*) boxes that contain the French expressions you'll need to communicate and **Vocabulaire** and **Grammaire/Note de grammaire** boxes that give you the French words and grammatical structures you'll need to know. Activities in each **étape** enable you to develop your skills in listening, reading, speaking, and writing.

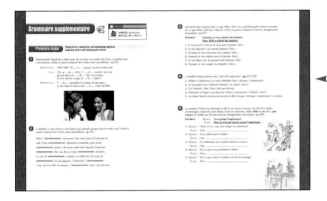

Panorama Culturel (*Cultural Panorama*) On this page are interviews with French-speaking people from around the world. You can watch these interviews on video or listen to them on audio CD. You can also watch them using the *CD-ROM Tutor* and the *DVD Tutor,* then check to see how well you understood by answering some questions about what the people say.

Rencontre culturelle (*Cultural Encounter*) This section, found in six of the chapters, gives you a firsthand encounter with some aspect of a French-speaking culture.

Note culturelle (*Culture Note*) In each chapter, there are notes with more information about the cultures of French-speaking people.

Lisons! (*Let's read!*) The reading section follows the three **étapes**. The selections are related to the chapter themes and help you develop your reading skills in French.

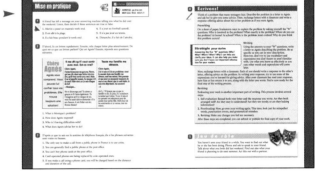

Grammaire supplémentaire (*Additional grammar practice*) This section begins the chapter review. You will find four pages of activities that provide additional practice on the grammar concepts you learned in the chapter.

Mise en pratique (*Review*) The activities on these pages practice what you've learned in the chapter and help you improve your listening, reading, and communication skills. You'll also review what you've learned about culture. A section called **Ecrivons!** (*Let's write!*) in Chapters 3–12 will help develop your writing skills.

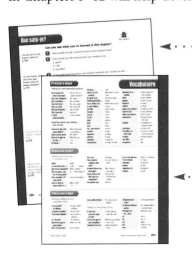

Que sais-je? (*Let's see if I can . . .*) This page at the end of each chapter contains a series of questions and short activities to help you see if you've achieved the chapter goals.

Vocabulaire (*Vocabulary*) On the French-English vocabulary list on the last page of the chapter, the words are grouped by **étape**. These words and expressions will be on the quizzes and tests.

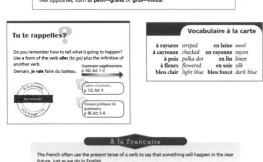

Organizing vocabulary in various ways can help you remember words. Group words by categories, like foods, sports, numbers, colors, and so forth. Try to associate words with a certain context, such as school (school subjects, classroom objects) or a store (items for sale, salesperson). Try to use associations like opposites, such as **petit—grand** or **gros—mince**.

Tu te rappelles?

Do you remember how to tell what is going to happen? Use a form of the verb **aller** (*to go*) plus the infinitive of another verb.
Demain, **je vais** faire du bateau.

Grammaire supplémentaire, p. 342, Act. 1–2

Cahier d'activités, p. 122, Act. 4

Travaux pratiques de grammaire, p. 90, Act. 5–6

Vocabulaire à la carte

à rayures	*striped*	en laine	*wool*
à carreaux	*checked*	en rayonne	*rayon*
à pois	*polka dot*	en lin	*linen*
à fleurs	*flowered*	en soie	*silk*
bleu clair	*light blue*	bleu foncé	*dark blue*

A la française

The French often use the present tense of a verb to say that something will happen in the near future, just as we do in English.
Samedi matin, je vais jouer au tennis. *Saturday morning, I'm going to play tennis.*
Samedi matin, je joue au tennis. *Saturday morning, I'm playing tennis.*

You'll also find special features in each chapter that provide extra tips and reminders.

De bons conseils (*Helpful advice*) offers study hints to help you succeed in a foreign language class.

Tu te rappelles? (*Do you remember?*) and **Si tu as oublié** (*If you forgot*) remind you of expressions, grammar, and vocabulary you may have forgotten.

A la française (*The French way*) gives you additional expressions to add more color to your speech.

Vocabulaire à la carte (*Additional Vocabulary*) lists extra words you might find helpful. These words will not appear on the quizzes and tests unless your teacher chooses to include them.

You'll also find French-English and English-French vocabulary lists at the end of the book. The words you'll need to know for the quizzes and tests are in boldface type.

At the end of your book, you'll find more helpful material, such as:
- a summary of the expressions you'll learn in the **Comment dit-on... ?** boxes
- additional vocabulary words you might want to use
- a summary of the grammar you'll study
- a grammar index to help you find where structures are presented

Allez, viens! Come along on an exciting trip to new cultures and a new language!

Bon voyage!

Explanation of Icons in *Allez, viens!*

Throughout Allez, viens!, you'll see these symbols, or icons, next to activities and presentations. The following key will help you understand them.

Video/DVD Whenever this icon appears, you'll know there is a related segment in the *Allez, viens! Video* and *DVD* Programs.

Listening Activities

Pair Work/Group Work Activities

Writing Activities

Interactive Games and Activities Whenever this icon appears, you'll know there is a related activity on the *Allez, viens! Interactive CD-ROM Tutor* and on the *DVD Tutor*.

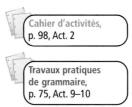

Cahier d'activités, p. 98, Act. 2

Travaux pratiques de grammaire, p. 75, Act. 9–10

Practice Activities These icons tell you which activities from the *Cahier d'activités* and the *Travaux pratiques de grammaire* practice the material presented.

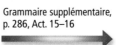
Grammaire supplémentaire, p. 286, Act. 15–16

Grammaire supplémentaire This reference tells you where you can find additional grammar practice in the review section of the chapter.

Internet Activities This icon provides the keyword you'll need to access related online activities at **go.hrw.com**.

En route! Contents

Come along—to a world of new experiences!

En route! offers you the opportunity to learn the language spoken by millions of people in countries in Europe, Africa, Asia, and around the world. Let's find out what those countries are.

Révisions

CHAPITRE 7
La famille.....198

ALLEZ, VIENS

à Abidjan!

LOCATION • CHAPITRE 8.....226

CHAPITRE 8
Au marché.....230

ALLEZ, VIENS

en Arles!

LOCATION • CHAPITRES 9, 10, 11.....260

CHAPITRE 9
Au téléphone.....264

CHAPITRE 10
Dans un magasin de vêtements 292

CHAPITRE 11
Vive les vacances! 322

ALLEZ, VIENS

à Fort-de-France!

LOCATION • CHAPITRE 12 350

CHAPITRE 12
En ville 354

CULTURAL REFERENCES

XV

LA FRANCE

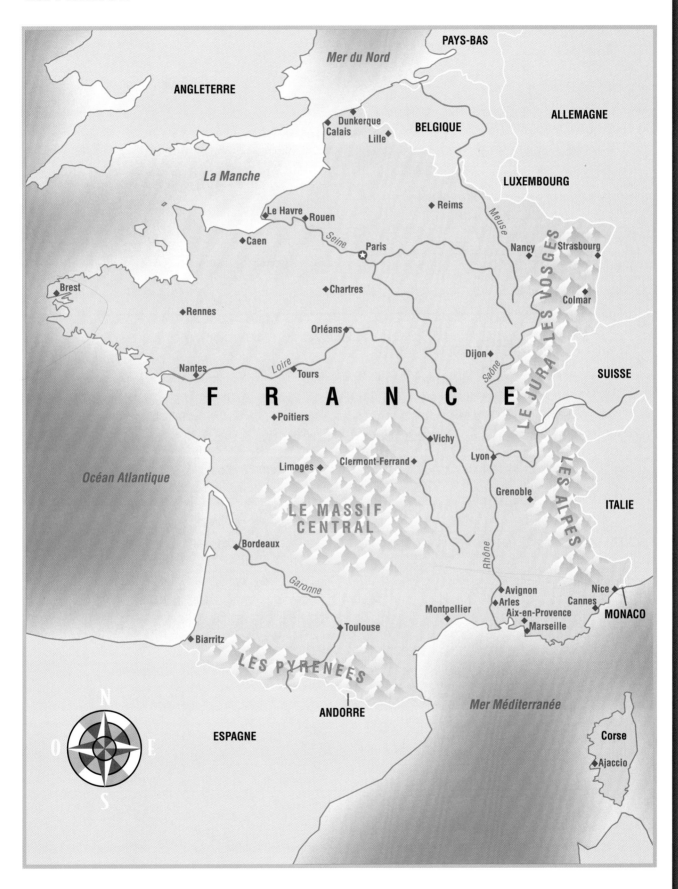

L'AFRIQUE FRANCOPHONE

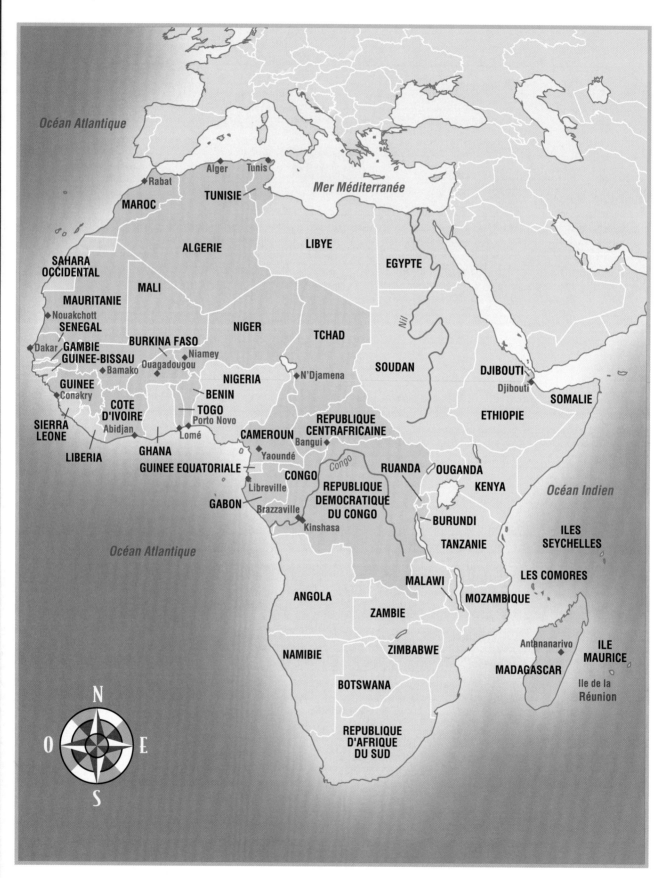

Océan Atlantique

Mer Méditerranée

MAROC
Rabat
Alger
Tunis
TUNISIE

ALGERIE
LIBYE
EGYPTE

SAHARA
OCCIDENTAL

MALI

MAURITANIE
Nouakchott
SENEGAL

NIGER
TCHAD

SOUDAN

Nil

DJIBOUTI
Djibouti

Dakar
GAMBIE
GUINEE-BISSAU
BURKINA FASO
Niamey
Ouagadougou
Bamako

NIGERIA
N'Djamena

SOMALIE

GUINEE
Conakry
BENIN
TOGO
Porto Novo

ETHIOPIE

COTE
D'IVOIRE
Abidjan
Lomé
CAMEROUN
Bangui
REPUBLIQUE
CENTRAFRICAINE

SIERRA
LEONE

LIBERIA
GHANA
Yaoundé
Congo

GUINEE EQUATORIALE
CONGO
RUANDA
OUGANDA

Libreville
REPUBLIQUE
DEMOCRATIQUE
DU CONGO
KENYA
Océan Indien

GABON
Brazzaville
Kinshasa
BURUNDI

TANZANIE

ILES
SEYCHELLES

MALAWI
LES COMORES

ANGOLA
MOZAMBIQUE

ZAMBIE

NAMIBIE
ZIMBABWE
Antananarivo
ILE
MAURICE

MADAGASCAR
Ile de la
Réunion

BOTSWANA

REPUBLIQUE
D'AFRIQUE
DU SUD

N
O
E
S

Océan Atlantique

L'AMERIQUE FRANCOPHONE

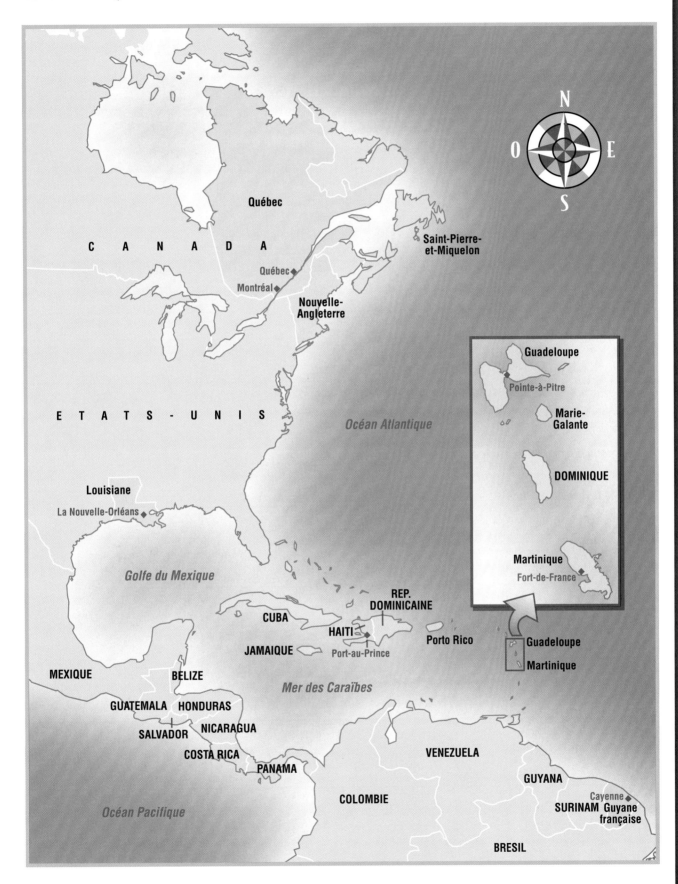

SECTION

Qui suis-je?

- Greetings and introductions
- Saying goodbye
- Likes and dislikes
- Numbers
- Sports and activities
- Regular *-er* verbs
- Expressions with *faire* and *jouer*

—Salut, Lisette! Ça va?

—Oui, et toi?

—Ça va très bien.

—Bonjour, Monsieur Balland.

—Bonjour, Marc. Ça va?

—Oui. Ça va, merci.

Comment dit-on...?

Greeting people and saying goodbye; asking how people are and telling how you are; asking someone's name and age and giving yours

CD-ROM 1
DVD 1

To greet people and say goodbye:

Bonjour.	Au revoir.
Salut.	A tout à l'heure.
	A demain.

To ask someone's name and age and give yours:

Tu t'appelles comment?	Je m'appelle...
Il/Elle s'appelle comment?	Il/Elle s'appelle...
Tu as quel âge?	J'ai... ans

To ask how people are and tell how you are:

Ça va?	Très bien.
	Comme ci comme ça.
	Pas terrible.

Travaux pratiques de grammaire, pp. 1–2, Act. 1–6

Cahier d'activités, p. 4, Act. 3

Vocabulaire

Les chiffres de 0 à 20

0 zéro	1 un	2 deux	3 trois	4 quatre	5 cinq	6 six
7 sept	8 huit	9 neuf	10 dix	11 onze	12 douze	13 treize
14 quatorze	15 quinze	16 seize	17 dix-sept	18 dix-huit	19 dix-neuf	20 vingt

Note culturelle

In France, girls kiss both girls and boys on the cheek when they meet or say goodbye. Boys shake hands with one another. To address adults who aren't family members, use the titles **madame**, **mademoiselle**, and **monsieur**.

1 Petite conversation

Parlons With a classmate, create a conversation between two French students who meet on the first day of school. Use as many expressions as possible from the box on the right.

Ça va? Je m'appelle... Très bien!
A demain! Au revoir.
Tu as quel âge?
J'ai... ans. Salut!
Bonjour!
Tu t'appelles comment? Pas terrible!

2 Les salutations

Ecrivons Imagine des conversations entre les personnes que tu vois sur ces photos.

EXEMPLE — Salut, Lisette!
— Salut, Camille. Ça va?

1.

2.

3.

4.

Cahier d'activités, p. 10, Act. 18–19

Travaux pratiques de grammaire, pp. 6–7, Act. 15–17

Vocabulaire

Likes and dislikes

danser

dormir

regarder la télé

écouter de la musique

étudier

faire les magasins

les vacances (f.)

3 Charades

Parlons Get together with a classmate and take turns acting out the things and activities from the **Vocabulaire**. The other person should guess the name of the thing or activity that is being acted out.

Comment dit-on...?

Expressing likes, dislikes, and preferences

Tu aimes... ?   J'aime mieux...
J'aime bien...   Je préfère...
J'adore...
J'aime pas...

Cahier d'activités, p. 9, Act. 16

4   Et toi?

Lisons/Ecrivons Anne adore la musique classique. Son cousin Marc aime beaucoup Elvis Presley. Complète la conversation entre Anne and Marc avec les expressions que tu connais. Utilise chaque *(each)* expression une fois.

MARC   ___**1**___ Elvis Presley, Anne? Moi, ___**2**___ Elvis! Il est super!

ANNE   Non, ___**3**___ Elvis. ___**4**___ Bach, Chopin et Mozart. Et ___**5**___ Beethoven! C'est mon musicien préféré.

MARC   ___**6**___ Beethoven à Elvis Presley, le champion du rock-and-roll?! Incroyable!

5   Qui ça?

Parlons Tell a classmate what each person in the photos likes to do, using the **je** form instead of the person's name. Your partner will guess the identity of the one you impersonate. Take turns until all of the people have been identified.

1. Thuy

2. Didier

3. Stéphane

4. Elodie et ses amis

5. Hélène

6. Pamela

Regular *-er* verbs

Most -er verbs, like **aimer** *(to like)* and **étudier** *(to study)*, follow the pattern below. Drop the **-er** and add the appropriate endings.

étudier

J'	étudi**e**	Nous	étudi**ons**
Tu	étudi**es**	Vous	étudi**ez**
Il/Elle/On	étudi**e**	Ils/Elles	étudi**ent**

Remember to use **tu** with a friend, family member, or someone your own age or younger. Use **vous** when addressing more than one person or someone older than you who is not a relative. **Elles** refers to a group of females, while **ils** refers to a group of males or a group of males and females.

Cahier d'activités, pp. 9–10, Act. 14, 17

Travaux pratiques de grammaire, pp. 7–9, Act. 18–23

6 **Grammaire en contexte**

Lisons/Ecrivons Amandine is talking on the phone with her friend Aurélie. She is trying to decide whom to invite to her birthday party on Saturday. Fill in the blanks with the correct forms of the verbs.

«J'aime beaucoup Sébastien. Nous ___1___ (parler) au téléphone cinq fois par semaine. Mais il ne ___2___ (danser) pas! Je/J' ___3___ (aimer) bien Victor mais il ___4___ (adorer) les films et il y a un film super à la télé samedi. Mathieu et Romain ___5___ (jouer) au foot samedi soir. Tu ___6___ (étudier) avec Julien Mercier le mercredi après-midi, n'est-ce pas? Est-ce qu'il est libre samedi?»

7 **Grammaire en contexte**

Parlons/Ecrivons Get together with two classmates and take turns interviewing one another about your interests, such as leisure activities, sports, music, or favorite television shows. Take notes and confirm with the group what each person being interviewed says. Finally, report your findings to the class.

EXEMPLE

Ashley, est-ce que tu aimes téléphoner?

Oui, j'aime téléphoner.

Ashley et Jason, est-ce que vous aimez lire?

Oui, nous aimons lire.

Bon. Ashley, tu aimes téléphoner.
Ashley et Jason, vous aimez lire.

Ashley aime téléphoner et lire et Jason aime lire.

Sports et activités

faire de la natation

faire du théâtre

faire du patin à glace

faire du vélo

jouer au foot(ball)

jouer à des jeux vidéo

Cahier d'activités, p. 38, Act. 4

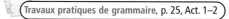

Travaux pratiques de grammaire, p. 25, Act. 1–2

8 De nouveaux amis

Parlons Your pen pal Christine sent you some photos of friends she met while at summer camp. Tell what her friends like to do based on the photos.

1. Ahmed

2. Michel

3. Irène et François

4. Mark, David et Thomas

9 Des activités variées

Parlons You're applying for a job at a summer camp in France. The director wants to know how well you can match people with activities. Tell the activities you would suggest for each of the following people.

1. Céline aime la plage.

2. Moustafa adore la nature.

3. Baptiste n'aime pas le sport.

4. Bertille aime les Jeux olympiques d'hiver.

5. Fabien et Noémie aiment les pièces de Shakespeare.

Grammaire

Expressions with *faire* and *jouer*

You use the irregular verb **faire** *(to make, to do)* followed by **de** with activities, including some sports. Remember to make the necessary contractions.

faire

Je	**fais**	Nous	**faisons**
Tu	**fais**	Vous	**faites**
Il/Elle/On	**fait**	Ils/Elles	**font**

Je fais **du** ski.   Elle fait **des** photos.   Vous faites **de la** natation.

You use **jouer** *(to play)* with games or sports that you play. **Jouer** is followed by **à.** Remember to make any necessary contractions. (See p. *Révisions* 22.)

Nous jouons **au** football.   Elle joue **à des** jeux vidéo.

> Travaux pratiques de grammaire, p. 26, Act. 3–4

---

10 Grammaire en contexte

Lisons/Ecrivons Read Mathilde's letter to an advice column. Fill in the blanks with the correct forms of either **faire** or **jouer.**

Chère Pauline,

J'ai un grand problème. Je ne ___1___ pas de sport! Tous mes copains adorent le sport. Mon ami Fabrice ___2___ au base-ball. Hugues et Rémi ___3___ de la natation. Mes amies Anne-Sophie et Chloé ___4___ très souvent au volley-ball! J'ai un ami qui n'aime pas le sport non plus. Nous ___5___ du théâtre ensemble à l'école et nous ___6___ un peu à des jeux vidéo. Mais je voudrais voir mes autres amis aussi! Qu'est-ce que je peux faire? Et toi, est-ce que tu ___7___ du sport?

Mathilde

---

11 Grammaire en contexte

Parlons You're organizing teams for an "Olympics" at your school. Choose four sports from the **Vocabulaire** and then interview your classmates to find at least three students to compete in each sport you have chosen.

EXEMPLE   **Tu aimes faire du vélo?**

REVISIONS

SECTION

Le Temps de l'école

- **School subjects and supplies**
- **Colors**
- **Times of the day**
- **Days of the week**
- **Months and seasons**
- **The weather**
- **The verb *avoir***
- **Adjective agreement and placement**
- **Adverbs of frequency**

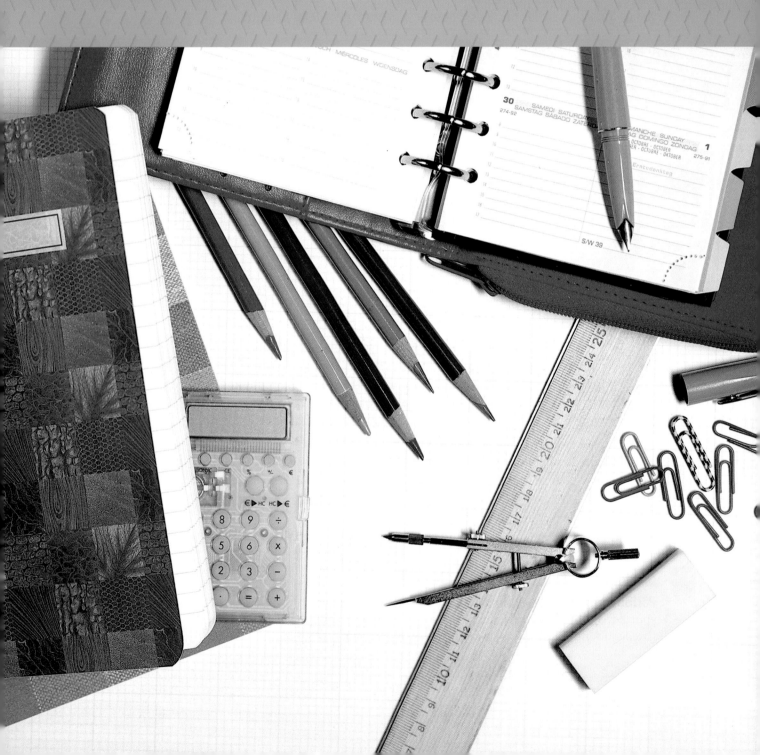

—Qu'est-ce qu'il te faut
pour l'anglais, Claire?

—Eh bien... il me faut
deux cahiers.

La récréation dans une
école de Côte d'Ivoire

Section B REVISIONS

Vocabulaire

Les matières

l'informatique (f.)
l'allemand (m.)
l'espagnol (m.)
les arts plastiques (m.)
la chimie
l'éducation physique et sportive (EPS) (f.)
les travaux pratiques (m.)

L'école

le cours
les devoirs (m.)
l'élève (m./f.)
le professeur
la récréation
la sortie
l'emploi du temps (m.)

Les jours de la semaine

lundi
mardi
mercredi
jeudi
vendredi
samedi
dimanche

CD-ROM 1
DVD 1

Cahier d'activités, pp. 14–16, Act. 2–5, 7; pp. 18–19, Act. 14–15

Travaux pratiques de grammaire, pp. 10–11, Act. 1–4; pp. 13–14, Act. 10–12

---

12 Quel cours?

Lisons/Ecrivons Based on what these people like, write the class each one would be most likely to teach.

1. Fabienne : «J'adore la natation et le volley-ball!»
2. Mélodie : «Moi, j'aime voyager, surtout au Mexique.»
3. Ludovic : «J'adore la sculpture.»
4. Jérémy : «Moi, j'aime faire des expériences dans le laboratoire.»
5. Malika : «J'aime beaucoup les ordinateurs.»

Grammaire

The verb _avoir_

Do you remember the irregular verb **avoir** _(to have)_? Here is its conjugation in the present tense.

J'	**ai**	Nous	**avons**
Tu	**as**	Vous	**avez**
Il/Elle/On	**a**	Ils/Elles	**ont**

CD-ROM 1
DVD 1

Cahier d'activités, p. 17, Act. 12

Travaux pratiques de grammaire, pp. 12–13, Act. 7–9

---

13 Grammaire en contexte

Ecrivons Fabien's best friend Ali moved to a new city. Read Ali's e-mail to Fabien and complete it with the correct forms of **avoir**.

> Salut, Fabien!
>
> Cette année, j' ___1___ beaucoup de cours intéressants. J' ___2___ maths le lundi à 8 heures! Mon prof de chimie est très sympa et notre lycée ___3___ un laboratoire super cool. En plus du sport normal, nous ___4___ la possibilité de faire de la natation ou de l'équitation! On ___5___ un parc et une piscine juste à côté du lycée. Est-ce que tu ___6___ Madame Bermondy en anglais cette année? A plus!

Asking for and giving information; telling when you have class

To ask about someone's classes:

Tu as quel cours maintenant?
Tu as quoi l'après-midi?
Vous avez biologie le matin?

To tell what classes you have:

J'ai maths aujourd'hui.
On a français et géographie.

Cahier d'activités,
pp. 17–18, Act. 12–13

Travaux pratiques
de grammaire,
p. 15, Act. 15–17

To find out at what time someone has a certain class:

Tu as allemand à quelle heure?

To tell at what time you have a certain class:

J'ai EPS à quatorze heures.

huit heures

dix heures quarante

neuf heures quinze

quatorze heures vingt

treize heures quarante-cinq

14 ## Méli-mélo!

Ecrivons/Parlons Antoine and Sébastien are passing each other in the hall between classes. Work with a classmate to unscramble their conversation. Then act out the conversation.

— Moi, j'ai chimie. La récréation est à quelle heure?

— Super! Tu as quel cours maintenant?

— Salut, ça va?

— J'ai espagnol, et toi?

—A deux heures.

— Alors, à toute à l'heure!

15 ## Tu as quoi comme cours?

Parlons Role-play a situation with a classmate in which you ask each other about your school schedules. Be sure to mention the times you have classes.

EXEMPLE

— **Tu as quoi le lundi?**

— **J'ai informatique, français, EPS, chimie et arts plastiques.**

— **Tu as informatique le matin?**

— **Oui, à dix heures.**

Note culturelle

In France, secondary school starts with the grade called **la sixième** (*sixth grade*) and continues with **la cinquième, la quatrième,** etc., ending with **la classe terminale,** which marks the end of high school **(le lycée).** At the end of **terminale,** students take a difficult comprehensive exam called **le baccalauréat,** or **le bac** for short. The **bac** is a prerequisite to enter a university. Students who want to pursue traditional studies choose a **bac général.** Other students might choose to focus on technical skills and prepare for a **bac technologique;** yet others might choose a **bac professionnel,** which focuses on a variety of professional skills.

Les fournitures scolaires

un cahier	un classeur
un crayon	un livre
une gomme	une feuille de papier
un taille-crayon	une règle
un stylo	un ordinateur
un sac (à dos)	un dictionnaire

Les couleurs

- ■ rouge
- ■ orange
- ■ jaune
- ■ rose
- ■ marron
- ■ vert(e)
- ■ bleu(e)
- ■ violet(te)
- ❑ blanc(he)
- ■ gris(e)
- ■ noir(e)

Travaux pratiques de grammaire, pp. 17–18, Act. 1–3

16 C'est pas vrai!

Ecrivons Sylvie's brother Jérôme has accused her of having borrowed his dictionary without asking. Complete Sylvie's response based on the images.

J'ai un ___1___ 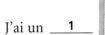, une ___2___ ,

une ___3___ , un ___4___ , un ___5___

et un ___6___ . Je t'assure, je n'ai pas ton dictionnaire!

Adjective agreement and placement

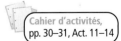

Usually, you add an **e** at the end of a masculine adjective to make it feminine and an **s** to make it plural.

	Singular	Plural
Masculine	le cahier noir	les cahiers noir**s**
Feminine	la montre noir**e**	les montres noir**e s**

- When a masculine adjective ends in an unaccentuated **e,** the spelling doesn't change in the feminine form: **rouge.**
- When a masculine adjective ends in an **s,** the spelling doesn't change in the masculine plural form: **gris.**
- Some adjectives don't change spelling in the feminine and plural forms. These include the adjectives **marron** and **orange.**
- Some adjectives follow a different spelling pattern: **blanc → blanche.**
- Most adjectives are placed after the nouns they modify.

Cahier d'activités, pp. 30–31, Act. 11–14

Travaux pratiques de grammaire, pp. 22–23, Act. 13–15

17 Grammaire en contexte

Lisons/Écrivons Vincent is having a bad day. Not only did he lose his backpack, but while he is reporting it to the secretary at the school office, she gets the colors of his items switched around. Help Vincent correct the secretary's statements.

— Alors, dans ton sac à dos, tu as une règle grise et un classeur noir?

— Non, madame, j'ai une règle ___1___ et un classeur ___2___.

— Et tu as aussi un stylo blanc et une feuille de papier verte?

— Non, madame, j'ai un stylo ___3___ et une feuille ___4___.

— Eh bien, tu as une gomme bleue et un cahier violet?

— Non, madame, j'ai une gomme ___5___ et un cahier ___6___.

— Et tu dis aussi que tu as des crayons jaunes et un taille-crayon marron, c'est ça?

— Non, madame, j'ai des crayons ___7___ et un taille-crayon ___8___.

18 Qu'est-ce qu'on a?

Parlons/Écrivons With three classmates, prepare a list of the school supplies you have. Each of you says what he or she owns. A volunteer writes who owns what. Another volunteer reads the list to the rest of the class. Don't forget to include the color of each item!

EXEMPLE   Caitlin a une règle jaune, un classeur vert, un stylo violet,...

Comment dit-on...?

Making and responding to requests; asking others what they need and telling what you need

To ask someone for something:

Tu as une gomme?

Vous avez des feuilles de papier?

To respond:

Oui. **Voilà.**

Non. **Je regrette. Nous n'avons pas de** feuilles.

To ask what someone needs:

Qu'est-ce qu'il te faut pour la biologie?

Qu'est-ce qu'il vous faut pour l'EPS?

To tell what you need:

Il me faut une calculatrice.

Il nous faut un short et des baskets.

Cahier d'activités, pp. 27–28, Act. 4–6

---

19 Au magasin

Parlons Tu veux acheter des fournitures scolaires mais le magasin n'a pas les choses que tu veux acheter. Avec un(e) camarade, imagine de petits dialogues entre le client et l'employé(e) du magasin. Jouez ces dialogues.

EXEMPLE   — Il me faut une gomme pour les arts plastiques.

— Je regrette, nous n'avons pas de gommes.

Les mois

janvier	février	mars	avril
mai	juin	juillet	août
septembre	octobre	novembre	décembre

Les saisons

le printemps

l'été

l'automne

l'hiver

CD-ROM 1
DVD 1

Quel temps fait-il?

Il fait beau.   Il fait frais.   Il fait froid.

Il fait chaud.   Il pleut.   Il neige.

Cahier d'activités, p. 42, Act. 12–14; p. 44, Act. 17

Travaux pratiques de grammaire, pp. 30–32, Act. 12–14, 16

---

20 **Jours de fête**

Parlons Dis le nom du mois qui correspond à chaque fête.

1. La fête du travail *(Labor Day)*
2. La Saint-Sylvestre *(New Year's Eve)*
3. Le jour de l'an *(New Year's Day)*
4. La fête nationale *(Independence Day)*
5. La fête des pères *(Father's Day)*
6. La Saint-Patrick *(St. Patrick's Day)*

21 **Ma correspondante**

Ecrivons Your pen pal Lili wants to visit the United States. She isn't sure what time of year to visit. Pick the image that best answers Lili's questions and describe it.

a.   b.   c.   d.

1. Quel temps fait-il en Alaska en hiver?
2. Quel temps fait-il à Seattle en automne?
3. Quel temps fait-il à New York en été?
4. Quel temps fait-il à Dallas au printemps?

22 **Mon mois préféré**

Parlons Avec deux camarades, parlez de votre mois préféré, selon *(based on)* les activités que vous aimez faire et le temps qu'il fait pendant ce mois-là.

EXEMPLE
— Quel mois est-ce que tu préfères, toi?
— Je préfère août. J'adore faire de la natation et il fait chaud en août.

Grammaire

Adverbs of frequency

These are adverbs you can use to tell how often you do something:

> **quelquefois** *(sometimes)*, **de temps en temps** *(from time to time)*, **souvent** *(often)*, **rarement** *(rarely)*, **ne... jamais** *(never)*, **d'habitude** *(usually)*, and **... fois par semaine** *(. . . time(s) a week)*.

• Short adverbs are usually placed just after the verb they modify.

> Je fais **rarement** du jogging en hiver.

• Longer adverbs go either at the beginning or at the end of a sentence.

> **D'habitude,** je joue au foot le mardi.
> Je joue au tennis une **fois par semaine.**

• In the case of adverbs with negation, **ne (n')** goes before the verb and the adverb goes after the verb.

> Tu **n'**as **jamais** de crayons!
> Vous **ne** faites **jamais** de patin?

Cahier d'activités, pp. 45–46, Act. 20–22

Travaux pratiques de grammaire, pp. 33–34, Act. 17–20

23 ## Grammaire en contexte

Lisons/Ecrivons   Anne-Marie is filling out a survey by a school committee asking how often she uses various items for her classes. Fill in her responses with appropriate phrases from the word box. Use each phrase only once.

1. Des crayons? J'ai arts plastiques quatre fois par semaine. Alors, je dis : ___**1**___ .
2. Un dictionnaire allemand-français? Je n'ai pas allemand. Donc, je dis : ___**2**___ .
3. Une règle? Il me faut une règle pour la géométrie une ou deux fois par semaine. Alors, je dis : ___**3**___ .
4. Une calculatrice? Mon prof de maths n'aime pas trop les calculatrices! On fait les devoirs sans calculatrice, ___**4**___ . Donc, je dis : ___**5**___ .

> de temps en temps   jamais
>   rarement
> d'habitude   souvent

24 ## Grammaire en contexte

Parlons   With a partner, discuss whether you like the activities below. Tell how often you do the activities that you like.

> **EXEMPLE**   — **Tu aimes jouer au volley-ball?**
>
>   — **Oui, je joue souvent au volley-ball.**

> faire de la natation   jouer au basket-ball   faire du vélo
>   faire du patin à glace
> jouer à des jeux vidéo   jouer au volley-ball

REVISIONS

SECTION

e

On sort?

- **Foods and beverages**
- **Things to do and places to go**
- **The verbs *prendre*, *aller*, and *vouloir***
- **Contractions with *à***
- **Information questions**
- **Making plans**
- **Expressions for eating in a restaurant**

—On peut aller au café.

—D'accord.

—Bonne idée!

—Qu'est-ce que tu vas faire samedi?

—Je vais aller au théâtre avec Nina.

Vocabulaire

J'ai faim! Je voudrais...

J'ai soif! Je voudrais...

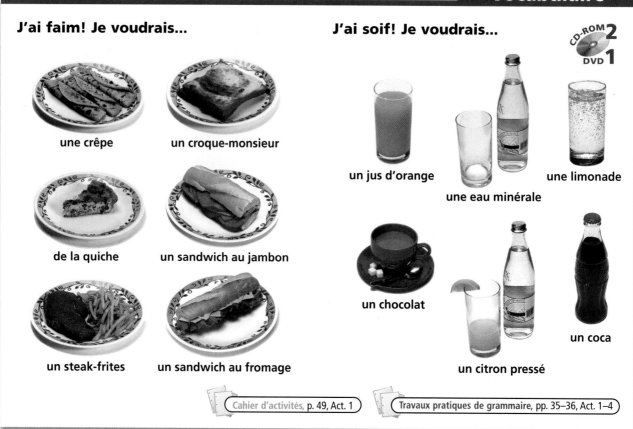

CD-ROM 2
DVD 1

une crêpe

un croque-monsieur

de la quiche

un sandwich au jambon

un steak-frites

un sandwich au fromage

un jus d'orange

une eau minérale

une limonade

un chocolat

un citron pressé

un coca

Cahier d'activités, p. 49, Act. 1

Travaux pratiques de grammaire, pp. 35–36, Act. 1–4

25 Des repas à la française

Parlons You overhear your friend Caroline talking out loud as she prepares a shopping list. Guess what foods and drinks she is planning to prepare for Roxanne, the French exchange student staying with her family.

1. "Let's see, I need flour, eggs, milk, butter, cheese . . ."
2. "I need to get some kind of fruit juice . . ."
3. "I need to pick up some bread, and I need ham . . ."
4. "Okay, maybe some French bread and some more cheese for lunch one day . . ."
5. "Since it's cold here, Roxanne might want to drink something hot . . ."

26 Moi aussi!

Écrivons/Parlons With a partner, create a comedy skit between two friends who are very competitive. They go to a restaurant and each one tries to "one-up" the other by ordering what the other ordered plus an additional item of food and drink. After you write the skit, perform it in front of the class.

EXEMPLE — J'ai faim! Je voudrais des crêpes!

— Moi aussi, j'ai faim! Je voudrais des crêpes et un steak-frites!

Grammaire

Do you remember the following irregular verbs?

prendre *(to have)*		**aller** *(to go)*		**vouloir** *(to want)*	
Je	prends	Je	vais	Je	veux
Tu	prends	Tu	vas	Tu	veux
Il/Elle/On	prend	Il/Elle/On	va	Il/Elle/On	veut
Nous	prenons	Nous	allons	Nous	voulons
Vous	prenez	Vous	allez	Vous	voulez
Ils/Elles	prennent	Ils/Elles	vont	Ils/Elles	veulent

Cahier d'activités, p. 51, Act. 5; p. 52, Act. 9; p. 63, Act. 7; pp. 66–67, Act. 15–16

Travaux pratiques de grammaire, p. 37, Act. 6–7; p. 43, Act. 5–6; p. 46, Act. 12–13

27 Grammaire en contexte

Lisons/Ecrivons Loïs, Alain, and Cécile are in a café. They are trying to decide what they are going to eat. Complete their conversation using the correct forms of the verbs **aller, prendre,** and **vouloir.**

LOÏS   Mmm... Moi, je ___**1**___ (aller) prendre un sandwich au jambon. Et vous, qu'est-ce que vous ___**2**___ (aller) prendre?

ALAIN   Moi, je ___**3**___ (prendre) un sandwich au fromage. Et toi, Cécile, qu'est-ce que tu ___**4**___ (prendre)? Tu ne ___**5**___ (vouloir) pas une pizza? Elles sont bonnes ici.

CÉCILE   Non, pas aujourd'hui. Je ___**6**___ (vouloir) un croque-monsieur plutôt. Au fait, Juliette et Sami ___**7**___ (aller) venir aussi. Ils ___**8**___ (aller) sûrement prendre des pizzas. Ils adorent ça. Et comme boisson, qu'est-ce que vous ___**9**___ (vouloir), les garçons?

LOÏS   Nous ___**10**___ (prendre) toujours du coca, tu sais bien! Madame, s'il vous plaît!

28 Pas d'accord!

Ecrivons/Parlons You and your partner are at a food stand in Paris. You'd like to share a food item and a drink, but you don't have the same tastes. Create a skit using the expressions below and the verbs **prendre, aller,** and **vouloir.** Then act out your skit in front of the class.

EXEMPLE   —Moi, je veux une crêpe et une limonade.

          —Ah, non! Je n'aime pas les crêpes. On prend un sandwich au jambon et un citron pressé?

un sandwich au jambon   de la quiche

un coca   une crêpe   un jus d'orange   un citron pressé

une limonade

un sandwich au fromage

un croque-monsieur   une eau minérale

Getting someone's attention; ordering food; paying the check

You might say . . .

Excusez-moi.

Monsieur! Madame! Mademoiselle!

La carte, s'il vous plaît.

Qu'est-ce qu'il y a à boire?

Vous avez des pizzas?

Je vais prendre une omelette, s'il vous plaît.

C'est combien, un sandwich?

Ça fait combien?

L'addition, s'il vous plaît.

The server might say . . .

Vous avez choisi?

Vous prenez?

Oui, tout de suite.

C'est douze euros.

Ça fait vingt euros cinquante.

CD-ROM **2**
DVD **1**

> Cahier d'activités, p. 53, Act. 10–12; p. 54, Act. 14; p. 55, Act. 16–17; pp. 57–58, Act. 23–24

---

29 En voyage avec mon oncle

Parlons Sarah is in a French restaurant with her Uncle Paul, who does not speak French. Tell what Sarah needs to ask the waiter based on what her uncle wants.

1. Uncle Paul would like to know what drinks they have.

2. He'd like to know if they have steaks and fries.

3. He is wondering how much the steak with fries costs.

4. He'd like to get the check.

5. The writing on the check is hard to read, so he'd like to know how much he owes.

Note culturelle

France, along with most other countries of the European Union, changed its currency to the **euro** in 2002. Euros are subdivided into **cents** (also called **centimes** in France). There are one hundred **cents** in each euro.

---

30 Jeu de rôle

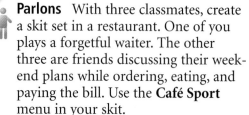

Parlons With three classmates, create a skit set in a restaurant. One of you plays a forgetful waiter. The other three are friends discussing their weekend plans while ordering, eating, and paying the bill. Use the **Café Sport** menu in your skit.

CAFE SPORT

Sandwiches		
Fromage	2,50 €	
Jambon	3,00 €	
Saucisson	3,00 €	
Hamburger	3,50 €	
Hot-dog	2,50 €	
Steak-frites	5,00 €	
Croque-monsieur	3,50 €	
Pizza	3,50 €	
Frites	1,50 €	
Glace	1,50 €	

BOISSONS	
Jus de fruit	2,00 €
orange, pomme, pamplemousse	
Limonade	1,50 €
Café	1,50 €
Cola	2,00 €
Eau minérale	1,50 €
Chocolat	2,50 €

Things to do and places to go

faire un pique-nique   faire les vitrines   au théâtre

aller voir un match   voir un film   à la plage

voir une pièce   au parc   au centre commercial

faire une promenade   au stade   au cinéma

Cahier d'activités,
p. 62, Act. 3–4

---

31 ## Qu'est-ce qu'on fait?

Lisons Céline is telling her friend Patrice what she and her friends are going to do this weekend. Match what she is saying with the photos you see.

a.

b.

c.

d.

1. Julien et Marie vont au stade. Il y a un bon match aujourd'hui.

2. Paula et Christelle vont faire les vitrines. Elles adorent ça!

3. Moi, je vais aller voir une pièce avec Emile.

4. Félicie va aller à la plage.

Comment dit-on...?

Making plans

To ask what a friend is planning to do:

    Qu'est-ce que tu vas faire cet après-midi?

    Tu vas faire quoi demain?

To tell what you're going to do:

    Dimanche, **je vais** jouer au tennis.

    Pas grand-chose.

    Rien de spécial.

---

32 ## Projets de week-end

Parlons Get with a classmate and discuss each other's plans for the weekend. Decide who has the best plans and share that person's plans with the rest of the class.

EXEMPLE

MIKE   Qu'est-ce que tu vas faire samedi?

ANDY   Je vais aller voir un match de foot. Et toi?

MIKE   Je vais faire le ménage.

Grammaire

Contractions with *à*

When you use the preposition **à** before **le** or **les,** make the following contractions:

à + le = **au**   **à + les** = **aux**

Cécile va **au** stade cet après-midi.

The preposition **à** doesn't contract with **l'** or **la** .

Il ne va pas **à la** piscine. Il va **à l'**école.

Cahier d'activités,
pp. 63–64, Act. 6, 8

Travaux pratiques de grammaire,
pp. 44–45, Act. 7–11

---

33 Grammaire en contexte

Ecrivons Use the images to complete these mini-conversations.

1. — **Est-ce que tu nages souvent... ?**
— **Oui, mais je préfère nager...**
2. — **Tu vas faire du jogging... ?**
— **Non, je vais voir un match...**

3. — **Moi, je veux aller...**
— **Moi, je préfère aller...**
4. — **Tu aimes aller... ?**
— **Non, pas trop. Mais j'aime bien aller...**

---

34 Tu y vas souvent?

Parlons With a classmate, ask one another how often you go to each place, using expressions from the list on the left. In your answers, use the expressions from the list on the right.

le cinéma	de temps en temps
le zoo	souvent
la bibliothèque	ne... jamais
la piscine	... fois par semaine
le centre commercial	rarement
le musée	

Extending and responding to invitations; arranging to meet someone

To extend an invitation:
> **Tu veux** aller au zoo **avec moi?**
> **On peut** faire du patin.

To accept an invitation:
> **D'accord.**
> **Bonne idée.**
> **Pourquoi pas?**

To refuse an invitation:
> **Ça ne me dit rien.**
> **J'ai des trucs à faire.**
> **Désolé(e), je ne peux pas.**

Cahier d'activités,
pp. 65–66,
Act. 11–14

Travaux pratiques
de grammaire,
pp. 47–48, Act. 14–17

To arrange to meet someone:
> **Quand?**
> **Avec qui?**
> **Où?**
> **A quelle heure?**

> **Demain matin.**
> **Avec** Paul.
> **Devant** le restaurant.
> **Vers** sept heures.

35 ### Méli-mélo!

Lisons/Parlons Unscramble the conversation between Saïd and Jules. Then act it out with a class-mate using a new day, place, activity, and meeting time.

> — Vers onze heures.
> — Tu veux aller à la plage? On peut nager.
> — Oui, d'accord! A demain, Saïd!
> — Pourquoi pas? A quelle heure?
> — Pas grand-chose.
> — Dis, Jules, qu'est-ce que tu vas faire demain?

Grammaire

Information questions

- To ask an information question, you can use just the question word or phrase.
  > **A quelle heure?**
- You can put the question word at the end of your statement.
  > Tu veux faire **quoi?**
- You can also begin your question with a question word or phrase followed by **est-ce que** or **est-ce qu'**.
  > **Où est-ce qu'**on se retrouve?

Cahier d'activités,
p. 69, Act. 21–22

Travaux pratiques de grammaire,
pp. 49–50, Act. 18–21

36 ### Grammaire en contexte

Parlons With a partner, create a conversation in which you make plans to do some-thing on Saturday. Use the places in the images for your conversation. Invite each other to go to different places and refuse the first suggestions. Once you agree on a place, make plans for when and where to meet.

a.

b.

c.

d.

REVISIONS

Le Monde francophone

Qu'est-ce que tu aimes faire après l'école?

Léontine, Côte d'Ivoire

J'aime lire les romans. J'aime regarder la télévision.

Tu as quels cours?

Morgan, France

J'ai français, mathématiques, géographie, anglais et sciences et c'est tout.

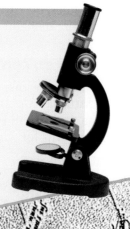

Qu'est-ce que tu fais comme sport?

Olivier, Martinique

J'aime la natation. J'aime beaucoup aller à la mer pour nager, me relaxer, me dorer au soleil. J'aime aussi le volley-ball, le badminton. J'aime pas le football par contre et... ni le basket.

Qu'est-ce que tu fais quand tu sors?

Léna, France

Je vais dans des cafés; je vais au cinéma, à la piscine; je vais voir des pièces de théâtre.

As-tu compris?

A. When does Léontine like to read?
B. What else does she like to do?
C. What classes does Morgan have?
D. What sports does Olivier enjoy?
E. Where does he go to swim?
F. Does he like soccer?
G. Where does Léna go to swim?
H. What else does she like to do when she goes out?

SONDAGE

Using the four questions asked in the interviews, create a survey (**un sondage**). Then pick six classmates and ask them the questions in your survey. They should answer in French. Write down their answers and tally them. You might present the results to the class. (Example: **Trois camarades aiment aller au cinéma, deux camarades aiment nager,...**)

REVISIONS

Réponds aux questions suivantes.

SECTION A

1 Tu t'appelles comment?

2 Tu as quel âge?

3 Quand tu parles à ton professeur de français, est-ce que tu lui dis «Bonjour, vous allez bien?» ou «Salut, ça va?»? Pourquoi?

4 Tes amis et toi, qu'est-ce que vous aimez faire le week-end?

5 Est-ce que tu aimes mieux étudier ou regarder la télé?

6 Comment s'appelle ton professeur de français?

SECTION B

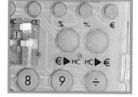

7 Tu as quoi comme cours le lundi?

8 Il est 22h et tu parles avec un autre élève du cours de français au téléphone. A la fin de la conversation, est-ce que tu lui dis «A tout à l'heure» ou «A demain»? Pourquoi?

9 Quels jours de la semaine est-ce que tu vas à l'école?

10 Vrai ou faux : Tu es plus âgé(e) (*older*) que les élèves de terminale.

11 Qu'est-ce qu'il y a dans ton sac pour l'école?

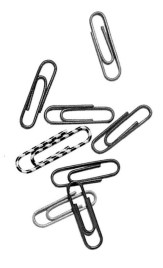

12 Tu as un sac à dos? Il est de quelle couleur?

13 Quelle est ta couleur préférée? *(Hint:* C'est le _____.)

14 Tu as des feuilles de papier pour prendre des notes *(to take notes)?* Elles sont de quelle couleur?

15 C'est quand, ton anniversaire *(birthday)?*

16 Quel temps fait-il dans ta région en été?

17 En quels mois sont les fêtes suivantes chez toi?
    a. la fête nationale
    b. la Saint-Patrick
    c. la fête du travail

18 Tu es au café et tu as très faim. Qu'est-ce que tu prends?

19 Quand toi et tes amis, vous avez soif, qu'est-ce que vous prenez?

20 Tu es au café et tu veux voir la carte. Qu'est-ce que tu demandes au serveur?

21 Qu'est-ce que tu proposes à tes amis quand vous avez du temps libre *(free time)?*

22 Qu'est-ce que tu vas faire ce week-end?

23 Qu'est-ce que tu fais comme sport?

24 A quelle heure est-ce que tu vas à l'école?

25 Quand tu veux faire une promenade, où est-ce que tu vas?

Pose les questions 2, 4, 12, 13, 22 et 23 à trois camarades de la classe de français. Note les réponses de tes camarades et donne-les au professeur.

7
La famille

Objectives

In this chapter you will learn to

Première étape

- identify and introduce people

Deuxième étape

- describe and characterize people

Troisième étape

- ask for, give, and refuse permission

◢ internet

ADRESSE: go.hrw.com
MOT-CLE: WA3 PARIS-7

◀ **Elle est comment, ta famille?**

MISE EN TRAIN · *Sympa, la famille!*

Stratégie pour comprendre
Look at the people pictured in the photo album. Can you guess how they're related to Isabelle?

Thuy

Isabelle

1
Thuy : Tiens, j'adore regarder les photos. Je peux les voir?
Isabelle : Bien sûr!

2 Ce sont mes grands-parents. Ils sont heureux sur cette photo. Ils fêtent leur quarantième anniversaire de mariage.

Ma tante Loïc Mon oncle
Julie Patricia

4 Là, c'est mon oncle et ma tante, le frère de ma mère et sa femme. Et au milieu, ce sont leurs enfants, mes cousins. Ils habitent tous en Bretagne. Ça, c'est Loïc. Il a 18 ans. C'est Julie. Elle a 8 ans. Elle est adorable. Et elle, c'est ma cousine Patricia. Elle est très intelligente. En maths, elle a toujours 18 sur 20!

3 C'est une photo de Papa et Maman

5

Là, c'est moi. Quel amour de bébé, n'est-ce pas? Je suis toute petite... peut-être un an et demi.

6

C'est mon frère Alexandre. Il a 11 ans. Il est parfois pénible.

7

C'est ma tante du côté de mon père. Elle s'appelle Véronique. Ça, c'est son chat Musica. Elle adore les animaux. Elle a aussi deux chiens!

8

Isabelle : Et toi, tu n'as pas de frères ou de sœurs?

Thuy : Non. Je suis fille unique.

Isabelle : Tu as de la chance.

Cahier d'activités, p. 73, Act. 1

MISE EN TRAIN

1 Tu as compris?

Réponds aux questions suivantes sur *Sympa, la famille!*

1. What are Isabelle and Thuy talking about?
2. Does Isabelle have brothers or sisters? If so, what are their names?
3. How many cousins does she have?
4. Who are some of the other family members she mentions?
5. How does Isabelle feel about her family? How can you tell?

2 Vrai ou faux?

1. Julie a huit ans.
2. Julie est blonde.
3. Les cousins d'Isabelle habitent à Paris.

4. Tante Véronique n'a pas d'animaux.
5. Thuy a un frère.

3 Quelle photo?

De quelle photo est-ce qu'Isabelle parle?

1. Il a onze ans.
2. En maths, elle a toujours 18 sur 20.
3. J'ai un an et demi, je crois...
4. Elle a huit ans.

a.

b.

c.

d.

4 Cherche les expressions

In *Sympa, la famille!*, what does Isabelle or Thuy say to . . .

1. ask permission?
2. identify family members?
3. describe someone?
4. pay a compliment?
5. tell someone's age?
6. complain about someone?

> Je peux... ?   C'est...
>
> Elle est très intelligente.
>
> Elle est adorable.   Il/Elle a... ans.
>
> Ce sont...
>
> Il est parfois pénible.   Ils sont heureux.

5 Et maintenant, à toi

Est-ce que la famille d'Isabelle est comme les familles que tu connais? Est-ce qu'elle est différente? Pourquoi?

Comment dit-on...?

Identifying people

To identify people:

C'est ma tante Véronique.
Ce sont mes cousins Loïc et Julie. *These/Those are . . .*
Voici mon frère Alexandre. *Here's . . .*
Voilà Patricia. *There's . . .*

6 C'est qui?

Parlons Avec un(e) partenaire, inventez des identités pour les personnes qui sont sur cette photo.

Les membres de la famille d'Isabelle

Other family relationships:
la femme *wife*
le mari *husband*
la fille *daughter*
le fils *son*
l'enfant *child*
le parent *parent, relative*

Ma grand-mère et mon grand-père,
Eugénie et Jean-Marie Ménard

Ma tante
Véronique, la
sœur de mon
père

Mon père et ma mère, Raymond
et Josette Guérin

Mon oncle et ma tante, Guillaume
et Micheline Ménard

Mon frère
Alexandre

C'est moi!

Mes cousines Patricia et Julie, et mon cousin Loïc

Mon chien   Mon chat

Mon canari   Mon poisson

Cahier d'activités, pp. 74–75, Act. 2a, 4a

Travaux pratiques de grammaire, p. 51, Act. 1–2

Note de grammaire

Use **de (d')** to indicate relationship or ownership.

C'est la mère **de** Paul.
That's Paul's mother.
Voici le chien **d'**Ophélie.
Here's Ophélie's dog.
C'est un ami **du** prof.
That's the teacher's friend.

Grammaire supplémentaire, p. 218, Act. 1

Cahier d'activités, pp. 74, 76, Act. 2b, 7b

Travaux pratiques de grammaire, p. 52, Act. 3–4

7 ### Grammaire en contexte

Parlons Quels membres de la famille d'Isabelle sont décrits dans les phrases suivantes?

EXEMPLE **Le frère de Véronique, c'est Raymond.**

1. C'est le père d'Alexandre.
2. C'est la femme de Guillaume.
3. C'est le grand-père de Julie.
4. C'est la mère de Patricia.
5. Ce sont les sœurs de Loïc.
6. C'est le cousin de Patricia.

8 La famille d'Alain

Ecoutons Alain montre des photos de sa famille à Jay. De quelle photo est-ce qu'il parle?

a.   b.   c.   d.   e.

Grammaire

Possessive adjectives

	Before a masculine singular noun	Before a feminine singular noun	Before a plural noun
my	mon	ma	mes
your	ton	ta	tes
his/her/its	son	sa	ses
our	notre } frère	notre } sœur	nos } frères
your	votre	votre	vos
their	leur	leur	leurs

- **Son, sa,** and **ses** may mean either *her* or *his.*

  C'est **son** père.   That's *her* father. *or* That's *his* father.
  C'est **sa** mère.   That's *her* mother. *or* That's *his* mother.
  Ce sont **ses** parents.   Those are *her* parents. *or* Those are *his* parents.

- **Mon, ton,** and **son** are used before all singular nouns that begin with a vowel sound, whether the noun is masculine or feminine.

  C'est **ton amie** Marianne?
  C'est **mon oncle** Xavier.

- Liaison is always made with **mon, ton,** and **son,** and with all the plural forms.

  mon école   **nos amis**

- Use **ton, ta,** and **tes** with people you would normally address with **tu.** Use **votre** and **vos** with people you would normally address with **vous.**

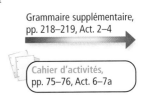

Grammaire supplémentaire, pp. 218–219, Act. 2–4

Cahier d'activités, pp. 75–76, Act. 6–7a

Travaux pratiques de grammaire, p. 53, Act. 5–7

9 Grammaire en contexte

Ecoutons Listen to Roland and Odile. Are they talking about their own pets or someone else's? Then, listen again to find out what kind of pets they're talking about.

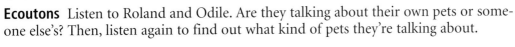

Note culturelle

Family life plays an important role in French society. Although modern times have brought changes to the family's daily life (more working mothers, less time for family activities, more divorces, and so on), France is working hard to maintain the family unit. To do this, the French government provides subsidies (**allocations familiales**) to all families with two or more children. Other social benefits also encourage larger families in a country with an ever-decreasing birth rate. These benefits include a paid maternity leave of at least 14 weeks, a renewable maternity or paternity leave of one year, free day-care, and a birth allowance (**allocation de naissance**) for every child after the second. Families also receive subsidies for each child attending school or college.

10 Grammaire en contexte

Parlons Tu habites avec une famille française. Tu montres une photo de ta famille à ton/ta camarade. Explique-lui qui sont les personnes sur la photo. Il/Elle va te poser des questions. Ensuite, changez de rôle.

EXEMPLE

—C'est qui, ça?

—C'est ma sœur.

—Elle joue souvent au tennis?

—Oui. Une fois par semaine.

11 Devine!

Parlons Identifie les personnes sur les images suivantes et explique leurs relations. Travaille avec un(e) camarade, puis changez de rôle.

EXEMPLE   C'est Nadine et son grand-père.

Hassan

Thierry

Monique et Annie

Nadine

Liliane

Introducing people

To introduce someone to a friend:

C'est Jean-Michel.
Je te présente mon ami Jean-Michel.
I'd like you to meet . . .

To introduce someone to an adult:

Je vous présente Jean-Michel.

To respond to an introduction:

Salut, Jean-Michel. **Ça va?**
Bonjour.
Très heureux (heureuse).
Pleased to meet you. (formal)

Cahier d'activités, p. 76, Act. 8

12 Les présentations

Ecoutons Are the people in these conversations identifying someone or introducing someone?

13 Je te présente...

Parlons Il y a un(e) nouvel(le) élève français(e) dans ton école. Il/Elle te demande comment tes camarades s'appellent et quel âge ils ont. Travaillez en groupe et faites les présentations. Ensuite, changez de rôle.

14 Mon journal

Ecrivons Ecris un paragraphe sur ta famille. Donne le nom et l'âge de chaque personne et explique ce que cette personne aime bien faire. Si tu préfères, tu peux aussi inventer une famille ou décrire une famille célèbre ou une famille de la télé.

Tu te rappelles?

Do you remember how to ask for and give people's name and age?

—Elle s'appelle comment?
—Magali.
—Elle a quel âge?
—Seize ans.

Vocabulaire à la carte

Here are some other words you might need to talk about your family.

des petits-enfants	*grandchildren*
un demi-frère	*stepbrother; half brother*
une demi-sœur	*stepsister; half sister*
un(e) enfant unique	*an only child*
une belle-mère	*stepmother/mother-in-law*
un beau-père	*stepfather/father-in-law*
un petit-fils	*grandson*
une petite-fille	*granddaughter*
une nièce	*niece*
un neveu	*nephew*

Vocabulaire

Ils sont comment?

PETITE   GRAND

BRUNE   BLOND   ROUX

JEUNE   AGÉE

MINCE   GROS

You can also use these descriptive words:

mignon(mignonne)(s) *cute*   **ne... ni grand(e)(s) ni petit(e)(s)** ... *neither tall nor short*

You can use these words to characterize people:

amusant(e)(s) *funny*	**intelligent(e)(s)** *smart*	**embêtant(e)(s)** *annoying*
timide(s) *shy*	**content(e)(s)** *happy*	**pénible(s)** *a pain in the neck*
gentil(le)(s) *nice*	**fort(e)(s)** *strong*	**méchant(e)(s)** *mean*
sympathique(s)/sympa(s) *nice*		

Cahier d'activités,
p. 77, Act. 9–10

Travaux pratiques de
grammaire, p. 54, Act. 8–9

DE BONS CONSEILS

Organizing vocabulary in various ways can help you remember words. Group words by categories, like foods, sports, numbers, colors, and so forth. Try to associate words with a certain context, such as school (school subjects, classroom objects) or a store (items for sale, salesperson). Try to use associations like opposites, such as **petit—grand** or **gros—mince.**

15 De qui est-ce qu'on parle?

Ecoutons Match the descriptions you hear with the students' names.

Roger   Denise   Julie   Martin   Carmen

Comment dit-on...?

Describing and characterizing people

To ask what someone is like:

Il est comment? *What is he like?*
Elle est comment? *What is she like?*
Ils/Elles sont comment? *What are they like?*

To describe someone:

Il n'est ni grand **ni** petit.
Elle est brune.
Ils/Elles sont âgé(e)s.

To characterize someone:

Il est pénible.
Elle est timide.
Ils/Elles sont amusant(e)s.

Cahier d'activités,
p. 78, Act. 13

16 Les cousins d'Ariane

Ecoutons Ariane is telling a friend about her cousins. Does she have a favorable or unfavorable opinion of them?

17 Des familles bizarres

Parlons Comment sont les membres de ces familles?

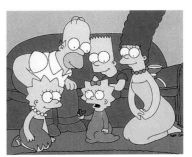

Adjective agreement

As you may remember from Chapter 3, you often change the pronunciation and spelling of adjectives according to the nouns they describe.

- If the adjective describes a feminine noun, you usually add an **e** to the masculine form of the adjective.

- If the adjective describes a plural noun, you usually add an **s** to the singular form, masculine or feminine.

- If an adjective describes both males and females, you always use the masculine plural form.

- Some adjectives have special (irregular) feminine or plural forms. Here are some irregular adjectives that you've seen in this chapter.

Il est **roux**.	Elle est **rousse**.
Ils sont **roux**.	Elles sont **rousses**.
Il est **mignon**.	Elle est **mignonne**.
Ils sont **mignons**.	Elles sont **mignonnes**.
Il est **gentil**.	Elle est **gentille**.
Ils sont **gentils**.	Elles sont **gentilles**.
Il est **gros**.	Elle est **grosse**.
Ils sont **gros**.	Elles sont **grosses**.
Il est **sympa**.	Elle est **sympa**.
Ils sont **sympas**.	Elles sont **sympas**.

Grammaire supplémentaire,
p. 219, Act. 5–6

Cahier d'activités,
pp. 77–78, Act. 11–12

Travaux pratiques de
grammaire,
pp. 55–57, Act. 10–14

- In the masculine forms, the final consonant sound is silent. In the feminine forms, the final consonant sound is pronounced.

- A few adjectives don't ever change. Here are some that you've already seen.

marron   **orange**   **cool**   **super**

---

18 ### Grammaire en contexte

Parlons Frédéric et Denise sont frère et sœur. Regarde l'image et dis s'ils sont semblables ou différents.

EXEMPLE   **Frédéric est grand,
mais Denise est petite.**

19 ### Grammaire en contexte

Parlons Décris ton/ta meilleur(e) ami(e) à un(e) camarade. Dis comment il/elle est physiquement. Décris sa personnalité et ce qu'il/elle aime. Ensuite, changez de rôle.

Grammaire

The verb *être*

Etre is an irregular verb.

Grammaire supplémentaire,
pp. 220–221, Act. 7–9

Cahier d'activités,
pp. 78–79, Act. 14–15

Travaux pratiques
de grammaire,
pp. 57–58, Act. 15–17

être *(to be)*

Je	**suis** intelligent(e).	Nous	**sommes** intelligent(e)s.
Tu	**es** intelligent(e).	Vous	**êtes** intelligent(e)(s).
Il/Elle/On	**est** intelligent(e).	Ils/Elles	**sont** intelligent(e)s.

20 Grammaire en contexte

Ecrivons Albain décrit tout le monde. Complète ses descriptions avec la forme appropriée du verbe **être**.

Je ___1___ blond, mais Rénato et Jacob, ils ___2___ bruns. Francette et Babette, vous ___3___ rousses. Et toi, Francette, tu ___4___ grande aussi. Rénato aussi ___5___ grand, et pénible. Babette ___6___ très gentille et mignonne. Mais les différences ne ___7___ pas importantes. Nous ___8___ tous intelligents.

21 Grammaire en contexte

Parlons Décris un membre de la famille Louvain à un(e) camarade. Attention! Ne dis pas comment il/elle s'appelle. Ton/Ta camarade doit deviner de qui tu parles. Ensuite, changez de rôle.

M. Louvain **Chantal** **Gabrielle** **Mme Louvain** **M. Louvain** **Mme Louvain** **Emile** **Philou et Chouchou** **Luc**

22 Mon journal

Ecrivons Ecris un paragraphe pour décrire une personne de ta famille que tu admires. Dis ce qu'il/elle aime faire et où il/elle aime aller. Si tu préfères, tu peux décrire un personnage de la télé.

Tu as un animal domestique? Il est comment?

We talked to some French-speaking people about their pets. Here's what they had to say.

Olivier,
Martinique

«Oui, j'ai un animal à la maison, un chien. Son nom, c'est Chopine. Il n'est pas trop gros, [il est] vivant. Il aime beaucoup s'amuser et beaucoup manger aussi.»

Onélia,
France

«J'ai un chat. Il s'appelle Fabécar. Il a trois ans. C'est un mâle. On le voit assez rarement. On le voit seulement quand il veut manger, sinon il se promène dans les jardins. Il est très affectueux.»

Marie-Emmanuelle,
France

«J'ai un cheval. Il est grand. Il fait 1 mètre 78 au garrot. Il est brun. Il s'appelle Viêt. Et on fait des balades à cheval.»

Qu'en penses-tu?

1. What names do these people give their pets?
2. Do you take your pets out in public? Why or why not? If so, where?
3. What kind of system is used in the United States to identify lost pets?

Savais-tu que...?

More than half of French households have pets. City dwellers often take them along when they shop. In many francophone countries, people sometimes carry small animals in baskets (**paniers**) made just for them! It isn't unusual to see dogs and cats on trains or in subways, restaurants, department stores, and other public places. Most pet owners have their four-legged friends tattooed with a number that allows them to be identified in case they are lost. Various groups in France have launched poster campaigns to encourage dog owners to teach their pets to use the gutter instead of the sidewalk: **Apprenez-leur le caniveau!**

Objective Asking for, giving, and refusing permission

Comment dit-on...?

Asking for, giving, and refusing permission

To ask for permission:

> Je voudrais aller au cinéma. **Tu es d'accord?**
> *Is that OK with you?*
> **(Est-ce que) je peux** sortir? *May I . . .*

To give permission:

> **Oui, si tu veux.** *Yes, if you want to.*
> **Pourquoi pas?**
> **Oui, bien sûr.**
> **D'accord, si tu** fais **d'abord** la vaisselle.
> *OK, if you . . . first.*

To refuse permission:

> **Pas question!** *Out of the question!*
> **Non, c'est impossible.** *No, that's impossible.*
> **Non, tu dois** faire tes devoirs.
> *No, you've got to . . .*
> **Pas** ce soir. *Not . . .*

Grammaire supplémentaire,
p. 221, Act. 10

Cahier d'activités,
p. 81, Act. 21

23 **Je peux... ?**

Ecoutons Listen to these people ask for permission. Are they given or refused permission?

Vocabulaire

débarrasser la table	*to clear the table*
faire les courses	*to do the shopping*
faire le ménage	*to clean house*
faire la vaisselle	*to do the dishes*
garder ta petite sœur	*to look after . . .*
laver la voiture	*to wash the car*
passer l'aspirateur	*to vacuum*
promener le chien	*to walk the dog*
ranger ta chambre	*to pick up your room*
sortir la poubelle	*to take out the trash*
tondre le gazon	*to mow the lawn*

Cahier d'activités,
pp. 80–82, Act. 17–18, 20, 22–23

Travaux pratiques de grammaire,
pp. 59–60, Act. 18–21

24 Permission donnée ou refusée

Ecoutons Listen to some French teenagers ask permission to go out with their friends. Which picture represents the outcome of each dialogue?

a.

b.

c.

d.

e.

f.

25 Qui doit le faire?

Parlons Demande à un(e) camarade qui fait les corvées ménagères dans sa famille. Ensuite, changez de rôle.

EXEMPLE   —Qui promène le chien?
               —Mon frère. Et moi aussi quelquefois.

26 Tu es d'accord?

Ecrivons Qu'est-ce que ces personnes disent?

1.

2.

3.

4.

27 **Et toi?**

Parlons Donne la permission ou refuse la permission dans les situations suivantes.

1. Ta petite sœur ou ton petit frère veut écouter ta cassette.

2. Ton ami(e) veut lire ton livre.

3. Ta petite sœur ou ton petit frère veut aller avec tes amis et toi au cinéma.

28
De l'école au travail

Parlons This summer, you're going to work for a French family as a babysitter. Your partner is going to play the role of one of the children, and he is going to ask you permission to do different things this weekend. Give permission for some activities and say no for others. Explain why you gave or refused permission. Then, change roles.

PRONONCIATION

The nasal sounds [ɔ̃], [ɛ̃], and [œ̃]

In Chapter 5 you learned about the nasal sound [ɑ̃]. Now listen to the other French nasal sounds [ɔ̃], [ɛ̃], and [œ̃]. As you repeat the following words, try not to put a trace of the consonant **n** in your nasal sounds.

on   hein   un

How are these nasal sounds represented in writing? The nasal sound [ɔ̃] is represented by a combination of **on** or **om.** Several letter combinations can represent the sound [ɛ̃], for example, **in, im, ain, aim, (i)en.** The nasal sound [œ̃] is spelled **un** or **um.** A vowel after these groups of letters or, in some cases, a doubling of the consonant **n** or **m** will result in a non-nasal sound, as in **limonade** and **ennemi.**

A. A prononcer

Repeat the following words.

1. ton   blond   pardon   nombre
2. cousin   impossible   copain   faim
3. un   lundi   brun   humble

B. A lire

Take turns with a partner reading the following sentences aloud.

1. Ils ont très faim. Ils vont prendre des sandwiches au jambon. C'est bon!
2. Allons faire du patin ou bien, allons au concert!
3. Ce garçon est blond et ce garçon-là est brun. Ils sont minces et mignons!
4. Pardon. C'est combien, cette montre?

C. A écrire

You're going to hear a short dialogue. Write down what you hear.

En direct des refuges

Stratégie pour lire

When you read something, it's important to separate the main idea from the supporting details. Sometimes the main idea is clearly stated at the beginning, other times it's just implied.

A. Which completion best expresses the main idea of these articles?

These articles are about . . .

1. animals that are missing.
2. animals that have performed heroic rescues.
3. animals that are up for adoption.
4. animals that have won prizes at cat and dog shows.

B. Now that you've decided what the main idea of the reading is, make a list of the kinds of details you expect to find in each of the articles.

C. How is Mayo different from the other animals? What is the main idea of the article about him? What other details are given?

D. Each of the articles includes a description of the animal. Look at the articles again and answer these questions.

1. Which animal is the oldest? The youngest?
2. Which animals get along well with children?

EN DIRECT DES REFUGES

IL VOUS ATTEND, ADOPTEZ-LE

CAMEL, 5 ANS

Ce sympathique bobtail blanc et gris est arrivé au refuge à la suite du décès accidentel de son maître. Il est vif, joyeux, a bon caractère et s'entend très bien avec les enfants. En échange de son dévouement et de sa fidélité, ce sportif robuste demande un grand espace afin de pouvoir courir et s'ébattre à son aise.

Continuez à nous écrire, et envoyez-nous votre photo avec votre protégé, une surprise vous attend!

Cet animal vous attend au refuge de la Société normande de protection aux animaux, 7 bis, avenue Jacques-Chastellain, Ile Lacroix 76000 Rouen. Tél.: (02) 35.70.20.36. Si Camel a été adopté, pensez à ses voisins de cage.

ELLE VOUS ATTEND, ADOPTEZ-LA

DADY, 2 ANS

Toute blanche, à l'exception de quelques petites taches et des oreilles noires bien dressées, Dady a un petit air de spitz, opulente fourrure en moins. Gentille, enjouée, très attachante, elle a été abandonnée après la séparation de ses maîtres et attend une famille qui accepterait de s'occuper d'elle un peu, beaucoup, passionnément.

Cet animal vous attend au refuge de l'Eden, Rod A'char, 29430 Lanhouarneau. Tél.: (02) 98.61.64.55. Colette Di Faostino tient seule, sans aucune subvention, ce havre exemplaire mais pauvre. Si Dady a été adoptée, pensez à ses compagnons de malchance !

Mayo a trouvé une famille

Mayo a été adopté à la SPA de Valenciennes par Françoise Robeaux qui rêvait d'un chat gris ! Il a ainsi rejoint l'autre «fils» de la famille, un superbe siamois âgé de 13 ans.

ELLE VOUS ATTEND, ADOPTEZ-LA
POUPETTE, 3 ANS

Cette jolie chatte stérilisée au regard tendre et étonné a été recueillie à l'âge de quelques semaines par une vieille dame, dont elle a été la dernière compagne. Sa maîtresse est malheureusement décédée après un long séjour à l'hôpital. Poupette, l'orpheline, ne comprend pas ce qui lui arrive et commence à trouver le temps long ! Elle a hâte de retrouver un foyer «sympa», des bras caressants et une paire de genoux pour ronronner.

Cet animal vous attend avec espoir au refuge Grammont de la SPA 30, av. du Général-de-Gaulle 92230 Gennevilliers. Tél.: (01) 47.98.57.40. Rens. sur Minitel: 36.15 SPA. Si Poupette est déjà partie, pensez aux autres!

IL VOUS ATTEND, ADOPTEZ-LE
JUPITER, 7 MOIS

Cet adorable chaton tigré et blanc vient tout juste d'être castré et est dûment tatoué. Très joueur et affectueux, il a été recueilli au refuge parce que, malheureusement, sa maîtresse a dû être hospitalisée pour un séjour de longue durée. Sociable, il s'entend très bien avec les jeunes enfants et accepterait volontiers un chien pour compagnon.

Cet animal vous attend au refuge de la fondation Assistance aux animaux, 8, rue des Plantes 77410 Villevaudé. Tél.: (01) 60.26.20.48 (l'après-midi seulement).

ELLE VOUS ATTEND, ADOPTEZ-LA
FLORA, 3 ANS

C'est une pure braque Saint Germain roux et blanc. Elle ne pense qu'à jouer, s'entend bien avec les enfants et témoigne d'une gentillesse infatigable. Flora a été abandonnée car elle ne s'intéressait pas à la chasse. Son sport passion : la course derrière la «baballe».

Elle vous attend au refuge de l'Eden, Rod A'char, 29430 Lanhouarneau. Tél.: (02) 98.61.64.55. Colette Di Faostino tient seule, sans aucune subvention, ce havre exemplaire mais pauvre. Si Flora a déjà été adoptée, pensez à ses compagnons !

Vous avez recueilli un animal par notre intermédiaire ? Envoyez-nous votre photo avec votre protégé, une surprise vous attend!

---

3. Which animal needs a lot of space?

4. Which animals love to play?

E. Make a list of all the adjectives of physical description that you can find in the articles. Now, list the adjectives that describe the animals' characteristics.

F. Each article also explains why these animals were sent to the animal shelter.
   1. Which animal wasn't interested in hunting?
   2. Whose owner was involved in an accident?
   3. Whose owner had to go to the hospital for a long time?
   4. Whose family got separated?

G. A third kind of detail tells where you can go to adopt these animals. Can you find the French word for *animal shelter*?

H. Now, write your own classified ad to try to find a home for a lost pet. Remember to give the animal's name and age, tell what the animal looks like, and describe his or her character.

   or

   Write a letter to the animal shelter telling them what kind of pet you would like to adopt.
   1. First, make a list of all of the characteristics you're looking for in a pet. Will you choose to adopt a cat or a dog? What will he or she look like? Act like? Like to do?
   2. Write a short letter, including all the important information about your desired pet.
   3. Don't forget to give your address and telephone number!

Cahier d'activités, p. 83, Act. 25

Grammaire supplémentaire

Première étape Objectives Identifying and introducing people

1 Ahmed est nouveau dans ton quartier. Aide-le à identifier certaines personnes. Pour répondre à ses questions, utilise **c'est** et **ce sont** et les mots entre parenthèses dans l'ordre où ils se trouvent. (**pp. 203, 204**)

EXEMPLE —C'est qui, Karim et Mohammed? (les oncles/Samira)
—Ce sont les oncles de Samira.

1. C'est qui, Claudette? (la grand-mère/Guy)
2. C'est qui, Arnaud et Martin? (les frères/Marie)
3. C'est qui, Mourad? (le fils/Fatima)
4. C'est qui, Jacqueline et Jeanne? (les tantes/Paul)
5. C'est qui, Ismaïl? (le grand-père/Saïdou)
6. C'est qui, Hélène? (la fille/Jean)
7. C'est qui, Stéphane? (le petit-fils/Mme Lominé)

2 Sabine and Claire are asking their younger brother Luc to bring them some items they forgot in their room. Complete their statements with the appropriate possessive adjectives. (**p. 205**)

EXEMPLE Luc, apporte-nous **nos** calculatrices, s'il te plaît!

1. Apporte-nous _____ stylos, s'il te plaît!
2. Apporte-moi _____ trousse, s'il te plaît!
3. Apporte-moi _____ cahiers, s'il te plaît!
4. Apporte-nous _____ dictionnaire, s'il te plaît!
5. Apporte-moi _____ calculatrice, s'il te plaît!
6. Apporte-nous _____ sacs, s'il te plaît!

3 Luc ne trouve pas ce que ses sœurs veulent. Il leur demande où ces choses se trouvent. Complète ses questions avec les adjectifs possessifs appropriés. (**p. 205**)

1. (à Claire et à Sabine) Ils sont où, _____ stylos?
2. (à Claire) Elle est où, _____ trousse?
3. (à Sabine) Ils sont où, _____ cahiers?
4. (à Sabine et à Claire) Il est où, _____ dictionnaire?
5. (à Claire) Elle est où, _____ calculatrice?
6. (à Sabine et à Claire) Ils sont où, _____ sacs?

4 Mazarine et Jean-Luc parlent de leurs animaux domestiques. Complète leurs phrases avec les adjectifs possessifs appropriés. (**p. 205**)

MAZARINE   Il a quel âge, ___1___ chien, Jean-Luc?

JEAN-LUC   ___2___ chien? Je n'ai pas de chien. Par contre, j'ai des poissons rouges!

MAZARINE   Ah, c'est cool, ça! Ils s'appellent comment, ___3___ poissons?

JEAN-LUC   Elvis et Presley. Tu aimes les poissons rouges, toi?

MAZARINE   Oui, beaucoup, mais j'aime mieux les chats et les canaris.
            ___4___ sœur a deux chats et trois canaris.

JEAN-LUC   Ils sont comment, les chats de ___5___ sœur?

MAZARINE   Très mignons!

JEAN-LUC   Et ___6___ canaris?

MAZARINE   Eh bien, ils sont jaunes.

JEAN-LUC   Ah! Très drôle! Est-ce que ___7___ parents aiment bien les animaux?

MAZARINE   Oui. Chez moi, tout le monde adore les animaux.

Deuxième étape   Objective Describing and characterizing people

5 Déchiffre chaque adjectif, et ensuite, fais l'accord avec le sujet, si c'est nécessaire. (**p. 210**)

1. Daniel est UNBR.
2. Ses amis sont LNBOD.
3. Ses tantes sont NILTEG.
4. Ses frères sont OFRT.
5. Ses sœurs sont TNSUAMA.

6. Son chien est BNTAMEET.
7. Sa grand-mère est ETPIT.
8. Ses chats sont ROGS.
9. Sa mère est XRUO.
10. Son cousin est ENBLEPI.

6 Complète chaque phrase avec l'adjectif approprié et fais l'accord nécessaire. (**p. 210**)

1. J'aime beaucoup ta cousine Mathilde. Elle est _____. (pénible/sympa)
2. Cette quiche est _____! (super/timide)
3. Tes yeux sont _____. (orange/marron)
4. J'aime bien ta grand-mère. Elle est _____. (embêtant/amusant)
5. Ta mère est _____, non? (roux/orange)

Grammaire supplémentaire

CD-ROM 2 DVD 1

go.
hrw
.com
WA3 PARIS-7

7 Complète chaque phrase logiquement. (**p. 211**)

1. Je...	**a.** est très gentille.
2. Elles...	**b.** suis grand et fort.
3. Tu...	**c.** sont embêtants.
4. Julien et moi, on...	**d.** sommes très minces.
5. Jeanne...	**e.** es méchant!
6. Alice et moi, nous...	**f.** êtes un peu pénibles!
7. Mes frères...	**g.** est roux.
8. Marie et toi, vous...	**h.** sont intelligentes.

8 Choose the expression from the box below that completes each sentence logically. Be sure to consider adjective agreement while making your choices. (**p. 211**)

1. _____ rousses mais toi, tu es blonde.

2. _____ très gentille. Tu l'invites à ma boum, d'accord?

3. _____ très cool. Je peux les écouter?

4. _____ brun mais toi, tu es blonde.

5. _____ mignon comme tout! Viens ici, Médor.

6. _____ timides et ne parlent jamais.

7. _____ orange. C'est bizarre.

Ton chien est	Tes CD sont
	Ton père est
Ta sœur est	Tes baskets sont
Tes cousines sont	Tes amis sont

9 Emma veut savoir comment sont les personnes qui sont dans l'album de photos de Gustave. Ecris ses questions en utilisant la forme correcte du verbe **être** et l'adjectif possessif approprié. (**pp. 205, 211**)

EXEMPLE   GUSTAVE   Ça, ce sont mes cousines Arianne et Aurélie.

               EMMA   **Elles sont comment, tes cousines?**

1. Ça, c'est mon cousin Jean-Pierre.
2. Voilà mes tantes Yvette et Claudette.
3. Ça, ce sont mes oncles André et Auguste.
4. Voilà mes grands-parents.
5. Voilà ma sœur Rosalie.

Troisième étape

Objective Asking for, giving, and refusing permission

10 Onélia veut faire beaucoup de choses, mais, d'abord, elle doit demander la permission à ses parents. Complète ses questions avec la forme appropriée du verbe **être**. (**pp. 211, 213**)

1. Je voudrais sortir avec mes copains. Tu _____ d'accord, Maman?
2. Je voudrais aller au cinéma. Vous _____ d'accord?
3. Je voudrais aller à la MJC. Tu _____ d'accord, Papa?
4. Je _____ invitée à la boum de Pierre. Vous _____ d'accord?

11 Mme Ménard demande à ses enfants de l'aider. Complète leurs réponses avec la forme correcte du verbe **être**. (**pp. 211, 213**)

1. MME MENARD   Fabienne, tu fais les courses, s'il te plaît?
      FABIENNE   Désolée, je _____ occupée. J'ai des devoirs à faire.

2. MME MENARD   Anne et Eva, vous faites la vaisselle, s'il vous plaît?
   ANNE ET EVA   Désolées, nous _____ occupées.

3. MME MENARD   Paul et Eric, vous pouvez débarrasser la table?
   PAUL ET ERIC   Désolés, on _____ occupés. On a des trucs à faire.

4. MME MENARD   Lise, tu peux promener le chien?
         LISE   Oui, bien sûr!
  MME MENARD   Merci. Tu _____ très gentille!

Mise en pratique

1   Ecoute Nathalie qui va te parler de sa famille. Puis, réponds aux questions.

1. Comment s'appelle le frère de Nathalie?
2. Il a quel âge?
3. Est-ce qu'elle a un chien ou un chat?
4. Comment est son animal?

2 D'abord, lis ces documents rapidement. Ensuite, relis chaque document et réponds aux questions suivantes.

1. What kind of document is this? How do you know?
2. Who is Michel Louis Raymond?
3. Who are Denise Morel-Tissot and Raymond Tissot?
4. What happened on May 20, 2003?

> *Nous avons la joie de vous annoncer la naissance de notre fils*
>
> **Michel Louis Raymond**
> **20 mai 2003**
>
> *Denise Morel-Tissot*
> *Raymond Tissot*

5. What kind of document is this? How do you know?
6. Who are Christelle and Nicolas?
7. What happened on February 15, 2003, at three o'clock?
8. Who do you think M. and Mme Lionel Desombre are?

> *Christelle et Nicolas*
>
> *ont le plaisir de vous faire part de leur mariage*
>
> *qui aura lieu le quinze février 2003 à 15 heures, en la Mairie de Saint-Cyr-sur-Loire*
>
> *M. et Mme Lionel Desombre*
> *305 Rue des Marronniers*
> *37540 Saint-Cyr-sur-Loire*

3 Est-ce que ces phrases décrivent la culture française, la culture américaine ou les deux?

1. Dogs are not allowed in restaurants or department stores.

2. The government gives money to all families with two or more children.

3. Pets are tattooed with an identification number.

4. Women have a paid maternity leave of 14 weeks.

4 # Ecrivons!

Write a paragraph describing the family in the picture. Give French names to all the family members, tell their ages, give brief physical descriptions, say something about their personalities, and mention one or two things they each like to do.

Stratégie pour écrire

Using details to describe people will enable you to help your reader develop a clearer mental picture of what you're writing about. The more detailed the writing, the sharper the mental image the reader gets of the subject.

A cluster diagram, like the one you created in Chapter 3, will help you organize your thoughts. Make a large circle for each family member, then attach smaller circles for age, physical description, and so on.

Using the information you organized in your cluster diagram, write a paragraph describing the family in the picture. Imagine that your readers have never seen this picture before. After reading your paragraph, they should feel as if they know the members of the family personally. Be sure to use descriptive words you learned in this chapter, but remember those you've learned in previous chapters as well!

5 # Jeu de rôle

Your friends arrive at your door and suggest that you go out with them. Your parent tells them that you can go out if you finish your chores, so your friends offer to help. As you work around the house, you discuss where to go and what to do. Create a conversation with your classmates. Be prepared to act out the scene, using props.

Que sais-je?

WA3 PARIS-7

Can you use what you've learned in this chapter?

Can you identify people?
p. 203

1 How would you point out and identify Isabelle's relatives? How would you give their names and approximate ages? See page 204.
1. her grandparents
2. her uncle
3. her cousin Loïc
4. her brother

Can you introduce people?
p. 207

2 How would you introduce your friend to . . .
1. an adult relative?
2. a classmate?

Can you describe and characterize people?
p. 209

3 How would you describe these people?

1.

2.

4 How would you . . .
1. tell a friend that he or she is nice?
2. tell several friends that they're annoying?
3. say that you and your friend are intelligent?

Can you ask for, give, and refuse permission?
p. 213

5 How would you ask permission to . . .
1. go to the movies?
2. go out with your friends?
3. go shopping?
4. go ice-skating?

6 How would you give someone permission to do something? How would you refuse?

7 What are three things your parents might ask you to do before allowing you to go out with your friends?

224 *deux cent vingt-quatre*   CHAPITRE 7   La famille

Première étape

Vocabulaire

Première étape

Identifying people

C'est...	This/That is . . .
Ce sont...	These/those are . . .
Voici...	Here's . . .
Voilà...	There's . . .

Family members

la famille	family
le grand-père	grandfather
la grand-mère	grandmother
la mère	mother
le père	father
le parent	parent, relative
la femme	wife
le mari	husband
la sœur	sister
le frère	brother
la fille	daughter
le fils	son
l'enfant (m./f.)	child
l'oncle (m.)	uncle
la tante	aunt
la cousine	girl cousin
le cousin	boy cousin
le chat	cat
le chien	dog
le canari	canary
le poisson	fish

Possessive adjectives

mon/ma/mes	my
ton/ta/tes	your
son/sa/ses	his, her
notre/nos	our
votre/vos	your
leur/leurs	their

Introducing people

C'est...	This is . . .
Je te/vous présente...	I'd like you to meet . . .
Très heureux (heureuse).	Pleased to meet you. (formal)

Other useful expressions

de	of (indicates relationship or ownership)

Deuxième étape

Describing and characterizing people

Il est comment?	What is he like?
Elle est comment?	What is she like?
Ils/Elles sont comment?	What are they like?
Il est...	He is . . .
Elle est...	She is . . .
Ils/Elles sont...	They're . . .
amusant(e)	funny
content(e)	happy
embêtant(e)	annoying
fort(e)	strong
gentil (gentille)	nice
intelligent(e)	smart
méchant(e)	mean
pénible	annoying; a pain in the neck
sympa(thique)	nice
timide	shy
âgé(e)	older
blond(e)	blond
brun(e)	brunette
grand(e)	tall
gros (grosse)	fat
jeune	young
mince	slender
mignon (mignonne)	cute
ne... ni grand(e) ni petit(e)	neither tall nor short
petit(e)	short
roux (rousse)	redheaded
être	to be

Troisième étape

Asking for, giving, and refusing permission

Tu es d'accord?	Is that OK with you?
(Est-ce que) je peux... ?	May I . . . ?
Oui, si tu veux.	Yes, if you want to.
Pourquoi pas?	Why not?
Oui, bien sûr.	Yes, of course.
D'accord, si tu... d'abord...	OK, if you . . . first.
Pas question!	Out of the question!
Non, c'est impossible.	No, that's impossible.
Non, tu dois...	No, you've got to . . .
Pas...	Not . . .

Chores

débarrasser la table	to clear the table
faire la vaisselle	to do the dishes
faire le ménage	to clean house
faire les courses	to do the shopping
garder...	to look after . . .
laver la voiture	to wash the car
passer l'aspirateur	to vacuum
promener le chien	to walk the dog
ranger ta chambre	to pick up your room
sortir la poubelle	to take out the trash
tondre le gazon	to mow the lawn

Allez, viens à Abidjan!

Ville principale de la République de Côte d'Ivoire

Population : plus de 2.100.000

Points d'intérêt : l'Assemblée nationale, le palais du Président, le parc national du Banco, le Musée national

Abidjanais célèbres : Bernard Dadié, Goffi Jadeau, Amon d'Aby, Abdoulaye Traoré

Ressources et industries : café, cacao, bananes, textiles, bois

Spécialités : foutou, aloco, kedjenou, attiéké, sauce arachide, sauce graine, sauce claire

WA3 ABIDJAN

VIDEO

CD-ROM 2
DVD 2

MALI

BURKINA FASO

GUINEE

Korhogo

CÔTE D'IVOIRE

Bouaké

GHANA

Yamoussoukro

LIBERIA

Abidjan

Océan Atlantique

La ville d'Abidjan ▶

Abidjan

Cette ville moderne est située sur la baie de Cocody en Côte d'Ivoire. C'est une ville pleine d'animation qu'on appelle souvent «le creuset de l'Afrique». Les bureaux et les hôtels du quartier du Plateau contrastent avec Treichville, un quartier pittoresque et très animé qui est le centre culturel d'Abidjan.

✈ internet

go.hrw.com

ADRESSE: go.hrw.com
MOT-CLE: WA3 ABIDJAN

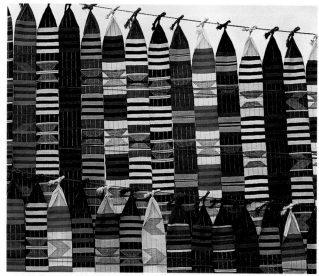

1 Les tissus colorés
La Côte d'Ivoire est connue pour ses tissus très colorés.

2 Les masques traditionnels
On peut voir beaucoup de masques traditionnels au Musée national d'Abidjan.

3 Le Plateau
C'est le centre des affaires et du gouvernement à Abidjan.

4 Le parc Banco

C'est un parc national depuis 1953, et une très belle réserve naturelle située dans la forêt tropicale.

5 Treichville

C'est le principal quartier commerçant d'Abidjan. On y découvre toutes sortes de couleurs, de sons et d'arômes. Ce quartier animé est un vrai plaisir pour les sens.

Au chapitre 8, on va faire la connaissance de Djeneba, de sa famille, de sa prof d'anglais et d'Aminata. Djeneba nous fait visiter le marché d'Abidjan et on apprend comment faire du foutou qui est une spécialité de Côte d'Ivoire. Abidjan est une ville de contrastes. C'est une grande ville moderne, mais riche en traditions africaines.

6 Le port d'Adjamé

C'est un des ports les plus importants de l'Afrique occidentale.

Objectives

In this chapter you will learn to

Première étape

- express need

Deuxième étape

- make, accept, and decline requests
- tell someone what to do

Troisième étape

- offer, accept, or refuse food

 internet

go.hrw.com ADRESSE: go.hrw.com
MOT-CLE: WA3 ABIDJAN-8

◀ **Un marché d'Abidjan**

MISE EN TRAIN · *Une invitée pour le déjeuner*

Stratégie pour comprendre
Where does Djeneba go to do the grocery shopping? Do you recognize any of the food items she buys?

 Djeneba

 Mme Diomandé

 Aminata

1 kilo de riz
250 grammes de pâte d'arachide
1 poisson
7 oignons
1 douzaine de tomates
3 citrons
un paquet de beurre
du pain

**Le matin chez les Diomandé, à Abidjan.
C'est l'heure du petit déjeuner.**

1

Mme Diomandé : Encore du pain, Aminata?

Aminata : Non, merci. Je n'ai plus faim.

Mme Diomandé : Je pense faire du foutou avec de la sauce arachide pour le déjeuner.

2

Plus tard...

Mme Diomandé : Tiens, te voilà, Djeneba. Tu me fais le marché?

Djeneba : Volontiers! Qu'est-ce qu'il te faut?

3

Mme Diomandé : Il me faut des légumes, du riz, du poisson... Tu me rapportes aussi du pain... Et prends de la pâte de tomates.

Djeneba : Bon, d'accord.

④ **Djeneba va au marché...**

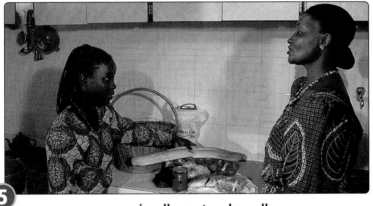

⑤ **... puis, elle rentre chez elle.**

Djeneba : Voilà le poisson, les 250 grammes de pâte d'arachide, les oignons, les tomates et les citrons. J'ai aussi acheté un paquet de beurre, de la pâte de tomates, du pain et du riz.

Mme Diomandé : Merci, chérie.

⑥ **Mme Diomandé fait la cuisine.**

⑦ **Mme Diomandé :** Viens. Goûte voir. C'est bon?

Djeneba : Oui, très bon.

⑧ *Toc toc toc!*

⑨ **Djeneba :** Ah, j'ai oublié... Devine qui j'ai vu au marché.

Mme Diomandé : Aucune idée... Va voir qui est à la porte.

Cahier d'activités, p. 85, Act. 1–2

1 Tu as compris?

1. What time of day is it?
2. What does Mme Diomandé want Djeneba to do? Why?
3. What are some of the things Djeneba buys?
4. What happens at the end of the story?
5. Judging from the story title, what do you think Djeneba forgot to tell Mme Diomandé?

2 Vrai ou faux?

1. Aminata va au marché.
2. Mme Diomandé va faire du foutou avec de la sauce arachide.
3. Djeneba ne veut pas aller au marché.
4. Djeneba achète des bananes au marché.
5. Djeneba oublie le pain.

3 Choisis la photo

Choisis les photos qui représentent ce que Djeneba a acheté.

1. du poisson   2. des tomates   3. des oignons   4. des citrons   5. du pain

a.

b.

c.

d.

e.

4 C'est qui?

1. «Non, merci. Je n'ai plus faim.»
2. «Tu me fais le marché?»
3. «J'ai aussi acheté un paquet de beurre, de la pâte de tomates, du pain et du riz.»
4. «Ah, j'ai oublié... »
5. «Va voir qui est à la porte.»

5 Cherche les expressions

In *Une invitée pour le déjeuner,* how does . . .
1. Mme Diomandé offer more food to Aminata?
2. Aminata refuse the offer?
3. Mme Diomandé ask Djeneba to do the shopping?
4. Mme Diomandé tell Djeneba what she needs?
5. Djeneba agree to do what Mme Diomandé asks?

> Volontiers!   Tu me fais le marché?
>
> Non, merci. Je n'ai plus faim.
>
> Bon, d'accord.
>
> Encore du pain?   Il me faut...

6 Et maintenant, à toi

Qui fait les courses dans ta famille? Où est-ce que vous faites les courses?

Première étape

Objective Expressing need

WA3 ABIDJAN-8

Vocabulaire

Qu'est-ce qu'on trouve au marché? Au supermarché?

Légumes

du maïs

des petits pois
(m.)

des pommes
de terre (f.)

des carottes (f.)

des gombos (m.)

Fruits

des fraises (f.)

des poires (f.)

des noix de
coco (f.)

des citrons (m.)

des goyaves (f.)

des papayes
(f.)

Produits laitiers

du beurre

du fromage

du lait

des pommes (f.)

des mangues (f.)

Viandes

du porc

du poulet

du bœuf

du raisin

des ananas (m.)

---

des yaourts (m.) *yogurt*

des œufs (m.) *eggs*

du poisson *fish*

du riz *rice*

du pain *bread*

de la farine *flour*

du sucre *sugar*

de la confiture *jam*

des gâteaux (m.) *cakes*

de la tarte *pie*

des oranges (f.) *oranges*

des bananes (f.) *bananas*

des pêches (f.) *peaches*

des tomates (f.) *tomatoes*

des avocats (m.) *avocados*

une/de la salade *a/some salad*

des salades (f.) *heads of lettuce*

des oignons (m.) *onions*

des haricots verts (m.) *green beans*

des champignons (m.) *mushrooms*

Travaux pratiques de grammaire,
pp. 61–62, Act. 1–4

Cahier d'activités,
pp. 86–87, Act. 3–5

7 **Qu'en penses-tu?**

Ecoutons Listen to the dialogues and decide if the people are talking about fruit, vegetables, fish, or poultry.

Grammaire

The partitive and indefinite articles

CD-ROM **2**
DVD **2**

You already know how to use **un** and **une** with singular nouns and **des** with plural nouns. Use **du, de la, de l'**, or **des** to indicate *some of* or *part of* something.

> Je voudrais **du** gâteau.
>
> Tu veux **de la** salade?
>
> Elle va prendre **de l'**eau minérale.
>
> Il me faut **des** oranges.

• If you want to talk about a whole item, use the indefinite articles **un** and **une.**

Il achète **une** tarte.

Il prend **de la** tarte.

Grammaire supplémentaire,
p. 252, Act. 1–3

• In a negative sentence, **du, de la, de l'**, and **des** change to **de/d'** *(none or any)*.

—Tu as **du** pain?

—Désolée, je n'ai pas **de** pain.

—Tu prends **de la** viande?

—Merci, je ne prends jamais **de** viande.

Cahier d'activités,
p. 87, Act. 6

• You can't leave out the article in French as you do in English.
Elle mange **du** fromage. *She's eating cheese.*

Travaux pratiques de
grammaire,
pp. 63–65, Act. 5–9

8 **Grammaire en contexte**

Lisons/Ecrivons Complète ce dialogue avec **du, de la, de l', de, d',** ou **des.**

ASSIKA	Dis, Maman, qu'est-ce qu'on mange à midi? J'ai très faim!
MAMAN	___1___ poisson, ___2___ riz et ___3___ haricots verts.
ASSIKA	Est-ce qu'on a encore ___4___ pain?
MAMAN	Non. Et on n'a pas ___5___ bananes non plus. Est-ce que tu peux aller en acheter?
ASSIKA	Bon, d'accord. C'est tout?
MAMAN	Non. Prends aussi ___6___ yaourts, ___7___ farine et ___8___ sucre. Je vais faire un gâteau pour ce soir.
ASSIKA	Super!
MAMAN	Merci, ma chérie.

Grammaire en contexte

Parlons Qu'est-ce que Prisca, Clémentine et Adjoua achètent au marché?

1.

2.

3.

Note culturelle

Shopping at a market in Côte d'Ivoire can be an exciting and colorful experience. Every city, town, and village has an open- air market where people come to buy and sell food, cloth, housewares, medicine, and herbal remedies.

Although French is the official language in Côte d'Ivoire, more than 60 different African languages are spoken there. To make shopping easier for everyone, there is a common market language called **Djoula**. Here are a few phrases in **Djoula**.

í ní sɔ̀gɔ̀ma	(ee nee so*goma*)	*Good morning.*
í ní wúla	(ee *nee* woulah)	*Good afternoon./Hello.*
í ká kέnε wá?	(ee kah keh*neh* wah)	*How are you?/How's it going?*
n ká kέnε kósobε	(nnkah keh*neh* kuh*sohb*eh)	*I'm fine.*

ETIENNE NANGBO

10 Qu'est-ce qu'il y a dans le chariot?

Parlons Ton/Ta camarade ne trouve plus son chariot. Il y a cinq autres chariots dans le magasin. Les listes suivantes décrivent le contenu des chariots. Demande à ton/ta camarade ce qu'il y a dans son chariot pour deviner quel est son chariot. Ensuite, changez de rôle.

EXEMPLE
— Tu as acheté des tomates? — Non.
— Tu as acheté du poisson? — Oui.
— Ton chariot, c'est le numéro...? — Oui.

1. du poisson
des tomates
des bananes
du fromage
du lait

2. du pain
des œufs
des oignons
du poisson
des haricots verts

3. du sucre
des ananas
du lait
du maïs
des tomates

4. des tomates
des haricots verts
des œufs
du sucre
du maïs

5. des ananas
des bananes
du fromage
des oignons
des haricots verts

6. des bananes
des œufs
du poisson
du pain
des tomates

Expressing need

— **Qu'est-ce qu'il te faut?**
— **Il me faut** des bananes, du riz et de l'eau minérale.

— **De quoi est-ce que tu as besoin?** *What do you need?*
— **J'ai besoin de** riz pour faire du foutou. *I need . . .*

Cahier d'activités, p. 88, Act. 8

Note de grammaire

The expression **avoir besoin de** can be followed by a noun or a verb. The partitive article is not used with this expression.

Tu **as besoin de** tomates?
Nous **avons besoin d'**œufs pour l'omelette.
J'**ai besoin d'**aller au marché.

Cahier d'activités, p. 88, Act. 9

Grammaire supplémentaire, p. 253, Act. 4

Travaux pratiques de grammaire, p. 65, Act. 10

11 ### Grammaire en contexte

Lisons/Parlons Sandrine fait une fête, mais le menu est secret. Regarde les listes suivantes et devine ce qu'elle prépare.

1. J'ai besoin de salade, de tomates, de carottes, d'oignons...

2. J'ai besoin de fromage, de pain, de jambon...

3. J'ai besoin d'œufs, de champignons, de fromage, de lait...

4. J'ai besoin de bananes, de pommes, d'oranges...

une tarte aux pommes

un banana split   une salade de fruits

un sandwich

une salade   une omelette

12 ### Grammaire en contexte

Ecrivons Tu as besoin de quoi pour faire...

1. un bon sandwich?

2. une quiche?

3. une salade?

4. une salade de fruits?

5. un banana split?

A la française

Many French expressions involve foods: **On est dans la purée** *(We're in trouble)*; **C'est pas de la tarte** *(It's not easy)*. Can you guess what **C'est du gâteau** means?*

13 ### Que faut-il?

Parlons Tu veux préparer un repas pour ta famille française. D'abord, fais un menu. Ensuite, va au supermarché et achète ce qu'il te faut. Ton/ta camarade va jouer le rôle du/de la marchand(e). Ensuite, changez de rôle.

Vocabulaire à la carte

Here are some additional words you may want to know:

du concombre	*cucumber*
des cornichons (m.)	*pickles*
de la mayonnaise	*mayonnaise*
de la moutarde	*mustard*
des noix (f.)	*nuts*
du poivre	*pepper*
du sel	*salt*

_____

* It means *It's easy; it's a piece of cake.*

PANORAMA CULTUREL

Où est-ce que tu aimes faire des provisions?

Where does your family go to shop for groceries? People in francophone countries have several options. We asked these people where they shop. Here's what they had to say.

Louise, France

«Je vais le plus souvent au supermarché, mais je préfère le marché, parce que le marché, c'est dehors et puis, l'ambiance est meilleure.»

Angèle, Côte d'Ivoire

«Je préfère aller au supermarché pour aller faire des achats parce que là-bas, c'est plus sûr et bien conservé.»

Micheline, Belgique

«Je préfère aller au marché, chez les petits commerçants, parce qu'il y a le contact personnel, il y a le choix, il y a les odeurs, les couleurs, le plaisir de la promenade aussi dans le marché.»

Qu'en penses-tu?

1. Where do these people shop for groceries?
2. What are the advantages and disadvantages of shopping in these different places?
3. Are there outdoor farmers' markets in your community? What can you buy there?
4. Does your family sometimes shop in small specialty stores? If so, what do they buy there?

Savais-tu que... ?

Many people in francophone countries grocery shop in supermarkets (**supermarchés**) or hypermarkets (**hypermarchés**) because it's convenient. Others prefer to shop in small grocery stores (**épiceries**) or outdoor markets (**marchés en plein air**). **Supermarchés** are similar to their American counterparts. **Hypermarchés** are very large stores that carry just about anything you can imagine—all under one roof! Americans may be surprised to learn, however, that stores are not open 24 hours a day or even late in the evening. **Epiceries** are usually closed between 12:30 P.M. and 4 P.M. and all day on either Sunday or Monday.

Comment dit-on...?

Making, accepting, and declining requests; telling someone what to do

To make requests:

> **Tu peux** aller faire les courses?
> *Can you . . . ?*
> **Tu me rapportes** des œufs?
> *Will you bring me . . . ?*

To accept:

> **Pourquoi pas?**
> **Bon, d'accord.**
> **Je veux bien.** *Gladly.*
> **J'y vais tout de suite.**
> *I'll go right away.*

To tell someone what to do:

> **Rapporte(-moi)** du beurre.
> *Bring (me) back . . .*
> **Prends** du lait. *Get . . .*
> **Achète(-moi)** du riz. *Buy (me) . . .*
> **N'oublie pas d'**acheter le lait.
> *Don't forget to . . .*

To decline:

> **Je ne peux pas maintenant.**
> **Je regrette, mais je n'ai pas le temps.**
> *I'm sorry, but I don't have time.*
> **J'ai des trucs à faire.**
> **J'ai des tas de choses à faire.**

Cahier d'activités, p. 89, Act. 10–12

14 **Un petit service**

a. Ecoutons Listen to these dialogues. Is the first speaker making a request or telling someone what to do?

b. Ecoutons Now, listen again. Does the second speaker accept or decline the request or command?

Grammaire

The verb *pouvoir*

Pouvoir is an irregular verb. Notice how similar it is to the verb **vouloir,** which you learned in Chapter 6.

pouvoir *(to be able to, can, may)*

Je	**peux**	Nous	**pouvons**
Tu	**peux**	Vous	**pouvez**
Il/Elle/On	**peut**	Ils/Elles	**peuvent**

Cahier d'activités, p. 90, Act. 13–14

Travaux pratiques de grammaire, p. 66, Act. 11–12

Grammaire supplémentaire, p. 253, Act. 5–6

15 **Grammaire en contexte**

Lisons/Ecrivons Complète la conversation avec les formes appropriées du verbe **pouvoir.**

M. BONFILS Sim, tu ___1___ aller au marché pour moi?

SIM Non, je ne ___2___ pas. J'ai des trucs à faire!

ARMANDE Papa, Julie et moi, nous ___3___ y aller si tu veux.

M. BONFILS Merci, les filles. Vous ___4___ me prendre un ananas et des mangues? Ah, et du pain aussi.

JULIE On ___5___ acheter les fruits, mais Sim et Marius ne font jamais rien. Ils ___6___ bien acheter le pain pour une fois!

16 **Grammaire en contexte**

Parlons Demande à tes camarades s'ils peuvent faire les choses suivantes pour toi ou avec toi.

regarder la télé après l'école

aller nager

faire des courses avec moi

me rapporter un sandwich

jouer au foot demain

sortir ce soir

EXEMPLE —Vous pouvez écouter de la musique après l'école?

—Non, nous ne pouvons pas.

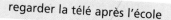

Vous en voulez combien?

un kilo(gramme) de pommes de terre et **une livre d'**oignons

une bouteille d'eau minérale

une douzaine d'œufs

une boîte de tomates

un paquet de sucre

une tranche de jambon

un morceau de fromage

un litre de lait

Cahier d'activités, pp. 90–91, Act. 15–17

Travaux pratiques de grammaire, p. 67, Act. 13

Note de grammaire

Notice that you use **de** or **d'** after these expressions of quantity.

Une tranche **de** jambon, s'il vous plaît.

Je voudrais un kilo **d'**oranges.

Travaux pratiques de grammaire, pp. 67–68, Act. 14–16

Grammaire supplémentaire, pp. 253–254, Act. 7–8

Note culturelle

The metric system was created shortly after the French Revolution and has since been adopted by nearly all countries in the world. Although the United States is officially trying to convert to the metric system, many people aren't yet used to it. In the metric system, lengths are measured in centimeters and meters, rather than inches and yards. Distances are measured in kilometers. Grams and kilograms are the standard measures of weight. **Une livre** is half a kilogram. Liquids, including gasoline, are measured in liters. To convert metric measurements, use the following table:

1 centimeter = .39 inches	1 gram = .035 ounces
1 meter = 39.37 inches	1 kilogram = 2.2 pounds
1 kilometer = .62 miles	1 liter = 1.06 quarts

17 Vous en voulez combien?

Ecoutons Listen to Sophie as she does her shopping. Write down the items and the quantities she asks for.

18 Grammaire en contexte

Lisons/Ecrivons Ta mère et ta grand-mère préparent un dîner. Elles te demandent d'aller au marché. Complète la conversation suivante avec une quantité logique de chaque article. Utilise les expressions proposées.

une boîte de/d'

une douzaine de/d'

un morceau de/d'

un litre de/d'

une bouteille de/d'

un paquet de/d'

une livre de/d'

un kilo de/d'

—Alors, Maman, qu'est-ce qu'il te faut?
—Il me faut ___1___ bœuf, ___2___ fromage et ___3___ eau minérale.
—Et pour le dessert?
—Achète-moi ___4___ farine, ___5___ pêches et ___6___ œufs.
—Et toi, Mémé, de quoi est-ce que tu as besoin?
—Rapporte-moi ___7___ oignons et ___8___ lait, s'il te plaît.
—D'accord. A tout à l'heure.

19 Allons au marché!

Parlons Tu fais les courses. Achète les articles sur ta liste. Demande une quantité logique pour chaque article. Ton/Ta camarade joue le rôle du/de la marchand(e). Ensuite, changez de rôle.

Vous avez choisi?

Voilà.

Et avec ça?

C'est tout?

Vous désirez?

Je voudrais...

Il me faut...

Je prends...

avocats
tomates
vinaigre
oignons
œufs
pain
huile d'olive
fromage
riz
haricots verts
raisin
sucre

20 Jeu de rôle

Parlons Tu fais des courses pour des personnes âgées. Fais une liste des articles que tu dois acheter. Donne aussi les quantités. Ton/Ta camarade va jouer le rôle de la personne âgée que tu aides. Ensuite, changez de rôle.

Rencontre culturelle

◄ **Le foutou,** the national dish of Côte d'Ivoire, is a paste made from boiled plantains, manioc, or yams. It is eaten with various sauces, such as peanut sauce or palm oil nut sauce.

▼ **La sauce arachide** is one of the many sauces eaten in Côte d'Ivoire. It is made from peanut butter with beef, chicken, or fish, hot peppers, peanut oil, garlic, onions, tomato paste, tomatoes, and a variety of other vegetables. It is usually served over rice.

▶ **L'aloco,** a popular snack food in Côte d'Ivoire, is a dish of fried plantain bananas. It is usually eaten with a spicy sauce (**sauce pimentée**).

Qu'en penses-tu?

1. Do these dishes resemble any that are eaten in the United States?
2. Which ingredients in these dishes can you find in your neighborhood grocery store? Which ingredients are unfamiliar?
3. What dishes are typical of your part of the country? Why are they more common than others?

Savais-tu que... ?

Yams (**ignames**) and plantains are abundant in the Republic of Côte d'Ivoire, which explains why **foutou** is a popular dish. A typical lunch consists of one main course — often **foutou,** rice, or **attiéké** (ground manioc root) with a sauce, and a dessert, usually tropical fruits such as guavas, pineapples, or papayas. Lunch is traditionally followed by an hour-long siesta. To accommodate this custom, stores are closed from noon until 3:00 P.M., even in large cities such as Abidjan. Unlike lunch, dinner tends to be a much lighter meal. Heavy foods are rarely eaten in the evening.

Qu'est-ce qu'on mange au...

petit déjeuner?

déjeuner?

goûter?

dîner?

Travaux pratiques de grammaire, p. 69, Act. 17–18

Cahier d'activités, p. 92, Act. 19–20

21 Le petit déjeuner

Ecoutons Listen to these people tell what they have for breakfast. Match each speaker with his or her breakfast.

a.

b.

c.

Note culturelle

In the morning, most people in francophone countries have a very light breakfast. Coffee with hot milk **(café au lait)** and hot chocolate are the drinks of choice. They are usually served with bread or croissants, butter, and jam. Children may eat cereal for breakfast as well, sometimes with warm milk. The largest meal of the day, **le déjeuner,** has traditionally been between noon and 1:00 P.M. Dinner **(le dîner)** is eaten after 7:00 P.M.

22 Un repas typique

Parlons Regarde les images suivantes et dis à quel(s) repas tu manges chaque plat. Ensuite, décide si ces plats sont typiquement américains, français ou les deux.

1.

2.

3.

4.

5.

6.

23 Quel repas?

Parlons Décris un des repas suivants à ton/ta camarade. Il/Elle doit deviner quelle image tu décris. Ensuite, changez de rôle.

EXEMPLE **Il y a du poulet,...**

1.

2.

3.

24 Devine!

Ecrivons/Parlons Fais des menus pour tes trois repas de demain. Utilise le **Vocabulaire** de la page 235. Ton/Ta camarade fait aussi trois menus. Ensuite, devinez le contenu de vos menus.

EXEMPLE —**Au petit déjeuner, tu vas manger... ?**
—**Oui, c'est ça.** *or* **Non, pas de...**

Comment dit-on...?

Offering, accepting, or refusing food

To offer food to someone:

Tu veux du riz?
Vous voulez de l'eau minérale?
Vous prenez du fromage?
Tu prends du fromage?
Encore du pain? *More . . . ?*

To accept:

Oui, s'il vous/te plaît.
Oui, j'en veux bien.
Yes, I'd like some.
Oui, avec plaisir.
Yes, with pleasure.

To refuse:

Non, merci.
Je n'en veux plus. *I don't want any more.*
Non, merci. Je n'ai plus faim.
No thanks. I'm not hungry anymore.

Cahier d'activités, pp. 92–93, Act. 21–22

25 A table

Ecoutons Is the speaker offering, accepting, or refusing food?

TROISIEME ETAPE

deux cent quarante-sept **247**

26 Encore du pain?

Parlons Un élève ivoirien dîne chez toi. Tu veux qu'il goûte plusieurs plats. Encourage-le. Ton ami accepte ou refuse poliment.

 **DE BONS CONSEILS**

Look for opportunities to practice your French wherever you go. Try to meet French-speaking people and talk with them. Ask your teacher to help you find a pen pal in a French-speaking country. Rent videocassettes of French films. See how many French products you can find at the grocery store and the cosmetic counter, and how many French dishes you can find on restaurant menus.

Grammaire

The pronoun *en*

En takes the place of a phrase beginning with **du, de la, de l', des,** or **de** to avoid repetition. **En** usually means *some (of it/of them)* or simply *it/them*.
— Tu veux **des mangues?**
— Oui, j'**en** veux bien.
— Tu manges **des légumes?**
— Oui, j'**en** mange souvent.

In a negative sentence, **en** means *any* or *none*.
— Tu veux **du beurre?**
— Merci, je n'**en** veux pas.

Grammaire supplémentaire, pp. 254–255, Act. 9–12

Cahier d'activités, p. 93, Act. 23

Travaux pratiques de grammaire, p. 70, Act. 19–20

27 Grammaire en contexte

Lisons/Ecrivons Regarde les articles dans le panier d'Aïssata. Combien est-ce qu'elle en a? Donne la quantité de chaque article.

EXEMPLE Des haricots? **Elle en a un kilo.**

1. Du lait?
2. Du beurre?
3. Des tomates?
4. Du riz?
5. Des œufs?
6. De l'eau minérale?
7. Des ananas?

28 Grammaire en contexte

 Parlons Demande à un(e) camarade s'il ou si elle aime les plats de l'activité 26. Utilise le pronom **en** dans tes questions. Ensuite, changez de rôle.

EXEMPLE
— **Tu manges du poulet?**
— **Oui, j'en mange souvent.**

 29 De l'école au travail

 Parlons/Ecrivons You work part-time in a French restaurant where the chef speaks mostly French. The chef, Pierre Leroux, asks you to go to the supermarket to buy some items he needs to prepare certain dishes. Make a list of what he needs and verify that you have all of the items. Your partner will play the role of the chef. Then switch roles.

PRONONCIATION

The sounds [o] and [ɔ]

The sound [o] is similar to the vowel sound in the English word *boat*. To make the sound [o], hold your mouth in a whistling position. Keep the lips and tongue steady to avoid the glide heard in *boat*. Repeat each of these words: **trop, kilo, mot.** The spellings **au, eau, ô,** and sometimes **o** represent the sound [o]. Now, repeat these words: **jaune, chaud, beau, rôle.**

The sound [ɔ] is between the vowel sounds in the English words *boat* and *bought*. Usually, this sound is followed by a consonant sound in the same syllable. The sound [ɔ] is more open, so hold your mouth in a semi-whistling position to produce it. This sound is usually spelled with the letter **o.** Now, repeat these words: **bof, donne, fort, carotte.**

A. A prononcer

Repeat the following words and phrases.

1. au revoir	un stylo jaune	au restaurant
2. un gâteau	moi aussi	des haricots verts
3. des pommes	d'abord	une promenade
4. encore	dormir	l'école

B. A lire

Take turns with a partner reading each of the following sentences aloud.
1. Elle a une gomme violette et un stylo jaune.
2. Tu aimes les carottes? Moi, j'adore. J'aime bien aussi les escargots et le porc.
3. Elle est occupée aujourd'hui. Elle a informatique et biologie.
4. Il me faut un short parce qu'il fait trop chaud.
5. Tu peux sortir si tu promènes d'abord le chien.

C. A écrire

You're going to hear a short dialogue. Write down what you hear.

LA CUISINE AFRICAINE

Stratégie pour lire

Remember to look for cognates to help you figure out what you're reading. Occasionally, you will encounter false cognates, words that look alike in two languages but have different meanings.

Context clues can sometimes help you recognize false cognates. An example of a false cognate is the French phrase **fruits de mer**. **Fruits de mer** may make you think of the English word *fruit,* but it means *seafood.*

A. You already know a few false cognates. Try to figure out the meaning of the false cognates in the sentences below.

1. Je vais à San Francisco à 11h00. Maintenant, il est 10h40, et **j'attends** le train.

   a. I'm attending

   b. I'm late for

   c. I'm waiting for

2. J'adore les sciences. Ce soir, je vais **assister** à une conférence sur l'ozone.

   a. to attend

   b. to assist

   c. to teach

Les desserts

Croissants au coco et au sésame   ✕ ∞
(Afrique occidentale)   Prép. : 30 mn. - Cuiss. : 10 mn.

Repos : 1 h. - 8 pers.

2 œufs	170 g de farine
140 g de sucre	Vanille en poudre
190 g de noix de coco râpée	Graines de sésame.

   Mélanger la noix de coco râpée, le sucre, la vanille et les œufs entiers. Incorporer la farine. Travailler la pâte. Former une boule. Laisser reposer 1 heure au frais.

   Etaler la pâte sur 1/2 cm. Découper en croissants. Les rouler dans le sésame. Cuire au four à 200 °C, (th. 6-7), 10 minutes.

—————————————————————— Les entrées

Mousseline africaine de petits légumes

✗ ◯◯

Prép. : 40 mn. - Cuiss. : 15 mn.

4 pers.

(Afrique occidentale - Bénin - Togo)

2 petits concombres	1 avocat
Ail	1 épi de maïs
1 lime	Graines de carvi
1 radis noir	4 petites brioches
1 / 2 papaye	Sel.

Eplucher les concombres. Les détailler en dés. Faire la même chose avec l'avocat. Débarrasser l'épis de maïs des feuilles et des barbes. Le faire cuire durant 15 minutes à l'eau bouillante. Saler en fin de cuisson.

Egréner le maïs. Débarrasser la papaye de ses graines. La découper en petits dés. Emincer le radis noir. **Parfumer de graines de carvi et d'ail haché. Arroser la salade de jus de lime.**

Retirer le chapeau des brioches. Les évider. Les garnir de la salade parfumée.

Les brioches ne doivent pas être sucrées. Si on les fabrique, il convient d'ôter le sucre. Ne pas saler l'épi de maïs au début de la cuisson mais à la fin afin d'éviter qu'il durcisse.

B. With a partner, scan the reading and write down all of the cognates you can find in these selections.

C. Did you find any false cognates? Were you able to figure out what they mean? If so, how?

D. Where would you expect to find these reading selections? Where are these dishes from?

E. Which of the dishes would make a good dessert?

F. Are these dishes easy or difficult to make? How do you know? Are they expensive or inexpensive to make? How do you know?

G. To make **croissants,** how long do you need to chill the dough? At what temperature do you bake them? What temperature is that on the Fahrenheit scale? (To convert from Celsius to Fahrenheit, multiply by $\frac{9}{5}$ and add 32.)

H. To make **mousseline,** how long do you have to cook the corn? Do you think this dish would taste sweet or salty? How many people does this dish serve?

I. Now, with a partner, write the instructions for an easy recipe that you know how to make. Include the ingredients, the steps required to prepare the dish, and the cooking and preparation time required.

Cahier d'activités, p. 95, Act. 25

Grammaire supplémentaire

CD-ROM 2
DVD 2

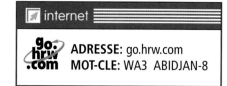

internet

ADRESSE: go.hrw.com
MOT-CLE: WA3 ABIDJAN-8

Première étape   Objective Expressing need

1 Eric is planning a party and has made a list of what he needs to do to get ready. Complete his list with **du, de la, de l', ** and **des** as needed. **(p. 236)**

Pour ma boum, je vais faire des sandwiches, alors je vais acheter ____1____ pain, ____2____ fromage et ____3____ jambon. Mes amis aiment manger ____4____ salade. Dans la salade, je vais mettre ____5____ tomates, ____6____ maïs et ____7____ champignons. Pour le dessert, je vais préparer une salade de fruits avec ____8____ oranges, ____9____ bananes et ____10____ pommes.

2 Lis les recettes ci-dessous. Ensuite, écris une note pour te rappeler les choses que tu dois acheter au marché. Utilise les articles **du, de la, de l'** et **des. (p. 236)**

EXEMPLE   **Il me faut de la farine...**

1.
Les crêpes bretonnes
500 g de farine
3 œufs
20 g de beurre
3 g de sel
5 g de levure
1 cl de jus de pomme
1/4 litre de lait

2.
La sauce arachide
4 oignons
2 tomates
5 cl d'huile d'arachide
100 g de pâte d'arachide
100 g de pâte de tomates
10 g de sel
3 piments rouges

3 Anne and Odile are talking about items they have to bring to a picnic. Complete their conversation with the partitive or indefinite articles. **(p. 236)**

—Alors, moi, j'ai ____1____ raisin, ____2____ pommes et ____3____ tomates. Je n'ai pas ____4____ avocats. Et toi, qu'est-ce que tu as?

—J'ai ____5____ confiture, ____6____ pain et ____7____ fromage. Je n'ai pas ____8____ jus de pomme, mais j'ai ____9____ eau minérale. Est-ce que tu veux acheter ____10____ tarte?

—Oui, c'est une bonne idée.

4 Rewrite the following sentences, using the expressions **avoir besoin de** or **il me/te faut** and the partitive article. (**pp. 236, 238**)

EXEMPLE Il me faut des bananes. **J'ai besoin de bananes.**
Tu as besoin de lait? **Il te faut du lait?**

1. Il me faut des noix de coco.
2. Il te faut des papayes?
3. Tu as besoin de confiture?
4. Il me faut du raisin.
5. J'ai besoin d'eau minérale.

6. Il te faut des ananas?
7. Tu as besoin de sucre?
8. Il te faut de la farine?
9. Il me faut des œufs, aussi.
10. Tu as besoin de pêches?

Deuxième étape

Objectives Making, accepting, and declining requests; telling someone what to do

5 Combine les expressions des deux colonnes pour faire des phrases complètes. (**p. 241**)

A	B
1. Est-ce que tu...	a. ne peuvent pas aller au cinéma ce soir. Ils sont occupés.
2. Elle...	b. ne peux pas sortir la poubelle. Je n'ai pas le temps.
3. Nous...	c. peux débarrasser la table, s'il te plaît?
4. Angèle et toi, vous...	d. ne pouvons pas faire la vaisselle. Nous avons des trucs à faire.
5. Moi, je...	e. ne peut pas sortir avec ses copines. Elle a des devoirs à faire.
6. Mes copains...	f. pouvez promener le chien?

6 Ton ami(e) et toi, vous allez faire une fête. Ecrivez les choses que les invités peuvent apporter. Utilise les formes correctes du verbe **pouvoir**. (**p. 241**)

1. Isabelle _____ acheter des avocats et des tomates.
2. Moi, je _____ acheter des tartes.
3. Henri, tu _____ acheter des fraises et des citrons?
4. Carol et Sylvain, vous _____ acheter de la salade et du pain.
5. Barbara, Serge et Françoise _____ acheter des boissons.

7 Unscramble the names of the food items. Then, combine the fragments to create sentences that tell Djeneba what to get you from the market. (**p. 242**)

EXEMPLE RUERBE / un paquet de/s'il te plaît/prends
Prends un paquet de beurre, s'il te plaît!

1. ITESPT OSPI / une boîte de/rapporte-moi/s'il te plaît
2. NDVAIE / s'il te plaît/un morceau de/achète-moi
3. EFOSU D' / prends/une douzaine
4. SJU ASANAN D' / une bouteille de/acheter/n'oublie pas de
5. AMCHNONPIGS / tu peux/s'il te plaît/une livre de/acheter
6. IRNAFE / un kilo de/s'il te plaît/rapporte-moi

Grammaire supplémentaire

CD-ROM 2
DVD 2
go.
hrw
.com
WA3 ABIDJAN-8

8 Your mom has asked you to pick up some items at the neighborhood grocery store. Write a sentence for each of the items on the list that you will need to purchase. Choose the appropriate quantity from the box for each item you request. (**p. 242**)

EXEMPLE   **Il me faut un paquet de sucre./J'ai besoin d'un paquet de sucre.**

une tranche	un litre	un morceau
un kilo	un paquet	
		une boîte
une douzaine	une bouteille	

sucre
farine
fromage
lait
eau minérale
œufs
pommes de terre
jambon

Troisième étape   **Objective** Offering, accepting, or refusing food

9 Tu demandes à Didier ce que sa famille aime manger. Ecris les réponses de Didier. Utilise **en** et le verbe **prendre**. (**pp. 149, 248**)

EXEMPLE   Tu prends du café au lait au petit déjeuner?
Oui, j'en prends.

1. Tu prends du lait au dîner? Non, ...
2. Tes parents prennent du pain avec leur fromage? Oui, ...
3. Ta sœur prend des légumes au déjeuner? Oui, ...
4. Ton petit frère prend des gâteaux au goûter? Non, ...
5. Ta cousine et toi, vous prenez de la viande au déjeuner? Non, ...
6. Tu prends de la sauce arachide avec ton riz? Oui, ...

10 Joël dîne avec sa famille française pour la première fois. Mets les morceaux de phrases dans le bon ordre pour recréer la conversation du dîner. Mets les formes correctes des verbes et ajoute les articles nécessaires. N'oublie pas la ponctuation! (**pp. 236, 247, 248**)

1. — petits pois/vouloir/tu
2. — en/bien/je/oui/vouloir
3. — vouloir/pain/tu
4. — plaisir/oui/avec
5. — tu/poulet/vouloir
6. — vouloir/ne...plus/merci/en/je/non
7. — vouloir/fromage/tu
8. — merci/je/non/laitiers/manger/ne...pas/produits

11 Lis les quatre phrases ci-dessous pour avoir des informations sur les amis d'Armelle. Utilise ces informations pour écrire leurs réponses aux questions d'Armelle. Utilise **en** et le verbe **vouloir** dans chaque réponse. (**p. 248**)

> Marius n'a plus faim, mais il a très soif.
>
> Irène aime les fruits, mais elle n'aime pas tellement le fromage.
>
> Isabelle n'aime pas la viande, mais elle adore le poisson.
>
> Léopold a très faim, mais il n'a plus soif.

EXEMPLE   Irène, encore du fromage? **Non, merci. Je n'en veux plus.**

1. Marius, tu veux de l'eau?
2. Irène, tu veux des pêches?
3. Isabelle, encore du rosbif?
4. Léopold, tu veux du gâteau?
5. Isabelle, tu veux du poisson?
6. Marius, encore du riz?

12 A nutritionist is visiting your school to interview students about their eating habits and to advise them on how to have a well-balanced diet. Complete the following sentences with the necessary articles. (**pp. 236, 238, 248**)

—Est-ce que tu manges ___1___ fruits?

—Oui, j'___2___ mange souvent.

—Est-ce que tu manges ___3___ bœuf?

—Non, je ne mange pas ___4___ viande, mais je mange ___5___ œufs de temps en temps.

—Est-ce que tu aimes ___6___ lait?

—Non, je n'___7___ bois jamais, mais je mange ___8___ yaourt et ___9___ fromage.

—Est-ce que tu bois ___10___ eau?

—Oui. J'___11___ bois beaucoup. Je bois au moins un litre ___12___ eau par jour.

—Bon, tu manges très bien, mais tu as besoin de manger ___13___ légumes.

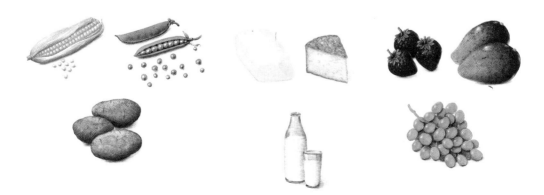

CD-ROM 2
DVD 2

internet

go.hrw.com
ADRESSE: go.hrw.com
MOT-CLE: WA3 ABIDJAN-8

1 Listen to this supermarket advertisement. List four of the foods that are on sale. Then, listen again for the prices of the four items you listed.

2

LES GROUPES D'ALIMENTS

Les aliments sont regroupés en 6 catégories selon leurs caractéristiques nutritionnelles :

- **Le lait et les produits laitiers** sont nos principaux fournisseurs de calcium.
- **Viandes, poissons et œufs** sont nos sources essentielles de protéines de bonne qualité.
- **Le groupe du pain, des féculents et des légumes secs** apporte les «glucides lents» libérant progressivement l'énergie nécessaire à notre organisme.
- **Légumes et fruits** sont nos sources de fibres, vitamines et minéraux.
- **Les matières grasses** sont les sources énergétiques les plus importantes pour notre corps.
- **Le sucre et ses dérivés** apportent les «glucides rapides» nécessaires au bon fonctionnement cérébral et musculaire.

Groupe	Lait Produits Laitiers	Viandes Poissons Œufs	Pains Féculents	Fruits Légumes	Matières Grasses	Sucre Dérivés
Intérêt Principal	Calcium	Protéines	Glucides	Fibres Vitamines A et B	Lipides	Glucides
Intérêt Secon-daire	Protéines Vitamines A, B, D	Fer Vitamine B	Fibres	Glucides	Vitamines (A, E, selon mat. grasses)	

L'ensemble de ces catégories permet, au sein d'une alimentation diversifiée, de couvrir tous nos besoins.

1. What kind of chart is this?

2. What do the six categories listed mean?

3. According to the chart, what are some of the nutrients found in . . .

    a. produits laitiers?   **d.** fruits et légumes?

    b. viandes?   **e.** matières grasses?

    c. pain?   **f.** sucre et ses dérivés?

4. Give some examples of foods you know in French that fall into each category.

5. Name three foods that are high in protein and three that are high in calcium.

3 Quelles différences est-ce qu'il y a entre les repas africains, français et américains?

4 ## Ecrivons!

Imagine that you're the producer of a certain food item that you're trying to market. Write an ad that encourages people to buy the item, telling when they might eat it and why it's good. Consider who would be likely to buy your product. Include logos and pictures in your ad as well.

Persuasive writing encourages people to do a certain thing or to think a certain way. Advertisements are a type of persuasive writing because advertisers try to convince people that their products are better than any others.

Stratégie pour écrire

Arranging your ideas spatially is a good way to organize ideas for your advertisement. First, brainstorm some catchy phrases and convincing arguments you might write in your ad to persuade people to buy your product. Also, decide what types of illustrations you might use (photos, logos, and so on) and where to place them in your ad. Then, create a sketch of how you want your ad to look.

Using the sketch you prepared, create the ad for your product. Structure is very important in persuasive writing. You should choose what you feel is the greatest benefit or most appealing characteristic of the product and draw attention to it. You can do this by writing it in larger print or in an eye-catching color. Less attention should be drawn to what you feel are your product's weaker points. However, try to avoid relying too heavily on illustrations and layout; your ad should be informative as well as eye-catching. Be sure to use descriptive terms that illustrate the qualities of your product.

5 ## Jeu de rôle

a. Make a list in French of what you've eaten for the last two days. Use the food vocabulary that you've learned in this chapter.

b. Now, you go to a nutrition counselor. The counselor will evaluate your diet, telling you what you need to eat more of and what you shouldn't eat anymore. Act out this scene with a partner. Then, change roles.

Can you use what you've learned in this chapter?

Can you express need?
p. 238

1 How would you tell someone that you need these things?

1.

2.

3.

4.

5.

Can you make, accept, and decline requests and tell someone what to do?
p. 240

2 How would you . . .
1. ask someone to go grocery shopping for you?
2. tell someone to bring back some groceries for you?

3 How would you accept the requests in Activity 2? How would you refuse?

4 How would you ask for a specific quantity of these foods?
1. œufs
2. lait
3. oranges
4. beurre
5. jambon
6. eau minérale

Can you offer, accept, or refuse food?
p. 247

5 How would you offer someone these foods?
1. some rice
2. some oranges
3. some milk

6 How would you accept the foods listed in number 5 if they were offered? How would you refuse them?

7 How would you tell someone what you have for . . .
1. breakfast?
2. lunch?
3. an afternoon snack?
4. dinner?

Expressing need

Qu'est-ce qu'il te faut?	What do you need?
Il me faut...	I need . . .
De quoi est-ce que tu as besoin?	What do you need?
J'ai besoin de...	I need . . .
du, de la, de l', des	some

Foods; Shopping

des ananas (m.)	pineapples
des avocats (m.)	avocados
des bananes (f.)	bananas
du beurre	butter
du bœuf	beef
des carottes (f.)	carrots
des champignons (m.)	mushrooms
des citrons (m.)	lemons
de la confiture	jam
de la farine	flour
des fraises (f.)	strawberries

du fromage	cheese
des fruits (m.)	fruit
des gâteaux (m.)	cakes
des gombos (m.)	okra
des goyaves (f.)	guavas
des haricots verts (m.)	green beans
du lait	milk
des légumes (m.)	vegetables
du maïs	corn
des mangues (f.)	mangoes
des noix de coco (f.)	coconuts
des œufs (m.)	eggs
des oignons (m.)	onions
des oranges (f.)	oranges
du pain	bread
des papayes (f.)	papayas
des pêches (f.)	peaches
des petits pois (m.)	peas
des poires (f.)	pears
du poisson	fish

des pommes (f.)	apples
des pommes de terre (f.)	potatoes
du porc	pork
du poulet	chicken
des produits (m.) laitiers	dairy products
du raisin	grapes
du riz	rice
une/de la salade	a/some salad
des salades	heads of lettuce
du sucre	sugar
de la tarte (f.)	pie
des tomates (f.)	tomatoes
de la viande	meat
des yaourts (m.)	yogurt
le marché	market
le supermarché	supermarket

Deuxième étape

Making, accepting, and declining requests

Tu peux... ?	Can you . . . ?
Tu me rapportes... ?	Will you bring me . . . ?
Bon, d'accord.	Well, OK.
Je veux bien.	Gladly.
J'y vais tout de suite.	I'll go right away.
Je regrette, mais je n'ai pas le temps.	I'm sorry, but I don't have time.

Je ne peux pas maintenant.	I can't right now.

Telling someone what to do

Rapporte(-moi)...	Bring (me) back . . .
Prends...	Get . . .
Achète(-moi)...	Buy (me) . . .
N'oublie pas de...	Don't forget to . . .
pouvoir	to be able to, can, may

Quantities

une boîte de	a can of
une bouteille de	a bottle of
une douzaine de	a dozen
un kilo(gramme) de	a kilogram of
un litre de	a liter of
une livre de	a pound of
un morceau de	a piece of
un paquet de	a package/box of
une tranche de	a slice of

Troisième étape

Offering, accepting, or refusing food

Tu veux... ?	Do you want . . . ?
Vous voulez... ?	Do you want . . . ?
Vous prenez... ?	Will you have . . . ?
Tu prends... ?	Will you have . . . ?
Encore de... ?	More . . . ?
Oui, s'il vous/te plaît.	Yes, please.

Oui, j'en veux bien.	Yes, I'd like some.
Oui, avec plaisir.	Yes, with pleasure.
Non, merci.	No, thank you.
Je n'en veux plus.	I don't want any more.
Non, merci. Je n'ai plus faim.	No thanks. I'm not hungry anymore.

en	some, of it, of them, any

Meals

le petit déjeuner	breakfast
le déjeuner	lunch
le goûter	afternoon snack
le dîner	dinner

Allez, viens en Arles!

Population : plus de 50.000

Points d'intérêt : la place Richelme, la place du Forum, les arènes romaines, les thermes de Constantin, les Alyscamps, le théâtre antique

Aux environs d'Arles : les Baux-de-Provence, les Antiques à St-Rémy-de-Provence, le moulin d'Alphonse Daudet

Personnages célèbres : Alphonse Daudet, Vincent Van Gogh, Frédéric Mistral

Musées : le musée Réattu, le musée de l'Arles Antique, le Museon Arlaten

Industries : riz, papier, industries chimiques et métalliques

go.hrw.com
WA3 ARLES

VIDEO

CD-ROM 3
DVD 2

ANGLETERRE ALLEMAGNE LUXEMBOURG
Paris
Chartres Strasbourg
Tours SUISSE
Poitiers
Océan Atlantique FRANCE
Lyon ITALIE
Bordeaux
Nice
Arles
Aix-en-Provence
N
CORSE
ESPAGNE Mer Méditerranée

La ville d'Arles ▶

Arles

Les Grecs ont fondé la ville d'Arles au cinquième siècle avant Jésus-Christ. Arles était la plus grande ville de Provence et la capitale de la Gaule ancienne. Arles est devenu une ville française en 1481. En 1888, Vincent Van Gogh est venu habiter en Arles. Il y a peint beaucoup de tableaux très célèbres. Aujourd'hui, Arles attire toujours les artistes, les historiens et les archéologues. De nombreux visiteurs viennent aussi en Arles chaque année pour ses festivals, ses musées et pour visiter ses environs. Arles est une ville très spéciale qu'on appelle souvent «le cœur de la Provence».

internet

go.hrw.com **ADRESSE:** go.hrw.com
MOT-CLE: WA3 ARLES

❶ Les Alyscamps
C'est un ancien cimetière chrétien très célèbre. Vincent Van Gogh et Paul Gauguin ont peint les Alyscamps dans plusieurs de leurs tableaux.

❷ Les arènes romaines
C'est un des plus anciens amphithéâtres romains. Les arènes romaines sont aussi parmi les plus grandes du monde. Elles mesurent 136 mètres de long et 107 mètres de large et peuvent contenir 12.000 spectateurs.

③ La Camargue

La Camargue est une région de marais magnifique. C'est un endroit protégé qui est célèbre pour ses flamants roses et ses chevaux sauvages.

Aux chapitres 9, 10 et 11,

tu vas faire la connaissance d'Hélène, de Magali et de leurs amis Florent et Ahmed. Ils vont te faire visiter la très belle ville d'Arles qui est située en Provence, dans le sud de la France. C'est une ville très ancienne, célèbre pour ses ruines romaines, mais aussi pour ses nombreux festivals et ses traditions provençales...

⑤ Le théâtre antique

On utilise encore aujourd'hui ce théâtre construit au premier siècle avant Jésus-Christ. Le Festival d'Arles, les Rencontres internationales de la photographie et d'autres spectacles ont lieu au théâtre antique.

④ les festivals

Arles est une ville célèbre pour ses nombreux festivals. On peut y admirer des danseurs en costumes traditionnels qui viennent de toute la Provence.

9

Au téléphone

Objectives

In this chapter you will learn to

Première étape

- ask for and express opinions
- inquire about and relate past events

Deuxième étape

- make and answer a telephone call

Troisième étape

- share confidences and console others
- to ask for and give advice

ADRESSE: go.hrw.com
MOT-CLE: WA3 ARLES-9

◀ **En France, les cabines téléphoniques sont nombreuses.**

MISE EN TRAIN ▪ *Un week-end spécial*

Stratégie
pour comprendre

Before you watch the video, think about the title of the story and look at the photos on these two pages. What is the subject of Hélène and Magali's telephone conversation? How did you figure that out?

Hélène   **Magali**   **Florent**   **Ahmed**

Hélène et Magali sont au téléphone et racontent ce qu'elles ont fait pendant le week-end. Magali a fait beaucoup de choses. La conversation dure...

1

Hélène : Allô?

Magali : Hélène? C'est Magali à l'appareil. Tu as passé un bon week-end?

Hélène : Bof, ça a été. Je n'ai rien fait de spécial.

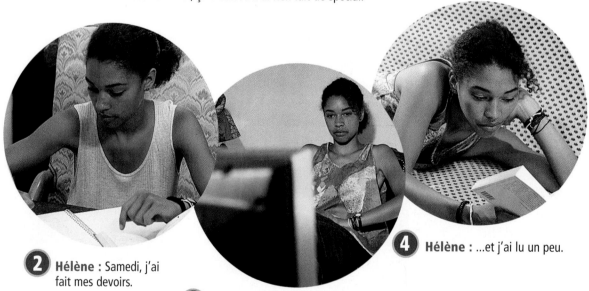

4 Hélène : ...et j'ai lu un peu.

2 Hélène : Samedi, j'ai fait mes devoirs.

3 Hélène : Dimanche, j'ai regardé la télévision...

5

Hélène : Et toi? Tu as passé un bon week-end?

Magali : Excellent! J'ai passé un week-end super!

Hélène : Ah oui? Qu'est-ce que tu as fait?

Magali : Je suis allée au théâtre antique avec Florent.

6 **Magali :** Il m'a présenté un garçon très sympa. Il s'appelle Ahmed. Il est super gentil.

7 **Magali :** Nous avons beaucoup parlé. Tu sais, il adore le sport. Il aime le tennis, comme moi.

8 **Magali :** Dimanche, nous sommes tous allés aux Baux-de-Provence.

9

Hélène : Qu'est-ce que vous avez fait là-bas?

Magali : Je vais te raconter une histoire incroyable!

Hélène : Je t'écoute.

Magali : Attends une seconde... Ecoute, Hélène, mon père veut téléphoner. Je te rappelle plus tard.

10 **Hélène :** Mais, qu'est-ce qui s'est passé aux Baux-de-Provence?

Cahier d'activités, p. 97, Act. 1

1 Tu as compris?

1. How was Hélène's weekend?
2. Did Magali have a good weekend? Why? Why not?
3. Do you think Magali likes Ahmed? How can you tell?
4. Why does Magali have to hang up?

2 Magali ou Hélène?

Qui a fait ça, Magali ou Hélène?

1. aller aux Baux
2. faire ses devoirs
3. lire
4. aller au théâtre antique
5. regarder la télévision
6. ne rien faire de spécial

3 Mets en ordre

Put Magali's activities in order according to *Un week-end spécial.*

1. Elle est allée au théâtre antique.
2. Elle est allée aux Baux-de-Provence.
3. Elle a parlé avec Hélène au téléphone.
4. Elle a rencontré un garçon sympa.

4 C'est qui?

A quelle personne correspond chaque phrase?

Magali

Hélène

Ahmed

le père de Magali

1. Cette personne veut téléphoner.
2. Cette personne a passé un bon week-end.
3. Cette personne est super gentille.
4. Pendant le week-end, cette personne n'a rien fait de spécial.
5. Cette personne va téléphoner plus tard.

5 Cherche les expressions

According to *Un week-end spécial,* what do you say in French . . .

1. to answer the phone?
2. to identify yourself on the phone?
3. to ask if someone had a good weekend?
4. to ask what someone did?
5. to tell someone to hold?
6. to ask what happened?

> C'est... à l'appareil.
>
> Attends une seconde.
>
> Allô?
>
> Qu'est-ce qui s'est passé?
>
> Qu'est-ce que tu as fait?
>
> Tu as passé un bon week-end?

6 Et maintenant, à toi

What do you think happened to Magali at les Baux?

Comment dit-on...?

Asking for and expressing opinions

To ask for someone's opinion:

Tu as passé un bon week-end?
Did you have a good weekend?

To express satisfaction:

Oui, très chouette. *Yes, super.*
Oui, excellent.
Oui, très bon.

To express indifference:

Oui, ça a été. *Yes, it was OK.*
Oh, pas mauvais.

To express dissatisfaction:

Très mauvais.
C'était épouvantable.
It was horrible.

Cahier d'activités, p. 98, Act. 2

---

7 ### Le week-end!

Ecoutons Listen to these people talk about their weekend. Tell if they had a really good time, a mildly good time, or no fun at all.

8 ### Tu as passé un bon week-end?

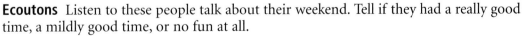

Parlons Demande à tes camarades s'ils ont passé un bon week-end ou pas. Ensuite, dis-leur si toi, tu as passé un bon week-end ou pas.

Comment dit-on...?

Inquiring about and relating past events

To inquire about past events:

Qu'est-ce qui s'est passé (hier)?
What happened (yesterday)?

Qu'est-ce que tu as fait vendredi?
What did you do . . . ?

Et après? *And then?*

Tu es allé(e) où? *Where did you go?*

To relate past events:

Nous avons parlé. *We talked.*

D'abord, j'ai fait mes devoirs.
First, . . .

Ensuite, j'ai téléphoné à un copain.
Then, . . .

Après, je suis sorti(e).
Afterwards, I went out.

Et après ça, j'ai téléphoné à Luc.
And after that, . . .

Finalement/Enfin, je suis allé(e)
chez Paul.
Finally, I went . . .

Cahier d'activités, p. 98, Act. 3

9 Méli-mélo!

Lisons Remets la conversation entre Albert et Marcel dans le bon ordre.

—Vendredi et samedi, rien de spécial.

—Et après ça?

—Pas mal. Dis, qu'est-ce que tu as fait ce week-end?

—Salut, Marcel! Ça va?

—Vous êtes allés où?

—Après, nous sommes allés au café et nous avons parlé jusqu'à minuit.

—Dimanche, j'ai téléphoné à Gisèle et nous avons décidé de sortir.

—Et dimanche?

—D'abord, nous avons fait un pique-nique. Ensuite, nous sommes allés au cinéma.

—Oui, ça va bien. Et toi?

CHAPITRE 9 Au téléphone

The *passé composé* with *avoir*

To tell what happened in the past, use the **passé composé** of the verb. The **passé composé** is composed of two parts: *(a)* a present-tense form of the helping verb **avoir** or **être**—which you've already learned—and *(b)* the past participle of the verb you want to use. You use **avoir** as the helping verb with most verbs. Only with a small number of French verbs, like **aller,** do you use **être** as the helping verb. You'll learn more about these verbs later.

Helping Verb	+	*Past Participle*

J'	**ai**
Tu	**as**
Il/Elle/On	**a**
Nous	**avons**
Vous	**avez**
Ils/Elles	**ont**

parlé au téléphone.

- To form the past participle of a verb that ends in **-er,** drop the **-er** and add **-é.**
- To make a verb in the **passé composé** negative, put **ne (n')... pas** around the helping verb.

Je n'ai pas étudié.

- Some French verbs have irregular past participles—that is, they don't follow a regular pattern. You'll have to memorize them when you learn the verb. Here are the past participles of some irregular verbs that you've already seen.

faire → **fait**	J'ai **fait** mes devoirs.
prendre → **pris**	Ils ont **pris** un taxi.
voir → **vu**	Il a **vu** sa grand-mère.
lire → **lu**	Elle a **lu** un roman français.

Grammaire supplémentaire,
pp. 284–285, Act. 1–3

Cahier d'activités,
pp. 98–99, Act. 4, 6–7

Travaux pratiques de grammaire,
pp. 71–74, Act. 1–7

---

10 ## Grammaire en contexte

Ecoutons Listen to these conversations and decide whether the speakers are talking about what they did last weekend or what they're going to do next weekend.

11 ## Grammaire en contexte

Parlons Qu'est-ce que Claire et ses amis ont fait à la plage?

1. 2. 3.

12 **Qu'est-ce qu'on a fait?**

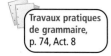 **Parlons** Avec un camarade, parlez de ce que vous avez fait et de ce que vous n'avez pas fait le week-end dernier. Ensuite, raconte le week-end de ton camarade à un troisième élève.

EXEMPLE   **J'ai promené le chien samedi matin.**

faire mes devoirs	laver la voiture	sortir la poubelle	promener le chien
acheter une montre		ranger ma chambre	prendre un café avec mes amis
voir un film français	faire le ménage	faire un pique-nique	lire un roman

Note de grammaire

When you use the **passé composé** with adverbs such as **trop, beaucoup, pas encore** (*not yet*), **bien** (*well*), **mal** (*badly*), and **déjà** (*already*), place the adverb before the past participle of the verb.

J'ai **déjà** mangé.

Nadine n'a **pas encore** vu ce film.

Travaux pratiques de grammaire, p. 74, Act. 8

Grammaire supplémentaire, p. 285, Act. 4–5 →

 **Note culturelle**

Arles est situé sur le Rhône, un fleuve du sud de la France. Pendant les premiers siècles après Jésus-Christ, Arles est devenu le port le plus important de la province romaine du sud de la Gaule appelée Provincia. Arles est aussi devenu le plus grand centre de commerce. Aujourd'hui, on peut toujours voir l'influence romaine en Arles. On peut y visiter l'amphithéâtre romain, un ancien théâtre, qui est toujours utilisé et les plus grands thermes de Provence.

13 **Grammaire en contexte**

Parlons Donne une raison logique pour expliquer pourquoi chaque chose est arrivée. Utilise les mots dans la boîte et le **passé composé**.

EXEMPLE   Céline a gagné le match de tennis.

Elle a bien joué.

1. Marie-Louise a eu 18 à son interro de maths!
2. Jérôme n'a pas d'énergie.
3. Sabine veut aller voir *Les Misérables*.
4. Luc n'a plus faim.
5. Etienne ne veut pas lire *Le Petit Prince*.

bien	étudier	travailler
		pas encore
déjà	voir	
		lire
trop	manger	beaucoup

Qu'est-ce que tu as fait aujourd'hui?

J'ai raté le bus.

J'ai trouvé vingt euros.

J'ai oublié mes devoirs.

J'ai déjeuné à la cantine.

J'ai rencontré une fille (un garçon) sympa.

J'ai chanté dans la chorale.

J'ai acheté un CD.

J'ai travaillé au fast-food.

Here are some other verbs and expressions you may want to use to talk about what you've done during your day.

apporter	*to bring*	**passer un examen**	*to take an exam*
chercher	*to look for*	**rater une interro**	*to fail a quiz*
commencer	*to begin, to start*	**répéter**	*to rehearse, to practice music*
dîner	*to have dinner*	**retrouver**	*to meet with*
gagner	*to win, to earn*	**visiter**	*to visit (a place)*
montrer	*to show*		

Travaux pratiques de grammaire, p. 75, Act. 9–10

14 Le week-end dernier

Parlons Dis ce que les personnes suivantes ont fait le week-end dernier.

 1.

 2.

 3.

 4.

 5.

 6.

15 Pierre a fait quoi?

Parlons Pierre a passé une semaine dans une colonie de vacances. Regarde les activités dans la boîte. Qu'est-ce qu'il a fait à ton avis? Qu'est-ce qu'il n'a pas fait?

chanter avec des copains

rater le bus

gagner un match   nager

faire du ski nautique   acheter un CD

rater un examen   manger des escargots

DE BONS CONSEILS

French words that look similar are often related in meaning, so you can use words you already know to guess the meanings of new words. If you already know what **chanter** means, you can probably guess the meaning of **une chanteuse.** You know what **commencer** means, so what do you think le **commencement** means? Likewise, you should be able to figure out **le visiteur** from the verb **visiter.**

16 Tu as déjà fait ça?

Ecrivons/Parlons Make a list of ten activities that you or a classmate might have done last week. Then, try to find a classmate who did each activity. When you find someone who did one of the activities, write his or her name on your list next to the activity. Try to find a different person for each activity.

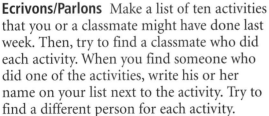

Activités	Nom
1. J'ai gagné cent dollars.	Jeff
2. J'ai chanté dans la chorale.	Lisa

17 Mon journal

Write down five things you did last weekend. Be sure to tell when you did each activity, with whom, and add as many other details as you can think of.

—Allô, Anita?
—Oui. C'est moi.
—Salut. C'est François.

—Allô? C'est Michel. Véronique est là,
  s'il vous plaît?
—Une seconde.
—Merci.

—Allô? Est-ce que Xuan est là, s'il vous
  plaît?
—Non, il est chez Robert.
—Est-ce que je peux laisser un message?
—Bien sûr.
—Vous pouvez lui dire qu'Emmanuelle
  a téléphoné?
—D'accord.
—Merci.

18 Au téléphone

Parlons Answer these questions about the
conversations.

1. What do the people say to begin the
   conversation?
2. Who has to wait a few seconds to speak
   to his or her friend?
3. Who gets to talk right away to the
   person he or she is calling?
4. Who isn't home?

Allô, allô?
Les spécialistes du téléphone

*Microcommutateurs • Téléphones sans fil • Téléphones
de voiture • Répondeurs • Télécopieurs personnels
• Interphones • Alarmes*

18, rue Lafayette — **13200 ARLES   04-90-96-45-75**
26, rue de la Liberté — **13200 ARLES 04-90-49-54-16**

Making and answering a telephone call

CD-ROM **3**
DVD **2**

To make a phone call:

Bonjour.
Je suis bien chez Véronique?
Is this . . . 's house?

C'est Michel.
(Est-ce que) Véronique **est là, s'il vous plaît?**

Je peux parler à Véronique?
Je peux laisser un message?
May I leave a message?

Vous pouvez lui dire que j'ai téléphoné?
Can you tell her/him that I called?

To answer a phone call:

Allô?
Qui est à l'appareil?
Who's calling?

Vous pouvez rappeler plus tard?
Can you call back later?

Une seconde, s'il vous plaît.
D'accord.

Bien sûr.

Here are some additional phrases you may need:

Ne quittez pas. *Hold on.*

Ça ne répond pas. *There's no answer.*

C'est occupé. *It's busy.*

Cahier d'activités,
p. 102, Act. 13–14

Travaux pratiques
de grammaire,
p. 76, Act. 11–12

19 **Un coup de fil**

Ecoutons Ecoute ces conversations téléphoniques. Qui téléphone? A qui
voudrait-il/-elle parler?

Note culturelle

En France, quand on veut téléphoner,
on peut aller à la poste. Il y a toujours des cabines
téléphoniques à la poste. On peut aussi téléphoner d'une
cabine publique. Pour réduire le vandalisme, France
Télécom remplace de plus en plus les téléphones à pièces
par des publiphones à cartes. Ces téléphones modernes
utilisent des télécartes. On peut acheter sa télécarte à la
poste ou dans un bureau de tabac. Chaque carte contient
un certain nombre d'unités. Pour téléphoner, on met sa
télécarte dans le publiphone. On utilise plusieurs unités à
chaque fois. Le publiphone a un écran qui dit combien
d'unités il reste sur la télécarte. On utilise plus d'unités si on
téléphone loin ou longtemps. Quand on a utilisé toutes les
unités d'une télécarte, il faut en acheter une autre.

20 Méli-mélo!

Lisons Mets cette conversation dans le bon ordre.

D'accord.

Allô?

C'est Aurélie.

Tu peux lui dire que j'ai téléphoné?

Salut, Aurélie. Désolée, elle n'est pas là.

Allô, bonjour. Je peux parler à Nicole?

Qui est à l'appareil?

Bien sûr.

Est-ce que je peux laisser un message?

21 Messages téléphoniques

Ecoutons During your exchange visit to France, you stay with a French family, **les Tissot.** You're the only one at home today. Several of their friends call and leave messages. Write down the messages and compare your notes with a classmate's.

22 Jeu de rôle

Parlons Tu téléphones à un(e) ami(e) mais il/elle n'est pas à la maison. Laisse un message pour ton ami(e). Ton (ta) camarade va jouer la rôle du père ou de la mère de ton ami(e). Ensuite, changez de rôle.

Grammaire

-re verbs

Like **-er** verbs, most verbs that end in **-re** follow a regular pattern. Drop the **-re** from the infinitive and add the endings indicated in the box to the right. Notice that you don't add an ending to the **il/elle/on** form of the verb.

- **Répondre** is followed by a form of the preposition **à**. Nathalie répond **à** Lucas. Je réponds **au** professeur.
- Some other **-re** verbs you might want to use are **vendre** (to sell), **attendre** (to wait for), and **perdre** (to lose).
- To form the past participle of an **-re** verb, drop the **-re** and add **-u**. Il a **répondu** à sa lettre.   Nous avons **perdu** nos cahiers.

répondre (to answer)

je répond**s**	nous répond**ons**
tu répond**s**	vous répond**ez**
il/elle/on répond	ils/elles répond**ent**

Grammaire supplémentaire, p. 286, Act. 6–8

Cahier d'activités, p. 103, Act. 15–16

Travaux pratiques de grammaire, p. 77, Act. 13–14

23 Grammaire en contexte

Ecrivons Sébastien overhears the following comments before class. Complete the comments with the appropriate forms of the verbs **répondre, vendre, attendre,** and **perdre.**

1. «Nous _____ le professeur. Il est en retard.»
2. «Attention, Luc! Tu _____ ton argent. Tu dois fermer ton sac à dos.»
3. «Ils _____ toujours bien aux questions du professeur!»
4. «Est-ce qu'on _____ des calculatrices à la Papeterie Simonet? Il me faut une calculatrice.»
5. «Je _____ à la lettre de Marianne. Elle est à Nice avec sa famille.»
6. «On va _____ des tee-shirts pour gagner de l'argent pour le Cercle français.»

Tu aimes téléphoner?

How often do you call your friends? We asked some francophone teenagers about their telephone habits. Here's what they told us.

Nicole,
Martinique

«Oui, j'aime beaucoup télé-phoner. Mes parents rous-pètent souvent parce que je reste longtemps au télé-phone, parce que ça coûte cher, le téléphone, et donc ils me demandent d'éviter de parler trop souvent au téléphone, de rester moins longtemps. Le plus souvent, je téléphone à peu près une heure de temps.»

Virgile,
France

«Ah oui, j'aime beaucoup téléphoner. Ça permet de discuter, de prendre des nouvelles un peu partout. C'est pratique.»

Marie,
France

«Ben, j'aime bien téléphoner... Ça dépend à qui, mes copines, mes copains. J'aime bien parce que j'aime bien leur parler, surtout à ma meilleure amie Caroline. J'aime beaucoup lui parler. On reste très longtemps. Mais sinon, téléphoner aux gens que je connais pas, j'aime pas trop.»

Qu'en penses-tu?

1. How do your phone habits compare with those of these people?
2. How might your life be different if you did or didn't have a phone in your room?
3. What restrictions on the use of the phone do you have at your house?

Savais-tu que... ?

The French telecommunications network is one of the best in the world. However, talking on the telephone in France and other francophone countries is still expensive, even when calling locally. For this reason, teenagers are not usually allowed to spend long periods of time on the phone, and most do not have a phone in their room.

Comment dit-on...?

Sharing confidences and consoling others; asking for and giving advice

To share a confidence:

> **J'ai un petit problème.** *I've got a little problem.*
> **Je peux te parler?** *Can I talk to you?*
> **Tu as une minute?** *Do you have a minute?*

To console someone:

> **Je t'écoute.** *I'm listening.*
> **Qu'est-ce que je peux faire?**
>   *What can I do?*
> **Ne t'en fais pas!** *Don't worry!*
> **Ça va aller mieux!** *It's going to get better!*

To ask for advice:

> **A ton avis, qu'est-ce que je fais?**
>   *In your opinion, what do I do?*
> **Qu'est-ce que tu me conseilles?**
>   *What do you advise me to do?*

To give advice:

> **Oublie-le/-la/-les!** *Forget him/her/it/them!*
> **Téléphone-lui/-leur!** *Call him/her/them!*
> **Tu devrais lui/leur parler.**
>   *You should talk to him/her/them.*
> **Pourquoi tu ne** téléphones **pas?**
>   *Why don't you . . . ?*

Cahier d'activités, pp. 104–105, Act. 18–22

---

24 Des conseils

Ecoutons Are these people giving advice or asking for advice?

Note de grammaire

In the expressions above, **le, la,** and **les** *(him, her, it, them)* are object pronouns that refer to people or things. The pronouns **lui** *(to him, to her)* and **leur** *(to them)* refer only to people. You will learn more about these pronouns later.

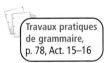

Travaux pratiques de grammaire, p. 78, Act. 15–16

Grammaire supplémentaire, p. 287, Act. 9–10 →

DE BONS CONSEILS

Many language students feel nervous about speaking. You might be worried about making mistakes, or you might think you won't sound right. To sharpen your speaking skills, practice aloud at home in French, using situations and material covered in class. You could role-play two friends talking on the phone about a problem that one person has. What would each person say? This is a good time to incorporate grammar points (like the object pronouns) that you covered in class in your conversation. These practice conversations will help prepare you to speak confidently in class.

25 Grammaire en contexte

Ecoutons Ecoute cette conversation entre Mireille et Simone. Simone a un problème. Quel est son problème?

26 J'ai un petit problème

Lisons Trouve la solution logique à chaque problème.

1. Mon frère ne me parle plus depuis cinq jours.
2. Je veux acheter un vélo, mais je n'ai pas d'argent.
3. J'ai oublié mes devoirs.
4. Je vais rater l'interro d'anglais.

a. Tu devrais étudier plus souvent.
b. Pourquoi tu ne travailles pas?
c. Refais-les!
d. Parle-lui!

27 Pauvre Hervé!

Ecrivons Console Hervé.

1. 2. 3.

28 Et à ton avis?

Parlons Your friend phones and asks to speak to you. He or she has some problems and wants to ask your advice about them. Console your friend and offer some advice. Then, change roles.

> Il/Elle...

n'a pas d'argent pour acheter des baskets.

n'a pas acheté de cadeau pour l'anniversaire de sa sœur.

n'aime pas le prof de biologie.

n'a pas parlé avec son petit ami (sa petite amie) depuis 3 jours.

ne peut pas trouver de travail pour l'été.

a raté un examen.

veut rencontrer de nouveaux copains.

n'a pas gagné son match de tennis.

veut faire une boum, mais ses parents ne sont pas d'accord.

29

De l'école au travail

Parlons You're the host of a radio talk show called *A l'écoute des jeunes.* You receive many calls from teenagers asking for your advice. Your job is to answer the phone, listen to their problems, ask them questions, and console them or give them some advice.

The vowel sounds [e] and [ɛ]

Listen to the vowels in the word **préfère.** How are they different? The first one is pronounced [e], and the second one [ɛ]. To make the vowel sound [e], hold your mouth in a closed, smiling position. Keep your lips and tongue steady to avoid the glide, as in the English word *day.* Repeat these words.

été désolé occupé répondre

Now, take a smiling position once again, but this time open your mouth wider. This will produce the vowel sound [ɛ]. Repeat these words.

règle algèbre achète frère

In the examples, you can see that **é** represents the sound [e], while **è** represents the sound [ɛ] in writing. You've probably noticed that **e** with no accent and some other letter combinations can represent these sounds as well. Repeat these words.

apportez trouver

You see that the spellings **ez** and **er** normally represent the sound [e]. This is true of all infinitives ending in **-er.**

Some spellings of the vowel sound [ɛ] are **ait, ais, ei,** and **ê.** An unaccented **e** is pronounced as open [ɛ] when it is followed by a double consonant, such as **ll** or **tt,** when followed by **x,** and, in most cases, when followed by **r,** or by any pronounced consonant. Now repeat these words.

fait français neige bête

elle cassette examen cherche

A. A prononcer

Repeat the following words.

1. délicieux   méchant   théâtre   vélo
2. après-midi   père   mère   très
3. février   chanter   chez   prenez
4. cette   française   treize   pêches

B. A lire

Take turns with a partner reading each of the following sentences aloud.

1. Ne quittez pas! Je vais chercher mon frère.
2. Marcel a visité Arles en mai. Il est allé au musée, à la cathédrale et aux arènes.
3. Elle n'aime pas trop l'algèbre et la géométrie, mais elle aime bien l'espagnol.
4. Tu ne peux pas aller au cinéma. Tu n'as pas fait la vaisselle.

C. A écrire

You're going to hear a short dialogue. Write down what you hear.

Je passe ma vie au téléphone

Stratégie pour lire

As you read, you use many different reading strategies at the same time. You may start by looking at illustrations, then move on to the titles and subtitles. You may need to skim the passage to get the general idea, then scan for specific details, and finally read the passage for more complete comprehension.

A. Skim the article. What kind of information do you expect to find?

B. What is the purpose of each section? How does the second section differ from the others?

Emmanuelle

C. How old was Emmanuelle when she started using the telephone? How did her parents feel about her using the telephone?

D. Read Emmanuelle's statement and list all the cognates you find. Then, match these terms with their English equivalents.

1. carte téléphonique	**a.** stationery
2. réprimander	**b.** phone card
3. remboursement	**c.** reprimand
4. cabine téléphonique	**d.** reimbursement
5. papier à lettres	**e.** telephone booth

Et moi, et moi...et eux!

Je passe ma vie au téléphone

Il y en a qui chantent : «Qui a eu cette idée folle, un jour, d'inventer l'école?» Moi, si j'en avais le talent, je chanterais : «Qui a eu cette idée folle, un jour, d'inventer le phone?»

Je ne pouvais plus me passer du téléphone. Et pourtant, j'ai tout essayé : punitions des parents, remboursement des communications, cures de quinze jours et plus en colonie… J'en ai découvert l'usage à dix ou onze ans, l'utilisation quasi quotidienne à treize ans. Et cela pour n'importe quel motif : discuter du travail scolaire, appeler les copains de colo qui habitent parfois à plus de 100 km de chez moi…

C'est à ce moment-là que mes parents sont intervenus. Au début, mes coups de fil ne se voyaient pas sur la note car mes parents restent assez longtemps, eux aussi, au téléphone. Mais du coup, j'ai pris l'habitude des longues conversations et des cris se sont fait entendre. Jusqu'au jour où, las de me réprimander, ils ont décidé de m'acheter une carte téléphonique et des timbres. J'ai vite eu la flemme d'aller à la cabine téléphonique et j'ai donc jeté mon dévolu sur le papier à lettres. En écrivant, j'utilise ma petite cervelle et quel plaisir de recevoir en retour une lettre que je peux lire et relire où et quand je veux!

Emmanuelle: «Qui a eu l'idée, un jour, d'inventer le phone?»

Il ne se passe pas une journée sans que je reçoive ma lecture préférée, celle qui vient du fond du cœur, celle des copains. D'accord, le téléphone est rapide et chaleureux, mais la lettre l'est peut-être encore plus. Bref, le téléphone est une gâterie à consommer avec modération.

Emmanuelle, 15 ans

Le bon usage du téléphone passe par une certaine maîtrise de l'appareil. Il faut savoir se présenter, être clair, précis, articuler... Après quelques années de pratique s'installe une véritable relation avec le combiné magique, merveilleux messager des peines et des espoirs. On attend une soirée entière une hypothétique sonnerie, on sursaute à chaque «Dring!», redoutant que Sylvain annule le rendez-vous pour lequel il a fallu passer trois heures dans la salle de bains. Combien de fois ai-je tourné, hésitante, autour de cet objet mystérieux au clavier soudain terrifiant? Combien de fois a-t-il, avec patience et sans jamais rien dire, recueilli mes rires et mes larmes? C'est pourquoi, aujourd'hui, je tiens à confesser publiquement et solennellement que j'aime mon téléphone!

Géraldine, 17 ans

Géraldine: «Je le confesse: mon téléphone, je l'aime!»

Pour dire bonjour, pour un rien...

Un quart d'heure, une demi-heure, une heure pendus au bout du fil... L'opération se répète quotidiennement. «Mes enfants téléphonent à leurs amis pour un rien, pour se dire bonjour et parfois pour faire leurs devoirs. Ça commence dès qu'ils rentrent du lycée et ça peut durer très longtemps... C'est à croire qu'ils sont nés avec un téléphone à l'oreille!», confie Véronique. Comme le dit Aurélie : «De retour chez soi, la seule façon de conserver un lien avec ceux qu'on vient de quitter, c'est le téléphone.»

Au sens propre comme au sens figuré, l'appareil est un fil qui vous relie au monde, qui vous rassure sur l'amitié des copains. C'est-à-dire sur ce qui est le plus important. Parce que dans l'amitié, on trouve la confiance, le respect, la tolérance et la sécurité dont on a tant besoin, à tout moment. Faute de lien, le risque est de se retrouver seul face à ses angoisses.

D'ailleurs, peu importe parfois qui vous appelez; quand l'interlocuteur décroche, vous finissez toujours par trouver quelque chose à raconter ou une confidence à partager.

Le téléphone, c'est un fil qui vous relie au monde, qui rassure sur l'amitié des copains. Et c'est ce qui est le plus important.

E. How did Emmanuelle break her telephone addiction? How does she communicate with her friends now? Why does she prefer this means of communication?

Géraldine

F. What advice does Géraldine give at the beginning of her statement? How does she describe her relationship with the telephone?

G. Who might have made each of the following statements?

"My telephone is my best friend."

"Finally, Arlette answered the letter I wrote her last week!"

"You may not make any more long-distance calls!"

H. Which people give the following reasons for talking on the phone?

1. to say hello to friends
2. to do homework

Pour dire bonjour, pour un rien...

I. In this section, Véronique and Aurélie each make a statement. Which person is a parent? How do you know?

J. Read the selection again and find three reasons why people enjoy talking on the phone. Which reason do you think is most important?

K. In English, write a statement similar to Emmanuelle's and Geraldine's in which you tell how you feel about the telephone. Give examples to show why you feel the way you do.

Cahier d'activités, p. 107, Act. 25

Grammaire supplémentaire

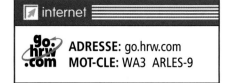

CD-ROM 3
DVD 2

internet

ADRESSE: go.hrw.com
MOT-CLE: WA3 ARLES-9

Première étape — **Objectives** Asking for and expressing opinions; inquiring about and relating past events

1 Emmanuelle téléphone à Julie pour lui raconter son week-end. Pour compléter leur conversation, utilise le passé composé des verbes entre parenthèses. (**p. 271**)

EMMANUELLE   Salut Julie. Tu ___**1**___ (passer) un bon week-end?

JULIE   Oh, oui. J'___**2**___ (regarder) un match de tennis, j'___**3**___ (parler) avec ma grand-mère et j'___**4**___ (lire) un roman. Et toi? Qu'est-ce que tu ___**5**___ (faire)?

EMMANUELLE   J'___**6**___ (prendre) la voiture de ma mère, et ma sœur et moi, nous ___**7**___ (voir) un film.

2 Complète ce que Pierre a écrit dans son journal à propos de son week-end. Utilise le passé composé des verbes entre parenthèses. (**p. 271**)

Hier, j'___**1**___ (retrouver) mes amis Jean et Françoise au café. Nous ___**2**___ (déjeuner) ensemble, puis, nous ___**3**___ (parler) de notre week-end. Samedi, Françoise ___**4**___ (lire) un livre et Jean ___**5**___ (étudier).

Le soir, ils ___**6**___ (acheter) un billet de loto mais ils ___**7**___ (ne pas gagner). Dimanche, j'___**8**___ (voir) un bon film et ensuite, j'___**9**___ (faire) mes devoirs.

3 Edouard veut toujours faire ce que Milo a fait. Lis ce qu'Edouard va faire et ensuite, dis ce que Milo a fait hier. Mets les verbes au passé composé et fais les changements nécessaires. (**p. 271**)

EXEMPLE   Demain, je vais acheter des baskets.
            Hier, Milo a acheté des baskets.

1. Je vais laver la voiture de mon père demain. Hier,...
2. Je vais déjeuner à la cantine demain. Hier,...
3. Demain, je vais retrouver mes copains. Hier,...
4. Demain, je vais répéter avec la chorale. Hier,...
5. Je vais dîner avec ma grand-mère demain. Hier,...
6. Demain, je vais ranger ma chambre. Hier,...

4 Complète chaque phrase avec l'adverbe approprié. (**pp. 271, 272**)

1. Hélène a (demain / pas encore / trop) mangé hier soir.
2. Tu vas parler avec Sullivan (demain / ce matin / hier)?
3. J'ai (bientôt / déjà / hier) fait mes devoirs.
4. Marianne et Roger, vous avez (maintenant / bien / hier) lu ce roman?
5. Les Saint-Martin ont pris un taxi pour aller à la gare (demain / maintenant / ce matin).

5 La maman d'Elissa lui demande si elle et ses frères et sœurs ont fait leur tâches domestiques. Réponds pour Elissa. Dans tes réponses, utilise **déjà** ou **ne (n')... pas encore**. N'oublie pas de faire tous les changements nécessaires. (**p. 272**)

EXEMPLE   MAMAN   Tu as passé l'aspirateur?
            ELISSA **Non, je n'ai pas encore passé l'aspirateur.**

1. MAMAN   Claire et toi, vous avez rangé vos chambres?
   ELISSA Non, _____

2. MAMAN   Tu as débarrassé la table?
   ELISSA Oui, _____

3. MAMAN   Et Guillaume, est-ce qu'il a fait les courses?
   ELISSA Oui, _____

4. MAMAN   Est-ce que tu as promené le chien?
   ELISSA Non, _____

5. MAMAN   Est-ce que Claire et Sophie ont fait le ménage?
   ELISSA Non, _____

Grammaire supplémentaire

WA3 ARLES-9

Deuxième étape — Objective Making and answering a telephone call

6 Ecris six phrases logiques en utilisant des mots de chaque colonne. Utilise le passé composé et n'oublie pas de faire tous les changements nécessaires. (**p. 277**)

Toi, tu		devant le cinéma
Moi, je	prendre	le bus de 10 h
Tes cousins	répondre	le téléphone
La mère de Serge	vendre	la question du professeur
Vous	perdre	la voiture
Nous	attendre	mon portefeuille
		pendant 15 minutes

7 Pierre, David et Yves parlent de ce que leurs amis vont faire aujourd'hui. Complète leur conversation avec les formes correctes des verbes **répondre** et **attendre**. (**p. 277**)

PIERRE   Tiens, salut! Vous ___**1**___ le bus?

YVES   Non, nous ___**2**___ Paul. Il va au stade avec nous.

PIERRE   Où est Lise?

DAVID   Elle est chez elle. Elle ___**3**___ sa mère pour aller au musée.

PIERRE   Ah oui! C'est vrai. Et Bruno, qu'est-ce qu'il fait ce matin?

YVES   Il ___**4**___ à la lettre de son correspondant américain. Et toi, qu'est-ce que tu fais, alors?

PIERRE   Rien de spécial.

DAVID   Tu ___**5**___ Paul avec nous?

PIERRE   Oui, pourquoi pas?

8 Mets chaque phrase dans un ordre logique. Utilise le passé composé quand c'est nécessaire. (**p. 277**)

1. hier/Paul/perdre/son portefeuille/au centre commercial

2. nous/répondre/au téléphone/quand/notre père/travailler

3. ne/pas/perdre/votre argent

4. mes parents/vendre/leur voiture/bleu/la semaine dernière

5. Michel/vendre/des bonbons/pour/gagner de l'argent

9   Léon appelle Magali pour lui demander son avis. Complète leur conversation avec **le, la, l'**, ou **lui**. (**p. 279**)

MAGALI   Allô?

LEON   Salut, Magali, ça va? J'ai un petit problème. Tu as une minute?

MAGALI   Oui. Bien sûr. Je t'écoute.

LEON   Ben, hier, au café, j'ai rencontré une fille. On a parlé pendant deux heures. Ce matin, elle m'a téléphoné pour me dire qu'elle veut sortir avec moi. A ton avis, qu'est-ce que je fais?

MAGALI   Elle est comment, cette fille? Tu ___**1**___ (l', les) aimes bien?

LEON   Oui. Je ___**2**___ (l', la) aime beaucoup. Elle est super sympa.

MAGALI   Qu'est-ce que tu ___**3**___ (lui, leur) as répondu, alors?

LEON   Je ne ___**4**___ (la, lui) ai pas répondu. A ton avis, qu'est-ce que je fais?

MAGALI   Téléphone- ___**5**___ (lui, leur) tout de suite!

LEON   Mais je ne trouve plus son numéro de téléphone!

MAGALI   Cherche- ___**6**___ (le, leur)!

LEON   Non, c'est pas possible. Je ne peux pas ___**7**___ (le, lui) téléphoner. Je suis trop timide!

MAGALI   Ah, bon! Alors, oublie- ___**8**___ (la, les)!

10   Ton ami Max et toi, vous donnez des conseils à Odile. Répète les conseils de Max et utilise les pronoms **le, la, les, lui** ou **leur**. (**p. 279**)

EXEMPLE   MAX   Achète les pommes rouges!
          TOI   **Oui. Achète-les!**

1. Téléphone à tes copains!   _____

2. Prends la trousse violette!   _____

3. Apporte tes disques compacts!   _____

4. Oublie ce garçon!   _____

5. Attends les vacances!   _____

6. Ecris à Caroline!   _____

7. Parle à tes parents!   _____

8. Achète ces stylos!   _____

Mise en pratique

 CD-ROM 3
DVD 2

internet

go.hrw.com

ADRESSE: go.hrw.com
MOT-CLE: WA3 ARLES-9

1 A friend has left a message on your answering machine telling you what he did over the weekend. Listen, then decide if these sentences are true or false.

1. Martin a passé un mauvais week-end.

2. Il est allé à la plage.

3. Il a fait beau pendant le week-end.

4. Il a joué au football samedi.

5. Il n'a pas joué au tennis.

6. Dimanche, il a fait de l'aérobic.

2 D'abord, lis ces lettres rapidement. Ensuite, relis chaque lettre plus attentivement. De quoi est-ce que ces lettres parlent? Qui est Agnès? Ensuite, réponds aux questions suivantes.

Chère Agnès	Il me dit qu'il veut sortir avec moi. Est-ce vrai?	Toute ma famille me déteste.
Agnès vous comprend. Vous pouvez lui confier tous vos problèmes. Elle trouve toujours une solution!	Chère Agnès, J'aime beaucoup un garçon, Pierre, qui me dit, dans une lettre très tendre, qu'il veut sortir avec moi. Mais il ne m'appelle jamais. Se moque-t-il de moi? Aide-moi car je suis dingue de lui! --Monique... Ne te décourage pas! Tu aimes ce garçon et il t'aime également. Tu t'imagines qu'il se moque de toi, mais lui aussi doit se demander s'il a ses chances. A toi d'aller vers lui. Bonne chance!	Chère Agnès, J'ai 14 ans et j'ai un problème : tout le monde dans ma famille me déteste, sauf ma mémé. Mes parents et ma sœur se moquent toujours de moi et me disent que je suis laide. Je suis très déprimée. Au secours! --S Ah S...! N'écoute pas ce que ta famille te dit. Et puis, il y a toujours ta mémé qui t'aime. Tu as 14 ans et tes parents ont sûrement peur de perdre leur petite fille. Parle-leur de tes sentiments et tu verras, tout ira mieux.

1. What is Monique's problem?

2. How does Agnès respond?

3. Who is S having difficulties with?

4. What does Agnès advise her to do?

3 D'après ce que tu sais sur le système de téléphone français, est-ce que les phrases suivantes sont vraies ou fausses?

1. The only way to make a call from a public phone in France is to use coins.

2. You can generally find a public phone at the post office.

3. You can't buy phone cards at the post office.

4. Card-operated phones are being replaced by coin-operated ones.

5. If you make a call using a phone card, you will be charged based on the distance and duration of the call.

4 **Ecrivons!**

Think of a problem that many teenagers face. Describe the problem in a letter to Agnès and ask her to give you some advice. Then, exchange letters with a classmate and write a response offering advice about his or her problem as if you were Agnès.

Prewriting

On a sheet of paper, brainstorm ways to explain the problem by asking yourself the "W" questions. Who is involved in the problem? What exactly is the problem? Where do you see the problem? At home? At school? When is the problem most evident? Why do you think this problem occurs?

Stratégie pour écrire

Answering the five "W" questions (Who? What? Where? When? Why?) can help you clarify your ideas. It can also help you make sure you don't leave out important information for your readers.

Writing

Using the answers to your "W" questions, write a letter to Agnès describing the problem. Be as specific as you can in your description. However, don't try to use vocabulary and expressions you don't know or aren't familiar with. Use what you know as effectively as you can; other words and expressions will come later.

Now, exchange letters with a classmate. Each of you should write a response to the other's letter, offering advice on the problem. In writing your response, try to use some of the expressions you've learned for giving advice. After your classmate has read your response, have him or her return it to you, along with the letter you wrote. You're now ready for the final step of the writing process.

Revising

Evaluating your work is another important part of writing. This process involves several steps:

1. Self-evaluation: Reread both your letter and the response you wrote. Are they both arranged well? Are they easy to understand? Are they too wordy, or are they lacking information?

2. Proofreading: Now, go over your writing again. This time, look just for misspelled words, punctuation errors, and grammatical mistakes.

3. Revising: Make any changes you feel are necessary.

After these steps are completed, you can submit or publish the final copy of your work.

5 **Jeu de rôle**

You haven't seen your friend in a while. You want to find out what he or she has been doing. Phone and ask to speak to your friend. Talk about what you both did last weekend. Find out also what your friend is planning to do next summer. Act this out with a partner.

Que sais-je?

Can you use what you've learned in this chapter?

Can you ask for and express opinions?
p. 269

1 How would you ask a friend how his or her weekend went?

2 How would you tell someone that your weekend was . . .
1. great?
2. OK?
3. horrible?

Can you inquire about and relate past events, using the passé composé?
p. 270

3 If you were inquiring about your friend's weekend, how would you ask . . .
1. what your friend did?
2. where your friend went?
3. what happened?

4 How would you tell someone that you did these things?

1.   2.   3.

Can you make and answer a telephone call?
p. 276

5 If you were making a telephone call, how would you . . .
1. tell who you are?
2. ask if it's the right house?
3. ask to speak to someone?
4. ask to leave a message?
5. ask someone to say you called?
6. tell someone the line's busy?

6 If you were answering a telephone call, how would you . . .
1. ask who's calling?
2. ask someone to hold?
3. ask someone to call back later?

Can you share confidences, console others, and ask for and give advice?
p. 279

7 How would you approach a friend about a problem you have?

8 What would you say to console a friend?

9 How would you ask a friend for advice?

10 How would you tell a friend what you think he or she should do?

Première étape

Asking for and expressing opinions

Tu as passé un bon week-end?	Did you have a good weekend?
Oui, très chouette.	Yes, super.
Oui, excellent.	Yes, excellent.
Oui, très bon.	Yes, very good.
Oui, ça a été.	Yes, it was OK.
Oh, pas mauvais.	Oh, not bad.
Très mauvais.	Very bad.
C'était épouvantable.	It was horrible.

Inquiring about and relating past events

Qu'est-ce qui s'est passé (hier)?	What happened (yesterday)?
Nous avons parlé.	We talked.
Qu'est-ce que tu as fait... ?	What did you do . . . ?
D'abord,...	First, . . .
Ensuite,...	Then, . . .

Après, je suis sorti(e).	Afterwards, I went out.
Et après (ça)...	And after (that) . . .
Finalement/Enfin,...	Finally, . . .
Tu es allé(e) où?	Where did you go?
Je suis allé(e)...	I went . . .
j'ai fait	I did, I made
j'ai pris	I took
j'ai vu	I saw
j'ai lu	I read
déjà	already
bien	well
mal	badly
ne... pas encore	not yet
acheter	to buy
apporter	to bring
chanter	to sing
chercher	to look for
commencer	to begin, to start
déjeuner à la cantine	to have lunch at the cafeteria

dîner	to have dinner
gagner	to win, to earn
montrer	to show
oublier	to forget
passer un examen	to take an exam
rater le bus	to miss the bus
rater une interro	to fail a quiz
rencontrer	to meet for the first time
répéter	to rehearse, to practice music
retrouver	to meet with
travailler au fast-food	to work at a fast-food restaurant
trouver	to find
visiter	to visit (a place)
une fille	girl
un garçon	boy

Deuxième étape

Making and answering a telephone call

Allô?	Hello?
Je suis bien chez...?	Is this . . . 's house?
Qui est à l'appareil?	Who's calling?
(Est-ce que)... est là, s'il vous plaît?	Is . . . there, please?
Une seconde, s'il vous plaît.	One second, please.

(Est-ce que) je peux parler à...?	May I speak to . . . ?
Bien sûr.	Certainly.
Vous pouvez rappeler plus tard?	Can you call back later?
Je peux laisser un message?	May I leave a message?
Vous pouvez lui dire que j'ai téléphoné?	Can you tell her/him that I called?

Ne quittez pas.	Hold on.
Ça ne répond pas.	There's no answer.
C'est occupé.	It's busy.
attendre	to wait for
perdre	to lose
répondre (à)	to answer
vendre	to sell

Troisième étape

Sharing confidences and consoling others

J'ai un petit problème.	I've got a little problem.
Je peux te parler?	Can we talk?
Tu as une minute?	Do you have a minute?
Je t'écoute.	I'm listening.
Qu'est-ce que je peux faire?	What can I do?
Ne t'en fais pas!	Don't worry!

Ça va aller mieux!	It's going to get better!

Asking for and giving advice

A ton avis, qu'est-ce que je fais?	In your opinion, what do I do?
Qu'est-ce que tu me conseilles?	What do you advise me to do?
Oublie-le/-la/-les!	Forget him/her/it/ them!

Téléphone-lui/ -leur!	Call him/her/them!
Tu devrais lui/leur parler.	You should talk to him/her/them.
Pourquoi tu ne... pas?	Why don't you . . . ?
le	him, it
la	her, it
les	them
lui	to him, to her
leur	to them

10
Dans un magasin de vêtements

Objectives

In this chapter you will learn to

Première étape

- ask for and give advice

Deuxième étape

- express need
- inquire

Troisième étape

- ask for an opinion
- pay a compliment
- criticize
- hesitate
- make a decision

 internet

 ADRESSE: go.hrw.com
MOT-CLE: WA3 ARLES-10

◄ **Je ne sais pas quoi mettre pour aller à la boum.**

MISE EN TRAIN ▪ *Chacun ses goûts*

DVD VIDEO

Stratégie pour comprendre
What event are Hélène and Magali discussing at the beginning of the story? Where does Magali go? Why do you think Hélène doesn't go with her?

Magali   **Hélène**   **La vendeuse**

1

Magali : Oh là là! Je ne sais pas quoi mettre demain. C'est l'anniversaire de Sophie. J'ai envie d'acheter quelque chose de joli. Et toi, qu'est-ce que tu vas mettre?

Hélène : Oh, je ne sais pas. Sans doute un jean et un tee-shirt.

2

Magali : Pourquoi est-ce que tu ne trouves pas quelque chose d'original? De mignon?

Hélène : Ecoute, Magali. Moi, j'aime bien être en jean et en tee-shirt. C'est simple et agréable à porter. Chacun ses goûts.

3

Au magasin...

La vendeuse : Bonjour. Je peux vous aider?

Magali : Je cherche quelque chose pour aller à une fête. J'aimerais quelque chose d'original et pas trop cher.

4

La vendeuse : Qu'est-ce que vous faites comme taille?

Magali : Je fais du 38.

La vendeuse : Nous avons des jupes, si vous voulez. Tenez, celle-ci fait jeune. Comment la trouvez-vous?

Magali : Bof. C'est pas tellement mon style.

Magali : J'aime bien cette jupe-ci. Est-ce que vous l'avez en vert?

La vendeuse : Elle est jolie, n'est-ce pas? Nous l'avons en bleu, en rouge et en vert. La voilà en 38.

Magali essaie la jupe...

La vendeuse : Très joli. Ça vous va très bien.

Magali : Oui, c'est pas mal, mais elle est un peu large, non? Est-ce que vous l'avez en 36?

Quelques minutes plus tard...

La vendeuse : Ah, très chic! C'est tout à fait votre style.

Magali : Vous trouvez? Mais, je ne sais pas quoi mettre avec.

La vendeuse : Nous avons ces chemisiers, si vous aimez. Taille unique. Ça va très bien avec la jupe.

Cahier d'activités, p. 109, Act. 1

1 Tu as compris?

1. Why does Magali want to buy something new?
2. What is Hélène going to wear? Why?
3. What type of clothing is Magali looking for?
4. What outfit does Magali like?

2 C'est qui?

Qui parle? C'est Magali, Hélène ou la vendeuse?

1. «J'aimerais quelque chose d'original et pas trop cher.»
2. «Je peux vous aider?»
3. «Moi, j'aime bien être en jean et en tee-shirt. C'est simple et agréable à porter.»
4. «Qu'est-ce que vous faites comme taille?»
5. «Chacun ses goûts.»
6. «Est-ce que vous l'avez en vert?»
7. «C'est tout à fait votre style.»
8. «Ce n'est pas tellement mon style.»

3 Chacun ses goûts

Qu'est-ce que Magali dit de ces vêtements?

1. le jean et le tee-shirt d'Hélène
2. la première jupe que la vendeuse propose.
3. la jupe verte en 38

4 Qu'est-ce qu'elle répond?

Qu'est-ce que Magali répond à la vendeuse?

1. Qu'est-ce que vous faites comme taille?
2. Comment la trouvez-vous?
3. Je peux vous aider?
4. Ah, très chic! C'est tout à fait votre style.

a. Vous trouvez? Mais, je ne sais pas quoi mettre avec.
b. Je fais du 38.
c. Je cherche quelque chose pour aller à une fête.
d. Bof. Ce n'est pas tellement mon style.

5 Cherche les expressions

According to *Chacun ses goûts,* how would you . . .

1. express indecision?
2. express satisfaction with your clothes?
3. tell a salesperson what you want?
4. tell what size you wear?
5. express dissatisfaction with clothes?
6. ask for a certain color or size?

> Je fais du...
>
> J'aimerais quelque chose de...
>
> C'est simple et agréable à porter.
>
> C'est pas tellement mon style.
>
> Je ne sais pas quoi mettre.
>
> Est-ce que vous l'avez en... ?

6 Et maintenant, à toi

Est-ce que tu préfères le style de Magali ou d'Hélène? Qu'est-ce que tu aimes comme vêtements?

Vocabu

Les vêtements

la chemise blanche
ou bleue 19,65€

la veste bleue
109,75€

le maillot
de bain bleu
et rouge
18,15€

le chemisier
blanc
22,70€

la robe
verte
à fleurs
66,90€

le blouson
bleu ou noir
141€

le blouson
marron
ou noir
176,80€

la jupe
grise
30,35€

les chaussures (f.)
marron
47,10€

les bottes noires
76,05€

Accessoires

noires
blanches
bleues

les lunettes de
soleil (f.) 9,35€

les boucles
d'oreilles (f.)
37,95€

pêche

les chaussettes
1,55€ la paire

la cravate bleue à
rayures 12,65€

la montre
noire 68,40€

l'écharpe rose
et blanche
15,45€

la ceinture noire
ou marron
15,20€

le chapeau
gris
38,85€

la casquette
rouge
24,50€

Here are some other words you may want to use to talk about what you're wearing.

un bracelet	un manteau *coat*	des sandales (f.)
un cardigan	un pantalon	un short
un jean	un pull(-over)	un sweat-shirt

Travaux pratiques de grammaire,
pp. 79–80, Act. 1–3

Cahier d'activités,
pp. 110–111, Act. 2–5

Qu'est-ce qu'Armelle a acheté?

Ecoutons Listen as Armelle tells her friend about her big shopping trip. Then, choose the illustration that represents her purchases.

a.　　　　　　　　b.　　　　　　　　c.

8 Des cadeaux

Parlons Regarde l'image et dis ce que Lise a acheté pour sa famille.

EXEMPLE　　**Elle a acheté... pour...**

9 Pas de chance!

Ecrivons Imagine que tu voyages en France. A l'arrivée, tu ne trouves pas tes bagages. Alors, la compagnie aérienne te donne 500 dollars pour acheter de nouveaux vêtements. Fais une liste de ce que tu vas acheter.

EXEMPLE　　**D'abord, je vais acheter...**

10 La fête

Parlons Tu es invité(e) à une fête. Dis quels vêtements tu vas porter. Choisis des articles de la liste de l'activité 9. Est-ce que tu vas avoir besoin d'autres vêtements?

EXEMPLE　　**Je vais mettre...**

Grammaire

The verbs *mettre* and *porter*

Mettre is an irregular verb.

mettre *(to put, to put on, to wear)*

Je	**mets**	Nous	**mettons**
Tu	**mets**	Vous	**mettez**
Il/Elle/On	**met**	Ils/Elles	**mettent**

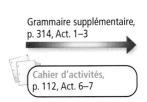

Grammaire supplémentaire,
p. 314, Act. 1–3

Cahier d'activités,
p. 112, Act. 6–7

Travaux pratiques de
grammaire,
pp. 80–81, Act. 4–6

- **Mets** and **met** are pronounced alike. You don't pronounce the final consonant(s) **ts** and **t**.
- The past participle of **mettre** is **mis**: Elle **a mis** une jupe.
- You can also use the regular **-er** verb **porter** to tell what someone is wearing: Elle **porte** une robe.

11 Grammaire en contexte

Parlons Dis ce que les personnes suivantes mettent pour sortir.

1. Pour aller à l'école, Sophie...

2. Pour aller à une boum, elles...

3. Pour aller au café, toi, tu...

4. Pour aller au stade, nous...

12 Grammaire en contexte

Parlons Demande à ton/ta camarade quels vêtements il/elle a mis hier et dis-lui ce que toi, tu as mis.

DE BONS CONSEILS

Although it's common to feel a little uncomfortable when speaking a new language, the best way to overcome it is to talk and talk and talk. Whenever you answer a question or have a conversation with a partner, try to keep the conversation going as long as possible. Don't worry about making a mistake. The more you think about making mistakes, the less likely you will be to talk.

Comment dit-on...?

Asking for and giving advice

To ask for advice:

Je ne sais pas quoi mettre pour
aller à la boum. *I don't know
what to wear for (to) . . .*
Qu'est-ce que je mets? *What shall
I wear?*

To give advice:

**Pourquoi est-ce que tu ne mets
pas** ta robe? *Why don't you
wear . . . ?*
Mets ton jean. *Wear . . .*

Cahier d'activités,
p. 112, Act. 8–9

 Des conseils

Ecoutons Are these people asking for or giving advice?

 Harmonie de couleurs

Parlons Demande à ton/ta camarade ce que tu devrais mettre avec les vêtements suivants. Il/Elle va te donner des conseils. Ensuite, changez de rôle.

EXEMPLE —Qu'est-ce que je mets avec ma jupe noire?

—Pourquoi est-ce que tu ne mets pas ton pull gris?

1. Avec mon pantalon bleu?   3. Avec mes baskets violettes?   5. Avec mon short orange?
2. Avec ma chemise rouge?   4. Avec mon pull gris?   6. Avec ma veste verte?

 Qu'est-ce que je mets?

Parlons Cette année, tu vas habiter avec une famille française. Dis à ton/ta camarade où tu vas aller en France et explique ce que tu vas faire. Demande-lui quels vêtements tu devrais porter pour les occasions suivantes. Il/Elle va te donner des conseils. Ensuite, changez de rôle.

EXEMPLE —Pour aller au café, qu'est-ce que je mets?

—Mets un jean et un sweat-shirt.

pour aller à une boum

pour aller à la plage   pour aller au café   pour dîner dans un restaurant élégant

pour jouer au football

pour aller au parc   pour aller au théâtre

pour faire du patin à glace

pour aller au musée   pour faire du ski

 Mon journal

Ecrivons Décris les vêtements que tu mets pour aller au lycée, pour aller à des fêtes, pour sortir avec tes amis et pour les grandes occasions.

Comment dit-on...?

Expressing need; inquiring

The salesperson might ask you:

> **Vous désirez?**
> **(Est-ce que) je peux vous aider?**
> *May I help you?*

BONJOUR, J'AIMERAIS UN PANTALON POUR ALLER AVEC MON TEE-SHIRT!

VOUS AVEZ CES CHAUSSURES EN 43?

To express need, you might answer:

> **Oui, il me faut** un chemisier vert.
> **Oui, vous avez** des chapeaux?
> **Je cherche quelque chose pour**
>   aller à une boum.
>   *I'm looking for something to . . .*
> **J'aimerais** un chemisier **pour aller**
>   **avec** ma jupe.
>   *I'd like . . . to go with . . .*
> **Non, merci, je regarde.**
>   *No, thanks, I'm just looking.*
> **Je peux l'/les essayer?**
>   *Can I try it/them on?*
> **Je peux essayer le/la/l'/les**
>   bleu(e)(s)?
>   *Can I try on the . . . ?*

To inquire about prices:

> **C'est combien,... ?**
> **Ça fait combien?**

To ask about sizes, colors, and fabrics:

> **Vous avez ça en (taille)** 36?
>   *Do you have that in (size) . . . ?*
> **en bleu?**
> **en coton?** *cotton?*
> **en jean?** *denim?*
> **en cuir?** *leather?*

| Travaux pratiques de grammaire, p. 82, Act. 7 | Cahier d'activités, p. 113, Act. 10–11 |

Note de grammaire

You can use colors and other adjectives as nouns by putting **le, la,** or **les** before them. Change their spelling according to the things they refer to: **le bleu, la bleue** = *the blue one;* **les verts, les vertes** = *the green ones.*

| Travaux pratiques de grammaire, p. 82, Act. 8 | Grammaire supplémentaire, p. 315, Act. 4 → |

Cahier d'activités, p. 114, Act. 12

17 ### Qui parle?

Ecoutons Listen and decide whether a customer or salesperson is speaking.

Couleur, prix ou taille?

Ecoutons Listen and decide whether these people are talking about the color, price, or size of the items they're looking at.

19 Méli-mélo!

Lisons Mets cette conversation dans le bon ordre.

—C'est combien?

—Oui. Nous les avons en bleu, en rouge et en orange.

—Voilà, ces maillots de bain sont très chic.

—Oh là là! C'est trop cher, ça!

—Je peux vous aider?

—C'est 68 €.

—Euh, je n'aime pas trop la couleur. Vous les avez en bleu?

—Oui, je cherche un maillot de bain.

20 Grammaire en contexte

Lisons/Ecrivons Blondine et Claire se préparent pour aller à une fête. Complète leur conversation avec **le, la, l'** ou **les** et une couleur.

—Et avec ma jupe bleue, est-ce que je mets mon chemisier orange ou mon chemisier blanc?

—Pas l'orange! Mets plutôt ___1___ .

—Et pour les chaussures? ___2___ vont mieux avec ma jupe, non?

—Mais non. Mets ___3___ .

—Et mon sac rose ou le noir? Le rose, non?

—Mmm... je n'aime pas ___4___ . Tu as une ceinture noire?

—Oui, mais j'ai aussi une ceinture jaune.

—Ah non! Pas la jaune! Mets ___5___ .

21 Préférences

 Parlons Tu regardes des vêtements dans un catalogue avec ton/ta camarade. Dites quels articles vous aimez et en quelle couleur.

EXEMPLE —J'aime bien ce polo bleu. Et toi?
         —Moi, j'aime mieux le noir.

COLLECTION D'ETE

LES POLOS à 24€

LES JEANS à 37€

rouge
jaune
bleu
blanc
orange
noir
noir
blanc
bleu

Note culturelle

The French don't use the same clothing sizes as Americans. Look at this size conversion chart to find the size you'd ask for if you were shopping in France.

TABLE DE COMPARAISON DE TAILLES

Robes, chemisiers et pantalons femmes.

France	34	36	38	40	42	44
USA	3	5	7	9	11	13

Chaussures femmes.

France	36	37	38	38½	39	40
USA	5-5½	6-6½	7-7½	8	8½	9

Tricots, pull-overs, pantalons hommes.

France	36	38	40	42	44	46
USA	26	28	30	32	34	36

Chemises hommes.

France	36	37	38	39	40	41
USA	14	14½	15	15½	16	16½

Chaussures hommes.

France	39	40	41	42	43	44
USA	6½-7	7½	8	8½	9-9½	10-10½

22 Jeu de rôle

Parlons Tu as besoin de quelque chose pour aller avec les vêtements proposés. Dis au vendeur/à la vendeuse ce que tu veux. Pose des questions sur les prix et sur les tailles. Joue cette scène avec ton/ta camarade. Ensuite, changez de rôle.

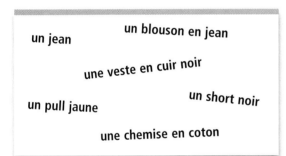

un jean
un blouson en jean
une veste en cuir noir
un pull jaune
un short noir
une chemise en coton

Vocabulaire à la carte

à rayures	*striped*	**en laine**	*wool*
à carreaux	*checked*	**en rayonne**	*rayon*
à pois	*polka dot*	**en lin**	*linen*
à fleurs	*flowered*	**en soie**	*silk*
bleu clair	*light blue*	**bleu foncé**	*dark blue*

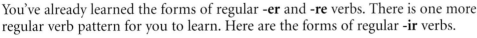

Grammaire

-ir verbs

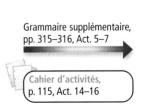

You've already learned the forms of regular -**er** and -**re** verbs. There is one more regular verb pattern for you to learn. Here are the forms of regular -**ir** verbs.

choisir *(to choose, to pick)*

Je	**choisis**	Nous	**choisissons**
Tu	**choisis**	Vous	**choisissez**
Il/Elle/On	**choisit**	Ils/Elles	**choisissent**

Je **choisis** un manteau noir.

* The past participle of regular -**ir** verbs ends in -**i**: Elle a choisi une belle robe.
* Other regular -**ir** verbs you might want to use when talking about clothes are: **grandir** *(to grow)*, **maigrir** *(to lose weight)*, and **grossir** *(to gain weight)*.

Grammaire supplémentaire, pp. 315–316, Act. 5–7

Cahier d'activités, p. 115, Act. 14–16

Travaux pratiques de grammaire, pp. 83–84, Act. 9–12

23 Grammaire en contexte

Parlons Qu'est-ce qu'ils choisissent pour aller avec leurs vêtements?

1. Elle...   2. Nous...   3. Il...   4. Vous...

24 Ça ne me va plus!

Parlons Pourquoi ces vêtements ne vont plus? Utilise le passé composé dans tes réponses.

1.

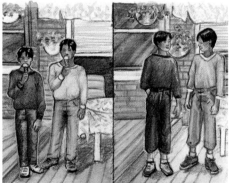

2.

3.

4.

25 Dans un grand magasin

Parlons Avec un(e) camarade, joue une scène entre un(e) client(e) et un vendeur/une vendeuse dans un grand magasin. Le/La client(e) va en vacances d'hiver. Il/Elle dit au vendeur/à la vendeuse ce qu'il/elle cherche. Il/Elle pose aussi des questions sur les tailles, les couleurs, les styles, les tissus et les prix. Il/Elle veut essayer plusieurs articles. Le vendeur/la vendeuse répond au/à la client(e). Ensuite, changez de rôle.

PANORAMA CULTUREL

Qu'est-ce que tu aimes comme vêtements?

We asked some francophone people what they like to wear. Here's what they said.

Marie-Emmanuelle,
France

«J'aime bien mettre des jeans, des tee-shirts, des affaires simples, mais de temps en temps, j'aime bien être originale et porter des jupes longues, ou euh... quelque chose de plus classique ou plus moderne.»

Thomas,
France

«J'aime les jeans, les chemises, les grosses chaussures et les casquettes aussi.»

Aminata,
Côte d'Ivoire

«J'adore beaucoup les jupes droites, les robes, les pagnes. J'aime beaucoup me mettre aussi en tissu.»

Qu'en penses-tu?

1. How do you and your friends like to dress? How is this different from the way these people like to dress?

2. Which of these people share your tastes in clothing?

Savais-tu que...?

In France and other francophone countries, it is common to see people dressed quite well on the streets, on trains, at work, and in restaurants, even fast-food restaurants. In Africa, women commonly drape themselves in brightly-colored fabrics called **pagnes.** Martinique is famous for its **madras** patterns, and southern France is known for its pretty **provençal** prints. Although Paris has the reputation of being a fashion capital, ordinary Parisians don't wear fashions created by well-known designers. Most young people like to wear jeans, just like American teenagers.

Comment dit-on...?

Asking for an opinion, paying a compliment, and criticizing

To ask for an opinion:

Comment tu trouves... ?
Elle me va, cette robe?
  Does . . . suit me?
Il te/vous plaît, ce jean?
  Do you like . . . ?
Tu aimes mieux le bleu **ou** le noir?

ÇA ME VA, CE JEAN?

IL VOUS VA TRÈS BIEN. C'EST TOUT À FAIT VOTRE STYLE!

To pay a compliment:

C'est parfait. *It's perfect.*
C'est tout à fait ton/votre style.
  It looks great on you!
Elle te/vous va très bien, cette jupe.
  . . . suits you really well.
Il/Elle va très bien avec ta chemise.
  It goes very well with . . .
Je le/la/les trouve... *I think it's/they're . . .*
        très à la mode. *in style.*
        chic.
        mignon(mignonne)(s). *cute.*
        sensationnel(le)/sensass. *fantastic.*
        rétro.

To criticize:

Il/Elle ne te/vous va pas du tout. *That doesn't look good on you at all.*
Il/Elle est (Ils/Elles sont) trop serré(e)(s). *It's/They're too tight.*
        large(s). *baggy.*
        petit(e)(s). *small.*
        grand(e)(s). *big.*
        court(e)(s). *short.*
        long(longue)(s). *long.*
Il/Elle ne va pas du tout avec tes chaussures. *That doesn't go at all with . . .*
Je le/la/les trouve moche(s). *I think it's/they're tacky.*
        démodé(e)(s). *out of style.*
        horrible(s). *terrible.*

> Cahier d'activités,
> pp. 116–117, Act. 17–20

> Travaux pratiques de grammaire,
> pp. 85–86, Act. 13–15

26 Compliment ou critique?

Ecoutons Listen to the following conversations and decide if the speakers are complimenting or criticizing each other's clothing.

27 Un après-midi au grand magasin

Parlons Tu es vendeur/vendeuse au magasin Le Printemps. Ces personnes ont besoin de conseils. Qu'est-ce que tu leur dis?

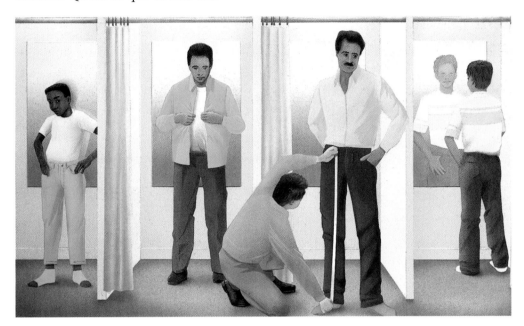

28 Sondage

Lisons/Parlons Fais ce petit test d'un magazine de mode français. Combien de points est-ce que tu as au total? Comment es-tu d'après le test? Compare ton résultat avec le résultat d'un(e) camarade.

ENQUETE : LA MODE

Es-tu à la mode?

Fais notre petit test pour savoir si tu es vraiment à la dernière mode.

En général, quelle sorte de vêtements est-ce que tu portes?
a. Des vêtements super chic. (3 points)
b. Ça dépend de l'occasion. (2 points)
c. Des jeans, des tee-shirts et des baskets. (1 point)

Tu achètes de nouveaux vêtements...
a. très souvent. (3 points)
b. quelquefois. (2 points)
c. presque jamais. (1 point)

Quand tu achètes des vêtements, en général, tu...
a. achètes ce qui est à la dernière mode. (3 points)
b. achètes quelque chose que tu aimes. (2 points)
c. achètes ce qui est en solde. (1 point)

Dans un magazine de mode, tu vois que les chemises en plastique fluorescentes sont très populaires. Tu...
a. achètes 4 chemises de 4 couleurs différentes. (3 points)
b. attends patiemment pour voir si les autres en portent. (2 points)
c. refuses d'en acheter! Tu ne veux pas être ridicule! (1 point)

Réponses :
10 -12 points : Tu es vraiment à la mode! Attention! Tu risques de perdre ton originalité.
5 - 9 points : Parfaitement raisonnable! Tu es à la mode tout en gardant ton propre style.
0 - 4 points : Tu ne t'intéresses pas à la mode! Tu sais, il y a quelquefois des styles uniques. Essaie de les trouver.

NE PRENDS PAS CE TEST TROP AU SERIEUX!

Read the following dialogues to find out how French people compliment one another.

—J'aime bien ta chemise.
—Ah oui?
—Oui, elle est pas mal.
—Tu trouves? Tu sais, c'est une vieille chemise.

—Il est super, ce chapeau!
—Tu crois?
—Oui, il te va très bien.
—C'est gentil.

—Tu es ravissante aujourd'hui!
—Vraiment? Je n'ai rien fait de spécial.

Qu'en penses-tu?

1. How do these people react to a compliment?
2. How do you usually react to a compliment? How is that different from the French reactions you've just read?

Savais-tu que...?

The French do not compliment freely and generally do so only in exceptional cases. It is common to respond to compliments with **Merci.** However, French people will often respond with a modest expression of disbelief, such as **Vraiment? Tu crois? Tu trouves? Ah oui?** or a comment downplaying the importance of the item complimented, such as **Oh, c'est vieux.**

29 **Fais des compliments!**

Parlons Fais des compliments à une(e) camarade sur deux vêtements qu'il/elle porte. Il/Elle va te répondre à la française.

EXEMPLE —Elles sont sensass, tes baskets!
—Vraiment?
—Oui, elles sont très à la mode!

Grammaire

The direct object pronouns *le, la,* and *les*

The pronouns **le**, *him* or *it*, **la**, *her* or *it*, and **les**, *them*, refer to people or things. In the sentences below, what do the pronouns **le, la,** and **les** refer to?*

— Ce pull, il te plaît? — Oui, je **le** trouve assez chic.
— Comment tu trouves cette robe? — Je **la** trouve démodée.
— Vous aimez ces chaussures? — Oui, je vais **les** prendre.

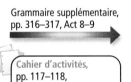

• You normally place the direct object pronouns <u>before</u> the conjugated verb.

Je **le** prends. Je **l'**ai pris.
Je ne **la** prends pas. Ne **les** prends pas!

• There are two exceptions to this rule. You place the direct object pronoun <u>after</u> the conjugated verb in a positive command and before an infinitive.

Prends-**le**!

Je vais **la** prendre.

• When **le** or **la** comes before a verb that starts with a vowel sound, it changes to **l'**.

Je vais essayer **le pull.** Je vais **l'**essayer.

_____
* the pullover, the dress, the shoes

Grammaire supplémentaire, pp. 316–317, Act 8–9

Cahier d'activités, pp. 117–118, Act. 21–22

Travaux pratiques de grammaire, pp. 86–87, Act 16–17

30 **Qu'en penses-tu?**

Lisons/Ecrivons Elise et Karim font des courses. Complète leur conversation avec **le, la, l',** et **les.**

ELISE Dis, Karim, tu aimes ce pantalon, toi?

KARIM Bof... Je ____1____ trouve un peu démodé, mais enfin...

ELISE Et cette chemise-là?

KARIM Oui, je ____2____ aime bien. Eh! Tu as vu ces chaussures? Elles sont super, non?

ELISE Oui! Tu vas ____3____ prendre?

KARIM Oh, je sais pas...

ELISE Si, allez! Prends- ____4____ !

KARIM Bon. Je vais ____5____ essayer. Et toi, essaie la chemise. Je ____6____ trouve vraiment chouette.

ELISE D'accord. Mmm... et ce pull violet, il est beau, non?

KARIM Oui, mais je ____7____ préfère en bleu.

Hesitating; making a decision

When the salesperson asks you:

Vous avez choisi?
Vous avez décidé de prendre ce pantalon?
Have you decided to take . . . ?
Vous le/la/les prenez?
Are you going to take it/them?

To hesitate, say:

Je ne sais pas.
Euh... J'hésite.
Oh, I'm not sure.
Il/Elle me plaît, mais il/elle est cher/chère.
I like it, but it's expensive.

To make a decision, say:

Je le/la/les prends.
I'll take it/them.
C'est trop cher.
It's too expensive.

Cahier d'activités,
p. 118, Act. 22

Note de grammaire

• Use **il/elle/ils/elles** when you are referring to a specific item. Comment tu trouves cette robe? **Elle** est chouette, non?

• Use **c'est** when you are speaking in general about an action or something that happened.

J'aime porter des pantalons parce que **c'est** pratique.

J'ai réussi à mon examen de maths! **C'est** super!

In the sentences above, **c'est** refers to the general ideas of wearing pants and passing a test.

Travaux pratiques
de grammaire,
p. 87, Act. 18

Grammaire supplémentaire,
p. 317, Act. 10

Cahier d'activités, p. 118, Act. 23

31

Oui ou non?

 Ecoutons Listen to these exchanges between a customer and a salesperson. Tell whether the customer takes the item, doesn't take it, or can't decide.

32

Qu'est-ce qu'ils disent?

Ecrivons/Parlons Ecris ce que tu crois que ces personnes disent. Ensuite, compare tes réponses avec les réponses d'un(e) camarade.

1.

2.

3.

4.

33 De l'école au travail

Parlons Tu travailles au rayon vêtements du grand magasin Le Printemps, à Paris. Un client/Une cliente veut acheter des vêtements pour aller à un mariage. Il/elle hésite, alors tu vas l'aider à trouver quelque chose et lui donner des conseils.

PRONONCIATION

The glides [j], [w], and [ɥ]

As you listen to people speak French, you may notice a sound that reminds you of the first sound in the English word *yes.* This sound is called a *glide,* because one sound glides into another. Now, try making the sound [j] in these common French words: **mieux, chemisier, bien.** Did you notice that this gliding sound often occurs when the letter **i** is followed by **e?** The sound is also represented by the letters **ill** in words such as **maillot** and **gentille.**

There are two more glides in French. [w] sounds similar to the *w* sound you hear in *west wind.* Listen to these French words: **moi, Louis, jouer.**

The last glide sound is the one you hear in the French word **lui.** It sounds like the French vowel sounds [y] and [i] together. This sound is often written as **ui.** Listen to the glide [ɥ] in these words: **cuir, huit, juillet.**

A. A prononcer

Repeat the following words.

1. travailler	monsieur	combien	conseiller
2. pouvoir	soif	poires	moins
3. suis	minuit	suite	juillet

B. A lire

Take turns with a partner reading each of the following sentences aloud.

1. J'aime bien tes boucles d'oreilles. Elles sont géniales!

2. Il me faut des feuilles de papier, un taille-crayon et un cahier.

3. Elle a choisi un blouson en cuir et une écharpe en soie. C'est chouette!

4. Tu as quoi aujourd'hui? Moi, j'ai histoire et ensuite, je vais faire mes devoirs.

5. —Tu veux promener le chien avec moi?

   —Pourquoi pas?

C. A écrire

You're going to hear a short dialogue. Write down what you hear.

LA MODE AU LYCÉE

A. Think for a moment about the role fashion plays in your life.

  1. Do you follow trends you see in magazines or at school?

  2. How much influence do your parents have on your wardrobe?

  3. Do you think clothing is a reflection of a person's personality or lifestyle?

B. How would you categorize styles that are popular at your school or in your town? What words would you use to describe them?

C. What can you tell about the people who wrote these essays?

D. Which of the students consider fashion important? Which consider it unimportant?

LA MODE AU LYCÉE

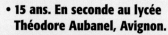

Mélanie

- **15 ans. En seconde au lycée Théodore Aubanel, Avignon.**

Ce que je trouve dommage aujourd'hui, c'est que les filles ressemblent de plus en plus à des garçons. Au lycée, presque toutes mes copines portent des jeans ou des pantalons avec des sweat-shirts. Moi aussi, j'aime bien les jeans, mais de temps en temps, je préfère m'habiller «en fille» avec des robes ou des jupes. Je porte aussi beaucoup de bijoux, surtout des boucles d'oreilles; j'adore ça. Et puis en même temps, ça fait plaisir à mes parents quand je suis habillée comme ça; ils préfèrent ça au look garçon manqué.

Christophe

- **17 ans. En terminale au lycée Henri IV, Paris.**

Moi, ce qui m'énerve avec la mode, c'est que si tu ne la suis pas, tout le monde te regarde d'un air bizarre au lycée. Moi, par exemple, le retour de la mode des années 70, les pattes d'eph et le look grunge, c'est vraiment pas mon truc. Je trouve ça horrible. Alors, je ne vois pas pourquoi je devrais m'habiller comme ça, simplement parce que c'est la mode. Je préfère porter des pantalons à pinces, des blazers et des chemises avec des cravates. Mes copains trouvent que ça fait trop sérieux, trop fils-à-papa, mais ça m'est égal. Je suis sûr que dans quelques années, quand ils travailleront, ils seront tous habillés comme moi et quand ils regarderont des photos de terminale, ils rigoleront bien en voyant les habits qu'ils portaient à 18 ans!

Serge

• **16 ans. En première au lycée Ampère de Lyon.**

Pour moi, ce qui est vraiment important, c'est d'avoir des vêtements confortables. Je suis très sportif et j'aime pouvoir bouger dans mes habits. Mais, je veux aussi des trucs cool. Pas question de porter des vêtements très serrés ou très chers, par exemple. Je ne vois pas l'intérêt d'avoir un blouson qui coûte 610 €. Je préfère un blouson bon marché dans lequel je peux jouer au foot avec les copains. Comme ça, si je tombe ou si je l'abîme, c'est pas tragique. En général, je mets des jeans parce que c'est pratique et sympa. En été, je porte des tee-shirts très simples et en hiver, des sweat-shirts. Et comme chaussures, je préfère les baskets.

Emmanuelle

• **17 ans et demi. Lycée Mas de Tesse, Montpellier.**

Pour moi, la façon dont quelqu'un s'habille est un reflet de sa personnalité. Au lycée, j'étudie les arts plastiques, et comme on le dit souvent, les artistes sont des gens originaux et créatifs. Je n'aime pas dépenser beaucoup pour mes vêtements. Je n'achète jamais de choses très chères, mais j'utilise mon imagination pour les rendre plus originales. Par exemple, j'ajoute toujours des accessoires sympas : bijoux fantaisie que je fabrique souvent moi-même, foulards, ceintures, sacs... Parfois, je fais même certains de mes vêtements, surtout les jupes car c'est facile. Et comme ça, je suis sûre que personne ne portera la même chose que moi!

E. Although many people consider France a fashion capital, the U.S. also influences fashion. What English words can you find in the essays?

F. Look for the words in the box below in the essays. Then, try to match them with their English equivalents.

1. bijoux	**a.** fashion
2. la mode	**b.** things
3. pattes d'eph	**c.** ruin
4. bouger	**d.** jewelry
5. abîme	**e.** to move
6. les trucs	**f.** bell-bottoms

G. Which student . . .
   1. likes clothes that are practical and comfortable?
   2. makes some of his or her clothing and jewelry?
   3. doesn't buy expensive clothes?
   4. thinks girls should wear feminine clothes sometimes?

H. Which of the following sentences are facts and which are opinions?
   1. En été, je porte des tee-shirts.
   2. Les artistes sont des gens originaux et créatifs.
   3. Les filles ressemblent de plus en plus à des garçons.
   4. Je n'achète jamais de choses très chères.
   5. La façon dont on s'habille est un reflet de sa personnalité.

I. Write a short paragraph in French telling what you like to wear. Mention colors and any other details you feel are important.

Cahier d'activités, p. 119, Act. 25

trois cent treize **313**

Grammaire supplémentaire

Première étape | **Objective** Asking for and giving advice

1 Complète les phrases suivantes avec le présent du verbe **mettre.** (**p. 299**)

1. Qu'est-ce que je __ E __ __ pour la boum de Charles?

2. Pourquoi tu ne M __ T __ pas ta robe blanche?

3. Odile et Béatrice __ __ T __ E __ __ souvent des robes à fleurs.

4. Boris et moi, nous __ E __ __ __ N __ des lunettes de soleil pour aller à des boums.

5. Vous __ __ T __ E __ des lunettes de soleil quand il pleut comme ça?

6. Oui, on __ E __ toujours des lunettes de soleil et des baskets.

2 Complète les phrases suivantes avec le sujet approprié. (**p. 299**)

je/j'	vous	nous
Sylvie	mes parents	Jeannette

1. _____ a mis une robe rouge pour aller à l'opéra.

2. _____ portent toujours des jeans le week-end.

3. Pour aller nager, _____ met son maillot de bain rose et blanc.

4. A la plage, _____ portons toujours des lunettes de soleil.

5. _____ mettez des bottes quand il pleut?

6. Il faisait froid hier, alors _____ ai mis mon cardigan noir pour aller à l'école.

3 Marie-France demande à Patricia ce qu'elle devrait porter pour aller au théâtre. Complète leur conversation avec la forme correcte des verbes entre parenthèses. N'oublie pas d'utiliser le **passé composé** quand c'est nécessaire. (**p. 299**)

MARIE-FRANCE Je ne sais pas quoi ___1___ (mettre) pour aller au théâtre.

PATRICIA ___2___ (mettre) ta jupe noire avec ton chemisier blanc.

MARIE-FRANCE Non, ce n'est pas très chic. Et j' ___3___ (déjà mettre) mon chemisier blanc avec ma veste cette semaine.

PATRICIA Pourquoi tu ne ___4___ (mettre) pas ton chemisier bleu avec une écharpe alors?

MARIE-FRANCE Non, j' ___5___ (déjà porter) mon écharpe à la boum de Jean-Marc.

PATRICIA ___6___ (mettre) ta robe noire.

MARIE-FRANCE Bonne idée. Et je vais ___7___ (mettre) aussi mes chaussures noires. Enfin, c'est décidé.

Objectives **Expressing need; inquiring**

4 Nadia demande à Clara ce qu'elle devrait mettre pour aller à la boum de Raphaël. Utilise le verbe **mettre** à l'impératif et la forme correcte de l'adjectif entre parenthèses. (**pp. 299, 301**)

EXEMPLE   NADIA   Je mets ma robe violette? (gris)
             CLARA   Je la trouve trop serrée. **Mets la grise!**

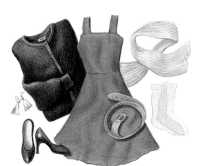

1. NADIA   Je mets mes sandales jaunes? (blanc)

  CLARA   Je les trouve un peu démodées. _____

2. NADIA   Je mets mon cardigan orange? (noir)

  CLARA   C'est pas ton style. _____

3. NADIA   Je mets mon écharpe rouge? (rose)

  CLARA   Elle ne te va pas. _____

4. NADIA   Je mets ma ceinture verte? (bleu)

  CLARA   Elle ne va pas avec ta robe. _____

5. NADIA   Je mets mes boucles d'oreilles marron? (vert)

  CLARA   Je les trouve trop grosses. _____

5 D'après ce que les personnes suivantes aiment porter, dis ce qu'elles vont mettre pour aller à la boum de Mélanie. Dans tes réponses, utilise le verbe **choisir** et n'oublie pas de faire tous les changements nécessaires. (**p. 303**)

EXEMPLE   Suzanne aime les jupes courtes. **Elle choisit une jupe courte.**

1. Pierre et Philippe aiment bien les cravates à pois.

2. Armelle adore les robes rétro.

3. Moi, j'aime les boucles d'oreilles noires.

4. Tu préfères les chemisiers à fleurs.

5. Elsa et toi, vous aimez bien les chaussures en cuir.

6. Toi et moi, nous adorons les blousons en jean.

6 Ecris des phrases complètes avec les mots suivants. N'oublie pas de mettre les verbes au présent et de faire tous les changements nécessaires. (**p. 303**)

1. vous/ne/pas/grossir/parce que/vous/faire du sport

2. on/grandir/si/on/manger/assez

3. tu/maigrir/parce que/tu/jouer au foot/tous les jours

4. nous/grossir/facilement/si/nous/ne/pas/faire du jogging

5. je/grossir/parce que/je/manger/beaucoup de gâteaux

6. mes petites sœurs/grandir/tous les jours

7. il/maigrir/si/il/ne/pas/manger/trois fois par jour

8. vous/grandir/quand/vous/manger vos légumes

9. ma sœur/maigrir/facilement/quand/elle/faire de l'aérobic

10. tu/manger/beaucoup/mais/tu/ne/jamais/grossir

Grammaire supplémentaire

7 Dis pourquoi les personnes suivantes ne peuvent plus mettre leurs vêtements. Utilise le **passé composé** des verbes entre parenthèses. (**p. 303**)

> **EXEMPLE**   Armelle, ce cardigan ne te va plus. (grandir)   **J'ai grandi.**

1. Sophie, ce pantalon ne te va plus. (maigrir)
2. Pierre et Jean, ces chemises ne vous vont plus. (grandir)
3. Valentine, cette robe ne te va plus. (grossir)
4. Ce pantalon ne me va plus. (grandir)
5. Ahmed et Karim, ces vestes ne vous vont plus. (maigrir)
6. Dis donc, ce blouson ne me va plus. (grossir)

Troisième étape

Objectives Asking for an opinion; paying a compliment; criticizing; hesitating; making a decision

8 Tu fais les magasins avec une amie et elle te demande ton avis sur les vêtements qu'elle voudrait acheter. Dans tes réponses, utilise **le, la, les** et **l'**. (**p. 309**)

1. Est-ce que tu aimes cette robe?
2. Comment tu trouves ce pantalon?
3. Je veux acheter cette veste, mais j'hésite.
4. J'aime bien cette veste, mais elle est chère et un peu grande.
5. Qu'est-ce que tu penses de ces chaussures?

9 Anne est dans un magasin de vêtements. Complète la conversation qu'elle a avec le vendeur. Utilise le pronom approprié **le, la, les** ou **l'** dans tes réponses. **(p. 309)**

EXEMPLE   ANNE   Ces bottes vont très bien avec mon manteau.
                         Je peux les essayer?
          VENDEUR Elles vous vont très bien, mademoiselle!
                         Vous les prenez?
          ANNE   Oui. **Je les prends.**

1. ANNE   Ce blouson va très bien avec mon pantalon noir.
              _____?
   VENDEUR Il vous va très bien, mademoiselle.
              _____?
     ANNE   Oui. _____.

2. ANNE   Ces sandales vont très bien avec ma jupe en jean.
              _____?
   VENDEUR Elles vous vont très bien, mademoiselle.
              _____?
     ANNE   Euh... J'hésite... Non. _____. Elles sont trop chères.

3. ANNE   Cette robe va très bien avec mes chaussures.
              _____?
   VENDEUR Elle vous va très bien, mademoiselle.
              _____?
     ANNE   Elle me plaît beaucoup. Oui. _____.

4. ANNE   Ces lunettes de soleil vont très bien avec mon maillot de bain. _____?
   VENDEUR Elles vous vont très bien, mademoiselle.
              _____?
     ANNE   Elles sont super cool. Oui. _____.

10 Complète les phrases suivantes avec **il est, elle est** ou **c'est**. **(p. 310)**

1. Comment tu trouves ce chapeau? _____ sensass, non?
2. Moi, j'aime beaucoup porter un chapeau parce que _____ sympa.
3. Cédric porte souvent une casquette. _____ en cuir, sa casquette. Très chic!
4. Tu aimes les choses en cuir, toi? Moi, non. Je préfère le jean. _____ plus pratique!
5. Tu dis? Ah, oui. J'adore le look rétro. _____ chouette, le rétro!
6. Moi, j'ai une chemise rétro! _____ super cool!
7. Je vais essayer le pull vert, mais je pense que/qu' _____ trop grand.
8. J'aime porter des jeans et des tee-shirts parce que _____ toujours à la mode.

Mise en pratique

1 Listen to this conversation between Philippe and a saleswoman at a French department store. Then, answer these questions.

1. What does Philippe want to buy?

2. What colors does he prefer?

3. What does the salesperson say about the first item Philippe tries on?

4. How does Philippe feel about the way the item fits?

5. Does he end up buying it?

2 Look over the advertisement below. Then, answer the questions that follow.

NOUVELLE COLLECTION ARIELLE DE LA BRETTINIERE

FEMME : Pantalon à pinces uni, 100 % soie. Du 36 au 44, **60€**. Existe en vert, bleu, rouge, blanc et noir. **Cardigan** en coton, taille unique, **45,50€**. Existe en noir et blanc cassé. **Tee-shirt** cache-cœur noir, manches courtes, **19,50€**. **Boucles d'oreilles** et **bracelet** fantaisie, **6,80€** et **9,90€**.
ENFANT : Robe bleu clair à fleurs multicolores, 100 % coton. De 2 à 8 ans, **12€**. **Tee-shirt** uni rose, 100 % coton, **4,40€**. De 2 à 8 ans. Existe en 17 coloris. **Sandales** en cuir blanc, **18,10€**. Du 24 au 34.
HOMME : Pantalon à pinces, 100 % lin. Du 38 au 52, **66,90€**. Existe en noir, bleu marine, beige et marron. **Chemise** en jean, manches longues. Du 2 au 6, **39,40€**. **Pull** rouge, 100 % coton. Du 2 au 6, **45,50€**.

VENDUE DANS LES GRANDS MAGASINS

1. Who does **Arielle de la Brettinière** make clothes for?

2. How many colors does the child's T-shirt come in?

3. The women's pants are available in what sizes?

4. What material is the men's shirt made of?

5. What's the most expensive men's item on the page? The most expensive women's item?

3 From what you know about French culture, are these statements true or false?

1. The French are famous for giving lots of compliments.

2. The French tend to downplay the compliments they receive.

3. **Merci** is the only appropriate response to a compliment.

4. A common French way to respond to a compliment on something you're wearing is to say **Tu trouves?**

4 | **Ecrivons!**

You've been hired by a French magazine to write about fashion trends among American teenagers today. Interview two or three classmates about their tastes in clothing. Then, write a short article in French based on your interviews.

Prewriting

First, brainstorm a list of interview questions that you might ask your classmates about their fashion preferences. You might ask what they like to wear, what they wear to parties (**les boums**), what colors they like, and what their favorite article of clothing is. Arrange your questions in a logical order. You may want to arrange them so that you begin with more general questions and progress to more specific ones.

> **Stratégie pour écrire**
>
> Paraphrasing is a useful tool for organizing and simplifying information for your readers. To paraphrase a quote or other piece of information you collect, you state the main points in your own words. At the same time, be sure you don't change the meaning of what was said.

Next, conduct your interview with two or three classmates. Be sure to take notes on their responses to each of your questions.

Before you begin your article, rearrange the information you've collected into a logical order. For example, you might group different answers to each question together.

Writing

Expository writing is a process of converting information you've collected into a readable or easily understandable form. Newspaper and magazine articles are good examples of expository writing. Reporters collect information on newsworthy events, fashion trends, etc., and then take that information and turn it into articles that readers can easily understand.

Now, referring to the information you've collected and organized, write a short article that reveals what you found out. It's not necessary to include every detail of the information you collect. For example, if a quote from your interview is too long, you may paraphrase the main points of the quote in your own words.

Revising

Peer evaluation is another helpful step in the evaluation process. Give your article to a classmate and have him or her give you suggestions on how to improve it. After your classmate evaluates your article, make any revisions you feel are necessary, including those you find in proofreading. Now you're ready to submit your finished article.

5 | **Jeu de rôle**

Choose one of the items from the advertisement on page 318 and ask the salesperson about it. Do they have it in your size? Can you try it on? The salesperson should compliment the way it looks, and you should decide whether to buy it or not. Take turns playing the role of the salesperson.

Que sais-je?

Can you use what you've learned in this chapter?

Can you ask for and give advice?
p. 300

1 How would you ask a friend what you should wear to a party?

2 How would you advise a friend to wear these clothes, using the verb **mettre**?

1.   2.

Can you express need and inquire?
p. 301

3 How would you tell a salesperson . . .
1. that you're just looking?   2. what you would like?

4 How would you ask a salesperson . . .
1. if you can try something on?
2. if they have what you want in a different size?
3. if they have what you want in a particular color?
4. how much something costs?

5 How would you tell what these people are choosing?

Charles   Jean-Marc et Farid   Astrid   Delphine et Camille

Can you ask for an opinion, pay a compliment, and criticize?
p. 306

6 If you were shopping with a friend, how would you ask . . .
1. if your friend likes what you have on?
2. if something looks good on you?
3. if it's too short?

7 How would you compliment a friend's clothing? How would you criticize it?

Can you hesitate and make a decision?
p. 310

8 How can you express your hesitation?

9 How would you tell a salesperson what you've decided to do?

Première étape

Clothes

un blouson	jacket
des bottes (f.)	boots
des boucles d'oreilles (f.)	earrings
un bracelet	bracelet
un cardigan	cardigan
une casquette	cap
une ceinture	belt
un chapeau	hat
des chaussettes (f.)	socks
des chaussures (f.)	shoes
une chemise	shirt (men's)
un chemisier	shirt (women's)
une cravate	tie
une écharpe	scarf
une jupe	skirt
des lunettes (f.) de soleil	sunglasses
un maillot de bain	bathing suit
un manteau	coat
un pantalon	(a pair of) pants
une robe	dress
des sandales (f.)	sandals
une veste	suit jacket, blazer
des vêtements (m.)	clothes

Asking for and giving advice

Je ne sais pas quoi mettre pour...	I don't know what to wear for (to) . . .
Qu'est-ce que je mets?	What shall I wear?
Pourquoi est-ce que tu ne mets pas... ?	Why don't you wear . . . ?
Mets...	Wear . . .
mettre	to put, to put on, to wear
porter	to wear

Deuxième étape

Expressing need; inquiring

Vous désirez?	What would you like?
(Est-ce que) je peux vous aider?	May I help you?
Je cherche quelque chose pour...	I'm looking for something to . . .
J'aimerais... pour aller avec...	I'd like . . . to go with . . .
Non, merci, je regarde.	No, thanks, I'm just looking.
Je peux l'/les essayer?	Can I try it/them on?
Je peux essayer le/la/les... ?	Can I try on the . . . ?
Vous avez ça... ?	Do you have that. . . ? (size, fabric, color)
en (taille)... ?	in size . . . ?
en bleu	in blue
en coton	cotton
en jean	denim
en cuir	leather

Other useful expressions

choisir	to choose, to pick
grandir	to grow
maigrir	to lose weight
grossir	to gain weight

Troisième étape

Asking for an opinion; paying a compliment; criticizing

Comment tu trouves... ?	How do you like . . . ?
Il/Elle me va?	Does . . . suit me?
Il/Elle te/vous plaît?	Do you like it?
C'est parfait.	It's perfect.
C'est tout à fait ton/votre style.	It looks great on you!
Il/Elle te/vous va très bien.	It suits you really well.
Il/Elle va très bien avec...	It goes very well with . . .
Il/Elle est (Ils/Elles sont) trop...	It's/They're too . . .
Je le/la/les trouve...	I think it's/they're . . .
très à la mode	in style
chic	chic
mignon(mignonne)(s)	cute
sensationnel(le)(s)/ sensass	fantastic
rétro	retro
serré(e)(s)	tight
large(s)	baggy
petit(e)(s)	small
grand(e)(s)	big
court(e)(s)	short
long(longue)(s)	long
moche(s)	tacky
démodé(e)(s)	out of style
horrible(s)	terrible
Il/Elle ne te/vous va pas du tout.	It doesn't look good on you at all.
Il/Elle ne va pas du tout avec...	It doesn't go at all with . . .

Hesitating; making a decision

Vous avez choisi?	Have you decided?
Vous avez décidé de prendre... ?	Have you decided to take . . . ?
Vous le/la/les prenez?	Are you taking it/them?
Je ne sais pas.	I don't know.
Euh... J'hésite.	Well, I'm not sure.
Il/Elle me plaît, mais il/elle est cher/chère.	I like it, but it's expensive.
Je le/la/les prends.	I'll take it/them.
C'est trop cher.	It's too expensive.

11
Vive les vacances!

Objectives

In this chapter you will learn to

Première étape

- inquire about and share future plans
- express indecision
- express wishes
- ask for advice
- make, accept, and refuse suggestions

Deuxième étape

- remind
- reassure
- see someone off

Troisième étape

- ask for and express opinions
- inquire about and relate past events

🗗 internet ▬▬▬▬▬▬▬▬▬▬▬

go.
hrw
.com   ADRESSE: go.hrw.com
       MOT-CLE: WA3 ARLES-11

◀ C'était formidable, les vacances en Provence!

trois cent vingt-trois   **323**

MISE EN TRAIN · *Bientôt les vacances!*

Stratégie pour comprendre
Judging from clues in this episode, what time of year is it? What do you think Magali, Florent, and Ahmed might be talking about? What is Florent's dilemma at the end?

Ahmed **Florent** **Magali**

1

Florent : Alors, les copains, qu'est-ce que vous allez faire pendant les vacances?

Magali : Moi, je pars en colonie de vacances.

Florent : C'est sympa!

2

Magali : Et en août, je vais voir mes cousins à la montagne. Ils habitent à Sisteron, dans les Alpes de Haute-Provence. C'est super joli là-bas.

3

Magali : Et toi, Ahmed, tu vas à l'étranger?

Ahmed : Non. En juillet, je vais faire du camping dans les gorges du Verdon.

4

Ahmed : En août, je travaille dans une station-service. J'aimerais bien acheter une mobylette.

Florent : C'est génial!

Magali : Et toi, Florent?

Florent : Je vais peut-être rester en Arles. J'ai envie d'être ici pour le Festival de la photographie. A part ça, je n'ai rien de prévu. Je n'ai pas encore décidé.

Ahmed : Pourquoi est-ce que tu ne travailles pas comme pompiste avec moi?

Florent : J'aimerais bien, mais je préfère partir en vacances.

Magali : Tu peux aller en colonie de vacances aussi.

Florent : C'est possible.

Magali : Bon, je dois m'en aller.

Ahmed : Moi aussi. Au revoir à tous!

Magali : Salut!

Florent : Tchao!

Florent : Qu'est-ce que je vais faire, moi?

Cahier d'activités, p. 121, Act.1

1 Tu as compris?

1. What time of year is it? How do you know?
2. Who is planning to travel during the vacation? Where?
3. Who is going to work during the vacation? Why?
4. What is Florent going to do?

2 C'est qui?

D'après *Bientôt les vacances!*, qui a l'intention de (d')...

Florent

Ahmed

Magali

aller dans les Alpes?

travailler en Arles?

rester en Arles?

partir en colonie de vacances?

aller voir ses cousins?

aller à la montagne?

faire du camping?

3 Vrai ou faux?

1. Les trois jeunes restent en France pendant les vacances.
2. Les cousins de Magali habitent à la montagne.
3. Ahmed va faire du camping dans les Alpes.
4. Ahmed va travailler dans un café.
5. Ahmed veut aller au Festival de la photographie.
6. Florent part en colonie de vacances.

4 Cherche les expressions

According to *Bientôt les vacances!*, what can you say in French. . .

1. to ask what someone is going to do?
2. to tell what a place looks like?
3. to express an opinion?
4. to express indecision?
5. to make a suggestion?
6. to express a preference?

> C'est génial!   C'est super joli...   Je préfère...
>
> Pourquoi est-ce que tu ne... pas?
>
> Qu'est-ce que vous allez faire... ?
>
> Je n'ai pas encore décidé.

5 Et maintenant, à toi

Quels projets de vacances est-ce que tu préfères? Pourquoi?

Première étape

Objectives Inquiring about and sharing future plans; expressing indecision; expressing wishes; asking for advice; making, accepting, and refusing suggestions

WA3 ARLES-11

Vocabulaire

Où est-ce que tu vas aller pendant tes vacances?

à la montagne

à la campagne

au bord de la mer

en forêt

en colonie de vacances

chez mes grands-parents

Qu'est-ce qu'on peut y faire? On peut y...

faire du camping.

faire de la randonnée.

faire du bateau.

faire de la plongée.

faire de la planche à voile.

faire de la voile.

Travaux pratiques de grammaire, pp. 88–89, Act. 1–4

Cahier d'activités, p. 122, Act. 2

---

6 **Les vacances**

Ecoutons Listen as Nathalie, Bruno, Pauline, and Emile tell about their vacation plans. What is each teenager going to do?

Although there are few hard-and-fast rules to help you remember if a noun is masculine or feminine, you can often predict the gender of a word by its ending. Some of the endings that usually indicate a feminine word are **-tion**, **-sion**, **-ie**, **-ette**, **-elle**, **-ine**, **-ude**, and **-ure**. Endings that often signal a masculine word are **-ment**, **-age**, **-oir**, **-ier**, **-et**, and **-eau**. But be careful! There are exceptions.

Tu te rappelles?

Do you remember how to tell what is going to happen? Use a form of the verb **aller** (to go) plus the infinitive of another verb.

Demain, **je vais** faire du bateau.

Grammaire supplémentaire, p. 342, Act. 1–2

Cahier d'activités, p. 122, Act. 4

Travaux pratiques de grammaire, p. 90, Act. 5–6

Si tu as oublié the verb *aller* *va à la page 174.*

7 En colonie de vacances

Parlons Qu'est-ce que Vincent et Roland vont faire en colonie de vacances?

1.

2.

3.

4.

5.

6.

Note culturelle

In francophone countries, many children and teenagers attend summer camps **(colonies de vacances)**, where they learn folklore, folk dances, arts and crafts, foreign languages, and learn about many other subjects. Of course, they also participate in sports. The camps are usually run by young adults called **animateurs**. In France alone there are hundreds of **colonies de vacances**.

Inquiring about and sharing future plans; expressing indecision; expressing wishes

> Qu'est-ce que tu vas faire pendant tes vacances?

> Je ne sais pas. J'hésite. Je voudrais bien aller à la montagne...mais j'ai aussi envie de rester ici pour voir mes grands-parents!

To inquire about someone's plans:

Qu'est-ce que tu vas faire cet été?
Où est-ce que tu vas aller pendant les vacances?

To share your plans:

En juillet, **je vais** travailler.
En août, **j'ai l'intention d'**aller en Italie.
. . . *I intend to* . . .

To express indecision:

J'hésite.
Je ne sais pas.
Je n'en sais rien. *I have no idea.*
Je n'ai rien de prévu. *I don't have any plans.*

To express wishes:

Je voudrais bien aller chez mes cousins.
J'ai envie de travailler.
I feel like . . .

(Cahier d'activités, p. 123, Act. 6)

---

8 ## Les projets de vacances

Ecoutons Listen to these speakers talk about their vacations. Do they have definite plans or are they undecided?

9 ## Les vacances en France

Parlons Imagine que tu vas aller en vacances en France cet été. Ton/Ta camarade va te poser des questions sur tes projets. Dis-lui ce que tu as envie de faire et ce que tu vas faire là-bas. Ensuite, changez de rôle.

EXEMPLE
— Qu'est-ce que tu vas faire cet été?
— Je vais faire du camping à la campagne.

visiter le Louvre faire des photos faire du ski rencontrer de jeunes Français
voir la tour Eiffel parler français aller à un concert de rock français aller au café

Note de grammaire

- To say *to* or *in* before the names of most cities, use **à**.

  Tu vas **à** Paris pendant les vacances?

- Names of countries are either masculine or feminine. Feminine countries end in **-e**, but there are exceptions, such as **le Mexique**. Use **au** (*to, in*) before masculine names, **en** (*to, in*) before feminine names and before names of countries that begin with a vowel. Before plural names, use **aux**.

  Vous allez **au** Canada?

  Hélène va **en** Allemagne.

  Nous allons **aux** Etats-Unis.

- States and provinces follow slightly different rules.

Grammaire supplémentaire, pp. 342–343, Act. 3–4

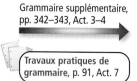

Travaux pratiques de grammaire, p. 91, Act. 7

Vocabulaire à la carte

en Angleterre	au Brésil	en Espagne	en Italie	au Sénégal
en Allemagne	en Californie	aux Etats-Unis	au Maroc	en Suisse
en Australie	en Chine	en France	au Mexique	au Texas
en Belgique	en Egypte	en Floride	en Russie	au Viêt-nam

10 Grammaire en contexte

Parlons Dans quel pays vont-ils passer leurs vacances?

1. Murielle va prendre des photos de la tour Eiffel.
2. Monique va visiter le château Frontenac.
3. Joseph va visiter la tour de Londres.
4. Mathieu va voir les pyramides.

au Canada	aux Etats-Unis	au Maroc
en Russie		en Angleterre
	en Egypte	
		en France

5. Than et Laure vont visiter le Texas.
6. Dominique va voir le Kremlin.
7. Paul et Gilles vont aller à Casablanca.

Tu te rappelles?

Do you remember how to ask for advice? Make, accept, and refuse suggestions?

To ask for advice:

Je ne sais pas quoi faire (où aller).

Tu as une idée?

Qu'est-ce que tu me conseilles?

To make suggestions:

Je te conseille de...

Tu devrais...

To accept suggestions:

C'est une bonne idée!

Pourquoi pas?

D'accord!

Allons-y!

To refuse suggestions:

Non, ce n'est pas possible.

Non, je ne peux pas.

Ça ne me dit rien.

C'est trop cher.

11 Grammaire en contexte

Parlons Choisis deux pays de l'activité 10. Avec un groupe de camarades, trouve au moins trois activités que tout le monde veut faire dans chaque pays.

12 Un voyage gratuit

Parlons Tu as gagné un voyage pour aller où tu veux dans le monde. Où est-ce que tu vas aller? Pourquoi? Qu'est-ce que tu vas y faire? Parle de ton voyage avec un(e) camarade. Ensuite, changez de rôle.

13 En vacances à la Martinique

Ecoutons Ecoute Alain et Valérie qui parlent de leurs vacances. Est-ce que ces phrases sont vraies ou fausses?

1. Alain ne sait pas quoi faire.
2. Valérie n'a pas d'idées.

3. Valérie est déjà allée à la Martinique.
4. Alain ne veut pas aller à la Martinique.

A la française

Use the words **alors** *(so, then, well, in that case)* and **donc** *(so, then, therefore)* to connect your sentences.

J'adore faire de la plongée, **donc** je vais en Australie.

Tu aimes faire du bateau? **Alors,** tu devrais aller à Marseille.

14 Des conseils

Parlons Ces élèves rêvent de ce qu'ils aiment. Ils ne savent pas où aller pendant les vacances. Tu as une idée?

EXEMPLE **Tu devrais aller...**

Je te conseille d'aller...

Malika

Marion

Hai

Christian

Adrienne

Ali

15 Où aller?

Parlons Dis à ton/ta camarade ce que tu aimes faire en vacances. Il/Elle va te dire où tu devrais aller pour faire ces choses. Accepte ou refuse ses suggestions et quand tu refuses, dis pourquoi. Ensuite, changez de rôle.

16 Mon journal

Ecrivons Décris un voyage que tu vas faire ou que tu voudrais faire. Où veux-tu aller? Quand? Avec qui? Qu'est-ce que tu vas y faire?

Qu'est-ce que tu fais pendant les vacances?

We asked some francophone people where they go and what they do on vacation. Here are their responses.

Nicole,
Martinique

«Pendant les vacances, alors, je vais généralement à la plage, au cinéma. Le soir, je sors, enfin je vais dans des fêtes, chez des amis. On danse. On s'amuse. On rigole. On joue aux cartes. Les vacances se passent comme ça.»

Quand est-ce que tu as des vacances?

«J'ai des vacances en juillet, à partir de juillet. Les vacances durent deux mois et nous reprenons l'école en septembre.»

Céline,
France

«Ben, pendant les vacances, bon, des fois je pars. L'année dernière, je suis partie en Espagne, cette année je pars en Corse. Je pars souvent avec des copains ou... sinon, je reste à Aix.»

Sim,
Côte d'Ivoire

«Pendant les vacances, d'habitude je vais au village chez les parents qui sont restés au village. Et après une année scolaire, il faut aller les voir parce que ça... il y a longtemps qu'on se voit pas. Donc, ça fait plaisir aux parents de revoir les enfants quand ils vont au village. Voilà. Ça fait changer de climat. On va se reposer un peu.»

Qu'en penses-tu?

1. Where do these people like to go and what do they like to do during their vacations?
2. Where do you go and what do you do on vacation? How does this differ from what these people do?

Savais-tu que...?

Salaried employees in France are guaranteed five weeks of vacation time per year. Most people take a month off in July or August and take the fifth week at some other time of the year, often in winter.

Vocabulaire

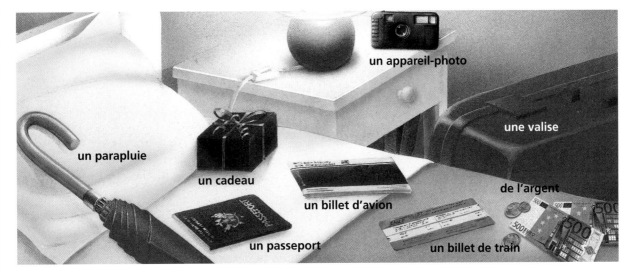

un appareil-photo

une valise

un parapluie

un cadeau

de l'argent

un billet d'avion

un passeport

un billet de train

Travaux pratiques de grammaire, p. 92, Act. 8–9

Cahier d'activités, p. 125, Act. 10–11

17 Qu'est-ce qu'il te faut?

Parlons Réponds aux questions suivantes.

1. Qu'est-ce qu'il faut quand il pleut?
2. Qu'est-ce qu'il faut pour prendre le train? L'avion?
3. Qu'est-ce qu'il faut pour acheter des souvenirs?
4. Qu'est-ce qu'il faut pour prendre des photos?

Comment dit-on...?

Reminding; reassuring

To remind someone of something:

N'oublie pas ton passeport!
Tu n'as pas oublié ton billet d'avion?
You didn't forget . . . ?
Tu ne peux pas partir sans ton écharpe!
You can't leave without . . . !
Tu prends ton manteau? *Are you taking . . . ?*

To reassure someone:

Ne t'en fais pas.
J'ai pensé à tout. *I've thought of everything.*
Je n'ai rien oublié. *I didn't forget anything.*

Cahier d'activités, p. 126, Act. 13

 18 Tu n'as rien oublié?

Ecoutons Listen to these speakers. Are they reminding or reassuring someone?

Si tu as oublié **clothing** va à la page 297.

19 Qu'est-ce qu'il a oublié?

Lisons/Parlons Regarde la liste de choses que Jean-Paul doit prendre avec lui pour son voyage. Fais une liste des choses qu'il a oubliées. Avec un(e) camarade, joue le rôle d'un parent de Jean-Paul et dis-lui ce qu'il doit prendre. Ensuite, changez de rôle.

Travaux pratiques de grammaire, p. 93, Act. 10

appareil-photo   casquette
billet d'avion   baskets
billet de train   shorts
passeport   chaussures
dictionnaire   chaussettes
magazines   cadeaux

 20 Jeu de rôle

Parlons Cet été, tu vas en vacances en France avec ton club de français. Ton ami(e) est allé(e) en France l'année dernière. Demande-lui ce que tu dois prendre. Il/Elle va te répondre. Joue cette scène avec un(e) camarade, puis, changez de rôle.

EXEMPLE —Qu'est-ce que je devrais prendre?
—N'oublie pas ton appareil-photo.

Grammaire

The verb *partir*

A small group of verbs whose infinitives end in **-ir** follow a pattern different than the one you learned in Chapter 10.

partir (*to leave*)

Je	**pars**	Nous	**partons**
Tu	**pars**	Vous	**partez**
Il/Elle/On	**part**	Ils/Elles	**partent**

Elles **partent** à dix heures.

- Don't pronounce the **s** or **t** in **pars** or **part**.
- **Sortir** (*to go out*) and **dormir** (*to sleep*) also follow this pattern.

Grammaire supplémentaire, pp. 343–344, Act. 5–7

Cahier d'activités, p. 125, Act. 12

Travaux pratiques de grammaire, pp. 93–94, Act. 11–12

À la française

French speakers often use the present tense to talk about the future.
Je **pars** à neuf heures. *I'm leaving/I'm going to leave/I will leave . . .*
Je **sors** avec Aline ce soir. *I'm going out/I'm going to go out/I will go out . . .*

21 **Grammaire en contexte**

Ecrivons Tu parles de ta routine quotidienne avec la famille française chez qui tu habites. Complète chaque phrase avec la forme correcte de **partir, sortir** ou **dormir.**

1. Je _____ pour l'école à huit heures du matin.

2. Ma sœur et moi, nous _____ jusqu'à dix heures le samedi matin.

3. Mon père et ma mère _____ toujours avant moi le matin.

4. Mon frère Emile _____ le vendredi soir avec son amie Agnès.

22 **Vacances en Provence**

Parlons Regarde l'itinéraire de Marianne. Ensuite, réponds aux questions.

1. D'où part Marianne samedi?

2. Où est-ce qu'elle va?

3. Son voyage va durer combien de temps?

4. Qu'est-ce qu'elle a l'intention de faire?

SAMEDI :
départ d'Arles, bus de 9h35;
arrivée aux Baux-de-Provence à 10h10;
* visite de la Cathédrale d'Images;
   dîner : Auberge de la Benvengudo

DIMANCHE :
départ pour Saint-Rémy-de-Provence, bus de 9h15;
arrivée à 9h45;
* visite du musée Van Gogh; déjeuner : pique-nique
   à Fontvieille;
* visite du moulin de Daudet; retour aux Baux-de-Provence;
   départ pour Avignon, bus de 18h16; arrivée à 19h10
   Hôtel le Midi; dîner

LUNDI :
* visite de la Cité des Papes, le Pont St-Bénezet,
   promenade du Rocher des Doms, le musée
   du Petit-Palais;
* spectacle folklorique; départ pour Grasse
   20h15; arrivée à 22h10 Hôtel les Arômes

MARDI :
* visite de la Parfumerie Fragonard;
* Musée d'Art et d'Histoire de Provence;
   départ de Grasse à 17h42; arrivée en
   Arles à 19h20

23 **Jeu de rôle**

Parlons Tu vas faire le même voyage que Marianne. Ton/Ta camarade va te poser des questions sur ton voyage et va te dire ce que tu dois prendre avec toi.

EXEMPLE   —**Tu vas aller aux Baux-de-Provence? N'oublie pas ton appareil-photo.**
   —**Ah! C'est une bonne idée.**

24 **Bonjour de Provence!**

Ecrivons Pendant ton voyage en Provence, écris une carte postale à ton ami(e), à tes camarades de classe ou à ton professeur.

Comment dit-on...?

Seeing someone off

To wish someone a good trip:

Bon voyage! *Have a good trip!*
Bonnes vacances! *Have a good vacation!*
Amuse-toi bien! *Have fun!*
Bonne chance! *Good luck!*

Cahier d'activités, p. 127, Act. 14–16

25 **On arrive ou on part?**

Ecoutons Ecoute ces conversations. On arrive ou on part?

26 **Au revoir!**

Parlons Ton ami(e) français(e) part en France. Tu vas à l'aéroport avec lui/elle. Dis-lui au revoir. Joue cette scène avec un(e) camarade.

27 **Un grand voyage**

Parlons Ton ami(e) et toi, vous allez faire un voyage dans un autre pays. Choisissez le pays où vous voulez aller et les activités que vous allez faire. Parlez du temps qu'il fait dans ce pays et dites quand vous voulez partir. Parlez aussi des vêtements et des autres choses que vous allez prendre.

28 **Un petit mot**

Ecrivons Ton ami(e) va partir en voyage demain. Ecris-lui une lettre pour lui dire bon voyage. Suggère des activités qu'il/elle peut faire pendant ses vacances.

Tu te rappelles?

Do you remember how to give commands? Use the **tu** or **vous** form of the verb without a subject pronoun.

> **Attends! Allez!**

When you use an **-er** verb, remember to drop the final **s** of the **tu** form.

> **Ecoute!**

When you use an object pronoun with a positive command, place it after the verb, separated by a hyphen in writing.

> **Donnez-moi votre billet, s'il vous plaît.**

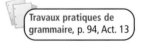 Travaux pratiques de grammaire, p. 94, Act. 13 — Grammaire supplémentaire, p. 344, Act. 8 →

Si tu as oublié **weather** va à la page 118.

Travaux pratiques de grammaire, p. 95, Act. 14–15

Comment dit-on...?

Asking for and expressing opinions

To ask someone's opinion:

Tu as passé un bon été?

Ça s'est bien passé?
Did it go well?

Tu t'es bien amusé(e)?
Did you have fun?

To express an opinion:

Oui, très chouette.
Oui, c'était formidable!
Yes, it was great!
Oui, ça a été.
Oh, pas mauvais.
C'était épouvantable.
Non, pas vraiment. *No, not really.*
C'était un véritable cauchemar!
It was a real nightmare!
C'était ennuyeux. *It was boring.*
C'était barbant.

Cahier d'activités, pp. 128–129, Act. 17–19

---

29 ### C'était comment, les vacances?

Ecoutons Listen to these conversations and then tell whether these people had a good, fair, or bad vacation.

30 ### Méli-mélo!

Lisons Remets la conversation entre Thierry et Hervé dans le bon ordre.

Tu te rappelles?

Do you remember how to inquire about and relate events that happened in the past?

Tu es allé(e) où?

Qu'est-ce que tu as fait?

D'abord,... Ensuite,... Après,... Finalement,...

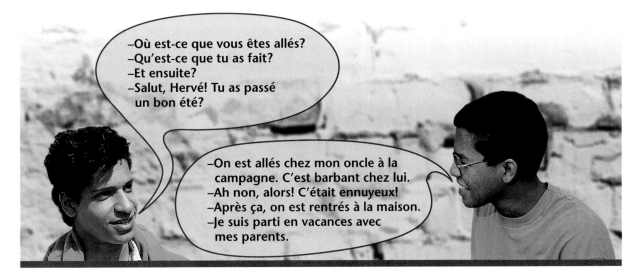

–Où est-ce que vous êtes allés?
–Qu'est-ce que tu as fait?
–Et ensuite?
–Salut, Hervé! Tu as passé un bon été?

–On est allés chez mon oncle à la campagne. C'est barbant chez lui.
–Ah non, alors! C'était ennuyeux!
–Après ça, on est rentrés à la maison.
–Je suis parti en vacances avec mes parents.

Tu te rappelles?

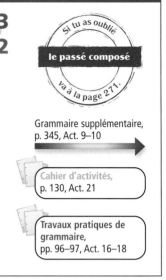

CD-ROM **3**
DVD **2**

Si tu as oublié
le passé composé
va à la page 271.

Do you remember how to form the **passé composé**? Use a form of **avoir** as a helping verb with the past participle of the main verb. The past participles of regular **-er**, **-re**, and **-ir** verbs end in **é**, **u**, and **i**.

Nous **avons** beaucoup **mangé**. J'**ai répondu** à leur lettre. Ils **ont fini**.

You have to memorize the past participles of irregular verbs.

J'**ai fait** du camping. Ils **ont vu** un film.

To make a verb in the **passé composé** negative, you place **ne... pas** around the helping verb.

Il **n'**a **pas** fait ses devoirs.

With **aller**, **partir**, and **sortir**, you use **être** as the helping verb instead of **avoir**.

Grammaire supplémentaire,
p. 345, Act. 9–10

Cahier d'activités,
p. 130, Act. 21

Travaux pratiques de
grammaire,
pp. 96–97, Act. 16–18

---

31 ## Qu'est-ce qu'elle a fait?

Lisons/Ecrivons Mets ces activités dans le bon ordre d'après l'itinéraire de Marianne à la page 335 en utilisant le passé composé.

EXEMPLE   D'abord, elle...

visiter le musée Van Gogh

voir un spectacle folklorique

visiter la Parfumerie Fragonard

visiter la Cité des Papes

voir le moulin de Daudet

faire la promenade du Rocher des Doms

faire un pique-nique

---

32 ## On fait la même chose?

Parlons Ton/Ta camarade et toi, vous avez pris ces photos pendant vos vacances en France l'année dernière. Expliquez où vous êtes allé(e)s et ce que vous avez fait. Donnez votre opinion sur chaque activité ou sur chaque endroit.

Un café sur le
Cours Mirabeau

Le palais des Papes,
c'est formidable.

La mer Méditerranée

Les arènes en Arles

La Côte d'Azur

33  **De l'école au travail**

 Écrivons You work for a company that organizes tours for young people. One of your clients has requested that you write him a note telling what he needs to bring on the trip. Study the itinerary on page 335 that you've put together for his tour group and write him a short fax detailing what he should pack.

EXEMPLE   **Le samedi 7 juin tu vas prendre le bus pour les Baux-de-Provence. N'oublie pas ton argent pour acheter le billet.**

PRONONCIATION

Aspirated h, th, ch, and gn

You've learned that you don't pronounce the letter **h** in French. Some words begin with an aspirated **h** (**h aspiré**). This means that you don't make elision and liaison with the word that comes before. Repeat these phrases: **le haut-parleur; le houx; les halles; les haricots.**

Haut and **houx** begin with an aspirated **h,** so you can't drop the **e** from the article **le. Halles** and **haricots** also begin with an aspirated **h,** so you don't pronounce the **s** in the article **les.** How will you know which words begin with an aspirated **h?** If you look the words up in the dictionary, you may find an asterisk (*) before an aspirated **h.**

How do you pronounce the combination **th?** Just ignore the letter **h** and pronounce the **t.** Repeat these words: **mathématiques, théâtre, athlète.**

What about the combination **ch?** In French, **ch** is pronounced like the English *sh,* as in the word *show.* Compare these English and French words: *change*/**change,** *chocolate*/**chocolat,** *chance*/**chance.** In some words, **ch** is pronounced like *k.* Listen to these words and repeat them: **chorale, Christine, archéologie.**

Finally, how do you pronounce the combination **gn?** The English sound /ny/, as in the word *onion* is similar. Pronounce these words: **oignon, montagne, magnifique.**

A. A prononcer

Repeat the following words.

1. le héros   la harpe   le hippie   le hockey
2. thème   maths   mythe   bibliothèque
3. Chine   choisir   tranche   pêches
4. espagnol   champignon   montagne   magnifique

B. A lire

Take turns with a partner reading each of the following sentences aloud.

1. J'aime la Hollande, mais je veux aller à la montagne en Allemagne.
2. Je cherche une chemise, des chaussures et un chapeau.
3. Il n'a pas fait ses devoirs de maths et de chimie à la bibliothèque dimanche.
4. Charles a gagné trois hamsters. Ils sont dans ma chambre! Quel cauchemar!

C. A écrire

You're going to hear a short dialogue. Write down what you hear.

TROISIEME ETAPE   *trois cent trente-neuf* **339**

Un guide touristique

Stratégie pour lire

When you read for a purpose, it's a good idea to decide beforehand what kind of information you want. If you're looking for an overview, a quick, general reading may be all that is required. If you're looking for specific details, you'll have to read more carefully.

A. The information at the top of both pages is from a book entitled *Le Guide du Routard.* Do you think this is

   1. a history book?

   2. a travel guide?

   3. a geography book?

B. You usually read a book like this to gather general information about what is going on, or to find details about a certain place or event. What general categories of information can you find? Under what titles?

C. Where should you stay if . . .

   1. you plan to visit Provence in November?

   2. you want a balcony?

   3. you want the least expensive room you can get?

   4. you have a tent and a sleeping bag?

D. Do you think the descriptions of the hotels were written by the hotel management? How do you know?

Où dormir?

Très bon marché

Auberge de jeunesse : 20, av. Foch. ☎ 04-90-96-18-25. Fax : 04-90-96-31-26. Fermée du 20 décembre au 10 février. 100 lits. 12,2€ la première nuit, 10,4€ les suivantes, draps et petit déjeuner compris. Fait aussi restaurant. Repas à 7,2€.

Prix modérés

Hôtel Gaugin : 5, place Voltaire. ☎ 04-90-96-14-35. Fax : 04-90-18-98-87. Fermé en novembre. De 27,5 à 32€ la chambre double. Chambres simples, bien aménagées. Les six qui donnent sur la place ont un balcon et la vue sur la place Voltaire. Peu de charme cependant dans ce quartier de l'après-guerre. Le petit plus : tous les matins la météo locale est affichée à la réception!

Plus chic

Hôtel du Musée : 11, rue du Grand-Prieuré. ☎ 04-90-93-88-88. Fax : 04-90-49-98-15. Fermé en janvier. De 45,7 à 61€ la chambre double. Joli patio pour le petit déjeuner. Dans une belle demeure du XVIIe siècle, face au musée Réattu et à deux pas du Rhône, une excellente adresse. Très bien situé et très bon accueil.

Camping

Camping City : 67, route de Crau. ☎ 04-90-93-08-86. Fax : 04-90-93-91-07. Fermé du 30 octobre au 1er mars. Assez ombragé, mais plutôt bruyant. Attention aux moustiques, car situé près d'un marécage. Piscine, épicerie, plats à emporter. Animations en été.

BATEAU «MIREIO»

Bateau restaurant de 250 places, chauffé, climatisé. Croisières déjeuner sans escale vers Châteauneuf-du-Pape ou avec escale en Arles – visite de la capitale de la Camargue –, à Roquemaure avec dégustation des vins de Côtes du Rhône, à Villeneuve avec visite du village et de ses monuments. Croisières dîner et soirées spectacle devant Avignon et Villeneuve. Animation dansante et commentaires sur toutes les croisières.

84000 AVIGNON -
Tél. : 04 90 85 62 25
Fax : 04 90 85 61 14

CATHEDRALE D'IMAGES

Aux Baux-de-Provence, dans les anciennes carrières du Val-d'Enfer, CATHEDRALE D'IMAGES propose un spectacle permanent en IMAGE TOTALE.4.000m2 d'écrans naturels, 40 sources de projection, 2 500 diapos créent une féerie visuelle et sonore où déambule le spectateur.–Couvrez-vous car les carrières sont fraîches!–

13520 LES BAUX-DE-PROVENCE -
Tél. : 04 90 54 38 65
Fax : 04 90 54 42 65

Où manger?

Bon marché

🍴 **Vitamine** : 16, rue du Docteur-Fanton, ☎ 04-90-93-77-36. derrière la place du Forum. Fermé le samedi soir et le dimanche sauf pendant la féria et le mois de la Photo. Une carte de 50 salades différentes, de 2,8 à 7,6€, 15 spécialités de pâtes de 5,3 à 7,3€, le tout dans une salle agréablement décorée (expos photos) et avec un accueil décontracté.

🍴 **Le Grillon** : 36, rond-point des Arènes. ☎ 04-90-96-70-97. Fermé le dimanche soir et le mercredi. Menu à 12,8€, très honnête, le midi, le soir et le week-end, avec soupe de poisson, fricassée de canard à la graine de moutarde, fromage ou dessert. À la carte, comptez 18,3 € pour un repas complet. Ce restaurant-brasserie-crêperie-glacier ne paie pas de mine, mais il y a une agréable terrasse avec une très belle vue sur les arènes. On y découvre de bons petits plats sympathiques.

🍴 **Le Poisson Banane** : 6, rue du Forum. ☎ 04-90-96-02-58. Ouvert uniquement le soir. Fermé le dimanche seulement hors saison. Menus à 12€ jusqu'à 21 h, 18,3 et 20,6€. Avec sa grande terrasse et sa tonnelle, ce petit resto caché derrière la place du Forum passe facilement inaperçu et c'est dommage. Il est agréable d'aller y goûter une cuisine sucrée-salée inventive avec une spécialité antillaise : le «poisson banane», bien sûr.

CHATEAU MUSEE DE L'EMPERI

Le CHATEAU DE L'EMPERI,

la plus importante forteresse médiévale en Provence, abrite une des plus somptueuses collections d'art et d'histoire militaire qui soit en Europe. Cette collection unique illustre l'évolution des uniformes et de l'art militaire de Louis XIV à 1918. La période napoléonienne est la plus présente. Le Château de l'Empéri est situé en plein cœur de la ville ancienne.

13300 SALON
DE PROVENCE -
Tél : 04 90 56 22 36

GROTTES DE THOUZON

Les décors de stalactites qui parent « le ciel » de ce réseau naturel forment des paysages souterrains merveilleux. (Photo : M. CROTET) Grotte réputée pour la finesse de ses stalactites (fistuleuses). Parcours aisé pour les personnes âgées et les enfants. Seule grotte naturelle aménagée pour le tourisme en Provence. Ouvert du 1/04 au 31/10. Groupe toute l'année sur rendez-vous.

84250 LE THOR
Tél. : 04 90 33 93 65
Fax : 04 90 33 74 90

E. Which restaurant should you try if . . .

1. you want the most expensive meal available?

2. you love salad?

3. you want to go out on Saturday night?

F. At the bottom of both pages, you will find descriptions of several tourist attractions in Provence. After you've read them, match attractions listed below with the sites where you would find them.

1. a dinner cruise
2. stalactites
3. thousands of projection screens
4. a collection of military art and uniforms

a. Cathédrale d'Images
b. Bateau «Miréio»
c. Grottes de Thouzon
d. Château Musée de l'Empéri

G. If you were working at a tourist information office, what would you recommend to someone who . . .

1. wants a comfortable cruise package?

2. would like to visit a medieval castle?

3. likes to explore caves?

4. is interested in military art?

H. Are there similar tourist attractions in your area? What are they?

I. You and your friend have three days to spend in Arles. You're on a very tight budget, but you still want to enjoy your trip. Where will you stay? Where will you eat your lunches and dinners? How much will you spend for these three days?

Cahier d'activités, p. 131, Act. 23

Grammaire supplémentaire

CD-ROM3 DVD2

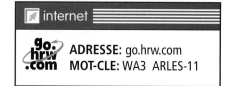

internet

go.hrw.com

ADRESSE: go.hrw.com
MOT-CLE: WA3 ARLES-11

Première étape

Objectives Inquiring about and sharing future plans; expressing indecision; expressing wishes; asking for advice; making, accepting, and refusing suggestions

1 Lis chaque phrase et décide si on parle d'une activité à faire quand il fait beau ou quand il pleut. Ensuite, écris les phrases dans la catégorie appropriée. (**p. 328**)

- je vais faire de la randonnée avec des copains.
- on va prendre des photos dans le parc.
- mes tantes vont regarder un film à la télévision.
- vous n'allez pas sortir de chez vous.
- nous allons passer la journée à la plage.
- tu vas lire un roman.

Il fait beau, alors...   Il pleut, alors...

1. . . .   4. . . .

2. . . .   5. . . .

3. . . .   6. . . .

2 Voici ce que ces gens font d'habitude en été. Mets ces phrases au futur en utilisant le verbe **aller**. (**pp. 174, 328**)

1. Antoine fait du bateau.

2. Sophie et sa sœur font de la voile.

3. Ma famille et moi, nous allons au bord de la mer.

4. Anne et toi, vous faites de la randonnée.

3 Le nom de ces étudiants étrangers commence par la première lettre de leur pays d'origine. Trouve le pays d'origine de chaque étudiant et dis où ils vont aller en vacances cet été. (**p. 330**)

EXEMPLE   Bélinda/**le Brésil** -> **Elle va aller au Brésil.**

1. ANNE/ _____ - _____

2. ERIN/_____ - _____

3. MARIA/_____ - _____

4. ISABELLA/_____ - _____

5. CÉLINE/ _____ - _____

le Canada   les Etats-Unis
     le Mexique
le Brésil   l'Australie   l'Italie

4 Jeanne et ses amis ne savent pas où aller en vacances et te demandent conseil. Lis ce qu'ils aiment faire et suggère-leur un des pays proposés. (**p. 330.**)

EXEMPLE J'aime faire de la randonnée! **Pourquoi tu ne vas pas en Suisse?**

1. J'adore les quiches et les croque-monsieur!

_____

2. Nous aimons la plage.

_____

3. Je voudrais visiter les pyramides.

_____

4. Nous adorons parler espagnol.

_____

la Californie

l'Egypte

la Suisse

le Mexique

la France

Deuxième étape

Objectives Reminding; reassuring; seeing someone off

5 Pour chaque phrase, choisis le sujet qui va avec le verbe, et ensuite, décide si ce qu'on dit est **une bonne idée** ou **une mauvaise idée.** (**p. 334**)

1. (Elle/Vous) partez à midi pour aller au lycée?

C'est une _____ idée.

2. (Tu/Nous) dors pendant que le prof parle?

C'est une _____ idée.

3. (Vous/Elle) part souvent en vacances.

C'est une _____ idée.

4. (Je/Nous) ne pars jamais sans mon parapluie quand il pleut.

C'est une _____ idée.

5. (Je/Ils) sortent souvent sans prendre leurs portefeuilles.

C'est une _____ idée.

6. (Nous/Ils) ne sortons jamais sans nos lunettes de soleil quand il fait beau.

C'est une _____ idée.

Grammaire supplémentaire

WA3 ARLES-11

6 Ecris cinq phrases pour dire quand tes amis et toi, vous allez à l'école. Utilise le verbe **partir**. (p. 334)

EXEMPLE Marianne (8h30) **Elle part à huit heures et demie.**

1. Antoine et moi (6h15)
2. Et toi, Maryse (7h00)
3. Lise et Marie (7h30)
4. Philippe et toi (8h00)
5. Stéphane (8h45)

7 Omar et Larissa se préparent pour aller chez leur grand-mère. Complète leur conversation avec les formes appropriées des verbes entre parenthèses. (p. 334)

OMAR   Dis, Larissa, tu ___**1**___ (dormir) toujours?

LARISSA   Oui. Je ___**2**___ (dormir)!

OMAR   Mais c'est pas possible! On ___**3**___ (partir) dans une heure!

LARISSA   On ___**4**___ (aller) où?

OMAR   Tu ne te rappelles pas? Nous ___**5**___ (partir) en vacances aujourd'hui! Au bord de la mer! Chez Mémé!

LARISSA   Ah, mais c'est vrai! J'avais oublié! C'est super! Qu'est-ce que je ___**6**___ (prendre)? Mon maillot de bain?

OMAR   Oui. ___**7**___ (prendre)-le! Il ___**8**___ (aller) faire chaud! Et n' ___**9**___ (oublier) pas une robe! On va ___**10**___ (sortir) avec les copains tous les soirs.

LARISSA   Je ___**11**___ (pouvoir) prendre la valise de Maman?

OMAR   Oui. Si tu ___**12**___ (vouloir).

LARISSA   Dis, Omar, tu n' ___**13**___ (avoir) pas oublié le cadeau pour Mémé?

OMAR   Mais non. Je n' ___**14**___ (avoir) rien oublié. J' ___**15**___ (avoir) pensé à tout.

8 Il y a des choses que tes amis et toi, vous devez prendre quand vous partez en vacances. Vos parents vous disent de les prendre. Ecris ce qu'ils vous disent et utilise le pronom approprié **le, la** ou **les**. (pp. 279, 336)

EXEMPLE Je ne peux pas partir sans mon blouson en jean.
Eh bien, prends-le!

1. Je ne peux pas partir sans ma valise!
2. Je ne peux pas partir sans mon passeport!
3. Nous ne pouvons pas partir sans nos chaussures en cuir!
4. Je ne peux pas partir sans mon appareil-photo!
5. Nous ne pouvons pas partir sans nos lunettes de soleil!
6. Je ne peux pas partir sans ma cravate à fleurs.

CHAPITRE 11   Vive les vacances!

9 Hélène raconte ce qu'elle a fait pendant ses vacances l'année dernière et parle de ce qu'elle va faire cette année. En lisant chaque phrase, décide de quelles vacances elle parle et ensuite, choisis la photo qui dépeint le mieux ses vacances. (**pp. 328, 338**)

1. Ça va être une aventure!

2. Je suis restée chez moi tout le temps.

3. Il va faire beau.

4. Je vais mettre un short et des lunettes de soleil dans ma valise avant de partir.

5. J'ai eu le temps de lire un roman.

6. Il n'a pas fait·beau.

7. Je vais aller à la plage.

8. J'ai regardé la télé.

a.

b.

10 Mets les mots dans un ordre logique pour dire ce que tes amis et toi, vous avez fait pendant les vacances. N'oublie pas de mettre les verbes au passé composé. (**pp. 271, 338**)

EXEMPLE   On/faire/ne/rien/de/spécial   **On n'a rien fait de spécial.**

1. Karim et moi/pièce/voir/une/super/nous

2. Tu/de/au bord de/la/faire/mer/voile/la/non?

3. Christelle/jusqu'à midi/dormir

4. Jacques et Simon/la télé/regarder/pendant des heures

5. Jonathan et toi/de/randonnée?/vous/la/faire

6. Larissa et moi/des/sensass/lire/romans/nous

7. Véra et Julie/visiter/le Louvre

8. Moi/à/des/répondre/lettres/je

Mise en pratique

 1 Listen to the radio advertisement and then answer the questions below.

1. What is being advertised?

2. Can you name two places that are mentioned in the advertisement?

3. What activities are mentioned in the advertisement?

4. For whom do they offer discounts?

2 Regarde cette brochure et réponds aux questions suivantes.

Le rêve américain devient réalité, en séjour Immersion avec EF

Vivre à l'américaine

Qui n'a rêvé un jour de vivre une autre vie ? Ce rêve devient réalité, grâce à la formule EF Immersion : pendant quelques semaines, vous devenez totalement américain. Parce que les familles d'accueil sont soigneusement séléctionnées par EF, votre intégration est immédiate, et vos progrès linguistiques sont aussi spectaculaires que durables. C'est, sans nul doute, la formule qui vous assure la connaissance la plus directe et la plus profonde du mode de vie américain.

Vacances de Printemps

N° de séjour	Date de départ	Date de retour	Durée du séjour	Région	Frais de séjour*
550	11 avril	25 avril	2 sem.	Côte Est	1.179
551	18 avril	2 mai	2 sem.	Côte Est	1.179
552	18 avril	2 mai	2 sem.	Sud-Est	1.246

1. Where do students go if they sign up for this trip?

2. Where do they stay?

3. What do they learn?

4. In what months can students make this trip?

5. How long does it last?

6. To what regions of the country can students go?

7. How much does this trip cost?

3 Dis si les phrases suivantes sont vraies ou fausses.

1. Only a few French children attend summer camp.

2. French children can study foreign languages at summer camp.

3. Most French people take a one-week summer vacation.

4 Ecrivons!

Write a letter to a French-speaking exchange student who is coming to your school. Tell him or her what there is to see and do where you live, what the weather is like there, and what to bring.

Prewriting

Before you begin your letter, arrange your ideas logically to make your letter flow more smoothly. You might want to divide a sheet of paper into columns and label each column with a subject you'll address in your letter (**le temps, il te faut...**, and so on). Write each of your ideas in the appropriate column.

> ### **Stratégie** pour écrire
> Using connecting words such as **donc** and **alors** to link your ideas can help your writing flow more naturally.

Writing

Using the ideas you organized, write a letter to describe the place where you live. Include a lot of detail in your description to help form an image of the places to visit. Try to use connecting words to tie sentences together in the letter.

Remember to use expressions you've learned for making suggestions and reminding someone to do something.

Revising

Proofreading is one of the most important steps in the evaluation process. It gives you a chance to correct any mistakes you might have made while you were writing. While writing your first draft, concentrate on being creative. You can make corrections to the grammar, punctuation, and spelling when you proofread.

It's a good idea to proofread in several passes. First, read through your letter to check only for grammar and punctuation mistakes. On your second pass, check for spelling errors. This way, there will be fewer errors in your final draft.

5 Jeu de rôle

a. You want to take a trip for your vacation, but you're not sure where. Tell your travel agent what you like to do and what you'd like to see. The travel agent will make some suggestions about where you might go and what there is to do there. He or she will also describe the weather conditions and tell you what clothes to take, where you can stay, and when and from where you can leave. The travel agent will also remind you of things you shouldn't forget to take. Act this out with your partner. Then, change roles.

b. You've returned from your trip and your friend wants to know how it went. Tell your friend about your trip and answer any questions he or she has about what you did. Act this out with your partner and then change roles.

Can you use what you've learned in this chapter?

Can you inquire about and share future plans? Express indecision and wishes?
p. 329

1 How would you ask where a friend is going on vacation and what he or she is going to do? How would you answer these questions?

2 How would you tell someone . . .
1. you're not sure what to do?
2. where you'd really like to go?

Can you ask for advice? Make, accept, and refuse suggestions?
p. 330

3 How would you ask a friend for advice about your vacation?

4 How would you suggest to a friend that he or she . . .
1. go to the country?
2. go camping?
3. work?
4. go to Canada?

5 How would you accept and refuse the suggestions in number 4?

Can you remind and reassure someone?
p. 333

6 How would you remind a friend to take these things on a trip?

1.

2.

3.

7 How would you reassure someone you haven't forgotten these things?

1.

2.
3.

Can you see someone off?
p. 336

8 How would you tell when these people are leaving, using the verb **partir**?
1. Didier / 14h28
2. Désirée et Annie / 20h46
3. Nous / 11h15
4. Tu / 23h59

9 How would you wish someone a good trip?

Can you ask for and express opinions?
p. 337

10 How would you ask a friend how his or her vacation went?

11 How would you tell how your vacation went?

Can you inquire about and relate past events?
p. 337

12 How would you find out what a friend did on vacation?

13 How would you tell what you did on vacation?

Première étape

Inquiring about and sharing future plans

Qu'est-ce que tu vas faire...?	What are you going to do . . . ?
Où est-ce que tu vas aller... ?	Where are you going to go . . . ?
Je vais...	I'm going to . . .
J'ai l'intention de/d'...	I intend to . . .

Expressing indecision

J'hésite.	I'm not sure.
Je ne sais pas.	I don't know.
Je n'en sais rien.	I have no idea.
Je n'ai rien de prévu.	I don't have any plans.

Expressing wishes

Je voudrais bien...	I'd really like to . . .
J'ai envie de/d'...	I feel like . . .

Vacation places and activities

à la montagne	to/in the mountains
en forêt	to/in the forest
à la campagne	to/in the countryside
en colonie de vacances	to/at a summer camp
au bord de la mer	to/on the coast
chez...	to/at . . . 's house
faire du camping	to go camping
faire de la randonnée	to go hiking
faire du bateau	to go boating
faire de la plongée	to go scuba diving
faire de la planche à voile	to go windsurfing
faire de la voile	to go sailing

à	to, in (a city or place)
en	to, in (before a feminine noun)
au	to, in (before a masculine noun)
aux	to, in (before a plural noun)

Asking for advice; making, accepting, and refusing suggestions

See Tu te rappelles? on page 330.

Deuxième étape

Travel items

un passeport	passport
un billet de train	train ticket
un billet d'avion	plane ticket
une valise	suitcase
de l'argent	money
un appareil-photo	camera
un cadeau	gift
un parapluie	umbrella

Reminding, reassuring

N'oublie pas...	Don't forget . . .
Tu n'as pas oublié... ?	You didn't forget . . . ?
Tu ne peux pas partir sans...	You can't leave without . . .
Tu prends... ?	Are you taking . . . ?
Ne t'en fais pas.	Don't worry.
Je n'ai rien oublié.	I didn't forget anything.

J'ai pensé à tout.	I've thought of everything.
partir	to leave

Seeing someone off

Bon voyage!	Have a good trip!
Bonnes vacances!	Have a good vacation!
Amuse-toi bien!	Have fun!
Bonne chance!	Good luck!

Troisième étape

Asking for and expressing opinions

Tu as passé un bon... ?	Did you have a good . . . ?
Ça s'est bien passé?	Did it go well?
Tu t'es bien amusé(e)?	Did you have fun?
Oui, très chouette.	Yes, very cool.
C'était formidable!	It was great!

Oui, ça a été.	Yes, it was OK.
Oh, pas mauvais.	Oh, not bad.
C'était épouvantable.	It was horrible.
Non, pas vraiment.	No, not really.
C'était un véritable cauchemar!	It was a real nightmare!

C'était ennuyeux.	It was boring.
C'était barbant.	It was boring.

Inquiring about and relating past events

See Tu te rappelles? on page 337.

Allez, viens à Fort-de-France!

Ville principale de la Martinique

Population : plus de 100.000

Langues : français, créole

Points d'intérêt : la bibliothèque Schœlcher, le musée départemental, le fort Saint-Louis, la cathédrale Saint-Louis

Parcs et jardins : la Savane, le Parc floral

Spécialités : crabes farcis, blanc-manger, boudin créole, acras de morue

Événements : Carnaval, le Festival de Fort-de-France, les Tours des yoles rondes de la Martinique

Océan Atlantique

N

Sainte-Marie •

• Saint-Pierre   • La Trinité

Mer des Caraïbes

• Le Robert

Fort-de-France ★   • Le Lamentin

• Le François

Océan Atlantique

MARTINIQUE

• Rivière-Pilote

go.hrw.com

WA3 FORT-DE-FRANCE

VIDEO

CD-ROM 3

DVD 2

La ville de Fort-de-France ▶

Fort-de-France

La ville de Fort-de-France est sur la baie des Flamands, entre les montagnes et la mer des Caraïbes. Presque un tiers de la population martiniquaise habite à Fort-de-France ou dans ses environs. C'est une ville où il y a un mélange de cultures. La Martinique est à 6.817 km (*4,261 miles*) de Paris, mais c'est un département français. L'influence française est évidente. Les bâtiments aux couleurs pastel et les balcons en fer forgé rappellent la Nouvelle-Orléans, mais les sons de la langue créole et de la musique zouk sont purement antillais.

🔗 internet

ADRESSE: go.hrw.com
MOT-CLE:
    WA3 FORT-DE-FRANCE

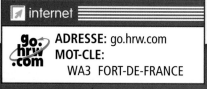

1 **La Savane**
C'est un magnifique parc plein d'arbres tropicaux, de fontaines, de bancs et de jardins. On y va pour rencontrer ses amis, se promener ou jouer au football.

2 **La bibliothèque Schœlcher**
C'est un bâtiment de styles divers (byzantin, égyptien et roman). Comme la tour Eiffel, elle a été construite pour l'Exposition universelle de 1889. Plus tard, on l'a démontée et reconstruite à Fort-de-France.

3 **Le clocher de la cathédrale Saint-Louis**
Il domine le centre-ville de Fort-de-France.

4 **Le madras**
La Martinique est connue pour ses tissus colorés qu'on appelle madras.

5 **Le fort Saint-Louis**
Il est construit sur une presqu'île rocheuse. Il domine la ville de Fort-de-France.

Au chapitre 12,

tu vas faire la connaissance de Lucien, de sa famille et de son amie Mireille. Ils vont te faire visiter Fort-de-France, la ville principale de la Martinique. C'est une ville moderne qui conserve ses traditions et l'art de vivre créole. Elle a toutes les caractéristiques d'une ville française, mais située sous le soleil des tropiques.

6 **Au marché**
On peut acheter des fruits et des légumes frais tous les jours. C'est un endroit pittoresque.

Objectives

In this chapter you will review and practice

Première étape

- pointing out places and things

Deuxième étape

- making and responding to requests
- asking for advice and making suggestions

Troisième étape

- asking for and giving directions

 internet

ADRESSE: go.hrw.com
MOT-CLE:
WA3 FORT-DE-FRANCE-12

◀ **Les rues animées de Fort-de-France**

MISE EN TRAIN · *Un petit service*

Stratégie
pour comprendre
What do you think **Un petit service** means? Can you guess what Lucien's mother, father, and sister are asking him to do?

Lucien

Lisette

La mère

Le père

Une voisine

1 **Lucien :** Maman, je vais en ville. J'ai rendez-vous avec Mireille. On va passer la journée à Fort-de-France. Je vais lui faire visiter le fort Saint-Louis.

2 **La mère :** Avant de rentrer, passe au marché et prends de l'ananas, des oranges et des caramboles.

3 **Lisette :** Ah, tu peux rendre ces livres à la bibliothèque aussi, s'il te plaît? Et en échange, tu me prends trois autres livres. Voilà ma carte.

4 **Le père :** Est-ce que tu peux aller à la poste et envoyer ce paquet?
Lucien : Je ne sais pas si je vais avoir le temps.

5   **Lucien :**   Je vais d'abord au fort Saint-Louis, puis je dois aller au marché et ensuite...
      Le père :   C'est important...
      Lucien :   Bon.

6   **Lisette :**   Tu peux passer chez le disquaire? J'ai commandé un disque compact.
      Lucien :   Bien. C'est tout?

7   **La mère :**   Au retour, tu peux aller à la boulangerie? Prends deux baguettes.

8   **Lucien :**   Bon, ça suffit pour aujourd'hui!

9   **Le père :**   Tu vas voir, c'est très intéressant, le fort Saint-Louis.
      Lisette :   Merci, Lucien. C'est sympa.

10   **Une voisine :**   Bonjour. Est-ce que par hasard vous allez en ville aujourd'hui?
       Lucien :   Au secours!

Cahier d'activités, p. 133, Act. 1

1 Tu as compris?

1. What are Lucien's plans for the day?
2. What are Lucien and his family talking about?
3. Is Lucien happy with the situation? Why or why not?
4. What happens at the end?

2 Qui dit quoi?

Lucien

Lisette

M. Lapiquonne

Mme Lapiquonne

1. «Tu peux aller à la boulangerie?»
2. «Tu peux rendre ces livres à la bibliothèque aussi, s'il te plaît?»
3. «Est-ce que tu peux aller à la poste et envoyer ce paquet?»

4. «Tu peux passer chez le disquaire?»
5. «Passe au marché et prends de l'ananas, des oranges et des caramboles.»
6. «C'est très intéressant, le fort Saint-Louis.»

3 Où va-t-il?

Où est-ce que Lucien va aller pour...

1. acheter des caramboles?
2. envoyer le paquet?
3. rendre les livres?

4. acheter le disque compact?
5. acheter des baguettes?

> à la boulangerie
> à la poste   chez le disquaire
> à la bibliothèque   au marché

4 Vrai ou faux?

1. Lucien va acheter des caramboles, des pêches et des pommes.
2. Il va rendre des livres à la bibliothèque.
3. Lucien va à la boulangerie.

4. Lisette lui donne de l'argent pour acheter un livre.
5. Lucien va chez le disquaire pour son père.
6. Il va acheter le journal pour la voisine.

5 Cherche les expressions

According to *Un petit service,* how do you . . .

1. say you're meeting someone?
2. say you don't know if you'll have time?
3. ask someone to do something for you?
4. express your annoyance?
5. call for help?

> Est-ce que tu peux... ?   Au secours!
>
> Ça suffit!   J'ai rendez-vous avec...
>
> Je ne sais pas si je vais avoir le temps.

6 Et maintenant, à toi

Quelles courses est-ce que tu fais pour ta famille et tes amis? Est-ce que tu vas aux mêmes endroits que Lucien?

Vocabulaire

Où est-ce qu'on va pour faire les courses? On peut aller à ces endroits :

CD-ROM 3
DVD 2

à **la boulangerie** pour acheter **des baguettes**

à **la pâtisserie** pour acheter **des pâtisseries**

à **l'épicerie** pour acheter de la confiture

à **la poste** pour acheter **des timbres** et **envoyer des lettres**

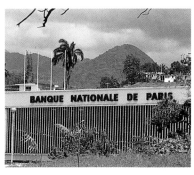

à **la banque** pour **retirer** ou **déposer** de l'argent

à **la librairie-papeterie** pour acheter des livres ou **des enveloppes**

à **la pharmacie** pour acheter **des médicaments**

chez le disquaire pour acheter des disques compacts ou des cassettes

à **la bibliothèque** pour **emprunter** ou **rendre** des livres

Cahier d'activités, pp. 134–135, Act. 2–5

Travaux pratiques de grammaire, pp. 98–99, Act. 1–4

7 Où sont-ils?

Ecoutons Listen to these conversations and tell where the people are.

Tu te rappelles?

Remember, **au, à la, à l'**, and **aux** mean *to the* or *at the*. Use **au** before a masculine singular noun, **à la** before a feminine singular noun, **à l'** before any singular noun beginning with a vowel sound, and **aux** before any plural noun.

Je vais { **au** musée. / **à la** boulangerie. / **à l'** épicerie.

Je vais { **à l'** hôtel. / **aux** Etats-Unis.

Grammaire supplémentaire, p. 376, Act. 1

Travaux pratiques de grammaire, pp. 100–101, Act. 5–8

---

8 Un petit mot

Lisons/Ecrivons Lis ce petit mot que Frédéric a écrit à un ami. Ensuite, fais une liste de trois endroits où Frédéric est allé et explique ce qu'il y a fait.

> Cher Pierre,
>
> Ici, rien de bien nouveau. Hier, mes parents sont allés passer la journée chez leurs amis, alors j'étais tout seul. J'en ai profité pour faire des courses. D'abord, je suis allé à la boulangerie acheter du pain. Ensuite, je suis allé à la poste parce que je n'avais plus de timbres, et j'en ai profité pour envoyer une lettre à Jules, mon correspondant québécois. Puis, je suis allé à la bibliothèque emprunter quelques livres parce que j'ai fini de lire toute ma collection. Je n'ai pas trouvé le dernier livre de Stephen King à la bibliothèque (il paraît qu'il est super!), alors je suis allé à la librairie pour l'acheter. Finalement, je suis passé à l'épicerie acheter des légumes et du fromage pour mon déjeuner. Voilà, c'est tout. Ecris-moi vite pour me dire comment tu trouves ton nouveau lycée. Salut.
>
> Frédéric

---

9 Des courses en ville

Lisons Yvette fait des courses en ville. Où est-elle?

1. «Je voudrais ce gâteau au chocolat, s'il vous plaît.»

2. «Je voudrais emprunter ces trois livres, s'il vous plaît.»

3. «Eh bien, je voudrais des médicaments pour ma mère.»

4. «C'est combien pour envoyer cette lettre aux Etats-Unis?»

5. «Zut, alors! Elle est fermée. Je ne peux pas déposer de l'argent!»

Note culturelle

Stores in France and Martinique don't stay open 24 hours a day. Between 12:30 P.M. and 3:30 P.M., very few small businesses are open; however, they usually remain open until 7:00 P.M. By law, businesses must close one day a week, usually Sunday. Only grocery stores, restaurants, and certain places related to culture and entertainment, such as museums and movie theaters, may stay open on Sunday.

---

10 **Il va où?**

a. **Lisons** Regarde la liste d'Armand. Où va-t-il?

b. **Lisons** Qu'est-ce qu'il peut acheter d'autre là où il va?

- classeurs
- gomme
- enveloppes
- CD
- livre
- aspirine
- timbres
- œufs
- tarte
- baguettes

You've already learned that an ending can often help you guess the gender of a word. An ending can also help you guess the meaning of a word. For example, the ending **-erie** often indicates a place where something is sold or made. Look at these words: **poissonnerie, fromagerie, chocolaterie, croissanterie.** What do you think they mean? Another common ending that carries a particular meaning is **-eur (-euse).** It indicates a person who performs a certain activity. In French, **chasser** means *to hunt.* A person who hunts is a **chasseur.** Since **chanter** means *to sing,* how do you think you would say *singer* in French? If **danser** means *to dance,* how would you say *dancer?**

11 **Devine!**

Parlons Pense à une chose que tu as achetée. Puis dis à ton/ta camarade où tu l'as achetée. Ton/Ta partenaire va essayer de deviner de quoi tu parles. Ensuite, changez de rôle.

Si tu as oublié
le passé composé
va à la page 271.

Grammaire supplémentaire,
pp. 376–377, Act. 2–3

EXEMPLE — **Je suis allé(e) à la boulangerie.**

— **Tu as acheté des croissants?**

— **Non.**

Comment dit-on...?

Pointing out places and things

Voici tes timbres.
Regarde, voilà ma maison.
Look, here/there is/are . . .

Ça, c'est la banque.
This/That is . . .

Là, c'est mon disquaire préféré.
There, that is . . .

Là, tu vois, c'est la maison de mes grands-parents.
There, you see, this/that is . . .

Cahier d'activités, p. 136, Act. 8

VOILÀ LA MAISON DE MES GRANDS-PARENTS.

*chanteur(euse), danseur(euse)

12 A la Martinique

Parlons Tu as pris les photos suivantes pendant ton voyage à la Martinique. Avec un(e) camarade, dites ce qu'il y a sur les photos.

le disquaire	la statue de Joséphine de Beauharnais
la pharmacie	la boulangerie
la bibliothèque Schœlcher	le marché

1.

2.

3.

4.

5.

6.

A la française

When you try to communicate in a foreign language, there will always be times when you can't remember or don't know the exact word you need. One way to get around this problem is to use *circumlocution*. Circumlocution means substituting words and expressions you <u>do</u> know to explain what you mean. For example, if you can't think of the French word for *pharmacy*, you might say **l'endroit où on peut acheter des médicaments** *(the place where you can buy medicine)*. Other expressions you can use are **la personne qui/que** *(the person who/whom)*, and **le truc qui/que** *(the thing that)*.

Cahier d'activités, p. 135, Act. 6

13 Mon quartier

Ecrivons Un(e) élève francophone va habiter avec ta famille pendant un semestre. Fais un plan de ton quartier et marque où se trouvent ton école, la poste, le supermarché, etc...

14 Jeu de rôle

Parlons L'élève francophone (ton/ta camarade) te demande où se trouvent plusieurs endroits. Montre-les sur le plan de l'activité 13. Explique ce qu'on y achète ou ce qu'on y fait. Ensuite, changez de rôle.

Rencontre culturelle

Look at the illustrations below. Where are these people? What are they talking about?

— **Et votre père, il va bien?**
— **Oui, merci. Il va beaucoup mieux depuis...**

— **Bonjour, Madame Perrot. Vous avez passé de bonnes vacances?**
— **Très bonnes. On est allés à la Guadeloupe. Vous savez, ma sœur habite là-bas, et...**

— **Qu'est-ce que vous allez faire avec ça?**
— **Ma voisine m'a donné une très bonne recette. C'est très simple. Tout ce qu'il faut faire, c'est...**

Qu'en penses-tu?

1. What are the topics of these conversations? What does this tell you about the culture of Martinique?
2. What kind of relationships do you or your family have with the people who work in your town? Do you know them? Do you often make "small talk" with them?

Savais-tu que... ?

In Martinique, as in many parts of France, people like to take the time to say hello, ask how others are doing, and find out what's going on in one another's lives. Of course, the smaller the town, the more likely this is to occur. While it may be frustrating to Americans in a hurry, especially when they are conducting business, in West Indian culture it is considered rude not to take a few minutes to engage in some polite conversation before talking business.

Comment dit-on...?

Making and responding to requests

CD-ROM 3
DVD 2

TU PEUX ALLER A L'EPICERIE POUR ACHETER DU JAMBON?

DIS, EST-CE QUE TU PEUX ALLER A LA POSTE POUR MOI?

To make a request:

(Est-ce que) tu peux aller au marché?
Tu me rapportes des timbres?
Tu pourrais passer à la poste acheter des timbres?
> *Could you go by . . . ?*

To accept requests:

D'accord.
Je veux bien.
J'y vais tout de suite.
Si tu veux. *If you want.*

Cahier d'activités, p. 137, Act. 9–11

To decline requests:

Je ne peux pas maintenant.
Je suis désolé(e), mais je n'ai pas le temps.

Tu te rappelles?

Use the partitive articles **du, de la,** and **de l'** when you mean some of an item. If you mean a whole item instead of a part of it, use the indefinite articles **un, une,** and **des. Du, de la, de l', des, un,** and **une** usually become **de/d'** in negative sentences.

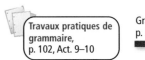

Travaux pratiques de grammaire, p. 102, Act. 9–10

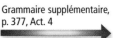

Grammaire supplémentaire, p. 377, Act. 4

15 **Est-ce que tu peux...?**

Ecoutons Listen to the following conversations and decide if the person agrees to or refuses the request.

16 Un petit service

Parlons Qu'est-ce que ces jeunes te disent pour te demander un service?

1.

2.

3.

4.

17 Il me faut...

Parlons Décide de quels articles tu as besoin et demande à ton/ta camarade d'aller les acheter au magasin approprié. Il/Elle va accepter ou refuser d'y aller. Ensuite, changez de rôle.

Si tu as oublié
expressing need
va à la page 238.

Grammaire supplémentaire, p. 377, Act. 5 →

1.

2.

3.

4.

5.

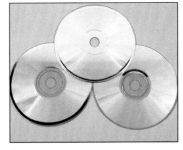
6.

18 Tu pourrais me rendre un service?

Parlons Demande à tes camarades de te rendre les services suivants. Ils vont accepter ou refuser et te donner une raison.

aller chercher un livre à la bibliothèque

acheter un dictionnaire de français à la librairie

acheter un CD chez le disquaire

acheter un sandwich au fast-food

acheter une règle à la papeterie

acheter des timbres à la poste

Si tu as oublié
making an excuse
va à la page 145.

Asking for advice and making suggestions

To ask for advice on how to get somewhere:

Comment est-ce qu'on y va?
How can we get there?

To suggest how to get somewhere:

On peut y aller en train.
We can go . . .
On peut prendre le bus.
We can take . . .

Vocabulaire

Comment est-ce qu'on y va?

CD-ROM**3**
DVD**2**

en bus (m.)

à pied (m.)

à vélo (m.)

en voiture (f.)

en taxi (m.)

en bateau (m.)

en avion (m.)

en train (m.)

en métro (m.)

Travaux pratiques de grammaire,
pp. 103–104, Act. 11–15

Cahier d'activités,
p. 138, Act. 12–14

19 On y va comment?

Ecoutons Listen to these conversations. Where are these people going and how are they going to get there?

20 Comment vont-ils voyager?

Parlons Dis comment ces gens voyagent.

1.   2.   3.   4.

Grammaire

The pronoun *y*

You've already seen the pronoun **y** *(there)* several times. Can you figure out how to use it?

—Je vais **à la bibliothèque.** Tu **y** vas aussi?
—Non, je n'**y** vais pas.
—Je vais **chez le disquaire.** Tu veux **y** aller?
—Non, j'**y** suis allé hier.

It can replace an entire phrase meaning *to, at,* or *in* any place that has already been mentioned. Place it before the conjugated verb, or, if there is an infinitive, place **y** before the infinitive: Je vais **y** aller demain.

Grammaire supplémentaire, p. 378, Act. 6–8

Cahier d'activités, p. 139, Act. 15–16

Travaux pratiques de grammaire, p. 105, Act. 16–17

21 Grammaire en contexte

Parlons Comment est-ce que tes amis et toi, vous allez aux endroits suivants?

EXEMPLE   **Au cinéma? Nous y allons en bus.**

au cinéma   au supermarché   à la poste
                                                à la bibliothèque
   à la piscine   au centre commercial
                                             au stade
   au parc   à la librairie   au lycée
                                       au concert

22 Qu'est-ce qu'on fait vendredi soir?

Parlons Tu téléphones à un(e) ami(e) pour l'inviter à sortir vendredi soir. Décidez où vous voulez aller et dites comment vous allez y aller.

Si tu as oublié *inviting* va à la page 179.

DEUXIEME ETAPE   *trois cent soixante-sept*   367

Qu'est-ce qu'il faut faire pour avoir un permis de conduire?

Here's what some francophone people told us about obtaining a driver's license where they live.

Emmanuel,
France

Lily-Christine,
Québec

«J'ai mon permis probatoire, temporaire. Je n'ai pas encore mon permis de conduire. Premièrement, pour avoir ton permis, tu suis les cours théoriques. Après ça, tu passes ton examen. Si tu passes l'examen, tu as ton permis temporaire. Après, tu suis des cours pratiques. Tu passes un examen sur route. Et puis, si tu as l'examen sur route, eh bien, tu as ton permis.»

«Non, je n'ai pas encore de permis de conduire parce que je n'ai pas encore 16 ans. Je l'aurai peut-être, [mon] permis accompagné, à 16 ans. Autrement, [pour avoir] un permis de conduire normal, il faut attendre 18 ans en France. Pour avoir un permis de conduire, il faut passer le code. C'est un examen, quoi, c'est le code de la route. Et [il] faut passer la conduite. On est avec un moniteur. On doit faire un trajet qu'il nous indique et puis, suivant si on le fait bien ou pas, on a notre permis.»

Charlotte,
France

«Il faut sans doute bien savoir ses signes, son code de la route. [Il ne faut] pas avoir la tête ailleurs souvent, enfin... [Il] faut être bien dans sa tête. Voilà.»

Qu'en penses-tu?

1. Are the requirements for a driver's license that these people mention the same as those in your state?

2. What means of public transportation are available in your area? Do you use them? Why or why not?

3. How does transportation influence your lifestyle? How would your lifestyle change if you lived where these people do?

Vocabulaire

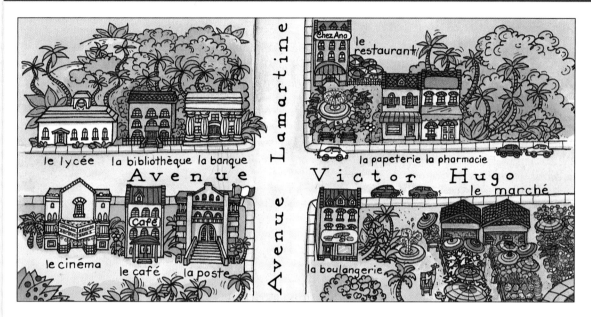

le lycée la bibliothèque la banque

Avenue

le cinéma le café la poste

Avenue Lamartine

Chez Ana le restaurant

la papeterie la pharmacie

Victor Hugo le marché

la boulangerie

La bibliothèque est **entre** le lycée et la banque.
La poste est **à droite du** café.
Le cinéma est **à gauche du** café.

Here are some other prepositions you may want to use to give directions:

à côté de	*next to*	**loin de**	*far from*
devant	*in front of*	**près de**	*near*
derrière	*behind*		

La boulangerie est **au coin de** la rue.
Le café est **en face de** la bibliothèque.

Cahier d'activités,
p. 140, Act. 18–20

Travaux pratiques de grammaire,
pp. 106–107, Act. 19–21

Note de grammaire

The preposition **de** usually means *of* or *from*.

• When you use **de** before **le** or **les,** make the following contractions:

de + le = du   C'est près **du** musée.

de + les = des   La ville est près **des** Alpes.

• **De** doesn't change before **l'** or **la:**

C'est au coin **de la** rue.

La poste est à côté **de l'**école.

Cahier d'activités,
p. 141, Act. 21

Grammaire supplémentaire,
p. 379, Act. 9–10

Travaux pratiques de grammaire, p. 106, Act. 18

23 Vrai ou faux?

Ecoutons Listen to the following statements and tell whether they are true or false, according to the **Vocabulaire**.

24 Qui est-ce?

Parlons Explique où un(e) camarade est assis(e) en classe. Les autres élèves de ton groupe vont essayer de deviner de qui tu parles.

EXEMPLE   Cette personne est derrière David est à côté d'Isabelle.

25 **Il est perdu!**

Parlons Ton ami Hervé n'a pas le sens de l'orientation. Tout ce qu'il décrit est dans la direction opposée de ce qu'il pense. Réponds aux questions d'Hervé pour l'aider.

EXEMPLE —La poste est loin de la bibliothèque?

—Mais non, elle est près de la bibliothèque.

1. Est-ce que la papeterie est près de la pharmacie?

2. Le cinéma est devant le centre commercial?

3. La bibliothèque est à droite?

4. Est-ce que le café est derrière le stade?

Note culturelle

Martinique is an overseas possession of France known as a **département d'outre-mer,** or **DOM.** It has the same administrative status as a department in France, and the people of Martinique, who are citizens of France, have the same rights and responsibilities as other French citizens. Other DOMs include Guadeloupe, French Guiana, and Reunion Island. France also has overseas territories, like New Caledonia and French Polynesia. These territories are called **territoires d'outre-mer,** or **TOMs.**

26 **La visite d'Arianne**

Ecrivons Arianne a pris des photos pendant sa visite chez son oncle et sa tante. Complète les descriptions des photos avec des prépositions.

1. C'est mon oncle et ma tante dans le jardin _____ leur maison.

2. Là, _____ ma tante, c'est mon cousin Daniel.

3. Et voilà ma cousine Adeline, _____ mon oncle.

4. Il y a une boulangerie _____ leur maison. Les croissants sont délicieux le matin!

5. Leur maison est _____ une autre maison et une épicerie.

6. Il y a un parc au coin de la rue, _____ leur maison.

Asking for and giving directions

To ask for directions:

> **Pardon, madame.** La poste, **s'il vous plaît?**
> **Pardon, mademoiselle. Où est** la banque, **s'il vous plaît?**
> **Pardon, monsieur. Je cherche** le musée, **s'il vous plaît.**
> *Excuse me, sir. I'm looking for . . . , please.*

To give directions:

> **Vous continuez jusqu'au prochain feu rouge.**
> *You keep going until the next light.*
> **Vous allez tout droit jusqu'au** lycée.
> *You go straight ahead until you get to . . .*
> **Vous tournez** à droite.
> *You turn . . .*
> **Prenez la rue** Lamartine, **puis traversez la rue** Isambert.
> *Take . . . Street, then cross . . . Street.*
> **Vous passez** devant la boulangerie.
> *You'll pass . . .*
> **C'est tout de suite à** gauche.
> *It's right there on the . . .*

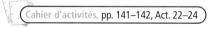

Cahier d'activités, pp. 141–142, Act. 22–24

27 **Pardon, je cherche...**

Ecoutons Guy is at the bus station (**la gare routière**) in Fort-de-France. Follow M. Robinet's directions, using the map on page 372. Where does Guy want to go?

Note culturelle

In many French towns, intersections have a traffic circle (**un rond-point**) at the center, which is often decorated with flowers, fountains, or statues. Vehicles enter and continue around the center island, turning off at the various streets that open into the circle. Most towns have at least one public square, often located in front of a public building or a church. Numerous cities have closed off some of the tiny streets in the **centre-ville** and made pedestrian areas where people can stroll freely, without having to worry about traffic.

28 **Où est-ce?**

Parlons Explique à ton/ta camarade comment aller de l'école à ton restaurant favori ou à ton magasin de disques préféré. Ton/Ta camarade va essayer de deviner le nom de l'endroit. Ensuite, changez de rôle.

29 Quel monument est-ce?

Lisons Ton/ta correspondant(e) martiniquais(e) te conseille certains endroits à visiter. Il/Elle te dit comment y aller. Suis ses explications sur le plan de Fort-de-France et dis de quel endroit il/elle parle.

la bibliothèque Schœlcher

la cathédrale Saint-Louis

Quand tu sors de la gare routière, va à droite sur le boulevard du Général de Gaulle. Prends la première à droite — c'est la rue Félix Eboué — et continue tout droit. Tu vas passer devant la préfecture. Traverse l'avenue des Caraïbes et va tout droit dans la rue de la Liberté jusqu'à la poste. Ensuite, tourne à droite rue Blénac et continue tout droit. Ça sera à droite, tout de suite après la rue Schœlcher.

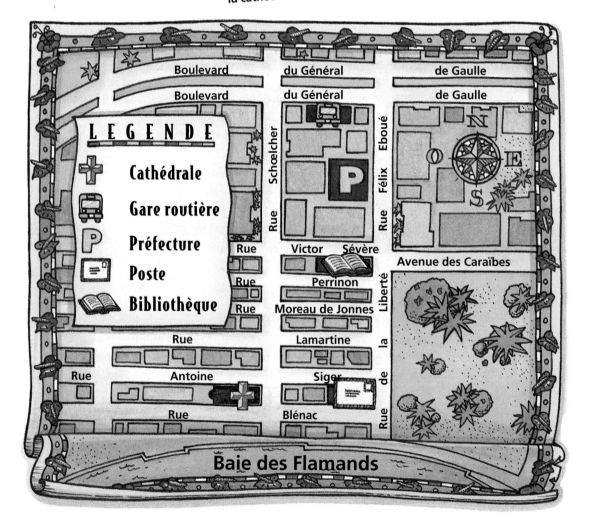

30

De l'école au travail

Parlons Imagine que tu travailles comme hôte ou comme hôtesse dans le restaurant Chez Ana. Le restaurant est situé dans un quartier très touristique et beaucoup de touristes te demandent des renseignements. Crée une conversation avec ton/ta camarade qui va te demander comment trouver deux endroits en ville. Utilise le plan à la page 369 pour expliquer comment on va à ces deux endroits, puis changez de rôle.

PRONONCIATION

Do you remember what you've learned about French pronunciation? Here is a quick pronunciation review. If you've forgotten how to produce any of these sounds, check the Pronunciation Index at the back of the book and go back to the chapters where they were introduced. Repeat these words.

[y]	du	étude	[u]	rouge	voudrais
[o]	escargots	gâteau	[ɔ]	pomme	carottes
[ø]	veut	heureux	[œ]	sœur	beurre
[e]	cinéma	trouver	[ɛ]	frère	anglaise
[ã]	anglais	il prend	[ɔ̃]	allons	poisson
[ɛ̃]	quinze	pain	[œ̃]	lundi	emprunter
[j]	papier	viande	[w]	moi	pouvoir
[ɥ]	lui	ensuite	[t]	maths	théâtre
[r]	très	roux	[ʃ]	chat	chercher
[']	le héros	le hockey	[ɲ]	montagne	Allemagne

A. A prononcer

Repeat the following words.

1. nourriture   boutique   bateau   poste
2. feu   déposer   près   derrière
3. devant   avion   timbre   emprunter
4. pied   voiture   envoyer   tout de suite
5. rue   gauche   prochain   bibliothèque

B. A lire

Take turns with a partner reading each of the following sentences aloud.

1. Quand le chat n'est pas là, les souris dansent.
2. Il est mieux de travailler que de s'amuser.
3. Beaucoup de bruit pour rien.
4. Un poisson n'est jamais trop petit pour être frit.
5. On n'attrape pas les mouches avec du vinaigre.

C. A écrire

You're going to hear a short dialogue. Write down what you hear.

Cheval de bois

A. Regarde le titre et les illustrations qui accompagnent le texte. Quel est le sujet de l'histoire? Où se passe l'histoire?

B. Scan the story to see if you can find the answers to these questions.

1. Who are the main characters in the story?
2. What is going on when the story starts?
3. Why does Congo come to help the horse?
4. How does Congo help the horse?

C. Lis l'histoire et ensuite mets ces événements dans le bon ordre.

1. Congo burns the blue horse.
2. A child is frightened by the blue horse.
3. Congo first comes to see the blue horse.
4. M. Quinquina and his sons play music.
5. The blue bird is freed.
6. The mayor goes to see Congo.

Cheval de bois

Cette année, la ville de Saint-Pierre accueille le manège de la famille Quinquina pour sa fête patronale. Le manège s'est installé sur la place du marché, face à la mer. Madame Quinquina tient une buvette où elle sert des limonades multicolores.

Monsieur Quinquina et ses deux fils jouent de la flûte de bambou et du "ti-bwa". Au rythme de cette musique, le manège de chevaux de bois, poussé par de robustes jeunes gens, tourne, tourne, tourne.

Cheval bleu, bleu comme l'océan.
Cheval noir, noir comme la nuit.
Cheval blanc, blanc comme les nuages.
Cheval vert, vert comme les bambous.
Cheval rouge, rouge comme le flamboyant.
Cheval jaune, jaune comme l'allamanda.

Les chevaux de bois tournent, tournent et, sur leur dos, tous les enfants sont heureux.

Mais quand la nuit parfumée caresse l'île, les chevaux de bois rêvent. Le cheval bleu, bleu comme l'océan, rêve de partir, partir loin, visiter les îles, visiter le monde. Il a entendu dire que la terre est ronde. Vrai ou faux? Il aimerait bien savoir ! Cela fait si longtemps qu'il porte ce rêve dans sa carcasse de bois que cette nuit-là, son rêve devient oiseau. L'oiseau bat des ailes dans le corps du cheval bleu, bleu comme l'océan.

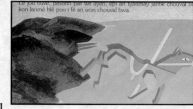

Au matin, un enfant monte sur le cheval bleu. Tout à coup, il commence à hurler :
— Maman, maman, il y a une bête dans le cheval. J'ai peur! Je veux descendre.

On arrête la musique, on arrête le manège. C'est un tollé général : les mères rassemblent leurs enfants. En quelques secondes, la place est vide. Le maire et ses conseillers décident d'aller chercher le sage Congo.

...Congo s'approche du manège et caresse les flancs du cheval bleu, bleu comme l'océan :
— Je vais te délivrer ! cheval bleu, bleu comme l'océan, car ton rêve est vivant, il s'est métamorphosé en oiseau.

Congo s'assied près du cheval bleu, bleu comme l'océan. Quand le maire voit Congo tranquillement assis, il sort de la mairie en courant et hurle :

— Que faites-vous?
— J'attends, dit doucement Congo.
— Vous attendez quoi? demande le maire.
— J'attends que la nuit mette son manteau étoilé et ouvre son œil d'or. Je ferai alors un grand feu.

Quand la nuit met son manteau étoilé et ouvre son œil d'or, Congo prend tendrement dans ses bras le cheval bleu, bleu comme l'océan, et le

dépose dans les flammes. Le feu crépite, chante, et l'or des flammes devient bleu, bleu comme l'océan. Les habitants de Saint-Pierre voient un immense oiseau bleu, bleu comme l'océan, s'élever dans la nuit étoilée et s'envoler vers l'horizon.
Congo, heureux, murmure :
-Bon vent, oiseau-rêve !

RAPPEL As you read the story, you probably came across some unfamiliar words. Remember, you don't have to understand every word to get a sense of what you're reading. If you decide that the meaning of a particular word is necessary to help you understand the story, there are two techniques you've learned that can help: using the context to figure out the meaning of the word, and trying to see a cognate in the word.

D. Below are some cognates that appear in *Cheval de bois*. See if you can match them with their English equivalents.

1. habitants	a. counselors
2. fête	b. to descend; to get down
3. flammes	c. island
4. conseillers	d. festival
5. île	e. flames
6. descendre	f. inhabitants, people who live in a certain area

E. Make a list of all of the other cognates you can find in *Cheval de bois.* You should be able to find at least six more. Watch out for false cognates!

F. How can you tell this story was written for a young audience?

G. What stories, fairy tales, or myths have you read or heard that are similar to this story? In what ways are they similar? In what ways are they different?

H. Do you think there really was a bird inside the horse? What do you think the bird represents?

I. Compose a fairy tale of your own. Write it out or record it in French. Keep it simple so that your teacher can use it in the future with students who are beginning to learn French! Illustrate your story to make it easier to understand.

Cahier d'activités, p. 143, Act. 25

trois cent soixante-quinze **375**

Première étape Objective Pointing out places and things

1 Ecris cinq phrases pour dire où ces gens vont aller pour trouver ce qu'ils veulent. Pour chaque phrase, utilise le présent d'**aller** et un des mot proposés. (**pp. 174, 177, 360**)

la boulangerie	la banque	la papeterie
la poste	l'épicerie	le marché	la pharmacie

EXEMPLE   J'ai besoin de pain. **Je vais à la boulangerie.**

1. Il me faut des feuilles de papier et des gommes.
2. Tu as besoin de retirer de l'argent.
3. Il vous faut des timbres.
4. Mme Bonjean a besoin de farine et de beurre.
5. Pierre et moi, nous avons besoin de médicaments.

2 Tu demandes à tes amis ce qu'ils ont fait pendant le week-end. Regarde les photos et écris leurs réponses au passé composé. (**pp. 271, 361**)

1. Hélène, qu'est-ce que tu as fait pendant le week-end?

   J'...

2. Sandra et Pamela, vous avez passé un bon week-end?

   Oui, nous...

3. Tu as passé un bon week-end, Martin?

   Oui, j'...

4. Ahmed, tu as passé un bon week-end?

   Oui, j'...

3 Delphine te raconte ses vacances à la Martinique. Complète les phrases avec les verbes indiqués au passé composé. (**pp. 271, 272, 277, 361**)

C'était chouette, mes vacances à la Martinique! Je n'ai pas reconnu mes cousins, ils
____1____ (beaucoup grandir)! Le premier jour, nous ____2____ (dîner) chez ma tante
Liliane. On ____3____ (parler) et on ____4____ (regarder) des photos après le dîner. La
première nuit, je/j' ____5____ (dormir) longtemps. Le deuxième jour, nous ____6____ (faire)
de la plongée. C'était magnifique! Malheureusement, je/j' ____7____ (perdre) mon
appareil-photo et je/j' ____8____ (ne pas prendre) de photos. Après, nous ____9____ (visiter)
la cathédrale Saint-Louis et la bibliothèque Schœlcher. Le dernier jour, nous ____10____
(faire) un tour en bateau. Et après, nous ____11____ (faire) des achats en ville où je/j'
____12____ (acheter) un disque de musique zouk pour toi.

Deuxième étape

Objectives **Making and responding to requests; asking for advice and making suggestions**

4 Récris les phrases suivantes. Remplace les quantités précises par les articles appropriés **du, de la, de l'**, ou **des**. (**pp. 236, 364**)

EXEMPLE   Tu pourrais me rapporter une bouteille de lait?
Tu pourrais me rapporter du lait?

1. Tu me rapportes un kilo de farine, s'il te plaît?
2. Tu me prends un paquet de beurre, s'il te plaît?
3. Tu m'achètes une livre de carottes?
4. Rapporte-moi trois tranches de jambon, s'il te plaît!
5. Tu me rapportes deux bouteilles d'eau minérale?
6. Tu pourrais m'acheter dix enveloppes et vingt timbres, s'il te plaît?
7. Tu peux m'acheter deux baguettes et cinq pâtisseries?
8. Tu peux aller à la poste et envoyer deux paquets pour moi?

5 Chaque personne a besoin de quelque chose. Ecris des phrases en utilisant **J'ai besoin de...** ou **Il me faut...**, pour dire ce qu'il leur faut. (**pp. 238, 365**)

1. Tu pourrais passer à la pharmacie?
2. Est-ce que tu peux aller à la boulangerie, s'il te plaît?
3. Est-ce que tu peux aller chez le disquaire?
4. Tu peux passer à la bibliothèque, s'il te plaît?
5. Tu pourrais aller à la librairie-papeterie, s'il te plaît?

6 Tu demandes à tes amis comment ils vont aller aux endroits suivants. Utilise le pronom **y** pour écrire leurs réponses. (**p. 367**)

    EXEMPLE   Philippe, comment est-ce que tu vas aux Etats-Unis? (en avion)
            J'y vais en avion.

1. Mohammed et Yasmina, comment est-ce que vous allez au bord de la mer? (en train)
2. Azzedine, comment tu vas à la campagne? (à vélo)
3. Comment est-ce que Fatima va en Angleterre? (en bateau)
4. Hannah et Raphaël, comment vous allez à la montagne? (en bus)
5. Aziz, comment est-ce que tu vas à Paris? (en voiture)
6. Comment est-ce qu'on va à la plage? (à pied)
7. Michel, quand tu vas à New York, comment est-ce que tu vas aux musées? (en taxi)
8. Agathe, quand tu vas à Paris avec ta mère, comment est-ce que vous allez de l'aéroport à l'hôtel? (en métro)

7 Récris les phrases suivantes en utilisant le pronom **y.** (**p. 367**)

1. Je vais passer à la boulangerie pour acheter des croissants.
2. Elle a rendu mes livres à la bibliothèque hier.
3. Nous avons acheté de l'aspirine à la pharmacie.
4. Ma mère a acheté des pâtisseries à la pâtisserie.
5. Nous allons à la banque pour retirer de l'argent.
6. On trouve de la musique zouk chez le disquaire Hit-Parade.

8 Complète les conversations suivantes avec **y** et la forme correcte du verbe entre parenthèses. Attention! Certains verbes vont être au présent et d'autres vont être au passé composé. (**p. 367**)

—Salut, Michèle, tu vas à la bibliothèque?

—Oui, je/j' ___1___ (y/aller) cet aprèm. J'ai des livres à rendre. Tu ___2___ (vouloir) venir?

—Oui, je veux bien. On ___3___ (y/aller) à quelle heure?

—Dis, Florence, c'est vrai que tu ___4___ (trouver) un billet de cent euros devant la banque?

—Pas tout à fait. Je/J' ___5___ (y/trouver) une pièce de cinq euros.

—Tu ___6___ (avoir) de la chance, quand même!

—Tu ___7___ (pouvoir) me rendre un service, ma chérie!

—Oui, Maman.

—Je/J' ___8___ (avoir) besoin de bananes et de citrons. Tu ___9___ (pouvoir) aller au marché, s'il te plaît?

—Au marché? C'est loin! Comment est-ce que je/j' ___10___ (y/aller)? A pied?

—Mais non. Pourquoi tu ne/n' ___11___ (y/aller) pas à vélo?

—Bonne idée. Je ___12___ (partir) tout de suite.

9   Unscramble the following location words. Then, combine the fragments to create five sentences telling where the places are located. Use the places in the order in which they are given. (**p. 369**)

     EXEMPLE   EN CEFA ED/l'école/le café   **L'école est en face du café.**

    1. REDEIRER/la poste/le stade

    2. ED TOIRDE A/la pharmacie/la boulangerie

    3. SERP ED/l'épicerie/le cinéma

    4. CHUGEA ED A/la pâtisserie/la bibliothèque

    5. ED NOIL/la banque/la papeterie

10   Complète les phrases suivantes. (**p. 369**)

     EXEMPLE   La poste est à droite **du** café.

    1. Le lycée est en face _____ cinéma.

    2. Le marché est loin _____ lycée.

    3. La pharmacie est à côté _____ arbres.

    4. Le café est entre _____ poste et _____ cinéma.

    5. La boulangerie est au coin _____ rue.

    6. Le lycée est à gauche _____ bibliothèque.

1 You're planning a trip to Martinique and you'll need some transportation. Look at these ads. What kinds of transportation are available?

LOCATION TROIS-ILETS
Anse à l'Ane - 97229 Trois-Ilets

68.40.37
Lundi à Vendredi
8 H - 13 H
et 15 H - 18 H
Week-end :
à la demande

Avec Location TROIS-ILETS, la moto que vous avez louée par téléphone, 48 heures plus tôt, vient à vous. Chez vous. Si vous vous trouvez dans la commune des Trois-Ilets. Location possible pour une semaine au moins.

TAXI
FORT-DE-FRANCE
102 Rue de la République -
97200 Fort-de-France

70.44.08 Tous les jours : 5 H - 20 H

Nos taxis répondent sans délais quand vous téléphonez à Taxi Fort-de-France. Déplacement dans toute l'île.

LOCA CENTER
3 Km Route de Schœlcher n. 63 -
97233 Schœlcher

Livraison de voiture (Opel Corsa, Peugeot 106) à domicile (Nord Caraïbe, Schœlcher, Fort-de-France) pour une durée minimum de trois jours. Pas de frais de déplacement. Pendant la haute saison, pour une location de 10 jours au moins, réserver un mois à l'avance. Pour une location d'une durée de 3 à 7 jours, réserver 48 heures à l'avance. Pendant la basse saison, réserver la veille ou le jour même.

61.05.95
61.40.12
Lundi à Vendredi
7 H 30 -
16 H 30
Week-end :
à la demande

---

1. Where can you call if you want a taxi? When is the latest you can call?

2. Where can you call if you want to rent a Peugeot? What about a motorcycle?

3. What's the minimum length of time you can rent these vehicles?

4. How far in advance do you need to make a reservation?

5. Are these places open on weekends?

2 Listen to Didier tell his family about his trip to Martinique. Put the pictures in order according to Didier's description.

a.

b.

c.

d.

③ Ecrivons!

Write a logical conversation to accompany the picture below.

Prewriting

To help form your writing plan, look at the illustration and jot down ideas that immediately come to mind. You might imagine the situation, names for the people, and things they might be saying. Think about the types of vocabulary and structures you will need.

Stratégie pour écrire

Making a writing plan before you begin is important. Study the illustration carefully. Do you know all the vocabulary you'll need? Will you need to use certain verbs or structures frequently? You might want to use your textbook as a reference.

Writing

Now, using the notes you created in your writing plan, create the conversation that goes with the picture. Keep in mind expressions you've learned, such as asking for and giving directions, and vocabulary for telling where something is located.

Revising

When you've completed your writing, set it aside for a while before you do your self-evaluation. This will give you a fresh perspective on how to make it better. Also, when you evaluate what you've written, focus on only one area at a time. For example, don't look for spelling and punctuation mistakes while you're checking to see how well your writing flows. Focus on finding such mistakes when you proofread.

After you've revised your work, let a classmate give you feedback. Then, you can concentrate on making any other necessary revisions.

④ Jeu de rôle

While visiting Fort-de-France, you stop and mail some postcards at the post office. You ask the employee for directions to two places in town: the library and the cathedral. Using the map on page 372, the employee gives you directions from the post office to each of these places. Be sure to ask questions if something is not clear. Then, ask the employee what means of transportation you should use to get to these places.

Can you use what you've learned in this chapter?

Can you point out places and things?
p. 361

1 How would you point out and identify . . .
1. a certain building?
2. a certain store?
3. a certain person?

Can you make and respond to requests?
p. 364

2 How would you ask someone to . . .
1. buy some stamps?
2. go to the bookstore?
3. deposit some money?

3 How would you agree to do the favors you asked in number 2? How would you refuse?

Can you ask for advice and make suggestions?
p. 366

4 How would you ask a friend what means of transportation you should use to get to a certain store?

5 How would you suggest these means of transportation?

1.

3.

2.

4.

Can you ask for and give directions?
p. 371

6 How would you tell someone that you're looking for a certain place?

7 How would you ask someone where a certain place in town is?

8 How would you give someone directions to your house from . . .
1. your school?
2. your favorite restaurant?

Première étape

Pointing out places and things

Voici...	Here is/are . . .
Regarde, voilà...	Look, here/there is/are . . .
Ça, c'est...	This/That is . . .
Là, c'est...	There, that is . . .
Là, tu vois, c'est...	There, you see, this/that is . . .
un endroit	place
chez	at (at the place of) . . .

Buildings

la banque	bank
la boulangerie	bakery
le disquaire	record store
l'épicerie (f.)	small grocery store
la librairie	bookstore
la papeterie	stationery store
la pâtisserie	pastry shop
la pharmacie	drugstore
la poste	post office

Things to do or buy in town

envoyer des lettres	to send letters
une baguette	long, thin loaf of bread
un timbre	stamp
retirer de l'argent (m.)	to withdraw money
déposer de l'argent	to deposit money
rendre	to return something
emprunter	to borrow
des médicaments (m.)	medicine
une enveloppe	envelope
une pâtisserie	pastry

Deuxième étape

Making and responding to requests

Tu peux... ?	Can you . . . ?
Tu me rapportes... ?	Will you bring me . . . ?
Tu pourrais passer à... ?	Could you go by . . . ?
D'accord.	OK.
Je veux bien.	Gladly.
J'y vais tout de suite.	I'll go right away.
Si tu veux.	If you want.
Je ne peux pas maintenant.	I can't right now.
Je suis désolé(e), mais je n'ai pas le temps.	I'm sorry, but I don't have time.

Asking for advice and making suggestions

Comment est-ce qu'on y va?	How can we get there?
On peut y aller...	We can go . . .
On peut prendre...	We can take . . .
y	there

Means of transportation

en bus (m.)	by bus
à pied (m.)	on foot
à vélo (m.)	by bike
en voiture (f.)	by car
en taxi (m.)	by taxi
en bateau (m.)	by boat
en avion (m.)	by plane
en train (m.)	by train
en métro (m.)	by subway

Troisième étape

Asking for and giving directions

Pardon, ..., s'il vous plaît?	Excuse me, . . . please?
Pardon, ... Où est..., s'il vous plaît?	Excuse me, . . . Where is . . . , please?
Pardon, ... Je cherche..., s'il vous plaît.	Excuse me, . . . I'm looking for . . . , please.
Vous continuez jusqu'au prochain feu rouge.	You keep going until the next light.
Vous allez tout droit jusqu'à...	You go straight ahead until you get to . . .
Vous tournez...	You turn . . .
Prenez la rue..., puis traversez la rue...	Take . . . Street, then cross . . . Street.
Vous passez...	You'll pass . . .
C'est tout de suite à...	It's right there on the . . .

Locations

à côté de	next to
loin de	far from
près de	close to
au coin de	on the corner of
en face de	across from
derrière	behind
devant	in front of
entre	between
à droite (de)	to the right (of)
à gauche (de)	to the left (of)

Reference Section

Function is another word for the way in which you use language for a specific purpose. When you find yourself in specific situations, such as in a restaurant, in a grocery store, or at school, you'll want to communicate with those around you. In order to communicate in French, you have to "function" in the language.

Each chapter in this book focuses on language functions. You can easily find them in boxes labeled **Comment dit-on... ?** The other features in the chapter—grammar, vocabulary, culture notes—support the functions you're learning.

Here is a list of functions and the French expressions presented in this book. You'll need them in order to communicate in a wide range of situations. Following each function entry, you will find the chapter and page number where each function is presented.

Socializing

Greeting people **Ch. 1, p. 22**
Bonjour.
Salut.

Saying goodbye **Ch. 1, p. 22**
Salut.   A bientôt.
Au revoir.   A demain.
A tout à l'heure.   Tchao.

Asking how people are and telling how you are **Ch. 1, p. 23**
(Comment) ça va?   Bof.
Ça va.   Pas mal.
Super!   Pas terrible.
Très bien.   Et toi?
Comme ci comme ça.

Expressing and responding to thanks **Ch. 3, p. 90**
Merci.
A votre service.

Extending invitations **Ch. 6, p. 179**
Allons... !
Tu veux... avec moi?
Tu viens?
On peut...

Accepting invitations **Ch. 6, p. 179**
Je veux bien.   D'accord.
Pourquoi pas?   Bonne idée.

Refusing invitations **Ch. 6, p. 179**
Désolé(e), je suis occupé(e).
Ça ne me dit rien.
J'ai des trucs à faire.
Désolé(e), je ne peux pas.

Identifying people **Ch. 7, p. 203**
C'est...
Ce sont...
Voici...
Voilà...

Introducing people **Ch. 7, p. 207**
C'est...
Je te/vous présente...
Très heureux (heureuse). (FORMAL)

Inquiring about past events **Ch. 9, p. 270**
Qu'est-ce que tu as fait... ?
Tu es allé(e) où?
Et après?
Qu'est-ce qui s'est passé?

Relating past events **Ch. 9, p. 270**
D'abord,...
Ensuite,...
Après,...
Je suis allé(e)...
Et après ça,...
Finalement,/Enfin,...

Inquiring about future plans **Ch. 11, p. 329**
Qu'est-ce que tu vas faire... ?
Où est-ce que tu vas aller... ?

Sharing future plans **Ch. 11, p. 329**
J'ai l'intention de...
Je vais...

Seeing someone off **Ch. 11, p. 336**
Bon voyage!
Bonnes vacances!
Amuse-toi bien!
Bonne chance!

Exchanging Information

Asking someone's name and giving yours
Ch. 1, p. 24
> Tu t'appelles comment?
> Je m'appelle...

Asking and giving someone else's name Ch. 1, p. 24
> Il/Elle s'appelle comment?
> Il/Elle s'appelle...

Asking someone's age and giving yours Ch. 1, p. 25
> Tu as quel âge?
> J'ai... ans.

Asking for information Ch. 2, p. 55
> Tu as quels cours... ?
> Tu as quoi... ?
> Vous avez... ?
> Tu as... à quelle heure?

Giving information Ch. 2, p. 55
> Nous avons...
> J'ai...

Telling when you have class Ch. 2, p. 58
> à... heure(s)
> à... heure(s) quinze
> à... heure(s) trente
> à... heure(s) quarante-cinq

Making requests Ch. 3, p. 80
> Tu as... ?
> Vous avez... ?

Responding to requests Ch. 3, p. 80
> Voilà.
> Je regrette.
> Je n'ai pas de...

Asking others what they need and telling what you need Ch. 3, p. 82
> Qu'est-ce qu'il te faut pour... ?
> Qu'est-ce qu'il vous faut pour... ?
> Il me faut...

Expressing need Ch. 8, p. 238; Ch. 10, p. 301
> Qu'est-ce qu'il te faut?
> Il me faut...
> De quoi est-ce que tu as besoin?
> J'ai besoin de...
> Oui, il me faut...
> Oui, vous avez... ?
> Je cherche quelque chose pour...
> J'aimerais... pour aller avec...

Asking for information Ch. 3, p. 90
> C'est combien?

Getting someone's attention
Ch. 3, p. 90; Ch. 5, p. 151
> Pardon...
> Excusez-moi.
> ... , s'il vous plaît.
> Monsieur!
> Madame!
> Mademoiselle!

Exchanging information Ch. 4, p. 116
> Qu'est-ce que tu fais comme sport?
> Qu'est-ce que tu fais pour t'amuser?
> Je fais...
> Je ne fais pas de...
> Je (ne) joue (pas)...

Ordering food and beverages Ch. 5, p. 151
> Vous avez choisi?
> Vous prenez?
> Je voudrais...
> Je vais prendre..., s'il vous plaît.
> ... , s'il vous plaît.
> Donnez-moi... , s'il vous plaît.
> Apportez-moi... , s'il vous plaît.
> Vous avez... ?
> Qu'est-ce que vous avez comme boissons?
> Qu'est-ce qu'il y a à boire?

Paying the check Ch. 5, p. 155
> L'addition, s'il vous plaît.
> Oui, tout de suite.
> Un moment, s'il vous plaît.
> Ça fait combien, s'il vous plaît?
> Ça fait... euros.
> C'est combien, ... ?
> C'est... euros.

Making plans Ch. 6, p. 173
> Qu'est-ce que tu vas faire... ?
> Tu vas faire quoi... ?
> Je vais...
> Pas grand-chose.
> Rien de spécial.

Arranging to meet someone Ch. 6, p. 183
> Quand (ça)?   et quart
> Tout de suite.   moins le quart
> Où (ça)?   moins cinq
> Devant...   midi (et demi)
> Au métro...   minuit (et demi)
> Chez...   Vers...
> Dans...   Quelle heure est-il?
> Avec qui?   Il est...
> A quelle heure?   On se retrouve...
> A cinq heures...   Rendez-vous...
> et demie   Entendu.

Describing and characterizing people
Ch. 7, p. 209
Il est comment?
Elle est comment?
Ils/Elles sont comment?
Il/Elle est...
Ils/Elles sont...
Il/Elle n'est ni... ni...

Making a telephone call Ch. 9, p. 276
Bonjour.
Je suis bien chez... ?
C'est...
(Est-ce que)... est là, s'il vous plaît?
(Est-ce que) je peux parler à... ?
Je peux laisser un message?
Vous pouvez lui dire que j'ai téléphoné?
Ça ne répond pas.
C'est occupé.

Answering a telephone call Ch. 9, p. 276
Allô?
Qui est à l'appareil?
Une seconde, s'il vous plaît.
D'accord.
Bien sûr.
Vous pouvez rappeler plus tard?
Ne quittez pas.

Inquiring Ch. 10, p. 301
(Est-ce que) je peux vous aider?
Vous désirez?
Je peux l'(les) essayer?
Je peux essayer... ?
C'est combien, ... ?
Ça fait combien?
Vous avez ça en... ?

Pointing out places and things Ch. 12, p. 361
Là, tu vois, c'est...
Ça, c'est...
Regarde, voilà...
Là, c'est...
Voici...

Asking for advice Ch. 12, p. 366
Comment est-ce qu'on y va?

Making suggestions Ch. 12, p. 366
On peut y aller...
On peut prendre...

Asking for directions Ch. 12, p. 371
Pardon, ..., s'il vous plaît?
Pardon, ... Où est..., s'il vous plaît?
Pardon, ... Je cherche..., s'il vous plaît.

Giving directions Ch. 12, p. 371
Vous continuez jusqu'au prochain feu rouge.
Vous tournez...
Vous allez tout droit jusqu'à...
Prenez la rue..., puis traversez la rue...
Vous passez...
C'est tout de suite à...

Expressing Feelings and Emotions

Expressing likes, dislikes, and preferences
Ch. 1, pp. 26, 32
J'aime (bien)...   J'aime mieux...
Je n'aime pas...   J'adore...
Je préfère...

Ch. 5, p. 154
C'est...
excellent!   bon!
pas mauvais!   délicieux!
pas terrible!   pas bon!
mauvais!   dégoûtant!

Telling what you'd like and what you'd like to do
Ch. 3, p. 85
Je voudrais...
Je voudrais acheter...

Telling how much you like or dislike something
Ch. 4, p. 114
Beaucoup.   Pas du tout.
Pas beaucoup.   surtout
Pas tellement.

Inquiring about likes and dislikes Ch. 1, p. 26
Tu aimes... ?

Ch. 5, p. 154
Comment tu trouves ça?

Sharing confidences Ch. 9, p. 279
J'ai un petit problème.
Je peux te parler?
Tu as une minute?

Consoling others Ch. 9, p. 279
Je t'écoute.
Ne t'en fais pas!
Ça va aller mieux!
Qu'est-ce que je peux faire?

Making a decision Ch. 10, p. 310
Vous avez décidé de prendre... ?
Vous avez choisi?
Vous le/la/les prenez?
Je le/la/les prends.
C'est trop cher.

SUMMARY OF FUNCTIONS

Hesitating **Ch. 10, p. 310**
Euh... J'hésite.
Je ne sais pas.
Il/Elle me plaît, mais il/elle est...

Expressing indecision **Ch. 11, p. 329**
J'hésite.
Je ne sais pas.
Je n'en sais rien.
Je n'ai rien de prévu.

Expressing wishes **Ch. 11, p. 329**
J'ai envie de...
Je voudrais bien...

Expressing Attitudes and Opinions

Agreeing **Ch. 2, p. 54**
Oui, beaucoup.
Moi aussi.
Moi non plus.

Disagreeing **Ch. 2, p. 54**
Moi, non.
Non, pas trop.
Moi, si.
Pas moi.

Asking for opinions **Ch. 2, p. 61**
Comment tu trouves... ?
Comment tu trouves ça?

Ch. 9, p. 269
Tu as passé un bon week-end?

Ch. 10, p. 306
Il/Elle me va?
Il/Elle te/vous plaît?
Tu aimes mieux... ou... ?

Ch. 11, p. 337
Tu as passé un bon... ?
Tu t'es bien amusé(e)?
Ça s'est bien passé?

Expressing opinions **Ch. 2, p. 61**
C'est...

facile.	pas terrible.
génial.	pas super.
super.	zéro.
cool.	barbant.
intéressant.	nul.
passionnant.	pas mal.
difficile.	

Ça va.

Ch. 9, p. 269
Oui, très chouette.

Oui, excellent.
Oui, très bon.
Oui, ça a été.
Oh, pas mauvais.
C'était épouvantable.
Très mauvais.

Ch. 11, p. 337
C'était formidable!
Non, pas vraiment.
C'était ennuyeux.
C'était un véritable cauchemar!

Paying a compliment **Ch. 10, p. 306**
C'est tout à fait ton/ votre style.
Il/Elle te/vous va très bien.
Il/Elle va très bien avec...
Je le/la/les trouve...
C'est parfait.

Criticizing **Ch. 10, p. 306**
Il/Elle ne te/vous va pas du tout.
Il/Elle ne va pas du tout avec...
Il/Elle est (Ils/Elles sont) trop...
Je le/la/les trouve...

Persuading

Making suggestions **Ch. 4, p. 122**
On... ?
On fait... ?
On joue... ?

Ch. 5, p. 145
On va... ?

Accepting suggestions **Ch. 4, p. 122**
D'accord.
Bonne idée.
Oui, c'est...
Allons-y!

Turning down suggestions; making excuses
Ch. 4, p. 122
Non, c'est...
Ça ne me dit rien.
Désolé(e), mais je ne peux pas.

Ch. 5, p. 145
Désolé(e). J'ai des devoirs à faire.
J'ai des courses à faire.
J'ai des trucs à faire.
J'ai des tas de choses à faire.
Je ne peux pas parce que...

Making a recommendation **Ch. 5, p. 148**
Prends...
Prenez...

Asking for permission **Ch. 7, p. 213**
Tu es d'accord?
(Est-ce que) je peux... ?

Giving permission **Ch. 7, p. 213**
Oui, si tu veux.
Pourquoi pas?
D'accord, si tu... d'abord...
Oui, bien sûr.

Refusing permission **Ch. 7, p. 213**
Pas question!
Non, c'est impossible.
Non, tu dois...
Pas ce soir.

Making requests **Ch. 8, p. 240**
Tu peux(aller faire les courses)?
Tu me rapportes... ?

Ch. 12, p. 364
Est-ce que tu peux... ?
Tu pourrais passer à... ?

Accepting requests **Ch. 8, p. 240**
Pourquoi pas?
Bon, d'accord.
Je veux bien.
J'y vais tout de suite.

Ch. 12, p. 364
D'accord.
Si tu veux.

Declining requests **Ch. 8, p. 240**
Je ne peux pas maintenant.
Je regrette, mais je n'ai pas le temps.
J'ai des tas de choses (trucs) à faire.

Ch. 12, p. 364
Je suis désolé(e), mais je n'ai pas le temps.

Telling someone what to do **Ch. 8, p. 240**
Rapporte(-moi)...
Prends...
Achète(-moi)...
N'oublie pas de...

Offering food **Ch. 8, p. 247**
Tu veux... ?
Vous voulez... ?
Vous prenez... ?
Tu prends... ?
Encore... ?

Accepting food **Ch. 8, p. 247**
Oui, s'il vous/te plaît.
Oui, avec plaisir.
Oui, j'en veux bien.

Refusing food **Ch. 8, p. 247**
Non, merci.
Non, merci. Je n'ai plus faim.
Je n'en veux plus.

Asking for advice **Ch. 9, p. 279**
A ton avis, qu'est-ce que je fais?
Qu'est-ce que tu me conseilles?

Ch. 10, p. 300
Je ne sais pas quoi mettre pour...
Qu'est-ce que je mets?

Giving advice **Ch. 9, p. 279**
Oublie-le/-la/-les!
Téléphone-lui/-leur!
Tu devrais...
Pourquoi tu ne... pas?

Ch. 10, p. 300
Pourquoi est-ce que tu ne mets pas... ?
Mets...

Reminding **Ch. 11, p. 333**
N'oublie pas...
Tu n'as pas oublié... ?
Tu ne peux pas partir sans...
Tu prends... ?

Reassuring **Ch. 11, p. 333**
Ne t'en fais pas.
J'ai pensé à tout.
Je n'ai rien oublié.

This list presents additional vocabulary you may want to use when you're working on the activities in the textbook and in the workbooks. It also includes the optional vocabulary labeled **Vocabulaire à la carte** that appears in several chapters. If you can't find the words you need here, try the French-English and English-French vocabulary lists beginning on page R31.

Adjectives

absurd	*absurde*
awesome (impressive)	*impressionnant(e)*
boring	*ennuyeux/ennuyeuse*
chilly (weather)	*froid, frais*
colorful (thing)	*vif/vive*
despicable	*ignoble*
eccentric	*excentrique*
incredible	*incroyable*
tasteful (remark, object)	*de bon goût*
tasteless (flavor)	*insipide*; (remark, object) *de mauvais goût*
terrifying	*terrifiant(e)*
threatening	*menaçant(e)*
tremendous (excellent)	*formidable*
unforgettable	*inoubliable*
unique	*unique*

Clothing

blazer	*un blazer*
button	*un bouton*
coat	*un manteau*
collar	*un col*
eyeglasses	*des lunettes* (f.)
gloves	*des gants* (m.)
handkerchief	*un mouchoir*
high-heeled shoes	*des chaussures* (f.) *à talons*
lace	*de la dentelle*
linen	*du lin*
necklace	*un collier*
nylon	*du nylon*
pajamas	*un pyjama*
polyester	*du polyester*
raincoat	*un imperméable*
rayon	*de la rayonne*
ring	*une bague*
sale (discount)	*des soldes* (m.)
silk	*de la soie*
sleeve	*une manche*
slippers	*des pantoufles* (f.)
suit (man's)	*un costume*; (woman's) *un tailleur*
suspenders	*des bretelles* (f.)
velvet	*du velours*
vest	*un gilet*
wool	*de la laine*
zipper	*une fermeture éclair®*

Colors and Patterns

beige	*beige*
checked	*à carreaux*
colorful	*coloré(e), vif/vive*
dark blue	*bleu foncé*
dark-colored	*foncé(e)*
flowered	*à fleurs*
gold (adj.)	*d'or, doré(e)*
light blue	*bleu clair*
light-colored	*clair(e)*
patterned	*à motifs*
polka-dotted	*à pois*
striped	*à rayures*
turquoise	*turquoise*

Computers

l'ordinateur   le lecteur de CD-ROM   le CD-ROM   la souris   le clavier

CD-ROM	*le CD-ROM, le disque optique compact*
CD-ROM drive	*le lecteur de CD-ROM, l'unité (f.) de CD-ROM*
to click	*cliquer*
computer	*l'ordinateur (m.)*
delete key	*la touche d'effacement*
disk drive	*le lecteur de disquette, l'unité de disquettes (f.)*
diskette, floppy disk	*la disquette, la disquette souple*
to drag	*glisser, déplacer*
e-mail	*le courrier électronique, la messagerie électronique*
file	*le dossier*
file (folder)	*le fichier*
hard drive	*le disque dur*
homepage	*la page d'accueil*
Internet	*Internet (m.)*
keyboard	*le clavier*
keyword	*le mot-clé*
log on	*l'ouverture (f.) de session*
modem	*le modem*
monitor	*le moniteur, le logimètre*
mouse	*la souris*

password	*le mot de passe*
to print	*imprimer*
printer	*l'imprimante (f.)*
to quit	*quitter*
to record	*enregistrer*
return key	*la touche de retour*
to save	*sauvegarder, enregistrer*
screen	*l'écran (m.)*
to search	*chercher, rechercher*
search engine	*le moteur de recherche, l'outil (m.) de recherche*
to send	*envoyer*
software	*le logiciel*
Web site	*le site du Web, le site W3*
World Wide Web	*le World Wide Web, le Web, le W3*

Entertainment

blues	*le blues*
CD player	*le lecteur de CD*
camera flash	*le flash*
folk music	*la musique folklorique*
headphones	*les écouteurs*

hit (song)	*le tube*
lens	*l'objectif (m.)*
microphone	*le micro(phone)*
opera	*l'opéra (m.)*
pop music	*la musique pop*
reggae	*le reggae*
roll of film	*la pellicule (photo)*
screen	*l'écran (m.)*
speakers	*les enceintes (f.), les baffles (m.)*
to turn off	*éteindre*
to turn on	*allumer*
turntable	*la platine*
walkman	*le balladeur*

Family

adopted	*adopté(e), adoptif/adoptive*
brother-in-law	*le beau-frère*
child	*un(e) enfant*
couple	*un couple*
daughter-in-law	*la belle-fille*
divorced	*divorcé(e)*
engaged	*fiancé(e)*
goddaughter	*la filleule*
godfather	*le parrain*
godmother	*la marraine*
godson	*le filleul*
grandchildren	*les petits-enfants*
granddaughter	*la petite-fille*
grandson	*le petit-fils*
great-granddaughter	*l'arrière-petite-fille (f.)*
great-grandfather	*l'arrière-grand-père (m.)*
great-grandmother	*l'arrière-grand-mère (f.)*
great-grandson	*l'arrière-petit-fils (m.)*
half-brother	*le demi-frère*
half-sister	*la demi-sœur*
mother-in-law	*la belle-mère*
only child	*un/une enfant unique*
single	*célibataire*
sister-in-law	*la belle-sœur*

son-in-law	le gendre; le beau-fils
stepbrother	le demi-frère
stepdaughter	la belle-fille
stepfather	le beau-père
stepmother	la belle-mère
stepsister	la demi-sœur
stepson	le beau-fils
widow	la veuve
widower	le veuf

Foods and Beverages

appetizer	une entrée
apricot	un abricot
asparagus	des asperges (f.)
bacon	du bacon
bowl	un bol
Brussels sprouts	des choux (m.) de Bruxelles
cabbage	du chou
cauliflower	du chou-fleur
cereal	des céréales (f.)
chestnut	un marron
cookie	un biscuit
cucumber	un concombre
cutlet	une escalope
fried egg	un œuf au plat; **hard-boiled egg** un œuf dur; **scrambled eggs** des œufs brouillés; **soft-boiled egg** un œuf à la coque

eggplant	une aubergine
French bread	une baguette
garlic	de l'ail (m.)
grapefruit	un pamplemousse
honey	du miel
liver	du foie
margarine	de la margarine
marshmallow	une guimauve
mayonnaise	de la mayonnaise
melon	un melon
mustard	de la moutarde
nuts	des noix (f.)
peanut butter	du beurre de cacahouètes
pepper (spice)	du poivre; (vegetable) un poivron
popcorn	du pop-corn
potato chips	des chips (f.)
raspberry	une framboise

salmon	du saumon
salt	du sel
shellfish	des fruits (m.) de mer
soup	de la soupe
spinach	des épinards (m.)
spoon	une cuillère
syrup	du sirop
veal	du veau
watermelon	une pastèque
zucchini	une courgette
bland	doux (douce)
hot (spicy)	épicé(e)
juicy (fruit)	juteux/juteuse; (meat) tendre
rare (cooked)	saignant(e)
medium (cooked)	à point
spicy	épicé(e)
well-done (cooked)	bien cuit(e)
tasty	savoureux/savoureuse

Housework

to clean	nettoyer
to dry	faire sécher
to dust	faire la poussière
to fold	plier
to hang	pendre
to iron	repasser
to put away	ranger
to rake	ratisser
to shovel	enlever à la pelle
to sweep	balayer

Pets

bird	un oiseau
cow	une vache
frog	une grenouille
goldfish	un poisson rouge
guinea pig	un cochon d'Inde
hamster	un hamster
horse	un cheval
kitten	un chaton
lizard	un lézard
mouse	une souris
parrot	un perroquet
pig	un cochon
puppy	un chiot
rabbit	un lapin
turtle	une tortue

Places Around Town

airport	l'aéroport (m.)
beauty shop	le salon de coiffure
bridge	le pont
church	l'église (f.)
consulate	le consulat
hospital	l'hôpital (m.)
mosque	la mosquée
police station	le commissariat de police
synagogue	la synagogue
tourist office	l'office de tourisme (m.)
town hall	l'hôtel (m.) de ville

Professions

Note: If only one form is given, that form is used for both men and women. Note that you can also say **une femme banquier, une femme médecin,** and so forth.

archaeologist	un(e) archéologue
architect	un(e) architecte
athlete	un(e) athlète
banker	un banquier
businessman/ businesswoman	un homme d'affaires (une femme d'affaires)
dancer	un danseur (une danseuse)
dentist	un(e) dentiste
doctor	un médecin
editor	un rédacteur (une rédactrice)
engineer	un ingénieur
fashion designer	un(e) styliste de mode
fashion model	un mannequin
hairdresser	un coiffeur (une coiffeuse)
homemaker	un homme au foyer (une femme au foyer)
lawyer	un(e) avocat(e)

manager (company)	un directeur (une directrice); (store, restaurant) un gérant (une gérante)
mechanic	un mécanicien (une mécanicienne)
painter (art)	un peintre; (buildings) un peintre en bâtiment
pilot	un pilote
plumber	un plombier
scientist	un(e) scientifique
secretary	un(e) secrétaire
social worker	un assistant social (une assistante sociale)
taxi driver	un chauffeur de taxi
technician	un technicien (une technicienne)
truck driver	un routier
veterinarian	un(e) vétérinaire
worker	un ouvrier (une ouvrière)
writer	un écrivain

School Subjects

accounting	la comptabilité
business	le commerce
foreign languages	les langues (f.) étrangères
home economics	les arts (m.) ménagers
marching band	la fanfare
orchestra	l'orchestre (m.)
social studies	les sciences (f.) sociales
typing	la dactylographie
woodworking	la menuiserie
world history	l'histoire (f.) mondiale

School Supplies

calendar	un calendrier
colored pencils	des crayons (m.) de couleur
compass	un compas
correction fluid	du liquide correcteur
glue	de la colle
gym uniform	une tenue de gymnastique
marker	un feutre
rubber band	un élastique
scissors	des ciseaux (m.)
staple	une agrafe
stapler	une agrafeuse
transparent tape	du ruban adhésif

Sports and Interests

badminton	*le badminton*
boxing	*la boxe*
fishing rod	*la canne à pêche*
foot race	*la course à pied*
to go for a ride	*faire une promenade,*
(by bike, car,	*faire un tour (à bicyclette,*
motorcycle, moped)	*en voiture, à moto, à*
	vélomoteur)
to do gymnastics	*faire de la gymnastique*
hunting	*la chasse*
to lift weights	*faire des haltères*
mountain climbing	*l'alpinisme* (m.)
to play checkers	*jouer aux dames*
to play chess	*jouer aux échecs*
to ride a skateboard	*faire de la planche à*
	roulettes
to sew	*coudre; faire de la*
	couture
speed skating	*le patinage de vitesse*
to surf	*faire du surf*

Weather

barometer	*le baromètre*
blizzard	*la tempête de neige*
cloudy	*nuageux*
drizzle	*la bruine*
fog	*le brouillard*
frost	*la gelée*
hail	*la grêle*
to hail	*grêler*
heat wave	*la canicule*
hurricane	*l'ouragan* (m.)
ice (on the road)	*le verglas*
It's pouring.	*Il pleut à verse.*
It's sleeting.	*Il tombe de la neige*
	fondue.
It's sunny.	*Il fait du soleil.*
lightning bolt	*l'éclair* (m.)
mist	*la brume*
shower (rain)	*l'averse* (f.)
storm	*la tempête*
thermometer	*le thermomètre*
thunder	*le tonnerre*
thunderstorm	*l'orage* (m.)
tornado	*la tornade*

Cities

Algiers	*Alger*
Brussels	*Bruxelles*
Cairo	*Le Caire*
Geneva	*Genève*
Lisbon	*Lisbonne*
London	*Londres*
Montreal	*Montréal*
Moscow	*Moscou*
New Orleans	*La Nouvelle-Orléans*
Quebec City	*Québec*
Tangier	*Tanger*
Venice	*Venise*
Vienna	*Vienne*

The Continents

Africa	*l'Afrique* (f.)
Antarctica	*l'Antarctique* (f.)
Asia	*l'Asie* (f.)
Australia	*l'Océanie* (f.)
Europe	*l'Europe* (f.)
North America	*l'Amérique* (f.) *du Nord*
South America	*l'Amérique* (f.) *du Sud*

Countries

Algeria	*l'Algérie* (f.)
Argentina	*l'Argentine* (f.)
Australia	*l'Australie* (f.)
Austria	*l'Autriche* (f.)
Belgium	*la Belgique*
Brazil	*le Brésil*
Canada	*le Canada*
China	*la Chine*
Côte d'Ivoire	*la République de Côte*
	d'Ivoire
Egypt	*l'Egypte* (f.)
England	*l'Angleterre* (f.)
France	*la France*
Germany	*l'Allemagne* (f.)

Greece	*la Grèce*
Holland	*la Hollande*
India	*l'Inde* (f.)
Ireland	*l'Irlande* (f.)
Israel	*Israël* (m.)
Italy	*l'Italie* (f.)
Jamaica	*la Jamaïque*
Japan	*le Japon*
Jordan	*la Jordanie*
Lebanon	*le Liban*
Libya	*la Libye*
Luxembourg	*le Luxembourg*
Mexico	*le Mexique*
Monaco	*Monaco* (f.)
Morocco	*le Maroc*
Netherlands	*les Pays-Bas* (m.)
North Korea	*la Corée du Nord*
Peru	*le Pérou*
Philippines	*les Philippines* (f.)
Poland	*la Pologne*
Portugal	*le Portugal*
Russia	*la Russie*
Senegal	*le Sénégal*
South Korea	*la Corée du Sud*
Spain	*l'Espagne* (f.)
Switzerland	*la Suisse*
Syria	*la Syrie*
Tunisia	*la Tunisie*
Turkey	*la Turquie*
United States	*les Etats-Unis* (m.)
Vietnam	*le Viêt-nam*

States

California	*la Californie*
Florida	*la Floride*
Georgia	*la Géorgie*
Louisiana	*la Louisiane*
New Mexico	*le Nouveau Mexique*
North Carolina	*la Caroline du Nord*
Pennsylvania	*la Pennsylvanie*
South Carolina	*la Caroline du Sud*
Texas	*le Texas*
Virginia	*la Virginie*

Oceans and Seas

Atlantic Ocean	*l'Atlantique* (m.), *l'océan* (m.) *Atlantique*
Caribbean Sea	*la mer des Caraïbes*
English Channel	*la Manche*
Indian Ocean	*l'océan* (m.) *Indien*
Mediterranean Sea	*la mer Méditerranée*
Pacific Ocean	*le Pacifique, l'océan* (m.) *Pacifique*

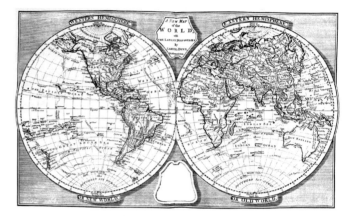

Other Geographical Terms

Alps	*les Alpes* (f.)
border	*la frontière*
capital	*la capitale*
continent	*le continent*
country	*le pays*
hill	*la colline*
lake	*le lac*
latitude	*la latitude*
longitude	*la longitude*
North Africa	*l'Afrique* (f.) *du Nord*
ocean	*l'océan* (m.)
plain	*la plaine*
Pyrenees	*les Pyrénées* (f.)
river	*la rivière, le fleuve*
sea	*la mer*
state	*l'état* (m.)
the North Pole	*le pôle Nord*
the South Pole	*le pôle Sud*
valley	*la vallée*

ADJECTIVES

REGULAR ADJECTIVES

In French, adjectives agree in gender and number with the nouns that they modify. A regular adjective has four forms: masculine singular, feminine singular, masculine plural, and feminine plural. To make a regular adjective agree with a feminine noun, add an -e to the masculine singular form of the adjective. To make one agree with a plural noun, add an -s to the masculine singular form. To make one adjective agree with a feminine plural noun, add -es to the masculine singular form. Adjectives ending in -é, like **désolé,** also follow these rules.

	SINGULAR	PLURAL
MASCULINE	un jean **vert**	des jeans **verts**
FEMININE	une ceinture **verte**	des ceintures **vertes**

ADJECTIVES THAT END IN AN UNACCENTED -E

When an adjective ends in an unaccented -e, the masculine singular and the feminine singular forms are the same. To form the plural of these adjectives, add an -s to the singular forms.

	SINGULAR	PLURAL
MASCULINE	un cahier **rouge**	des cahiers **rouges**
FEMININE	une trousse **rouge**	des trousses **rouges**

ADJECTIVES THAT END IN -S

When the masculine singular form of an adjective ends in an -s, the masculine plural form does not change. The feminine forms follow the regular adjective rules.

	SINGULAR	PLURAL
MASCULINE	un sac **gris**	des sacs **gris**
FEMININE	une robe **grise**	des robes **grises**

ADJECTIVES THAT END IN -EUX

Adjectives that end in **-eux** do not change in the masculine plural. The feminine singular form of these adjectives is made by replacing the **-x** with **-se.** To form the feminine plural, replace the **-x** with **-ses.**

	SINGULAR	PLURAL
MASCULINE	un garçon **heureux**	des garçons **heureux**
FEMININE	une fille **heureuse**	des filles **heureuses**

ADJECTIVES THAT END IN -IF

To make the feminine singular form of adjectives that end in **-if,** replace **-if** with **-ive.** To make the plural forms of these adjectives, add an **-s** to the singular forms.

	SINGULAR	PLURAL
MASCULINE	un garçon **sportif**	des garçons **sportifs**
FEMININE	une fille **sportive**	des filles **sportives**

ADJECTIVES THAT END IN -IEN

To make the feminine singular and feminine plural forms of adjectives that end in **-ien** in their masculine singular form, add **-ne** and **-nes.** Add an **-s** to form the masculine plural.

	SINGULAR	PLURAL
MASCULINE	un garçon **canadien**	des garçons **canadiens**
FEMININE	une fille **canadienne**	des filles **canadiennes**

ADJECTIVES THAT DOUBLE THE LAST CONSONANT

To make the adjectives **bon, gentil, gros, mignon, nul,** and **violet** agree with a feminine noun, double the last consonant and add an **-e.** To make the plural forms, add an **-s** to the singular forms. Note that with **gros,** the masculine singular and masculine plural forms are the same.

	SINGULAR					
MASCULINE	bon	gentil	gros	mignon	nul	violet
FEMININE	bonne	gentille	grosse	mignonne	nulle	violette

	PLURAL					
MASCULINE	bons	gentils	gros	mignons	nuls	violets
FEMININE	bonnes	gentilles	grosses	mignonnes	nulles	violettes

Grammar Summary

INVARIABLE ADJECTIVES

Some adjectives are invariable. They never change form. **Cool, marron, orange,** and **super** are examples of invariable adjectives.

Il me faut une montre **marron** et des baskets **orange.**

IRREGULAR ADJECTIVES

The forms of some adjectives must simply be memorized. This is the case for **blanc, sympa,** and **roux.**

Note that **sympathique,** the long form of the adjective, follows the rules for adjectives that end in an unaccented -e, like **rouge.**

	SINGULAR	PLURAL
MASCULINE	blanc	blancs
FEMININE	blanche	blanches

	SINGULAR	PLURAL
MASCULINE	roux	roux
FEMININE	rousse	rousses

	SINGULAR	PLURAL
MASCULINE	sympa	sympas
FEMININE	sympa	sympas

POSITION OF ADJECTIVES

In French, adjectives are usually placed after the noun that they modify.

C'est une femme **intelligente.**

Certain adjectives precede the noun. Some of these are **bon, jeune, joli, grand,** and **petit.**

C'est un **petit** village.

DEMONSTRATIVE ADJECTIVES

This, that, these, and *those* are demonstrative adjectives. There are two masculine singular forms of these adjectives in French: **ce** and **cet. Cet** is used with masculine singular nouns that begin with a vowel sound. Some examples are **cet ordinateur** and **cet homme.** Demonstrative adjectives always precede the noun that they modify.

	Singular Before a Consonant	Singular Before a Vowel Sound	Plural
MASCULINE	**ce** livre	**cet** ordinateur	**ces** posters
FEMININE	**cette** montre	**cette** école	**ces** gommes

POSSESSIVE ADJECTIVES

Possessive adjectives come before the noun that they modify and agree in gender and number with that noun. All nouns that begin with a vowel sound use the masculine singular form, for example **mon ami(e), ton ami(e), son ami(e).**

	Masculine Singular	Feminine Singular	Masc./Fem. Singular Before a Vowel Sound	Masc./Fem. Plural
my	**mon** père	**ma** mère	**mon** oncle	**mes** cousines
your	**ton** livre	**ta** montre	**ton** écharpe	**tes** cahiers
his, her, its	**son** chien	**sa** sœur	**son** école	**ses** cours

The possessive adjectives for *our, your,* and *their* have only two forms, singular and plural.

	Masc./Fem. Singular	Masc./Fem. Plural
our	**notre** frère	**nos** tantes
your	**votre** classeur	**vos** amis
their	**leur** copain	**leurs** trousses

ADJECTIVES AS NOUNS

To use an adjective as a noun, add a definite article before the adjective. The article that you use agrees in gender and number with the noun that the adjective is replacing.

—Tu aimes les chemises rouges ou **les blanches?**

Do you like the red shirts or the white ones?

—J'aime **les blanches.**

I like the white ones.

ADVERBS

POSITION OF ADVERBS

Most adverbs follow the conjugated verb. In the **passé composé,** they usually precede the past participle.

Nathalie fait **souvent** des photos.   Je n'ai pas **bien** mangé ce matin.

Adverbs that are made up of more than one word can be placed at the beginning or at the end of a sentence. When you use **ne (n')... jamais,** place it around the conjugated verb.

D'habitude, je fais du tennis le soir.

J'aime faire de l'aérobic **deux fois par semaine.**

Je **n'ai jamais** fait de ski.

ARTICLES

DEFINITE ARTICLES

French has four definite articles: **le, la, l'**, and **les.** The form that you use depends on the gender and number of the noun it modifies. Use **le** with masculine singular nouns, **le livre; la** with feminine singular nouns, **la chemise;** and **les** with both masculine and feminine nouns that are plural, **les crayons.** The form **l'** is used with both masculine and feminine nouns that begin with a vowel sound: **l'ami, l'amie, l'homme.** In French, you sometimes use a definite article when no article is required in English.

> J'aime **le** chocolat et toi, tu préfères **le** café.

	Singular Before a Consonant	Singular Before a Vowel Sound	Plural
MASCULINE	**le** professeur	**l'**ami	**les** livres
FEMININE	**la** pharmacie	**l'**école	**les** pommes

INDEFINITE ARTICLES

In English, there are three indefinite articles: *a, an,* and *some.* In French there are also three: **un, une,** and **des.** The indefinite articles agree in number and gender with the nouns they modify.

	SINGULAR	PLURAL
MASCULINE	**un** poisson	**des** chats
FEMININE	**une** orange	**des** lunettes

PARTITIVE ARTICLES

To say that you want *part* or *some* of an item, use the partitive articles. Use **du** with a masculine noun and **de la** with a feminine noun. Use **de l'** with singular nouns that begin with a vowel sound whether they are masculine or feminine.

> Je veux **de la** tarte aux pommes. *I want some apple pie.*

To indicate the whole as opposed to a part of the item, use the indefinite articles **un, une,** and **des.**

> Pour la fête, il me faut **des** tartes. *I need (some) pies for the party.*

NEGATION AND THE ARTICLES

When the main verb of a sentence is negated, the indefinite and the partitive articles change to **de/d'.** Definite articles remain the same after a negative verb.

J'ai **le** livre de maths.	—> Je n'ai pas **le** livre de maths.
J'ai **des** stylos.	—> Je n'ai pas **de** stylos.
J'ai mangé **de la** pizza.	—> Je n'ai pas mangé **de** pizza.

INTERROGATIVES

QUESTION FORMATION

There are several ways to ask yes-no questions. One of these is to raise the pitch of your voice at the end of a statement. The other is to place **est-ce que** in front of a statement.

Tu aimes le chocolat. —> **Tu aimes le chocolat?** (intonation) *or*
Est-ce que tu aimes le chocolat?

NEGATIVE QUESTIONS

The answer to a yes-no question depends on the way the question was stated. If the verb in a question is positive, then the answer is **oui** if you agree, and **non** if you don't. If the verb in a question is negative, then **non** is used to agree with the question and **si** to disagree.

Question	Agreeing with the Question	Disagreeing with the Question
Tu aimes lire?	**Oui,** j'aime lire.	**Non,** je n'aime pas lire.
Tu n'aimes pas lire?	**Non,** je n'aime pas lire.	**Si,** j'aime lire.

INFORMATION QUESTIONS

To ask for specific kinds of information, use the following question words:

A quelle heure?	*At what time?*	**Où?**	*Where?*
Avec qui?	*With whom?*	**Quand?**	*When?*

These words can be used by themselves, at the beginning of a question, at the beginning of a question, followed by **est-ce que,** or at the end of a question.

Avec qui?   **Avec qui** est-ce qu'on va au cinéma?
Avec qui on va au cinéma?   On va au cinéma **avec qui?**

NOUNS

PLURAL FORMS OF NOUNS

In French, you make most nouns plural by adding an **-s** to the end of the word, unless they already end in **-s** or **-x.** Nouns that end in **-eau** are made plural by adding an **-x,** and nouns that end in **-al** are generally made plural by replacing the **-al** with **-aux.**

	Regular Nouns	-s or -x	-eau	-al
SINGULAR	table	bus	manteau	hôpital
PLURAL	tables	bus	manteaux	hôpitaux

PREPOSITIONS

THE PREPOSITIONS A AND DE

The preposition **à** means *to, at,* or *in,* and **de** means *from* or *of.* When **à** and **de** are used in front of the definite articles **le** and **les,** they form contractions. If they precede any other definite article, there is no contraction.

> Il va **à** l'école et **au** musée. *He's going to school and to the museum.*
>
> Nous sommes loin **du** musée. *We are far from the museum.*

	Masculine Article	Feminine Article	Vowel Sound	Plural
à	à + le = **au**	à + la = **à la**	à + l' = **à l'**	à + les = **aux**
de	de + le = **du**	de + la = **de la**	de + l' = **de l'**	de + les = **des**

De can also indicate possession or ownership.

> C'est le livre **de** Laurent. *It's Laurent's book.*
>
> C'est le stylo **du** prof. *It's the professor's pen.*

PREPOSITIONS AND PLACES

To say that you are at or going to a place, you need to use a preposition. With cities, use the preposition **à : à Paris.** One notable exception is **en Arles.** When speaking about masculine countries, use **au : au Maroc.** With plural names of countries, use **aux : aux Etats-Unis.** Most countries ending in **-e** are feminine; in these cases, use **en : en France. Le Mexique** is an exception. If a country begins with a vowel, like **Israël,** use **en : en Israël.**

Cities	Masculine Countries	Feminine Countries or Masculine Countries that Begin with a Vowel	Plural Countries
à Nantes à Paris en Arles	au Canada au Maroc au Mexique	en Italie en Espagne en Israël	aux Etats-Unis aux Philippines aux Pays-Bas

PRONOUNS

In French, as in English, a pronoun can refer to a person, place, or thing. Pronouns are used to avoid repetition. In French, pronouns agree in gender and number with the noun that they replace.

SUBJECT PRONOUNS

Subject pronouns replace the subject in a sentence.

je (j')	*I*	**nous**	*we*
tu	*you* (familiar)	**vous**	*you* (plural or formal)
il	*he / it*	**ils**	*they*
elle	*she / it*	**elles**	*they*
on	*we / one / they*		

THE IMPERSONAL PRONOUN IL

Many statements in French begin with the personal pronoun **il.** In these statements, **il** does not refer to any particular person or thing. For this reason, these statements are called impersonal statements.

Il fait beau.　　*It's nice out.*

Il est huit heures.　　*It's eight o'clock.*

Il me/te faut... *I/You need . . .*

Il y a... *There is/are . . .*

DIRECT OBJECT PRONOUNS: LE, LA, LES

A direct object is a noun that receives the action of the verb. It answers the questions *What?* or *Whom?* To say *him, her, it,* or *them,* use the pronouns **le, la,** and **les.** In French, you place the direct object pronoun in front of the conjugated verb.

　　Il regarde **la télé.** —> Il **la** regarde.

If there is an infinitive in the sentence, the direct object pronoun comes before the infinitive.

　　Je vais attendre **Pierre.** —> Je vais **l'**attendre.

In an affirmative command, the direct object pronoun follows the verb and is connected to it with a hyphen.

　　Regarde **la télévision.** —> Regarde-**la**!

	SINGULAR	PLURAL
MASCULINE	le / l'	les
FEMININE	la / l'	les

INDIRECT OBJECT PRONOUNS: LUI, LEUR

The indirect object answers the question *To whom?* and refers only to people. In French an indirect object follows the preposition **à: Il parle à Marie.** The indirect object pronoun replaces the prepositional phrase **à + a person,** and precedes the conjugated verb.

> Nous téléphonons **à Mireille.** —> Nous **lui** téléphonons.

If there is an infinitive in the sentence, the indirect object pronoun comes before the infinitive.

> Il n'aime pas parler **à ses parents.** —> Il n'aime pas **leur** parler.

In an affirmative command, the indirect object pronoun follows the verb and is connected to it with a hyphen.

> Téléphone **à ta sœur.** —> Téléphone-**lui!**

THE PRONOUN Y

To replace a phrase meaning *to, on, at,* or *in* any place that has already been mentioned, you can use the pronoun **y.** It can replace phrases beginning with prepositions of location such as **à, sur, chez, dans,** and **en + a place or thing.** Place **y** before the conjugated verb.

> Elle va **à la pharmacie.** —> Elle **y** va.

If there is an infinitive, place **y** before the infinitive.

> Elle va aller **à la poste** demain. —> Elle va **y** aller demain.

THE PRONOUN EN

The pronoun **en** replaces a phrase beginning with **de, du, de la, de l',** or **des.** It usually means *about it, some (of it/of them),* or simply *it/them,* and is placed before the conjugated verb.

> Tu achètes **des haricots verts?** —> Oui, j'**en** achète pour le dîner.

En in a negative sentence means *not any* or *none.*

> Tu ne bois pas **de café.** —> Tu n'**en** bois pas.

En is placed before the conjugated verb.

> Je parle **de mes vacances.** —> J'**en** parle.

If there is an infinitive, place **en** before the infinitive.

> Vous aimez manger **des fruits.** —> Vous aimez **en** manger.

Notice that with the **passé composé, en** precedes the helping verb.

> Il a mangé **du pain.** —> Il **en** a mangé.

VERBS

THE PRESENT TENSE OF REGULAR VERBS

To conjugate a verb in French, use the following formulas. Which formula you choose depends on the ending of the infinitive. There are three major verb categories: **-er, -ir,** and **-re.** Each one has a different conjugation. Within these categories, there are regular and irregular verbs. To conjugate regular verbs, you drop the infinitive endings and add these endings.

Subject	aimer (to love, to like) Stem	Ending	choisir (to choose) Stem	Ending	vendre (to sell) Stem	Ending
je/j'		-e		-is		-s
tu		-es		-is		-s
il/elle/on	aim	-e	chois	-it	vend	—
nous		-ons		-issons		-ons
vous		-ez		-issez		-ez
ils/elles		-ent		-issent		-ent

VERBS WITH STEM AND SPELLING CHANGES

Verbs listed in this section are not irregular, but they do have some stem and spelling changes.

With **acheter** and **promener**, add an **accent grave** over the second-to-last **e** for all forms except **nous** and **vous**. Notice that the accent on the second **e** in **préférer** changes from é to è in all forms except the **nous** and **vous** forms.

	acheter (to buy)	préférer (to prefer)	promener (to walk (an animal))
je/j'	achète	préfère	promène
tu	achètes	préfères	promènes
il/elle/on	achète	préfère	promène
nous	achetons	préférons	promenons
vous	achetez	préférez	promenez
ils/elles	achètent	préfèrent	promènent
Past Participle	acheté	préféré	promené

The following verbs have different stems for **nous** and **vous.**

	appeler *(to call)*	essayer *(to try)*
je/j' tu il/elle/on	appelle appelles appelle	essaie essaies essaie
nous vous ils/elles	appelons appelez appellent	essayons essayez essaient
Past Participle	appelé	essayé

The following verbs show a difference only in the **nous** form.

	commencer *(to start)*	manger *(to eat)*
je/j' tu il/elle/on	commence commences commence	mange manges mange
nous vous ils/elles	commençons commencez commencent	mangeons mangez mangent
Past Participle	commencé	mangé

	nager *(to swim)*	voyager *(to travel)*
je/j' tu il/elle/on	nage nages nage	voyage voyages voyage
nous vous ils/elles	nageons nagez nagent	voyageons voyagez voyagent
Past Participle	nagé	voyagé

VERBS LIKE DORMIR

These verbs follow a different pattern from the one you learned for regular -ir verbs.
These verbs have two stems: one for the singular subjects, and one for the plural ones.

	dormir *(to sleep)*	**partir** *(to leave)*	**sortir** *(to go out, to take out)*
je/j'	dors	pars	sors
tu	dors	pars	sors
il/elle/on	dort	part	sort
nous	dorm**ons**	part**ons**	sort**ons**
vous	dorm**ez**	part**ez**	sort**ez**
ils/elles	dorm**ent**	part**ent**	sort**ent**

VERBS WITH IRREGULAR FORMS

Verbs listed in this section do not follow the pattern of verbs like **aimer, choisir,** or
vendre. Therefore, they are called *irregular verbs.* The following four irregular verbs are
used frequently.

	aller *(to go)*	**avoir** *(to have)*
je/j'	vais	ai
tu	vas	as
il/elle/on	va	a
nous	allons	avons
vous	allez	avez
ils/elles	vont	ont

	être *(to be)*	**faire** *(to do, to make, to play)*
je/j'	suis	fais
tu	es	fais
il/elle/on	est	fait
nous	sommes	faisons
vous	êtes	faites
ils/elles	sont	font

Devoir, pouvoir, and **vouloir** are also irregular. They are usually followed by an infinitive.

Je peux chanter. *I can sing.*

	devoir *(must, to have to)*	**pouvoir** *(to be able to, can)*	**vouloir** *(to want)*
je/j'	dois	peux	veux
tu	dois	peux	veux
il/elle/on	doit	peut	veut
nous	devons	pouvons	voulons
vous	devez	pouvez	voulez
ils/elles	doivent	peuvent	veulent

These verbs also have irregular forms.

	dire *(to say)*	**écrire** *(to write)*	**lire** *(to read)*
je/j'	dis	écris	lis
tu	dis	écris	lis
il/elle/on	dit	écrit	lit
nous	disons	écrivons	lisons
vous	dites	écrivez	lisez
ils/elles	disent	écrivent	lisent
Past Participle	dit	écrit	lu

	mettre *(to put, to put on, to wear)*	**prendre** *(to take, to have food or drink)*	**voir** *(to see)*
je/j'	mets	prends	vois
tu	mets	prends	vois
il/elle/on	met	prend	voit
nous	mettons	prenons	voyons
vous	mettez	prenez	voyez
ils/elles	mettent	prennent	voient
Past Participle	mis	pris	vu

THE NEAR FUTURE (FUTUR PROCHE)

Like the past tense, the near future is made of two parts. The future tense of a verb consists of the present tense of **aller** plus the infinitive:

Vous **allez sortir** avec vos copains demain. *You're going to go out with your friends tomorrow.*

THE PAST TENSE (PASSE COMPOSE)

The past tense of most verbs is formed with two parts: the present tense form of the helping verb **avoir** and the past participle of the main verb. To form the past participle, use the formulas below. To make a sentence negative in the past, place the **ne... pas** around the helping verb **avoir.**

INFINITIVE	aimer *(to love, to like)*		choisir *(to choose)*		vendre *(to sell)*	
	Stem	Ending	Stem	Ending	Stem	Ending
PAST PARTICIPLE	aim aimé	-é	chois choisi	-i	vend vendu	-u
PASSE COMPOSE	j'ai aimé		j'ai choisi		j'ai vendu	

J'**ai mangé** de la pizza.   Nous **avons choisi** le livre.

Elle n'**a** pas **vendu** sa voiture.   Nous n'**avons** pas **mangé** de pizza.

Some verbs have irregular past participles.

faire —> fait   **prendre —> pris**   **avoir —> eu**

lire —> lu   **voir —> vu**   **mettre —> mis**

With some verbs, such as **aller,** you use the helping verb **être** instead of **avoir.** The past participle of these verbs agrees in gender and number with the subject of the sentence.

Je **suis allé(e)** à l'école.   Ils **sont allés** à la poste.   Elle **est allée** au café.

THE IMPERATIVE (COMMANDS)

To make a request or a command of most verbs, use the **tu, nous,** or **vous** form of the present tense of the verb without the subject. Remember to drop the final **-s** in the **tu** form of an -er verb.

Mange!

Ecoute le professeur!

Faites vos devoirs!

Prenons un sandwich!

aimer *(to love, to like)*		choisir *(to choose)*		vendre *(to sell)*	
Stem	Ending	Stem	Ending	Stem	Ending
aim	-e -ons -ez	chois	-is -issons -issez	vend	-s -ons -ez

Chapter	Letter Combination	IPA Symbol	Example
Ch. 1, p. 35 Intonation			
Ch. 2, p. 63 Liaison			vous‿avez des‿amis
Ch. 3, p. 91 The **r** sound	the letter **r**	/ʀ/	rouge vert
Ch. 4, p. 125 The sounds [y] and [u]	the letter **u** the letter combination **ou**	/y/ /u/	une nous
Ch. 5, p. 157 The nasal sound [ɑ̃]	the letter combination **an** the letter combination **am** the letter combination **en** the letter combination **em**	/ɑ̃/	anglais jambon comment temps
Ch. 6, p. 187 The vowel sounds [ø] and [œ]	the letter combination **eu** the letter combination **eu**	/ø/ /œ/	deux heure
Ch. 7, p. 215 The nasal sounds [ɔ̃], [ɛ̃], and [œ̃]	the letter combination **on** the letter combination **om** the letter combination **in** the letter combination **im** the letter combination **ain** the letter combination **aim** the letter combination **(i)en** the letter combination **un** the letter combination **um**	/ɔ̃/ /ɛ̃/ /œ̃/	pardon nombre cousin impossible copain faim bien lundi humble
Ch. 8, p. 249 The sounds [o] and [ɔ]	the letter combination **au** the letter combination **eau** the letter **ô** the letter **o**	/o/ /ɔ/	jaune beau rôle carotte
Ch. 9, p. 281 The vowel sounds [e] and [ɛ]	the letter combination **ez** the letter combination **er** the letter combination **ait** the letter combination **ais** the letter combination **ei** the letter **ê**	/e/ /ɛ/	apportez trouver fait français neige bête
Ch. 10, p. 311 The glides [j], [w], and [ɥ]	the letter **i** the letter combination **ill** the letter combination **oi** the letter combination **oui** the letter combination **ui**	/j/ /w/ /ɥ/	mieux maillot moi Louis huit
Ch. 11, p. 339 **h aspiré, th, ch,** and **gn**	the letter **h** the letter combination **th** the letter combination **ch** the letter combination **gn**	/ˈ/ /t/ /ʃ/ /ɲ/	les halls théâtre chocolat oignon
Ch. 12, p. 373 Review			

Numbers

LES NOMBRES CARDINAUX

0	zéro	20	vingt	80	quatre-vingts
1	un(e)	21	vingt et un(e)	81	quatre-vingt-un(e)
2	deux	22	vingt-deux	82	quatre-vingt-deux
3	trois	23	vingt-trois	90	quatre-vingt-dix
4	quatre	24	vingt-quatre	91	quatre-vingt-onze
5	cinq	25	vingt-cinq	92	quatre-vingt-douze
6	six	26	vingt-six	100	cent
7	sept	27	vingt-sept	101	cent un
8	huit	28	vingt-huit	200	deux cents
9	neuf	29	vingt-neuf	201	deux cent un
10	dix	30	trente	300	trois cents
11	onze	31	trente et un(e)	800	huit cents
12	douze	32	trente-deux	1.000	mille
13	treize	40	quarante	2.000	deux mille
14	quatorze	50	cinquante	3.000	trois mille
15	quinze	60	soixante	10.000	dix mille
16	seize	70	soixante-dix	19.000	dix-neuf mille
17	dix-sept	71	soixante et onze	40.000	quarante mille
18	dix-huit	72	soixante-douze	500.000	cinq cent mille
19	dix-neuf	73	soixante-treize	1.000.000	un million

- The word **et** is used only in 21, 31, 41, 51, 61, and 71.
- **Vingt** (**trente, quarante,** and so on) **et une** is used when the number refers to a feminine noun: **trente et une cassettes.**
- The **s** is dropped from **quatre-vingts** and is not added to multiples of **cent** when these numbers are followed by another number: **quatre-vingt-cinq; deux cents,** *but* **deux cent six.** The number **mille** never takes an **s** to agree with a noun: **deux mille insectes.**
- **Un million** is followed by **de** + a noun: **un million de francs.**
- In writing numbers, a period is used in French where a comma is used in English.

LES NOMBRES ORDINAUX

1er, 1ère	premier, première	9e	neuvième	17e	dix-septième
2e	deuxième	10e	dixième	18e	dix-huitième
3e	troisième	11e	onzième	19e	dix-neuvième
4e	quatrième	12e	douzième	20e	vingtième
5e	cinquième	13e	treizième	21e	vingt et unième
6e	sixième	14e	quatorzième	22e	vingt-deuxième
7e	septième	15e	quinzième	30e	trentième
8e	huitième	16e	seizième	40e	quarantième

French-English Vocabulary

English-French Vocabulary

French-English Vocabulary

This list includes both active and passive vocabulary in this textbook. Active words and phrases are those listed in the **Vocabulaire** section at the end of each chapter. You are expected to know and be able to use active vocabulary. All entries in heavy black type in this list are active. All other words are passive. Passive vocabulary is for recognition only.

The number after each entry refers to the chapter where the word or phrase is introduced. Nouns are always given with an article. If it is not clear whether the noun is masculine or feminine, *m.* (masculine) or *f.* (feminine) follows the noun. Some nouns that are generally seen only in the plural, as well as ones that have an irregular plural form, are also given with gender indications and the abbreviation *pl.* (plural) following them. An asterisk (*) before a word beginning with *h* indicates an aspirate *h*. Phrases are alphabetized by the key word(s) in the phrase.

The following abbreviations are also used in this vocabulary: *pp.* (past participle), *inv.* (invariable), and *adj.* (adjective).

à *to, in (a city or place),* 11; **à côté de** *next to,* 12; **à la** *to, at,* 6; **A bientôt.** *See you soon.* 1; à carreaux *checked,* 10; **A demain.** *See you tomorrow.* 1; à fleurs *flowered,* 10; à la carte *pick and choose,* 3; à la française *French-style,* 1; **à la mode** *in style,* 10; à part ça *aside from that,* 11; à pois *polka dot,* 10; à propos de *in regard to, about,* 4; **A quelle heure?** *At what time?* 6; à rayures *striped,* 10; **A tout à l'heure!** *See you later!* 1; **A votre service.** *At your service; You're welcome.* 3; Et maintenant, à toi. *And now, it's your turn.* 1
l' abbaye (f.) *abbey,* 6
abîmer *to ruin,* 10
s' abonner *to subscribe;* abonnez-vous à... *subscribe to . . . ,* 3
l' abricot (m.) *apricot,* 5
abriter *to house,* 11
absent(e) *absent,* 2
accepter *to accept,* 6
accompagner *to accompany,* 4
l' accord (m.) *agreement;* Fais l'accord... *Make the agreement . . . ,* 7
l' accueil (m.) *reception, welcome,* 4
accueille (accueillir) *to welcome*
l' achat (m.) *purchase,* 3
acheter *to buy,* 9; **Achète (-moi)...** *Buy (me) . . . ,* 8; Je n'achète pas... *I don't buy / I'm not buying . . . ,* 3
l' acra de morue (m.) *cod fritter*

l' activité (f.) *activity,* 4
l' **addition** (f.) *check, bill,* 5; **L'addition, s'il vous plaît.** *The check, please.* 5
adhésif (-ive) *adhesive,* 3
admirer *to admire,* 7
adorable *adorable,* 7
adorer *to adore,* 1; **J'adore...** *I adore . . .* 1; J'adorerais... *I would adore . . . ,* 1
l' **aérobic** (f.) *aerobics,* 4; **faire de l'aérobic** *to do aerobics,* 4
l' aéroport (m.) *airport,* 11
les affaires (f.) *business, business affairs,* 8
affectueux (-euse) *affectionate,* 7
afin de *in order to,* 7
l' Afrique (f.) *Africa,* 8
l' **âge** (m.) *age,* 1; **Tu as quel âge?** *How old are you?* 1
âgé(e) *older,* 7
l' agenda (m.) *planner,* 4
agit : il s'agit de *it's concerned with; it's about,* 6
agréable *pleasant,* 4
ai : J'ai... *I have . . . ,* 2; **J'ai... ans.** *I am . . . years old.* 1; **J'ai besoin de...** *I need . . . ,* 8; **J'ai faim.** *I'm hungry.* 5; **J'ai l'intention de...** *I intend to . . . ,* 11; **J'ai soif.** *I'm thirsty.* 5; **Je n'ai pas de...** *I don't have . . . ,* 3
l' aide-mémoire (m.) *memory aid,* 3
aider *to help,* 10; **(Est-ce que) je peux vous aider?** *May I help you?* 10
l' ail (m.) *garlic,* 8
les ailes (f.) *wings,* 12
aimé(e) (pp. of aimer) *loved,* 1

aimer *to like,* 1; **J'aime mieux...** *I prefer . . . ,*1; **J'aimerais... pour aller avec...** *I'd like . . . to go with . . . ,*10; **Je n'aime pas...** *I don't like . . . ,* 1; **Moi, j'aime (bien)...** *I (really) like . . . ,* 1; **Tu aimes...?** *Do you like . . . ?* 1
l' aire de pique-nique aménagée (f.) *equipped picnic area,* 6
l' aise (f.) *ease,* 7
ajouter *to add,* 10
l' **algèbre** (f.) *algebra,* 2
l' Algérie (f.) *Algeria,* 0
l' alimentation (f.) *food,* 12
les aliments (m.) *nutrients,* 8
allé(e) (pp. of aller) *went,* 9; **Je suis allé(e)...** *I went . . . ,* 9; **Tu es allé(e) où?** *Where did you go?* 9
l' allée (f.) *path, driveway,* 4
l' **allemand** (m.) *German (language),* 2
aller *to go,* 6; **Ça va aller mieux!** *It's going to get better!* 9; **On peut y aller...** *We can go there . . . ,* 12
allez : Allez au tableau! *Go to the blackboard!* 0; **Allez, viens!** *Come along!* 0
Allô? *Hello?* 9
l' allocation de naissance (f.) *money provided as a birth allowance by the French government,* 7; l'allocation familiale (f.) *money provided by the French government to large families,* 7
allons : Allons-y! *Let's go!* 4; **Allons...** *Let's go . . . ,* 6
l' aloco (m.) *dish from West Africa made from fried plantain bananas and usually eaten as a snack,* 5
alors *well, then,* 3
l' alphabet (m.) *alphabet,* 0

l' ambiance (f.) *atmosphere*, 2
aménagé(e) *equipped*, 6
américain(e) *American (adj.)*, 0
l' **ami(e)** *friend*, 1
amical(e) (pl. amicaux) *friendly*, 2
amicalement *sincerely (to close a letter)*, 1
l' amitié (f.) *friendship*, 1
l' amour (m.) *love*, 1
l' amphithéâtre (m.) *amphitheater*, 9
amusant(e) *funny*, 7
s' amuser *to have fun*, 11; **Amuse-toi bien!** *Have fun!* 11; **Qu'est-ce que tu fais pour t'amuser?** *What do you do to have fun?* 4; **Tu t'es bien amusé(e)?** *Did you have fun?* 11
l' **an** (m.) *year*, 1; **J'ai... ans.** *I am . . . years old.* 1
l' **ananas** (m.) *pineapple*, 8
ancien(ne) *old; former*, 6; l'ancienne gare *the former train station*, 6
l' Andorre (article not commonly used) *Andorra*, 0
l' **anglais** (m.) *English (language)*, 1
l' animal (m.) *animal*, 1; animal domestique *pet*, 7
l' animateur (m.) *camp counselor*, 11
les animations (f.) *activities*, 11
animé(e) *animated, lively*, 8
l' année (f.) *year*, 4
l' année scolaire (f.) *school year*, 2
l' anniversaire (m.) *anniversary; birthday*, 7
annoncer *to announce*, 7
les annonces (f.) *ads*, 1; les petites annonces *personal or business ads*, 1
anthracite *charcoal grey*, 10
antillais(e) (adj.) *Antillean, from the Antilles (islands in the Caribbean Sea)*, 12
antique *ancient*, 9
les antiquités (f.) *antiquities, antiques*, 6
août *August*, 4; **en août** *in August*, 4
l' **appareil** (m.) *phone*, 9; **Qui est à l'appareil?** *Who's calling?* 9
l' **appareil-photo** (m.) *camera*, 11
appartient (appartenir) à *to belong to*, 9
s' **appeler** *to call oneself, to be called*, 1; **Il/Elle s'appelle comment?** *What's his/her name?* 1; **Il/Elle s'appelle...** *His/Her name is . . . ,* 1; **Je m'appelle...** *My name is . . . ,* 1; **Tu t'appelles comment?** *What's your name?* 1
apporter *to bring*, 9; **Apportez-moi... , s'il vous plaît.** *Please bring me . . . ,* 5
apprendre *to learn*, 0
approprié(e) *appropriate*, 7
l' **aprèm** (m.) *afternoon*, 2; cet aprèm *this afternoon*, 2

après *after, afterward*, 9; **Et après?** *And afterwards?* 9
l' après-guerre (m.) *post-war*, 11
l' **après-midi** (m.) *afternoon; in the afternoon*, 2; **l'après-midi libre** *afternoon off*, 2
l' arabe (m.) *Arabic (language)*, 1
l' arbre (m.) *tree*, 12
l' archéologue (m.) *archaeologist*, 9
l' ardoise (f.) *writing slate*, 3
l' arène (f.) *amphitheater*, 9
l' **argent** (m.) *money*, 11
l' arôme (m.) *aroma, odor*, 8
l' arrivée (f.) *arrival*, 6
arroser *to sprinkle*, 8
l' art (m.) *art*, 1
l' article (m.) *article, item*, 8
l' artiste (m./f.) *artist*, 0
les **arts plastiques** (m. pl.) *art class*, 2
as : Tu as... ? *Do you have . . . ?* 3; **Tu as quel âge?** *How old are you?* 1; **De quoi est-ce que tu as besoin?** *What do you need?* 8
l' ascenseur (m.) *elevator*, 6
l' ascension (f.) *ascent, climb*, 6; ascension en haut de la tour *ascent/climb to the top of the tower*, 6
l' **aspirateur** (m.) *vacuum cleaner*, 7; **passer l'aspirateur** *to vacuum*, 7
l' aspirine (f.) *aspirin*, 12
Asseyez : Asseyez-vous! *Sit down!* 0
assez *enough, fairly*, 2
assis(e) *seated, sitting*, 12
assidu(e) *regular (punctual)*, 2
l' **assiette** (f.) *plate*, 5
assuré(e) (pp. of assurer) *assured*, 1
l' **athlétisme** (m.) *track and field*, 4; **faire de l'athlétisme** *to do track and field*, 4
attachant(e) *loving*, 7
attendre *to wait for*, 9
Attention! *Watch out!* 7
attentivement *attentively*, 9
l' attiéké (m.) *ground manioc root*, 8
attirer *to attract*, 9
au *to, at*, 6; *to, in (before a masculine noun)*, 11; **au métro...** *at the . . . metro stop*, 6; au milieu *in the middle*, 7; **au revoir** *goodbye*, 1; Au secours! *Help!* 9
l' auberge de jeunesse (f.) *youth hostel*, 11
aucun(e) *none*, 7
aujourd'hui *today*, 2
aussi *also*, 1; **Moi aussi.** *Me too.* 2
l' **automne** (m.) *autumn, fall*, 4; **en automne** *in the fall*, 4
autour de *around*, 8
autre *other*, 4
aux *to, in (before a plural noun)*, 6
Av. (abbrev. of avenue) (f.) *avenue*, 6
avant *before*, 1

avec *with*, 1; **avec moi** *with me*, 6; **Avec qui?** *With whom?* 6
l' aventure (f.) *adventure*, 11
avez : Qu'est-ce que vous avez comme ... ? *What kind of . . . do you have?* 5; **Vous avez... ?** *Do you have . . . ?* 2
l' **avion** (m.) *plane*, 12; **en avion** *by plane*, 12, **un billet d'avion** *plane ticket*, 11
l' **avis** (m.) *opinion*, 9; **A ton avis, qu'est-ce que je fais?** *In your opinion, what do I do?* 9
l' **avocat** (m.) *avocado*, 8
avoir *to have*, 2; **avoir faim** *to be hungry*, 5; avoir hâte de *to be in a hurry (to do something)*, 7; avoir la flemme *to be lazy*, 9; avoir lieu *to take place*, 7; avoir raison *to be right*, 2; **avoir soif** *to be thirsty*, 5
avons : Nous avons... *We have . . . ,* 2
avril April, 4; **en avril** *in April*, 4
ayant : ayant pu donner *having been able to give*, 2

le baby (foot) *table soccer game*, 5
le bac(calauréat) *secondary school exam for entering a university*, 2
le bachelier *someone who has passed the **bac***, 2
le bagage *luggage*, 10
la **baguette** *long, thin loaf of bread*, 12
la baie *bay*
la balade à cheval *horseback ride*, 7
se balader *to stroll*, 6
le balcon *balcony*, 12
le ballon *ball*, 4
le bambou *bamboo*, 12
la **banane** *banana*, 8
le banc *(park) bench*, 12
les bandes dessinées (f.) *comic strips*, 2
la **banque** *bank*, 12
barbant(e) *boring*, 2
le **base-ball** *baseball*, 4; **jouer au base-ball** *to play baseball*, 4
le basilic *basil*, 5
le **basket(-ball)** *basketball*, 4; **jouer au basket(-ball)** *to play basketball*, 4
les **baskets** (f.) *sneakers*, 3
le **bateau** *boat*, 11; **en bateau** *by boat*, 12; **faire du bateau** *to go boating*, 11
le bateau-mouche *river boat*, 6
le bâtiment *building*, 12
bd (abbrev. of boulevard) (m.) *boulevard*, 6

beau (belle) *nice, pretty,* 4; **Il fait beau.** *It's nice weather.* 4
Beaucoup *A lot.* 4; **Oui, beaucoup.** *Yes, very much.* 2; **Pas beaucoup.** *Not very much.* 4
le **beau-père** *stepfather; father-in-law,* 7
le **bébé** *baby,* 7
belge *Belgian* (adj.), 1
la **Belgique** *Belgium,* 0
la **belle-mère** *stepmother; mother-in-law,* 7
le **besoin** *need,* 8; **De quoi est-ce que tu as besoin?** *What do you need?* 8; **J'ai besoin de...** *I need . . . ,* 8
la **bête** *animal,* 12
le **beurre** *butter,* 8
la **bibliothèque** *library,* 6
le **bic** *ballpoint pen,* 3
bien *well,* 1; **Je veux bien.** *Gladly.* 8; **Je veux bien.** *I'd really like to.* 6; **J'en veux bien.** *I'd like some.* 8; **Moi, j'aime (bien)...** *I (really) like . . . ,* 1; **Très bien.** *Very well.* 1
Bien sûr. *Of course.* 3; *certainly,* 9; **Oui, bien sûr.** *Yes, of course.* 7
bientôt *soon,* 1; **À bientôt.** *See you soon.* 1
Bienvenue! *Welcome!* 0
le **bien-vivre** *good living, the good life,* 6
le **bifteck** *steak,* 8
les **bijoux** (m.) *jewelry,* 10
le **billet** *ticket,* 11; **un billet d'avion** *plane ticket,* 11; **un billet de train** *train ticket,* 11
la **biologie** *biology,* 2
bizarre *strange,* 7
blanc(he) *white,* 3
le **blanc-manger** *coconut pudding*
bleu(e) *blue,* 3; **bleu clair** *light blue,* 10; **bleu foncé** *dark blue,* 10
blond(e) *blond,* 7
le **blouson** *jacket,* 10
le **bœuf** *beef,* 8
Bof! *(expression of indifference),* 1
boire *to drink,* 5; **Qu'est-ce qu'il y a à boire?** *What is there to drink?* 5
le **bois** *wood,* 12
la **boisson** *drink, beverage,* 5; **Qu'est-ce que vous avez comme boissons?** *What do you have to drink?* 5
la **boîte** *box, can,* 8; **une boîte de** *a can of,* 8
le **bon** *coupon,* 6
bon(ne) *good,* 5; **Bon courage!** *Good luck!* 2; **Bon voyage!** *Have a good trip!* 11; **Bon, d'accord.** *Well, OK.* 8; **de bons conseils** *good advice,* 1; **Oui, très bon.** *Yes, very good.* 9; **pas bon** *not good,* 5
Bonjour *Hello,* 1
bonne (f. of **bon**) *good,* 5; **Bonne chance!** *Good luck!* 11; **Bonne idée.** *Good idea.* 4; **Bonnes**

vacances! *Have a good vacation!* 11
le **bord** *side, edge;* **au bord de la mer** *to/on the coast,* 11
les **bottes** (f.) *boots,* 10
les **boucles d'oreilles** (f.) *earrings,* 10
le **boudin créole** *spicy Creole sausage,* 12
bouger *to move,* 10
bouillant(e) *boiling,* 8
la **boulangerie** *bakery,* 12
la **boule** *ball,* 8
la **boum** *party,* 6; **aller à une boum** *to go to a party,* 6
le **bouquiniste** *bookseller who has a stand along the Seine River in Paris,* 5
la **bouteille** *bottle,* 8; **une bouteille de** *a bottle of,* 8
la **boutique** *store, shop,* 3; **une boutique de souvenirs** *souvenir shop,* 3
le **bracelet** *bracelet,* 3
la **Bretagne** *Brittany (region of northwest France),* 7
la **brioche** *brioche, light, slightly sweet bread made with a rich yeast dough,* 8
la **brochure** *brochure,* 4
la **broderie** *embroidery,* 10
brun(e) *brunette,* 7
le **bulletin trimestriel** *report card,* 2
le **bureau** *office, desk,* 8; **bureau de tabac** *newsstand,* 9
le **bus** *bus,* 12; **en bus** *by bus,* 12; **rater le bus** *to miss the bus,* 9
la **buvette** *refreshment stand,* 12
byzantin(e) *Byzantine; of the style of art and architecture developed in Eastern Europe between the 4th and 15th centuries (characterized by domes and elaborate mosaics),* 12

C'est... *It's . . . ,* 2; **C'est...** *This is . . . ,* 7; **C'est qui?** *Who is it?* 2; **C'est combien?** *How much is it?* 3; **C'est du gâteau.** *It's a piece of cake.* 8; **C'est pas de la tarte.** *It's not easy.* 8; **C'est tout.** *That's all.* 1; **Ça, c'est...** *This/That is . . . ,* 12; **Non, c'est impossible.** *No, that's impossible.* 7
C'était barbant! *It was boring!* 11
ça *that; it;* **Ça boume?** *How's it going?* 2; **Ça va.** *Fine.* 1; **Ça va?** *How are things going?* 1; **Ça, c'est...** *This/That is . . . ,* 12; **Ça m'est égal** *It doesn't matter; I don't care.* 10; **Ça ne me dit rien.** *That doesn't*

interest me. 4; *I don't feel like it.* 6; **ça suffit** *that's enough,* 12; **Et après ça...** *And after that, . . . ,* 9; **Oui, ça a été.** *Yes, it was fine.* 9
ça fait : Ça fait combien, s'il vous plaît? *How much is it, please?* 5;
la **cabine téléphonique** *phone booth,* 9
le **cabinet de toilette** *small room with a sink and counter,* 11
caché(e) (pp. of *cacher*) *hidden,* 11
le **cadeau** *gift,* 11
le **café** *coffee, café,* 5; **le café au lait** *coffee with hot milk,* 8; **le café crème** *coffee with cream,* 5
le **cahier** *notebook,* 0
la **calculatrice** *calculator,* 3; **une calculatrice-traductrice** *translating calculator,* 3
le **caleçon** *leggings,* 4
le **calendrier** *calendar,* 6
la **Californie** *California,* 4
le **camarade** (la **camarade**) *friend;* **camarade de classe** *classmate,* 7
le **camembert** *Camembert cheese,* 5
le **caméscope** *camcorder,* 4
le **camp de sport** *sports camp,* 9
la **campagne** *countryside,* 11; **à la campagne** *to/in the countryside,* 11
le **camping** *camping,* 11; **faire du camping** *to go camping,* 11
le **Canada** *Canada,* 4
le **canal** *channel,* 3
le **canari** *canary,* 7
le **caniveau** *sidewalk gutter,* 7
la **cantine** *cafeteria,* 9; **à la cantine** *at the school cafeteria,* 9
la **capitale** *capital,* 5
car *because,* 4
la **caractéristique** *characteristic,* 8
la **carambole** *star fruit,* 12
la **carcasse** *body,* 12
le **cardigan** *sweater,* 10
le **carnaval** *carnival,* 11
la **carotte** *carrot,* 8
la **carrière** *quarry,* 11
la **carte** *map,* 0; *menu,* 12; **à la carte** *pick and choose,* 3; **La carte, s'il vous plaît.** *The menu, please.* 5
les **cartes** (f.) *cards,* 4; **jouer aux cartes** *to play cards,* 4
la **cartouche** *cartridge,* 3; **cartouche d'encre** *ink cartridge,* 3
le **carvi** *cumin (Afrique),* 8; **graines de carvi** *cumin seeds,* 8
la **casquette** *cap,* 10
la **cassette** *cassette tape,* 3
la **cassette vidéo** *videocassette,* 4
le **catalogue** *catalog,* 10
la **catégorie** *category,* 8
la **cathédrale** *cathedral,* 1
le **cauchemar** *nightmare,* 11; **C'était un véritable cauchemar!** *It was a real nightmare!* 11

ce *this; that,* 3; **Ce sont...** *These/Those are . . . ,* 7
la ceinture *belt,* 10
célèbre *famous, well-known,* 4
cent *one hundred,* 3; **deux cents** *two hundred,* 3
la centaine *a hundred or so;* des centaines d'années *hundreds of years,* 9
le centre *center,* 4
le centre commercial *mall,* 6
le centre-ville *city center,* 12
cependant *however,* 11
le cercle *circle, group,* 6; au cercle français *at French Club,* 4
certain(e) *certain, some,* 7
ces *these, those,* 3
cet *this, that,* 3
cette *this; that,* 3
chacun *each (person),* 5; Chacun ses goûts! *To each his own!* 1
la chaise *chair,* 0
chaleureux (-euse) *warm,* 9
la chambre *room,* 7; **ranger ta chambre** *to pick up your room,* 7
le champignon *mushroom,* 8
la chance *luck,* 11; **Bonne chance!** *Good luck!* 11
le changement *change,* 10
changer *to change,* 7
chanter *to sing,* 9
le chanteur *singer (male),* 9
la chanteuse *singer (female),* 9
Chantilly : la crème Chantilly *sweetened whipped cream,* 5
le chapeau *hat,* 10
le chapitre *chapter,* 9
chaque *each,* 4
chargé(e) *busy,* 2
le chariot *shopping cart,* 8
la chasse *hunting,* 7; une chasse au trésor *treasure hunt,* 3
le chat *cat,* 7
le chaton *kitten,* 7
chaud(e) *hot,* 4; **Il fait chaud.** *It's hot.* 4
chauffé(e) *heated,* 11
les chaussettes (f.) *socks,* 10
les chaussures (f.) *shoes,* 10; les chaussures à crampons *spikes,* 4
le chef-d'œuvre *masterpiece,* 6
la chemise *shirt (man's),* 10
la chemise *folder,* 3
le chemisier *shirt (woman's),* 10
le chèque *check,* 0
cher (chère) *dear,* 1; *expensive,* 3; **C'est trop cher.** *It's too expensive.* 10
chercher *to look for,* 9; **Je cherche quelque chose pour...** *I'm looking for something for . . . ,* 10
chéri(e) (noun) mon chéri/ma chérie *darling, sweetie,* 8
le cheval *horse,* 12; le cheval de bois *wooden horse, carousel horse,* 12

chez... *to/at . . . 's house,* 6; **chez le disquaire** *at the record store,* 12; **Je suis bien chez... ?** *Is this . . . 's house?* 9
chic *chic,* 10
le chien *dog,* 7; **promener le chien** *to walk the dog,* 7
le chiffre *number,* 0
la chimie *chemistry,* 2
chimique *chemical,* 9
le chocolat *chocolate,* 1; **un chocolat** *hot chocolate,* 5
la chocolaterie *chocolate shop,* 12
choisi (pp. of choisir) *decided, chosen;* **Vous avez choisi?** *Have you decided/chosen?* 5
choisir *to choose, to pick,* 10
le choix *choice,* 8
la chorale *choir,* 2
la chose *thing,* 5; **J'ai des tas de choses (trucs) à faire.** *I have lots of things to do.* 5
le chou *cabbage,* 1; mon chou *my darling, dear,* 1
chouette *cool,* 9; **Très chouette.** *Very cool.* 9
chrétien(ne) *Christian,* 9
la chute *waterfall,* 4
ci-dessous *below,* 8
le cimetière *cemetery,* 9
le cinéma *movie theater,* 6; *movies,* 1
cinq *five,* 9
cinquième *fifth,* 9
la Cité des Papes *monument in Avignon, France; a citadel of palaces where French popes lived and ruled in the 14th century,* 11
le citron *lemon,* 8
le citron pressé *lemonade,* 5
clair(e) *light (color),* 10
le classeur *loose-leaf binder,* 3
classique *classical,* 4
le client (la cliente) *customer,* 5
le climat *climate,* 11
climatisé(e) *air-conditioned,* 11
le clocher *steeple,* 12
le club *club,* 11
le coca *cola,* 5
le coco *coconut,* 8
le code de la route *rules of the road; test,* 12
le cœur *heart,* 9
le coin *corner,* 12; **au coin de** *on the corner of,* 12
le col *collar,* 10; au col montant *with turtleneck,* 10
le collant *hose,* 10
la colle *glue,* 3; un pot de colle *container of glue,* 3
la collection *collection,* 10
le collège *junior high school,* 2
la colonie de vacances *summer camp,* 11
coloré(e) *colorful,* 8
le coloris *color, shade,* 3

combien *how much, how many,* 3; **C'est combien,... ?** *How much is . . . ?* 5; **C'est combien?** *How much is it?* 3; **Ça fait combien, s'il vous plaît?** *How much is it, please?* 5
le combiné *(telephone) receiver,* 9
comique *comic, comical;* un film comique *comedy (movie),* 6
commander *to order,* 5
comme *like, as,* 4; **Comme ci comme ça.** *So-so.* 1; Qu'est-ce qu'ils aiment comme cours? *What subjects do they like?* 2; **Qu'est-ce que tu fais comme sport?** *What sports do you play?* 4; **Qu'est-ce que vous avez comme... ?** *What kind of . . . do you have?* 5
le commencement *beginning,* 9
commencer *to begin, to start,* 9
comment *what,* 0; *how,* 1; **(Comment) ça va?** *How's it going?* 1; Comment dit-on? *How do you say it?* 1; Comment le dire? *How should you say it?* 1; **Comment tu trouves... ?** *What do you think of . . . ?* 2; **Comment tu trouves ça?** *What do you think of that/it?* 2; **Il/Elle est comment?** *What is he/she like?* 7; **Ils/Elles sont comment?** *What are they like?* 7; **Tu t'appelles comment?** *What is your name?* 0
le commentaire *commentary,* 9
le commerçant *store owner,* 8
la Communauté financière africaine (CFA) *African Financial Community; the group of African countries that share a common currency (the CFA franc),* 3
la compagnie aérienne (f.) *airline company,* 10
le compagnon *companion,* 7
comparer *to compare,* 10
le compas *compass,* 3
compétent(e) *competent,* 2
compléter *to complete,* 4
le compliment *compliment,* 10
comprends : Tu comprends? *Do you understand?* 2
compris(e) *included,* 5
compris (pp. of comprendre): Tu as compris? *Did you understand?* 1
le concert *concert,* 1
le concombre *cucumber,* 8
conçu(e) (pp. of concevoir) *conceived,* 9
confier *to confide,* 9
la confiture *jam,* 8
connais : Tu les connais? *Do you know them?* 0; Tu connais ces nombres? *Do you recognize these numbers?* 2

la connaissance *acquaintance;* **Faisons connaissance!** *Let's get acquainted.* 1
connu(e) (pp. of connaître) *knew; known;* **le plus connu** *the best-known* (adj.), 6
le conseil *advice,* 1; **de bons conseils** *good advice,* 1; **demander conseil** *to ask for advice,* 11
conseiller *to advise, to counsel;* **Qu'est-ce que tu me conseilles?** *What do you advise me to do?* 9
le conseiller *adviser,* 12
la conseillère *adviser,* 12
conservé (pp. of conserver) *kept,* 2; **ce bulletin doit être conservé(e)** *this report card must be kept,* 2; *preserved (food);* **c'est plus sûr et bien conservé** *it's safer and better preserved,* 8
consoler *to console (someone), to make (someone) feel better, to comfort,* 9
construit(e) (pp. of construire) *constructed, built,* 9
contenir *to contain,* 9
content(e) *happy, pleased,* 7
le contenu *contents,* 8
continuer *to continue,* 12; **Vous continuez jusqu'au prochain feu rouge.** *You keep going until the next light.* 12
le contraste *contrast,* 8
contraster *to contrast,* 8
contre *against,* 2
la conversation *conversation,* 7
cool *cool,* 2
le copain (la copine) *friend,* 1
le cordon *cord, string;* **le cordon de serrage** *drawstring,* 10
le cornichon *pickle,* 8
le corps *body,* 8
correct(e) *correct, proper,* 9
le correspondant (la correspondante) *pen pal,* 1
correspondre *to write; to correspond,* 1; **Fais correspondre...** *Match...,* 6
la corvée ménagère *household chore,* 7
le costume *costume, traditional dress,* 9
la côte *coast,* 11
le côté *side;* **à côté de** *next to,* 12; **du côté de mon père** *on my father's side (of the family),* 7
le coton *cotton,* 10; **en coton** *(made of) cotton,* 10
la couleur *color,* 3; **De quelle couleur est...?** *What color is...?* 3
le coup *hit, blow;* **le coup de fil** *phone call,* 9
la coupe *dish(ful),* 5
la coupe Melba *vanilla ice cream, peaches, whipped cream, and fruit sauce,* 5

courir *to run,* 7
le cours *course,* 2; **le cours de développement personnel et social (DPS)** *health,* 2; **Tu as quels cours...?** *What classes do you have...?* 2
les courses (f.) *shopping, errands,* 7; **faire les courses** *to do the shopping,* 7; **J'ai des courses à faire.** *I have errands to do.* 5
court(e) *short (length),* 10
le cousin *male cousin,* 7
la cousine *female cousin,* 7
coûteux (-euse) *expensive,* 8
le crabe *crab,* 5; **les crabes farcis** *deviled land crabs,* 9
la cravate *tie,* 10
le crayon *pencil,* 3; **des crayons de couleur** *colored pencils,* 3
créer *to create,* 11
la crème fraîche *thick cream like sour cream but without the sour flavor; used to make sauces and toppings,* 5
le créole *creole language,* 12
la crêpe *very thin pancake,* 5
la crêperie *café or restaurant which specializes in crêpes,* 5
crépiter *to crackle,* 12
le creuset *melting pot;* **le creuset de l'Afrique** *the melting pot of Africa,* 8
croire *to believe;* **Tu crois?** *Do you think so?* 10
la croisière *cruise,* 11
le croissant *croissant; flaky, buttery roll eaten at breakfast,* 5
la croissanterie *croissant shop,* 12
le croque-monsieur *toasted ham and cheese sandwich,* 5
cru(e) *uncooked,* 5
le cuir *leather,* 10; **en cuir** *(made of) leather,* 10
cuire *to cook, to bake,* 8
la culture *culture,* 7
culturel(le) *cultural,* 0

D'abord, ... *First, ...,* 9
D'accord. *O.K.* 4; **Bon, d'accord.** *Well, O.K.* 8; **D'accord, si tu... d'abord...** *O.K. if you..., first.* 7; **Tu es d'accord?** *Is that O.K. with you?* 7
d'après *according to,* 4
d'habitude *usually,* 4
dans *in,* 6
danser *to dance,* 1
la danse *dance,* 2
le danseur (la danseuse) *dancer,* 9
de *from,* 0; *of,* 0; **de l'** *some,* 8;

de la *some,* 8; **Je n'ai pas de...** *I don't have...,* 3; **Je ne fais pas de...** *I don't play/do...,* 4
déambuler *to stroll,* 11
débarrasser la table *to clear the table,* 7
le débutant (la débutante) *beginner,* 4
décaféiné(e) *decaffeinated,* 5
décédé(e) *deceased,* 7
décembre *December,* 4; **en décembre** *in December,* 4
le décès *death,* 7
déchiffrer *to decode,* 7
décider *to decide,* 5; **Vous avez décidé de prendre...?** *Have you decided to take...?* 10
décontracté(e) *relaxed,* 11
la découverte *discovery,* 3
découvrir *to discover,* 8
décrire *to describe,* 7
décrocher *to take down; to unhook;* **quand l'interlocuteur décroche** *when the speaker picks up (the phone),* 9
dedans *inside,* 3
défavorable *unfavorable, disapproving,* 7
dégoûtant(e) *gross,* 5
dehors *outside,* 8
déjà *already,* 9
déjeuner *to have lunch,* 9; **le déjeuner** *lunch,* 9
délicieux (-euse) *delicious,* 5
délirer *to be delirious;* **La techno me fait délirer.** *I'm wild about techno music.* 1
délivré(e) (pp. of délivrer) : **il n'en sera pas délivré de duplicata** *duplicates will not be issued,* 2
le deltaplane *hang-glider;* **faire du deltaplane** *to go hang-gliding,* 4
demain *tomorrow,* 2; **À demain.** *See you tomorrow.* 1
demander *to ask, to ask for,* 7; **demander conseil** *to ask for advice,* 11
demi(e) *half;* **et demi** *half past (after **midi** and **minuit**),* 6; **et demie** *half past,* 6
le demi-frère *stepbrother,* 7; *half-brother,* 7
la demi-sœur *stepsister,* 7; *half-sister,* 7
démodé(e) *out of style,* 10
démonté(e) *dismantled,* 12
le dentiste (la dentiste) *dentist,* 1
le départ *departure,* 6
le département d'outre-mer *overseas department,* 12
dépêchez : **Dépêchez-vous de...** *hurry up and...,* 1
déplorable *deplorable,* 2
déposer *to deposit,* 12
déprimé(e) *depressed,* 9

depuis   *for (a certain amount of time)*, 9; *since*, 12
le **dérivé**   *derivative, by-product;* le sucre et ses dérivés   *sugar and its by-products*, 8
dernier (-ière)   *last;* la semaine dernière   *last week*, 9
derrière   *behind*, 12
des   *some*, 3
les **dés** (m.)   *dice;* découper en dés   *to dice*, 8
dès que   *as soon as*, 9
désagréable   *unpleasant*, 4
la description   *description*, 7
désirer   *to desire, to want;* **Vous désirez?**   *What would you like?* 10
désolé(e) : Désolé(e), je suis occupé(e).   *Sorry, I'm busy.* 6; **Désolé(e), mais je ne peux pas.**   *Sorry, but I can't.* 4
le dessert   *dessert*, 0
le dessin   *drawing*, 3
le détail   *detail*, 9
détailler   *to slice*, 8
détester   *to hate, to detest*, 6
deux   *two*, 0; les deux   *both*, 7
la deuxième étape   *second step*, 1
devant   *in front of*, 6
devenir   *to become*, 9
devez : vous devez   *you must*, 11
deviennent : Que deviennent... ?   *What happened to . . . ?* 7
deviner   *to guess*, 7; Devine!   *Guess!* 0
devoir   *to have to, must*, 7
les **devoirs** (m.)   *homework*, 2; **J'ai des devoirs à faire.**   *I've got homework to do.* 5
le dévouement   *devotion*, 7
devrais : Tu devrais...   *You should . . . ,* 9
la diapo(sitive)   *photographic slide*, 11
la dictée   *dictation*, 0
le dictionnaire   *dictionary*, 3
la différence   *difference*, 2
différent(e)   *different*, 7
difficile   *difficult*, 2
dimanche   *Sunday*, 2; **le dimanche**   *on Sundays*, 2
dîner   *to have dinner*, 9; **le dîner**   *dinner*, 8
dingue   *crazy*, 1; Je suis dingue de...   *I'm crazy about . . . ,* 1
dire   *to say;* 1; *to tell*, 9; Comment le dire?   *How should you say it?* 1; Dis,...   *Say, . . . ,* 2; **Ça ne me dit rien.**   *That doesn't interest me.* 4; Comment dit-on... ?   *How do you say . . . ?* 1; Jacques a dit...   *Simon says . . . ,* 0; Qu'est-ce qu'on se dit?   *What are they saying to themselves?* 2; **Vous pouvez lui dire que j'ai téléphoné?**   *Can you tell her/him that I called?* 9
direct(e)   *direct;* en direct   *live*, 7

la direction   *direction*, 12
la discothèque   *dance club*, 6
discuter   *to discuss*, 7; Ne discute pas!   *Don't argue!* 3
disponible   *available*, 8
le disquaire   *record store*, 12; **chez le disquaire**   *at the record store*, 12
le disque compact/CD   *compact disc/CD*, 3
distant(e)   *distant*, 2
la distribution   *cast (of a movie, play, etc.)*, 1; une distribution étincelante   *a brilliant cast*, 1
divers(e)   *various*, 3
le document   *document*, 7
dois : Non, tu dois...   *No, you've got to . . . ,* 7
le dolmen   *dolmen*, 1
le dom-tom   *abbreviation of départements et territoires d'outre-mer; overseas departments and territories of France such as Martinique and Réunion*, 3
domestique : animal domestique   *pet*, 7
le domicile   *place of residence*, 4
la domination   *domination*, 9
dominer   *to tower over*, 12
dommage   *too bad*, 10
donc   *so, therefore*, 11
donner   *to give*, 5; **Donnez-moi..., s'il vous plaît.**   *Please give me . . . ,* 5
donner sur   *to overlook*, 11
dont   *of which*, 7
dormir   *to sleep*, 1
le dos   *back*, 12; **un sac à dos**   *backpack*, 3
doucement   *gently*, 12
la douche   *shower*, 11; avec douche ou bains   *with shower or bath*, 11
doué(e)   *gifted, talented*, 2
la douzaine   *dozen*, 8; **une douzaine de**   *a dozen*, 8
les draps (m.)   *linens, sheets*, 11
dressé(e)   *pointed*, 7
droit(e)   *straight*, 10
la droite   *right (direction);* **à droite (de)**   *to the right*, 12
du   *some*, 8
le duplicata (inv.)   *duplicate;* il n'en sera pas délivré de duplicata   *duplicates will not be issued*, 2
durable   *long-lasting*, 11
durcir   *to harden*, 8
la durée   *duration*, 7
durer   *to last*, 11

E

l' eau (f.)   *water*, 5; **l'eau minérale**   *mineral water*, 5; **le**

sirop de fraise (à l'eau)   *water with strawberry syrup*, 5
s' **ébattre**   *to frolic*, 7
l' **échange** (m.)   *exchange*, 7; en échange de   *in exchange for*, 7
l' **échantillon** (m.)   *sample*, 2
l' **écharpe** (f.)   *scarf*, 10
l' **échelle** (f.)   *scale*, 6
s' **éclater**   *to have fun, to have a ball*, 4
l' **école** (f.)   *school*, 1; A l'école   *At school*, 0
l' **écolier** (m.), l'écolière (f.)   *schoolboy/schoolgirl*, 3
l' **économie** (f.)   *economics*, 2
écouter   *to listen*, 1; Ecoute!   *Listen!* 0; **écouter de la musique**   *to listen to music*, 1; **Ecoutez!**   *Listen!* 0; Je t'écoute.   *I'm listening.* 9
l' **écran** (m.)   *screen*, 11
l' **écrin** (m.)   *case*, 6
écrire   *to write*, 2; Ecris-moi.   *Write me.* 1
écris : Ecris cinq phrases...   *Write five sentences . . . ,* 12
l' **édifice** (m.)   *edifice, building*, 6
l' **éducation physique et sportive (EPS)** (f.)   *physical education*, 2; l'éducation civique et morale (f.)   *civics class*, 2
efficace   *efficient*, 9
égrener   *to shell*, 8
égyptien(ne)   *Egyptian (adj.)*, 6
Eh bien...   *Umm . . . (expression of hesitation)*, 5
élastique   *elastic (adj.)*, 3
élémentaire   *elementary; basic*, 8
l' **éléphant** (m.)   *elephant*, 0
l' **élève** (m./f.)   *student*, 2
l' **emballage** (m.)   *packaging*, 9
embêtant(e)   *annoying*, 7
émincer   *to slice thinly*, 8
l' **émission** (f.)   *TV program*, 4
empêche (empêcher)   *to prevent, to keep from doing*, 2
l' **emploi**   *use, job;* un emploi du temps   *schedule*, 2
emprunter   *to borrow*, 12
en   *in*, 1; **en**   *some, of it, of them, any, none*, 8; **en**   *to, in (before a feminine country)*, 11; **en coton**   *(made of) cotton*, 10; **en cuir**   *(made of) leather*, 10; en français   *in French*, 1; **en jean**   *(made of) denim*, 10; en retard   *late*, 2; en solde   *on sale*, 10; **en vacances**   *on vacation*, 4; **Je n'en veux plus.**   *I don't want anymore*, 8; **Oui, j'en veux bien.**   *Yes, I'd like some.* 8; Qu'en penses-tu?   *What do you think (about it)?* 1; **Vous avez ça en... ?**   *Do you have that in . . . ? (size, fabric, color)*, 10
encore   *again, more;* **Encore de... ?**   *More. . . ?* 8; *still*, 9

encourager *to encourage,* 8

l' **endroit** (m.) *place,* 12

énerver *to annoy,* 2

l' **enfant** (m./f.) *child,* 7; l'enfant unique *only child,* 7

enfin *finally,* 9

enjoué(e) *playful,* 7

ennuyer *to bore,* 2

ennuyeux (-euse) *boring,* 11; **C'était ennuyeux.** *It was boring,* 11

l' **enquête** (f.) *survey,* 1

l' **enseignement** (m.) *teaching,* 2

ensemble *together,* 4

l' **ensemble** (m.) *collection, ensemble,* 3

ensuite : Ensuite, ... *Next,/Then, ...,* 9

entendre *to hear;* s'entendre avec *to get along with,* 7

Entendu. *Agreed.* 6

entendu dire que : Il a entendu dire que... *He heard that ...,* 12

l' **enthousiasme** (m.) *enthusiasm,* 2

entier (-ière) *whole, entire;* le monde entier *all over the world,* 1

entrant *entering,* 2

entre *between,* 12

l' **entrée** (f.) *entry, entrance;* Entrée libre *"Browsers welcomed,"* 3

l' **enveloppe** (f.) *envelope,* 12

l' **envie** (f.) *desire; need;* **J'ai envie de...** *I feel like ...,* 11

les **environs** (m. pl.) *surroundings,* 9

s' envoler *to fly away,* 12

envoyer *to send,* 12; **envoyer des lettres** *to send letters* 12

l' épi (m.) *ear (of a plant),* 8; l'épi de maïs *ear of corn,* 8

l' **épicerie** (f.) *grocery store,* 12

éplucher *to clean, to peel,* 8

l' **éponge** (f.) *sponge,* 3

épouvantable *terrible, horrible,* 9; **C'était épouvantable.** *It was horrible.* 9

l' **EPS (l'éducation physique et sportive)** *gym class,* 3

l' **équipe interscolaire** (f.) *school team,* 4

l' **équitation** (f.) *horseback riding,* 1; **faire de l'équitation** *to go horseback riding,* 1

es : Tu es d'accord? *Is that OK with you?* 7

l' **escale** (f.) *docking (of a boat),* 11

l' **escalier** (m.) *staircase,* 6

les **escargots** (m.) *snails,* 1

l' **espace** (m.) *space, area,* 7

l' **espagnol** (m.) *Spanish (language),* 2

espère : J'espère que oui. *I hope so.* 1

l' **espoir** (m.) *hope,* 7

essayer *to try; to try on,* 10; **Je peux essayer...?** *Can I try on ...? 10;*

Je peux l'/les essayer? *Can I try it/them on?* 10

est : Il/Elle est... *He/She is ...,* 7; **Quelle heure est-il?** *What time is it?* 6; **Qui est à l'appareil?** *Who's calling?* 9

Est-ce que *(Introduces a yes-or-no question),* 4; **(Est-ce que) je peux...?** *May I ...?* 7

et *and,* 1; **Et après ça...** *And after that, ...,* 9; **Et toi?** *And you?* 1

l' **étage** (m.) *floor, story (of a building),* 6

était : C'était épouvantable. *It was horrible.* 9

étaler *to spread,* 8

l' **étape** (f.) *part,* 1; première étape *first part,* 1; deuxième étape *second part,* 1; troisième étape *third part,* 1

l' **état** (m.) *state,* 0

les **Etats-Unis** (m. pl.) *United States,* 0

l' **été** (m.) *summer,* 4; **en été** *in the summer,* 4

été (pp. of être) *was,* 9

étincelant(e) *brilliant,* 1

étoilé(e) *starry,* 12

étonné(e) (pp. of étonner) *surprised,* 7

étranger (-ère) *foreign,* 11

l' **étranger** (m.) *foreign countries;* à l'étranger *abroad,* 11

être *to be,* 7; **C'est...** *This is ...,* 7; **Ce sont...** *These (those) are ...,* 7; **Elle est...** *She is ...,* 7; **Il est...** *He is ...,* 7; **Il est...** *It is ... (time),* 6; **Ils/Elles sont...** *They're ...,* 7; **Oui, ça a été.** *Yes, it was fine.* 9

l' **étude** (f.) *study hall,* 2

l' **étudiant(e)** (m./f.) *student,* 0

étudier *to study,* 1

eu (pp. of avoir) *had, got,* 9

l' **euro** *European Community monetary unit,* 3; Ça fait... euros./C'est... euros. *It's ... euros.* 5

l' **Europe** (f.) *Europe,* 0

l' **événement** (m.) *event,* 9

évident(e) *evident, obvious,* 12

évider *to scoop out,* 8

éviter *to avoid,* 9

exactement *exactly,* 9

l' **examen** (m.) *exam,* 1; **passer un examen** *to take a test,* 9

excellent(e) *excellent,* 5; **Oui, excellent.** *Yes, excellent.* 9

excusez : Excusez-moi. *Excuse me.* 3

exemplaire *exemplary,* 7

l' **explication** (f.) *explanation,* 12

expliquer *to explain,* 7

l' **exposition** (f.) *exhibit,* 12

l' **expression** (f.) *expression,* 1

F

la **face** *face, side;* **en face de** *across from,* 12

facile *easy,* 2

la **façon** *way, manner,* 10

la **faim** *hunger;* **avoir faim** *to be hungry,* 5; **Non, merci. Je n'ai plus faim.** *No thanks. I'm not hungry anymore.* 8

faire *to do, to make, to play,* 4; **Désolé(e), j'ai des devoirs à faire.** *Sorry, I have homework to do.* 5; **J'ai des courses à faire.** *I have errands to do.* 5; **Qu'est-ce que tu vas faire...?** *What are you going to do ...?* 6; **Tu vas faire quoi...?** *What are you going to do ...?* 6; **faire de l'équitation** *to go horseback riding,* 1; faire de la course *to race (running),* 4; faire de la gymnastique *to do gymnastics,* 4; faire des haltères *to lift weights,* 4; **faire du bateau** *to go sailing,* **faire du sport** *to play sports,* 1; faire du surf *to surf,* 4; **faire la cuisine** *to cook, do the cooking,* 8; **faire la vaisselle** *to do the dishes,* 7; **faire le ménage** *to do housework,* 1; faire les boutiques *to go shopping,* 1; **faire les courses** *to do the shopping,* 7; **faire les magasins** *to go shopping,* 1; **faire les vitrines** *to window-shop,* 6; **faire un pique-nique** *to have a picnic,* 6; **faire une promenade** *to go for a walk,* 6

fais : A ton avis, qu'est-ce que je fais? *In your opinion, what do I do?* 9; **Fais-moi...** *Make me ...,* 3; **Je fais...** *I play/do ...,* 4; **Ne t'en fais pas!** *Don't worry!* 9; **Qu'est-ce que tu fais comme sport?** *What sports do you play?* 4; **Qu'est-ce que tu fais pour t'amuser?** *What do you do to have fun?* 4; **Qu'est-ce que tu fais...?** *What do you do ...?* 4

faisons : Faisons connaissance! *Let's get acquainted.* 1

fait : Quel temps fait-il? *What's the weather like?* 4; **Il fait beau.** *It's nice weather.* 4; **Il fait chaud.** *It's hot.* 4; **Il fait frais.** *It's cool.* 4; **Il fait froid.** *It's cold.* 4

fait (pp. of faire) *done, made,* 9; **J'ai fait...** *I did/made ...,* 9; **Qu'est-ce que tu as fait?** *What did you do?* 9

la **famille** *family,* 7

la fantaisie *fancy,* 10

le fantôme *ghost,* 0

la **farine**   *flour*, 8
le **fast-food**   *fast-food restaurant*, 6
favorable   *favorable, approving*, 7
favori(te)   *favorite*, 12
faut : Il me faut...   *I need . . .* , 3;
Qu'est-ce qu'il te faut pour...?
What do you need for . . . ?
(informal), 3; **Qu'est-ce qu'il te
faut?**   *What do you need?* 8;
Qu'est-ce qu'il vous faut pour...?
What do you need for . . . ?
(formal), 3
le **fauve**   *wildcat*, 6
faux (fausse)   *false*, 2
les **féculents** (m.)   *starches*, 8
la **féerie**   *extravaganza*, 11
la femme   *wife*, 7
la fenêtre   *window*, 0
le **fer forgé**   *wrought iron*, 12
ferai : je me ferai une joie de...   *I'll
gladly . . .* , 1
fermez : Fermez la porte.   *Close the
door.* 0
le **festival**   *festival*, 9
la **fête**   *party*, 1; **faire la fête**   *to live it
up*, 1
fêter   *to celebrate*, 7
le **feu**   *fire*, 12
le **feu rouge**   *traffic light*, 12; **Vous
continuez jusqu'au prochain feu
rouge.**   *You keep going until the
next light.* 12
la **feuille**   *sheet; leaf;* **une feuille de
papier**   *sheet of paper*, 0
le **feutre**   *marker*, 3
février   *February*, 4; **en février**   *in
February*, 4
la **fidélité**   *loyalty*, 7
le **fil**   *cord, thread;* **sans fil**   *cordless*, 9
le **filet**   *a type of net or mesh bag*, 3
la **fille**   *girl*, 0; **la fille**   *daughter*, 7
le film   *movie*, 6; **voir un film**   *to see
a movie*, 6; **un film d'aventures**
adventure film, 1
le fils   *son*, 7; **fils-à-papa**   *daddy's
boy*, 10
la **fin**   *end*, 4
finalement   *finally*, 9
fistuleux (-euse)   *hollow*, 11
le **flamant**   *flamingo;* **flamant rose**
pink flamingo, 9
la **flamme**   *flame*, 12
le **flanc**   *side, flank*, 12
la **fleur**   *flower*, 1
le **fleuve**   *river*, 9
le **flipper**   *pinball*, 5
la **flûte**   *flute*, 0
la **fois**   *time;* **une fois par semaine**
once a week, 4
folklorique   *folkloric, traditional*,
11
follement   *madly*, 1
foncé(e)   *dark (color)*, 10
fonder   *to found*, 9
la **fontaine**   *fountain*, 12
le foot   *soccer*, 4

le football   *soccer*, 1; **le football
américain**   *football*, 4; **jouer au
foot(ball)**   *to play soccer*, 4; **jouer
au football américain**   *to play
football*, 4
la **forêt**   *forest*, 0; **en forêt**   *to/in the
forest*, 11
la **forme**   *form, structure*, 7
formidable : C'était formidable!
It was great! 11
le **fort**   *fort*, 12
fort(e)   *strong*, 7
fou (folle)   *crazy*, 9
le **foulard**   *scarf*, 10
le **four**   *oven*, 8
le **fournisseur**   *supplier*, 8
les **fournitures** (f. pl.) **scolaires**   *school
supplies*, 3
la **fourrure**   *fur*, 7
le **foutou**   *a paste made from
boiled plantains, manioc, or
yams; it is common in Côte
d'Ivoire.* 8
le **foyer**   *home*, 7
fraîche   *cool, cold*, 5
le **frais**   *cool place*, 8; **au frais**   *in a
cool place*, 8
les **frais** (m. pl.)   *cost, expenses*, 11
frais   *cool (temperature)*, 4; **Il
fait frais.**   *It's cool.* 4 ; *fresh*,
12; **des fruits et des légumes
frais**   *fresh fruits and vegetables*, 12
la **fraise**   *strawberry*, 8; **un sirop de
fraises (à l'eau)**   *water with
strawberry syrup*, 5
le **franc**   *(former monetary unit of
France) franc*, 3
le **franc de la Communauté financière
africaine (CFA)**   *the currency of
francophone Africa*, 8
le français   *French (language)*, 1;
français(e)   *French (adj.)*, 0; **A la
française**   *French-style*, 2
francophone   *French-speaking*, 0
la **fréquence**   *frequency*, 4
le frère   *brother*, 7
les **friandises** (f.)   *sweets*, 6
les frites (f. pl.)   *French fries*, 1
froid(e)   *cold*, 4; **Il fait froid.**   *It's
cold.* 4
le fromage   *cheese*, 5
la **fromagerie**   *cheese shop*, 12
les fruits (m.)   *fruit*, 8
fui (pp. of fuir)   *fled*, 1
le **fun**   *fun*, 4; **C'est l' fun!** (in Canada)
It's fun! 4

gagner   *to win, to earn*, 9
la **garantie**   *guarantee*, 3

le **garçon**   *boy*, 9
garder   *to look after*, 7
la **gare**   *train station*, 6 ; **la gare
routière**   *bus station*, 12
le **garrot**   *withers, shoulder height of
an animal such as a horse*, 7
le gâteau   *cake*, 8
la **gâterie**   *little treat*, 9
la gauche   *left (direction);* **à gauche**
to the left, 12
la **Gaule**   *Gaul; the division of the
ancient Roman Empire (in
Western Europe) occupied by the
Gauls*, 9
le gazon   *lawn*, 7; **tondre le
gazon**   *to mow the lawn*, 7
généralement   *in general,
usually*, 11
génial(e)   *great*, 2
le **génie**   *genius*, 6
les **genoux** (m.)   *knees*, 7; **une paire de
genoux**   *pair of knees, lap*, 7
les **gens** (m. pl.)   *people*, 9
gentil(le)   *nice*, 7
la **géographie**   *geography*, 2
la **géométrie**   *geometry*, 2
la **glace**   *ice cream*, 1
la **glace**   *ice;* **faire du patin à glace**
to ice-skate, 4
le golf   *golf*, 4; **jouer au golf**   *to play
golf*, 4
les gombos (m.)   *okra*, 8
la gomme   *eraser*, 3
les **gorges** (f.)   *canyons*, 11
la/le **gosse**   *kid*, 2; **être traité comme
un gosse**   *to be treated like
a kid*, 2
la **gouache**   *paint*, 3
le **goût**   *taste*, 4
le goûter   *afternoon snack*, 8
goûter   *to taste*, 8
le **gouvernement**   *government*, 8
la **goyave**   *guava*, 8
grâce à   *thanks to*, 11
gradué(e)   *graduated*, 3; **une règle
graduée**   *graduated ruler*, 3
la **graine**   *seed*, 8
la **grammaire**   *grammar*, 1; **grammaire
en contexte**   *grammar in context*, 1
le **gramme**   *gram (unit of
measurement)*, 8
grand(e)   *tall*, 7; *big*, 10
grand-chose : Pas grand-chose.
Not much. 6
grandir   *to grow*, 10
la grand-mère   *grandmother*, 7
le grand-père   *grandfather*, 7
gratuit(e)   *free*, 6
grec(que)   *Greek (adj.)*, 6
gris(e)   *grey*, 3
gros(se)   *fat*, 7
grossir   *to gain weight*, 10
la **grotte**   *cave*, 11
le **groupe**   *musical group*, 2; **le groupe**
group, 7
le **gruyère**   *Gruyère cheese*, 5

la Guadeloupe *Guadeloupe,* 0
le guichet *ticket window,* 6
la Guyane française *French Guiana,* 0

habitant : habitant le monde entier *living all over the world,* 1
habite : J'habite à... *I live in . . . ,* 1
l' habitude (f.) *habit,* 4; **d'habitude** *usually,* 4
habituellement *usually,* 2
* haché(e) (pp. of hacher) *minced,* 8
Haïti (no article) *Haiti,* 0
***le hamburger** *hamburger,* 1
***les haricots** (m.) *beans,* 8; **les haricots verts** (m. pl.) *green beans,* 8
l' harmonie (f.) *harmony,* 10
***la harpe** *harp,* 11
***la hâte** *hurry, haste;* Elle a hâte de... *She can't wait to . . . ,* 7
* haut(e) *tall, high,* 6
***le haut-parleur** *loudspeaker,* 11
***le havre** *haven,* 7
l' hébergement (m.) *lodging,* 6
l' hélicoptère (m.) *helicopter,* 0
***le héros** *hero,* 11
hésite : Euh... J'hésite. *Well, I'm not sure.* 10
hésiter *to hesitate,* 10
l' **heure** (f.) *hour; time,* 1; **à l'heure de** *at the time of,* 1; **A quelle heure?** *At what time?* 6; **A tout à l'heure!** *See you later!* 1; l'heure officielle *official time (24-hour system),* 2; **Quelle heure est-il?** *What time is it?* 6; **Tu as... à quelle heure?** *At what time do you have . . . ?* 2
heures *o'clock,* 2; **à... heures** *at . . . o'clock,* 2; **à... heures quarante-cinq** *at . . . forty-five,* 2; **à... heures quinze** *at . . . fifteen,* 2; **à... heures trente** *at . . . thirty,* 2
heureusement *luckily, fortunately,* 4
heureux (-euse) *happy;* **Très heureux(-euse).** *Pleased to meet you.* 7
hier *yesterday,* 9
l' **histoire** (f.) *history,* 2
l' historien (m.) *historian,* 9
l' **hiver** (m.) *winter,* 4; **en hiver** *in the winter,* 4
***le hockey** *hockey,* 4; **jouer au hockey** *to play hockey,* 4
l' hôpital (pl. -aux) *hospital,* 0
l' horreur (f.) *horror;* un film d'horreur *horror movie,* 6
horrible *terrible,* 10
***le hot-dog** *hot dog,* 5

l' hôtel (m.) *hotel,* 0; l'hôtel de ville (m.) *town hall,* 1
*le houx *holly,* 11
l' huile d'olive (f.) *olive oil,* 5
* hurler *to shriek, to cry out,* 12
l' hypermarché (m.) *hypermarket,* 8

l' **idée** (f.) *idea,* 4; **Bonne idée.** *Good idea.* 4
identifier *to identify, to point out,* 7
l' identité (f.) *identity;* une photo d'identité *photo ID,* 1
l' igloo (m.) *igloo,* 0
l' igname (f.) *yam,* 8
il y a *there is, there are,* 5; il y a du soleil/du vent *it's sunny/windy,* 4; **Qu'est-ce qu'il y a à boire?** *What is there to drink?* 5
l' île (f.) *island,* 0
illogique *illogical,* 3
l' image (f.) *image,* 7
imagines : Tu imagines? *Can you imagine?* 4
l' impératif (m.) *command (verb form), imperative,* 10
important(e) *important,* 8
imprimé(e) *printed,* 10
inaperçu(e) *unnoticed,* 11
incompétent(e) *incompetent,* 2
inclus(e) *included,* 6
incroyable *unbelievable,* 9
l' industrie (f.) *industry,* 4
l' influence (f.) *influence,* 12
l' **informatique** (f.) *computer science,* 2
l' instrument de géométrie (m.) *instrument for geometry (compass, etc.),* 3
intelligent(e) *smart,* 7
l' **intention** (f.) *intention;* **J'ai l'intention de...** *I intend to . . . ,* 11
l' interclasse (m.) *break (between classes),* 2
intéressant(e) *interesting,* 2
international(e) *international,* 5
l' interphone (m.) *intercom,* 9
l' **interro(gation)** (f.) *quiz,* 9; **rater une interro** *to fail a quiz,* 9
intervenu(e) (pp. of intervenir) *intervened,* 9
l' interviewé(e) (m./f.) *interviewee,* 2
intime *personal,* 1
l' intonation (f.) *intonation,* 1
inventer *to invent,* 7
l' invitation (f.) *invitation,* 6
l' invité(e) (m./f.) *guest,* 8
inviter *to invite,* 7
ivoirien(ne) *from the Republic of Côte d'Ivoire,* 1

jamais : ne... jamais *never,* 4
le jambon *ham,* 5
janvier *January,* 4; **en janvier** *in January,* 4
le jardin *garden,* 0
jaune *yellow,* 3
le jazz *jazz,* 4
je *I,* 0
le jean *(pair of) jeans,* 3; **en jean** *made of denim,* 10
le **jeu** *game;* un jeu de rôle *role-playing exercise,* 1; **jouer à des jeux vidéo** *to play video games,* 4
jeudi *Thursday,* 2; **le jeudi** *on Thursdays,* 2
jeune *young,* 7; les jeunes *youths,* 4
le **jogging** *jogging,* 4; **faire du jogging** *to jog,* 4
la joie *joy,* 1
joignant (joindre) *attached,* 1
joli(e) *pretty,* 4
jouer *to play,* 4; **Je joue...** *I play . . . ,* 4; **Je ne joue pas...** *I don't play . . . ,* 4; **jouer à...** *to play (a game) . . . ,* 4
joueur (-euse) *playful,* 7
le **jour** *day,* 2; le jour férié (m.) *holiday,* 6
le journal *journal,* 1; *newspaper,* 12
la journée *day,* 2
juillet *July,* 4; **en juillet** *in July,* 4
juin *June,* 4; **en juin** *in June,* 4
la **jupe** *skirt,* 10
le jus d'orange *orange juice,* 5
le jus de fruit *fruit juice,* 5
le jus de pomme *apple juice,* 5
jusqu'à *up to, until,* 12; **Vous allez tout droit jusqu'à...** *You go straight ahead until you get to . . . ,* 12
juste *just,* 4

le kangourou *kangaroo,* 0
le **kilo(gramme)** *kilogram,* 8; **un kilo de** *a kilogram of,* 8
le kilomètre *kilometer,* 12

la *the,* 1; *her, it* (f.), 9
là *there,* 12; **-là** *there (noun suffix),* 3; **(Est-ce que)... est là, s'il**

vous plaît? *Is . . . , there, please?* 9;
là-bas *there; over there,* 8
là-bas *there, over there,* 9
laid(e) *ugly,* 9
la **laine** *wool,* 10
laisser *to leave,* 9; **Je peux laisser
un message?** *Can I leave a
message?* 9
le **lait** *milk,* 8
laitier (-ière) *dairy,* 8; **les produits
laitiers (m.)** *dairy products,* 8
la **langue** *language,* 1
large *baggy,* 10; *large wide;*
107 mètres de large *107 meters
wide,* 9
le **latin** *Latin (language),* 2
laver *to wash,* 7; **laver la voiture**
to wash the car, 7
le *the,* 1; *him, it,* 9
la **légende** *map key,* 12
la **légèreté** *lightness,* 6
les **légumes** (m.) *vegetables,* 8
les *the,* 1; *them,* 9
la **lettre** *letter,* 12; **envoyer des lettres**
to send letters, 12
leur *to them,* 9
leur/leurs *their,* 7
levez : Levez la main! *Raise your
hand!* 0; **Levez-vous!** *Stand up!* 0
la **levure** *yeast,* 8
la **liaison** *liaison; pronunciation of a
normally silent consonant at the
end of a word as if it were the first
letter of the word that follows,* 2
la **librairie** *bookstore,* 12
la **librairie-papeterie** *bookstore and
stationery store,* 3
libre *free,* 2
liégeois : café ou chocolat liégeois
*coffee or chocolate ice cream with
whipped cream,* 5
le **lieu** *place;* avoir lieu *to take
place,* 7; *... aura lieu... ... will
take place . . . ,* 7
la **limonade** *lemon soda,* 5
le **lin** *linen,* 10
le **lion** *lion,* 0
le **liquide correcteur** *correction
fluid,* 3
lire *to read,* 1
lisant : en lisant *while reading,* 11
lisons : Lisons! *Let's read!* 1
la **liste** *list,* 8
la **litote** *understatement,* 5
le **litre** *liter,* 8; **un litre de** *a liter of,* 8
la **livraison** *delivery,* 12
la **livre** *pound,* 8; **une livre de** *a
pound of,* 8
le **livre** *book,* 0
le **livret scolaire** *a student's personal
gradebook,* 3
la **location** *rental,* 4
logique *logical,* 3
loin *far,* 12; **loin de** *far from,* 12
long(ue) *long,* 10
longtemps (adv.) *a long time,* 9

la **longueur** *length,* 10
louer *to rent,* 12
la **Louisiane** *Louisiana,* 0
lu (pp. of lire) *read,* 9
lui *to him, to her,* 9
lumineux (-euse) *luminous, lit up,* 3
lundi *Monday,* 2; **le lundi** *on
Mondays,* 2
les **lunettes de soleil** (f. pl.)
sunglasses, 10
le **Luxembourg** *Luxembourg,* 0
le **lycée** *high school,* 2
le **lycéen** *high school student,* 2

ma *my,* 7
madame (Mme) *ma'am, Mrs.,* 1;
Madame! *Waitress!* 5
mademoiselle (Mlle) *miss, Miss,* 1;
Mademoiselle! *Waitress!* 5
le **madras** *madras (fabric or
pattern),* 10
le **magasin** *store,* 1; **faire les
magasins** *to go shopping,* 1; grand
magasin *department store,* 10
le **magazine** *magazine,* 3
le **magnétoscope** *videocassette
recorder, VCR,* 0
magnifique *magnificent, splendid,* 9
mai *May,* 4; **en mai** *in May,* 4
maigrir *to lose weight,* 10
le **maillot de bain** *bathing suit,* 10
la **main** *hand,* 0
maintenant *now,* 2; **Je ne peux
pas maintenant.** *I can't right
now.* 8
le **maire** *mayor,* 12
la **mairie** *city hall,* 4
mais *but,* 1
le **maïs** *corn,* 8
la **Maison des jeunes et de la culture
(MJC)** *recreation center,* 6
le **maître** *master, owner,* 7
maîtriser *to master,* 4
la **majorité** *majority,* 2
mal *bad,* 1; **Pas mal.** *Not
bad.* 1
la **malchance** *misfortune,* 7
le **mâle** *male (refers to animals),* 7
malheureusement *unfortunately,* 7
le **Mali** *Mali,* 0
la **manche** *sleeve,* 10
le **manchot** *penguin,* 6
le **manège** *carousel,* 12
manger *to eat,* 6
la **mangue** *mango,* 8
manque : Qu'est-ce qui manque?
What's missing? 2
manqué(e) (pp. of manquer)
missed; garçon manqué *tomboy,*
10

le **manteau** *coat,* 10
le **maquis** *maquis; kind of outdoor
restaurant in Côte d'Ivoire,* 5
le **marchand (la marchande)**
merchant, shopkeeper, 8
le **marché** *market,* 8
mardi *Tuesday,* 2; **le mardi** *on
Tuesdays,* 2
le **mari** *husband,* 7
le **mariage** *marriage,* 7
le **Maroc** *Morocco,* 0
marocain(e) *Moroccan (adj.),* 1
marron (inv.) *brown,* 3
mars *March,* 4; **en mars** *in
March,* 4
martiniquais(e) *from Martinique,* 1
la **Martinique** *Martinique,* 0
le **masque** *mask,* 8
le **match** *game,* 6; **regarder un
match** *to watch a game (on TV),*
6; **aller voir un match** *to go see a
game (in person),* 6
les **maths (les mathématiques)** (f. pl.)
math, 1
la **matière** *school subject,* 2; *fabric,* 10
les **matières grasses** (f.) *fat,* 8
le **matin** *morning, in the morning,* 2
mauvais(e) *bad,* 5; **C'est pas
mauvais!** *It's pretty good!* 5; **Oh,
pas mauvais.** *Oh, not bad.* 9;
Très mauvais. *Very bad.* 9
méchant(e) *mean,* 7
mécontent(e) *unhappy,* 2
les **médicaments** (m.) *medicine,* 12
meilleur(e) *best,* 7; les meilleurs
amis *best friends,* 7
le **mélange** *mixture,* 12
mélanger *to mix,* 8
méli-mélo *mishmash,* 1
le **membre** *member;* le membre de la
famille *family member,* 7
même *same,* 4
la **mémé** *granny, grandma,* 9
le **ménage** *housework,* 1; **faire le
ménage** *to do housework,* 1
le **mensuel** *monthly publication,* 9
la **menthe à l'eau** *beverage made with
mint syrup and water,* 5
le **menu** *meal, menu,* 8
méprisant(e) *contemptuous,* 2
la **mer** *sea;* **au bord de la mer** *to/on
the coast,* 11
Merci. *Thank you,* 3; **Non, merci.**
No, thank you. 8
mercredi *Wednesday,* 2; **le
mercredi** *on Wednesdays,* 2
la **mère** *mother,* 7
mes *my,* 7
le **message** *message,* 9; **Je peux laisser
un message?** *May I leave a
message?,* 9
mesurer *to measure,* 9
le **mètre** *meter,* 9
le **métro** *subway,* 12; **au métro...** *at
the . . . metro stop,* 6; **en métro** *by
subway,* 12

métropolitain(e) *metropolitan*, 2
mets : mets en ordre *put into order*, 6
mettre *to put, to put on, to wear,* 10; **Je ne sais pas quoi mettre pour...** *I don't know what to wear for (to) . . .* , 10; **Mets... Wear . . .** , 10; **Qu'est-ce que je mets?** *What shall I wear?* 10
meublé(e) *furnished*, 11
mexicain(e) (adj.) *Mexican*, 5
miam-miam *yum-yum*, 5
midi *noon*, 6; **Il est midi.** *It's noon.* 6; **Il est midi et demi.** *It's half past noon.* 6
mieux *better*, 9; **Ça va aller mieux!** *It's going to get better!* 9; **J'aime mieux...** *I prefer . . .* , 1
mignon(ne) *cute*, 7
le **milieu** *middle*; **au milieu** *in the middle*, 7
millier (m.) *a thousand or so*; **des milliers d'autres visiteurs** *thousands of other tourists*, 9
mince *slender*, 7
minuit *midnight*, 6; **Il est minuit.** *It's midnight.* 6; **Il est minuit et demi.** *It's half past midnight.* 6
la **minute** *minute*, 9; **Tu as une minute?** *Do you have a minute?* 9
mis (pp. of mettre) *put, placed*, 10
la **mise** *putting, setting*; **mise en pratique** *putting into practice*, 1; **mise en train** *getting started*, 1
la **mise en scène** *production*, 1
mixte *mixed*, 5
le **mobilier** *furniture*, 6
la **mobylette** *motor scooter*, 11
moche *tacky*, 10
la **mode** *style*, 10; **à la mode** *in style*, 10; **à la dernière mode** *in the latest fashion*, 10
le **mode d'emploi** *instructions*, 9
modéré(e) *moderate*, 11
moderne *modern*, 8
moi *me*, 2; **Moi aussi.** *Me too.* 2; **Moi, non.** *I don't.* 2; **Moi non plus.** *Neither do I.* 2; **Moi, si.** *I do.* 2; **Pas moi.** *Not me.*
moins (with numbers) *minus, lower*, 6; **moins cinq** *five to*, 6; **moins le quart** *quarter to*, 6
le **mois** *month*, 4
le **moment** *moment*, 5; **Un moment, s'il vous plaît.** *One moment, please.* 5
mon *my*, 7
Monaco *Monaco*, 0
le **monde** *world*, 0
le **moniteur** *monitor*, 12
monsieur (M.) *sir, Mr.,* 1; **Monsieur!** *Waiter!* 5
le **monstre** *monster*, 0
la **montagne** *mountain*, 4; **à la montagne** *to/in the mountains*, 11

la **montée** *ascent*, 6
monter *to climb, to rise*, 6
la **montre** *watch*, 3
montrer *to show*, 9
le **monument** *monument*, 6
se **moquer de** *to make fun of*, 9
le **moral** *morale*, 2
le **morceau** *piece*, 8; **un morceau de** *a piece of*, 8
le **mot** *word*, 11; **un petit mot** *a little note*, 5
le **motif** *reason, pattern*, 9
le **moulin** *windmill*, 9
la **mousseline** *chiffon*, 8
la **moutarde** *mustard*, 8
moyen(ne) *average*, 2; **travail moyen** *average work*, 2
le **Moyen Age** *Middle Ages*, 9
la **moyenne** *average*, 2
le **musée** *museum*, 6
la **musique** *music*, 2; **écouter de la musique** *to listen to music*, 1; **la musique classique** *classical music*, 4
le **mystère** *mystery*, 5

nager *to swim*, 1
le **nain** *dwarf*, 6
la **naissance** *birth*, 7
la **natation** *swimming*, 4; **faire de la natation** *to swim*, 4
national(e) *national*, 8
naturel(le) *natural*, 3
nautique *nautical*; **faire du ski nautique** *to water-ski*, 4
ne : ne... pas *not*, 1; **ne... pas encore** *not yet*, 9; **ne... jamais** *never*, 4; **ne... ni grand(e) ni petit(e)** *neither tall nor short*, 7; **n'est-ce pas?** *isn't that so? (tag question added to the end of a declarative phrase to make it a question)*
né(e) (pp. of naître) *born*, 9
la **Négritude** *movement which asserts the values and spirit of black African civilizations*, 0
la **neige** *snow*, 4
neige : Il neige. *It's snowing.* 4
le **neveu** *nephew*, 7
niçois(e) (adj.) *from Nice, France*, 5
la **nièce** *niece*, 7
le **Niger** *Niger*, 0
le **niveau** *level*, 6
le **nocturne** *late-night opening*, 6
le **Noël** *Christmas*, 0
noir(e) *black*, 3
la **noisette** *hazelnut*, 5

la **noix** *nut*, 5
la **noix de coco** *coconut*, 8
le **nom** *name*, 1; **nom de famille** *last name*
le **nombre** *number*, 2
nombreux(-euse) *numerous, many*, 9
non *no*, 1; **Moi non plus.** *Neither do I.* 2; **Moi, non.** *I don't.* 2; **Non, c'est...** *No, it's . . .* , 4; **Non, merci.** *No, thank you.* 8; **Non, pas trop.** *No, not too much.* 2
nos *our*, 7
la **note** *note*; **la note culturelle** *culture note*, 1
notre *our*, 7
nouveau (nouvelle) *new*, 7
la **Nouvelle-Angleterre** *New England*, 0
les **nouvelles (f.)** *news*, 9
novembre *November*, 4; **en novembre** *in November*, 4
le **nuage** *cloud*, 12
nul(le) *useless*, 2
le **numéro** *number*, 0; **un numéro de téléphone** *telephone number*, 3; **les numéros** *issues (for magazines, etc.)*, 3
nutritionnel(le) *nutritive, having to do with nutrition*, 8

l' **objet (m.)** *object*, 6; **objets trouvés** *lost and found*, 3
l' **observation (f.)** *observation*, 2
l' **occasion (f.)** *occasion*, 10
occupé(e) : C'est occupé. *It's busy.* 9; **Désolé(e), je suis occupé(e).** *Sorry, I'm busy.* 6
s' **occuper de** *to take care of*, 7
octobre *October*, 4; **en octobre** *in October*, 4
l' **odeur (f.)** *aroma, smell*, 8
l' **œil (m.)** *eye*, 12
l' **œuf (m.)** *egg*, 8
offre (offrir) *to offer*; **Le plus grand centre du sport au Canada offre...** *The largest sports center in Canada offers . . .* , 4
l' **oignon (m.)** *onion*, 8
l' **oiseau (m.)** *bird*, 12
ombragé(e) (pp. of ombrager) *shaded*, 11
l' **omelette (f.)** *omelette*, 5
on *one, we, you, they*, 1; **Comment dit-on...?** *How do you say . . . ?* 1; **On est dans la purée.** *We're in trouble.* 8; **On fait du ski?** *How about skiing?* 5; **On joue au base-ball?** *How about playing baseball?* 5; **On peut...** *We can . . .* ,

6; **On va au café?** *Shall we go to the café?* 5; **On...?** *How about . . . ?* 4

l' **oncle** (m.) *uncle*, 7

l' **opéra** (m.) *opera house*, 10

l' **opinion** (f.) *opinion*, 7

opposé(e) *opposite*, 12

opulent(e) *rich*, 7

l' **or** (m.) *gold*, 12

orange (inv.) *orange (color)*, 3

l' **orange** (f.) *orange*, 8; **le jus d'orange** *orange juice*

l' **ordinateur** (m.) *computer*, 3

l' **ordre** (m.) *order*, 9; l'**ordre chronologique** (m.) *chronological order*, 3

l' **organisation** (f.) *organization*, 1

original(e) *original*, 10

l' **otarie** (f.) *sea lion*, 6

ôter *to cut out*, 8

ou *or*, 1

où *where*, 6; **Où (ça)?** *Where?* 6; **Où est-ce que tu vas aller...?** *Where are you going to go . . . ?* 11; **Tu es allé(e) où?** *Where did you go?* 9

oublier *to forget*, 9; **Je n'ai rien oublié.** *I didn't forget anything.* 11; **Oublie-le/-la/-les!** *Forget him/her/them!* 9; **J'ai oublié.** *I forgot.* 3; **N'oublie pas de...** *Don't forget . . . ,* 8; **Tu n'as pas oublié...?** *You didn't forget . . . ?* 11

l' **ouest** *West*, 8

oui *yes*, 1; **Oui, c'est...** *Yes it's . . . ,* 4; **Oui, s'il te/vous plaît.** *Yes, please.* 8

ouvert(e) *open*, 6

l' **ouverture** (f.) *opening*, 6

ouvrez : Ouvrez vos livres à la page... *Open your books to page . . . ,* 0

la **page** *page*, 0

le **pagne** *a piece of dyed African cloth*, 10

le **pain** *bread*, 8

la **paire** *pair*, 5; **une paire de genoux** *pair of knees, lap*, 7

le **palais** *palace*, 1; **le palais de justice** *court, courthouse*, 1

le **pamplemousse** *grapefruit*, 5

le **panier** *basket*, 3

le **pantalon** *pair of pants*, 10

la **papaye** *papaya*, 8

la **papeterie** *stationery store*, 12; **librairie-papeterie** *bookstore/stationery store*, 3

le **papier** *paper*, 0; **des feuilles** (f.) **de papier** *sheets of paper*, 3

le **paquet** *package, box*, 8; **un paquet de** *a package/box of*, 8

par *by*, 12; *per*, 6; **par hasard** *by chance*, 12; **prix par personne** *price per person*, 6

le **parachute** *parachute*, 0

le **paragraphe** *paragraph*, 7

paraître *to appear; seem*, 12

le **parapluie** *umbrella*, 11

le **parc** *park*, 6

parce que *because*, 5; **Je ne peux pas parce que...** *I can't because . . . ,* 5

Pardon. *Pardon me.* 3; **Pardon, madame... , s'il vous plaît?** *Excuse me, ma'am . . . , please?* 12; **Pardon, monsieur. Je cherche... , s'il vous plaît.** *Excuse me, sir. I'm looking for. . . , please.* 12

le **parent** *parent, relative*, 7

paresseux (-euse) *lazy*, 2

parfait(e) *perfect*, 3; **C'est parfait.** *It's perfect.* 10

parfois *sometimes*, 4

parfumer *to flavor*, 8

la **parfumerie** *perfumery, perfume shop*, 11

parisien(ne) (adj.) *Parisian*, 5

parlé (pp. of parler) *talked, spoke*, 9; **Nous avons parlé.** *We talked.* 9

parler *to talk*, 1; *to speak*, 9; **(Est-ce que) je peux parler à...?** *Could I speak to. . . ?* 9; **Je peux te parler?** *Can I talk to you?* 9; **parler au téléphone** *to talk on the phone*, 1; **Parlons!** *Let's talk!* 2

parmi *among*, 9

partagé(e) *split, shared*, 6

le **partenaire** (la partenaire) *partner*, 7

partir *to leave*, 11; **Tu ne peux pas partir sans...** *You can't leave without . . . ,* 11

pas *not*, 1; **pas bon** *not good*, 5; **Pas ce soir.** *Not tonight.* 7; **pas content du tout** *not happy at all*, 2; **Il/Elle ne va pas du tout avec...** *It doesn't go at all with . . . ,* 10; **Pas grand-chose.** *Not much.* 6; **Pas mal.** *Not bad.* 1; **pas mauvais** *not bad*, 9; **Pas question!** *Out of the question!* 7; **pas super** *not so hot*, 2; **Pas terrible.** *Not so great.* 1; **pas du tout** *not at all*, 4

le **passeport** *passport*, 1

les **passe-temps** (m. pl.) *pastimes*, 4

passé (pp. of passer) : **Ça s'est bien passé?** *Did it go well?* 11; **Qu'est-ce qui s'est passé?** *What happened?* 9; **Tu as passé un bon week-end?** *Did you have a good weekend?* 9

passer *to pass*, 12; *to go by*, 12; **Tu pourrais passer à...?** *Could you go by . . . ?* 12; **Vous passez...** *You'll pass . . . ,*

12; **passer l'aspirateur** *to vacuum*, 7; **passer un examen** *to take a test*, 9

passerais : je passerais le bac... *I would take the bac . . . ,* 2

passionnant(e) *fascinating*, 2

la **pastille** *tablet*, 3

la **pâte** *dough*, 8; **la pâte d'arachide** *peanut butter*, 8; **la pâte de tomates** *tomato paste*, 8

le **pâté** *pâté*, 0

les **pâtes** (f. pl.) *pasta*, 11

le **patin** *skating*, 1; **faire du patin à glace** *to ice-skate*, 4

le **patin à roulettes** *rollerskating*, 4

le **patinage** *skating*, 4

patiner *to skate*, 4

la **patinoire** *skating rink*, 6

la **pâtisserie** *pastry shop, pastry*, 12

le **patrimoine** *heritage*, 6

patronal(e) *having to do with saints*; **la fête patronale** *patron saint's holiday*, 12

les **pattes d'eph** (f. pl.) *bell-bottoms*, 10

pauvre *poor*, 7

le **pays** *country*, 6

le **paysage** *landscape*, 11

la **pêche** *peach*, 8

peindre *to paint*, 9

la **peinture** *painting*, 6

pendant *during*, 1

pénible *annoying*, 7

penser *to think*; **J'ai pensé à tout.** *I've thought of everything.* 11; **Qu'en penses-tu?** *What do you think (about it)?* 1

perdre *to lose*, 9

perdu(e) (pp. of perdre) *lost*, 1

le **père** *father*, 7

permettre *to allow*, 9

le **permis de conduire** *driver's license*, 12; **le permis accompagné** *learner's permit (driving)*, 12; **le permis probatoire** *learner's permit (driving)*, 12

la **permission** *permission*, 7

le **personnage** *individual, character*, 9

la **personnalité** *personality*, 7

la **personne** *person*, 7

personnel(le) *personal*, 4

petit(e) *short (height)*, 7; *small (size)*, 10; **petites annonces** *classified ads*, 1

le **petit copain** *boyfriend*, 2

le **petit déjeuner** *breakfast*, 8

le **petit-fils** *grandson*, 7

la **petite copine** *girlfriend*, 2

la **petite-fille** *granddaughter*, 7

les **petits-enfants** (m.) *grandchildren*, 7

les **petits pois** (m.) *peas*, 8

peu *not very*, 2; **à peu près** *about, approximately*, 9; **peu content** *not very happy*, 2; **un peu** *a little*, 6

peut : On peut... *We can . . . ,* 6

peut-être *maybe, perhaps*, 11

peux : Désolé(e), mais je ne peux pas. *Sorry, but I can't.* 4; **Tu peux...?** *Can you...?* 8

la pharmacie *drugstore,* 12

la philosophie *philosophy,* 2

le phoque *seal,* 6

la photo *picture, photo,* 4; **faire de la photo** *to do photography,* 4; **faire des photos** *to take pictures,* 4

la photographie *photography,* 1

les photographies (f. pl.) *photographs,* 6

la phrase *sentence,* 4

la physique *physics,* 2

physiquement *physically,* 7

la pièce *play,* 6; **voir une pièce** *to see a play,* 6

le pied *foot,* 12; **à pied** *on foot,* 12

la Pierre Levée *name of a megalith in Poitiers, France,* 1

la pince : des pantalons à pinces *pleated pants,* 10

le pinceau *paintbrush,* 3

le pingouin *penguin,* 0

le pique-nique *picnic,* 6; **faire un pique-nique** *to have a picnic,* 6

la piscine *swimming pool,* 6

pittoresque *picturesque,* 8

la pizza *pizza,* 1

la place *place;* Services... de location sur place *On-site rentals,* 4

la plage *beach,* 1

la plaine *plain,* 4

le plaisir *pleasure, enjoyment,* 4; **Oui, avec plaisir.** *Yes, with pleasure.* 8

plaît : Il/Elle me plaît, mais il/elle est cher/chère. *I like it, but it's expensive.* 10; **Il/Elle te/vous plaît?** *Do you like it?* 10; **Ça te plaît?** *Do you like it?* 2; **s'il vous/te plaît** *please,* 3

la planche *board;* **faire de la planche à voile** *to go windsurfing,* 11

la plaque *plate (of metal or glass);* **la plaque d'immatriculation** *license plate,* 0

le plat *dish (food),* 5; les plats à emporter (m.) *food to go,* 11

plein(e) de *a lot of,* 8; une ville pleine d'animation *a city full of life,* 8

pleut : Il pleut. *It's raining.* 4

la plongée *diving;* **faire de la plongée** *to go scuba diving,* 11

plus *plus (math),* 2; *(with numbers)* *higher,* 0; **Je n'en veux plus.** *I don't want any more,* 8; **Moi non plus.** *Neither do I.* 2; **Non, merci. Je n'ai plus faim.** *No thanks. I'm not hungry anymore.* 8

plusieurs (inv.) *several,* 7

la poche *pocket,* 10

le poème *poem,* 0

le point *point,* 10; le point d'intérêt *tourist attraction,* 4

la poire *pear,* 8

le poisson *fish,* 7

la poissonnerie *fish shop,* 12

la poitrine *chest,* 10

le poivre *pepper,* 8

le poivron *green or red pepper,* 5

poliment *politely,* 8

la pollution *pollution,* 1

la pomme *apple,* 8; **jus de pom**me *apple juice,* 5

la pomme de terre *potato,* 8

le pompiste *gas pump attendant,* 11

la population *population,* 4

le porc *pork,* 8

le port *port,* 8

la porte *door,* 0

le portefeuille *wallet,* 3

le porte-monnaie *change purse,* 5

porter *to wear,* 10

le portugais *Portuguese (language),* 2

poser des questions *to ask questions,* 7

possible *possible,* 3

la poste *post office,* 12

le poster *poster,* 0

le pot de colle *container of glue,* 3

la poubelle *trashcan,* 7; **sortir la poubelle** *to take out the trash,* 7

la poudre *powder,* 8

la poule *(animal) chicken,* 8

le poulet *chicken (meat),* 8

pour *for,* 2; **Qu'est-ce qu'il te faut pour...** *What do you need for...?* *(informal),* 3; **Qu'est-ce que tu fais pour t'amuser?** *What do you do to have fun?* 4

pourquoi *why,* 0; **Pourquoi est-ce que tu ne mets pas...?** *Why don't you wear...?* 10; **Pourquoi pas?** *Why not?* 6; **Pourquoi tu ne... pas?** *Why don't you...?* 9

pourrais : Tu pourrais passer à...? *Could you go by...?* 12

pourtant *yet, nevertheless,* 9

pouvoir *to be able to, can,* 8; **(Est-ce que) je peux...?** *May I...?* 7; **Tu peux...?** *Can you...?* 8; **Je ne peux pas maintenant.** *I can't right now.* 8; **Je peux te parler?** *Can I talk to you?,* 9; **Non, je ne peux pas.** *No, I can't.* 12; **On peut...** *We can...,* 6; **Qu'est-ce que je peux faire?** *What can I do?* 9; **(Est-ce que) tu pourrais me rendre un petit service?** *Could you do me a favor?* 12; **Tu pourrais passer à...?** *Could you go by...?,* 12

pratique *practical,* 3

précieusement *carefully,* 2

précisant : en précisant *specifying,* 1

préféré(e) *favorite,* 4

la préfecture (de police) *police station,* 12

la préférence *preference,* 3

préférer *to prefer,* 1; **Je préfère...** *I prefer...,* 1

premier (-ière) *first,* 1; la première étape *first step,* 1

prendre *to take or to have (food or drink),* 5; **Je vais prendre..., s'il vous plaît.** *I'm going to have..., please.* 5; **On peut prendre...** *We can take...,* 12; **Prends...** *Get...,* 8; **Have...,** 5; **Je le/la/les prends.** *I'll take it/them.* 10; **Tu prends...?** *Will you have...?,* 8; *Are you taking...?,* 11; **Prenez une feuille de papier.** *Take out a sheet of paper.* 0; **Vous prenez...?** *What are you having?* 5; *Will you have...?,* 8; **Prenez la rue... puis traversez la rue...** *You take... Street, then cross... Street,* 12; **Vous avez décidé de prendre...?** *Have you decided to take...?* 10; **Vous le/la/les prenez?** *Are you going to take it/them?* 10

le prénom *first name,* 1

préparer *to prepare (something),* 8; se préparer *to prepare (oneself), to get ready,* 10

près *close,* 12; **près de** *close to,* 12

la présentation *presentation, introduction,* 7

présenter *to introduce;* **Je te (vous) présente...** *I'd like you to meet...,* 7; Présente-toi! *Introduce yourself!* 0

presque *almost,* 12

la presqu'île *peninsula,* 12

prévoir *to anticipate,* 4

prévu(e) (pp. of prévoir) *planned;* **Je n'ai rien de prévu.** *I don't have any plans.* 11

principal(e) *main;* la ville principale *main city,* 12

le printemps *spring,* 4; **au printemps** *in the spring,* 4

pris (pp. of prendre) *took, taken,* 9

le prisonnier *prisoner,* 4

le prix *price,* 6

le problème *problem,* 9; **J'ai un petit problème.** *I've got a little problem.* 9

prochain(e) *next,* 12; **Vous continuez jusqu'au prochain feu rouge.** *You keep going until the next light.* 12

les produits laitiers (m.) *dairy products,* 8

le prof(esseur) *teacher,* 0

les progrès (m.) *progress,* 11

le projet *project,* 6

la promenade *walk,* 6; **faire une promenade** *to go for a walk,* 6

promener *to walk,* 6; **promener le chien** *to walk the dog,* 7; se promener *to take a walk,* 12

promets (promettre) *to promise,* 1

le pronom *pronoun,* 8

prononcer *to pronounce,* 1; ne se

prononcent pas *no response*, 2

la prononciation *pronunciation*, 2

proposé(e) (pp. of proposer) *given, suggested*, 5

proposer *to propose, to suggest*, 5

prospérer *to prosper, to do well*, 9

protéger *to protect*, 9

la protéine *protein*, 8

provençal(e) *Provençal; from the Provence region of France*, 9

la Provence *Provence; region in southeast France on the Mediterranean Sea*, 9

la publicité *advertisment*, 10

le publiphone à cartes *card-operated telephone*, 9

puis *then*, 12; **Prenez la rue... puis traversez la rue...** *Take . . . Street, then cross . . . Street*, 12

le pull(-over) *pullover sweater*, 3

la punition *punishment*, 9

purement *purely*, 12

la pyramide *pyramid*, 11

qu'est-ce que *what*, 1; **Qu'est-ce qu'il te faut pour... ?** *What do you need for . . . ? (informal)*, 3; **Qu'est-ce qu'il vous faut pour... ?** *What do you need for . . . ? (formal)*, 3; Qu'est-ce qu'il y a dans...? *What's in the . . . ?* 3; Qu'est-ce qu'il y a? *What's wrong?* 2; Qu'est-ce qu'on fait? *What are we/they doing?* 4; **Qu'est-ce que je peux faire?** *What can I do?* 9; **Qu'est-ce que tu as fait... ?** *What did you do . . . ?* 9; **Qu'est-ce que tu fais... ?** *What do you do . . . ?* 4; **Qu'est-ce que tu vas faire... ?** *What are you going to do . . . ?* 6; **Qu'est-ce que vous avez comme boissons?** *What do you have to drink?* 5; **Qu'est-ce qu'il y a à boire?** *What is there to drink?* 5; Qu'est-ce qui manque? *What's missing?* 2

qu'est-ce qui *what (subj.)*, 9; **Qu'est-ce qui s'est passé?** *What happened?* 9

quand *when*, 6; **Quand (ça)?** *When?* 6

la quantité *quantity*, 8

quarantième *fortieth*, 7

le quart *quarter*, 6; **et quart** *quarter past*, 6; **moins le quart** *quarter to*, 6

que *that; what*, 1; Que sais-je? *self-check (What do I know?)*, 1

le quartier *neighborhood*, 4

le Québec *Quebec*, 0

québécois(e) *from Quebec*, 1

quel(le) *what, which*, 1; Ils ont quels cours? *What classes do they have?* 2; **Tu as quel âge?** *How old are you?* 1; **Tu as quels cours... ?** *What classes do you have . . . ?* 2; **Tu as... à quelle heure?** *At what time do you have . . . ?* 2; **Quelle heure est-il?** *What time is it?* 6; **Quel temps fait-il?** *What's the weather like?* 4

quelque *some*, 10

quelqu'un *someone*, 1

quelque chose *something*, 6; **Je cherche quelque chose pour...** *I'm looking for something for . . .*, 10

quelquefois *sometimes*, 4

la question *question*, 0

le questionnaire *questionnaire, survey*, 4

qui *who*, 0; **Avec qui?** *With whom?* 6; C'est qui? *Who is it?* 2; Qui suis-je? *Who am I?* 0

la quiche *quiche: a type of custard pie with a filling, such as ham, bacon, cheese, or spinach*, 5

quittez : Ne quittez pas. (telephone) *Hold on.* 9

quoi *what*, 10; **De quoi est-ce que tu as besoin?** *What do you need?* 5; **Je ne sais pas quoi mettre pour...** *I don't know what to wear for/to . . .*, 10; **Tu as quoi... ?** *What do you have . . . ?* 2 **Tu vas faire quoi?** *What are you going to do?* 6

quotidien(ne) *everyday*, 6

le rabat *flap*, 3

le raccourci *shortcut*, 2

raconter *to tell*, 9

la radio *radio*, 3

le radis *radish*, 8

le raisin *grapes*, 8

la randonnée *hike*, 11; **faire de la randonnée** *to go hiking*, 11

ranger *to arrange, straighten;* **ranger ta chambre** *to pick up your room*, 7

le rap *rap music*, 1

râpé(e) (pp. of râper) *grated*, 8

rapidement *rapidly, quickly*, 7

rappeler *to call back*, 9; **Vous pouvez rappeler plus tard?** *Can you call back later?* 9; Tu te rappelles? *Do you remember?* 3; *to remind*, 12

le rapport *relationship*, 7

rapporter *to bring back*, 8; **Rapporte-moi...** *Bring me*

back . . . , 8; **Tu me rapportes... ?** *Will you bring me . . . ?* 8

rarement *rarely*, 4

rater *to fail*, 9; *to miss*, 9; **rater le bus** *to miss the bus*, 9; **rater une interro** *to fail a quiz*, 9

le rayon *department*, 3; au rayon de musique *in the music department*, 3

la rayonne *rayon*, 10

la réalité *reality*, 11

la recette *recipe*, 8

recevoir *to receive*, 1

reconstruit(e) (pp. of reconstruire) *reconstructed*, 12

la récré(ation) *break*, 2

recueilli (pp. of recueillir) *to take in*, 7

refaire *to redo, remake*, 8

réfléchir *to think about*, 2; *to reflect;* Réfléchissez. *Think about it.* 2

le reflet *reflection*, 10

le refuge *animal shelter*, 7

le réfugié *refugee*, 1

le refus *refusal*, 6

refuser *to refuse*, 7

le regard *look*, 7

regarder *to look*, 10; *to watch*, 1; **Non, merci, je regarde.** *No, thanks, I'm just looking.* 10; **Regarde, voilà...** *Look, here's/there's/it's . . .*, 12; **regarder la télé** *to watch TV*, 1; **regarder un match** *to watch a game (on TV)*, 6; **Regardez la carte!** *Look at the map!* 0

la règle *ruler*, 3

regrette : Je regrette. *Sorry.* 3; **Je regrette, mais je n'ai pas le temps.** *I'm sorry, but I don't have time.* 8

regroupé(e) *rearranged*, 6

rejoint (pp. of rejoindre) *rejoined*, 7

la relation *relation*, 7

relier *to connect*, 9

religieux(-euse) *religious*, 9

relire *to re-read, to read again*, 7

remarquable *remarkable, exceptional*, 3

le remboursement *repayment*, 9

la rencontre *encounter*, 1

rencontrer *to meet*, 9

le rendez-vous *rendez-vous, date, appointment*, 12

rendre *to return something*, 12; rendre un service *to do (someone) a favor*, 12; **Rendez-vous...** *We'll meet . . .*, 6; pour les rendre plus originales *to make them more original*, 10

le renfort *reinforcement; renforts aux épaules reinforced shoulder seams*, 10

les renseignements (m.) *information*, 9

la rentrée *back to school*, 2

rentrer *to go home*, 8

le repas *meal*, 8

le répertoire   *index*, 9
répéter   *to rehearse, practice*, 9;
   Répétez!   *Repeat!* 0
le répondant   *respondent*, 4
le répondeur   *answering machine*, 9
répondre   *to answer*, 9; **Ça ne**
   répond pas.   *There's no answer.* 9
la réponse   *response, answer*, 2
reposer   *to rest, to relax*; laisser
   reposer   *to let stand*, 8;
   se reposer   *to relax*, 11
représenté(e) (pp. of représenter)
   represented, 7
représenter   *to represent*, 8
la république de Côte d'Ivoire   *the*
   Republic of Côte d'Ivoire, 0
la réserve   *reserve*, 8
respectueux (-euse)   *respectful*, 2
ressemblez : si vous me ressemblez
   if you're like me, 1
la ressource   *resource*, 4
le restaurant   *restaurant*, 6
la restauration   *dining*, 6
rester   *to stay, to remain*, 11
le resto   *restaurant*, 11
le résultat   *result*, 10
retard : en retard   *late*, 2
retirer   *to take out, to remove*;
   retirer de l'argent   *to withdraw*
   money, 12
le retour   *return*, 6
rétro (inv.)   *retro*, 10
retrouve : Bon, on se retrouve...
   OK, we'll meet . . ., 6
retrouver   *to find again*, 6
la Réunion   *the island of Réunion*, 0
rêvait (imp. of rêver)   *to dream*, 7
le rêve   *dream*, 11
revenir   *to come back*, 5
riche   *rich*, 8
ridicule   *ridiculous*, 10
rien   *nothing*, 6; *anything*, 11;
   Ça ne me dit rien.   *I don't feel like*
   it. 4; **Je n'ai rien oublié.**   *I didn't*
   forget anything. 11; **Rien de**
   spécial.   *Nothing special.* 6
rigoler   *to laugh*, 10
le riz   *rice*, 8
la robe   *dress*, 10
le rocher   *rock*, 11
rocheux (-euse)   *rocky*, 12
le rock   *rock (music)*, 4
le rôle   *role*, 7
le roller   *skating;* **faire du roller en**
   ligne   *to in-line skate*, 4
romain(e)   *Roman (adj.)*, 9
le roman   *novel*, 3
   roman(e)   *Romanesque; of the style*
   of architecture developed in Europe
   in the 11th and 12th centuries
   (characterized by heavy, massive
   walls and arches, etc.), 12
rond(e)   *round*, 12
le rond-point   *traffic circle*, 12
ronronner   *to purr*, 7
le rosbif   *roast beef*, 5

rose   *pink*, 3
la rose   *rose*, 0
le rôti   *roast*, 5
rouge   *red*, 3
le rouleau   *roll*, 3; un rouleau protège-
   livres   *a roll of plastic material to*
   protect books, 3
rouspètent (rouspéter)   *to*
   complain, 9
la routine quotidienne   *daily*
   routine, 11
roux (rousse)   *redheaded*, 7
le ruban   *ribbon, tape*; ruban adhésif
   transparent   *transparent adhesive*
   tape, 3
la rue   *street*, 12
la ruine   *ruin*, 9
le rythme   *rhythm*, 4

s'il te plaît (informal)   *please*, 3;
   Oui, s'il te plaît.   *Yes, please.*
   (informal), 8
s'il vous plaît   *please*, 3 *(formal)*;
   Oui, s'il vous plaît.   *Yes, please.*
   (formal), 8
sa   *his, her*, 7
le sac   *bag;* **le sac à dos**   *backpack*, 3
le sachet   *bag, packet*, 3
sage   *wise*, 12
sais : Je n'en sais rien.   *I have no*
   idea. 11; **Je ne sais pas.**   *I don't*
   know. 10; **Que sais-je?**   *self-check*
   (What do I know?), 1
la saison   *season*, 4; la basse saison
   off season, 12; la haute saison
   tourist season, 12
la salade   *salad*, 8
les salades (f.)   *heads of lettuce*, 8
salé(e)   *salty, salted*, 5
saler   *to salt*, 8
la salle   *room*, 2; la salle de classe
   classroom, 2
Salut   *Hi!* or *Goodbye!* 1
samedi   *Saturday*, 2; **le samedi**   *on*
   Saturdays, 2
les sandales (f.)   *sandals*, 10
le sandwich   *sandwich*, 5; **un**
   sandwich au fromage   *cheese*
   sandwich, 5; **un sandwich au**
   jambon   *ham sandwich*, 5; **un**
   sandwich au saucisson   *salami*
   sandwich, 5
sans   *without*, 3; sans doute
   probably, 10
la sauce   *sauce*, 5
la sauce arachide   *sauce made of*
   peanut butter with beef, chicken, or
   fish, hot peppers, peanut oil, garlic,
   onions, tomato paste, tomatoes, and
   other vegetables, 8

la sauce pimentée   *spicy sauce*, 8
le saucisson   *salami*, 5
le saumon   *salmon*, 5
sauvage (adj.)   *savage*, 9
savais : Savais-tu que... ?   *Did you*
   know . . . ?, 2
savoir   *to know*, 1
scellé(e) (pp. of sceller)   *sealed*, 9
la science-fiction   *science fiction*, 1
les sciences naturelles (f. pl.)   *natural*
   science, 2
scolaire   *having to do with school*, 2;
   la vie scolaire   *school life*, 2
la séance   *showing (at the movies)*, 6
la seconde   *second*, 9; **Une seconde,**
   s'il vous plaît.   *One second,*
   please. 9
le secours   *aid, help*; le poste de
   secours   *first-aid station*, 6
secret (secrète)   *secret*, 8
le séjour   *stay, residence*, 7
le sel   *salt*, 8
selon   *according to*, 8
la semaine   *week*, 4; **une fois par**
   semaine   *once a week*, 4
semblable   *similar, the same*, 7
le semestre   *semester*, 12
le Sénégal   *Senegal*, 0
le sens   *sense*, 8; le sens de
   l'orientation   *sense of direc-*
   tion, 12
   sensass (sensationnel)   *fantas-*
   tic, 10
sept   *seven*, 0
septembre   *September*, 4; **en**
   septembre   *in September*, 4
sera : ce sera   *it will be*, 6
le serpent   *snake*, 0
serré(e)   *tight*, 10
le serveur (la serveuse)
   waiter/waitress, 5
le service   *service*, 3; rendre un service
   to do (someone) a favor, 12; **A votre**
   service.   *At your service; You're*
   welcome, 3
service compris   *tip included*, 5
ses   *his, her*, 7
le sésame   *sesame*, 8
sévère   *severe, harsh*, 0
le short   *(pair of) shorts*, 3
   si   *yes (to contradict a negative*
   question), 2; **Moi, si.**   *I do.* 2;
   Oui, si tu veux.   *Yes, if you want*
   to. 7
sicilien(ne) (adj.)   *Sicilian*, 5
le siècle   *century*, 6
le signe   *sign*, 12
la similarité   *similarity*, 2
simple   *simple*, 10
simplement   *simply*, 6
sinon   *otherwise; other than*
   that, 9
le sirop de fraise (à l'eau)   *water with*
   strawberry syrup, 5
la situation   *situation*, 7
situé(e)   *situated, located*, 8

le ski *skiing*, 1; **faire du ski** *to ski*, 4; **faire du ski nautique** *to water-ski*, 4
la sœur *sister*, 7
la soie *silk*, 10
la soif *thirst*; **avoir soif** *to be thirsty*, 5
soigné(e) *with attention to detail*, 10
soigneusement *carefully*, 11
le soir *evening*; *in the evening*, 4; **Pas ce soir.** *Not tonight.* 7
sois (command form of être) : Ne sois pas découragée! *Don't be discouraged!* 9
soit *either*; soit chez moi, ou bien chez eux *whether at my house or at theirs*, 5
les soldes (m.) *sales*, 6
le soleil *sun, sunshine*, 4
le solfège *music theory*, 4
la solution *solution*, 9
le sommet *top, summit*, 6
le son *sound*, 8
son *his, her*, 7
le sondage *poll*, 1
la sonnerie *ringing (of the telephone)*, 9
sont : Ce sont... *These/Those are . . .*, 7; **Ils/Elles sont...** *They are . . .*, 7; **Ils/Elles sont comment?** *What are they like?* 7
la sorte *kind*; toutes sortes de *all kinds of*, 8
sorti(e) (pp. of sortir) *went out*, 9; **Après, je suis sorti(e).** *Afterwards, I went out.* 9
la sortie *dismissal (when school gets out)*, 2
sortir *to go out*, 1; *to take out*, 7; **sortir avec les copains** *to go out with friends*, 1; **sortir la poubelle** *to take out the trash*, 7
souterrain(e) *underground*, 11
le souvenir *souvenir*, 11
souvent *often*, 4
spécial(e) *special*, 6; **Rien de spécial.** *Nothing special.* 6
la spécialité *specialty dish*, 4
le spectacle *show*, 11
le spectateur *spectator, audience member*, 9
le sport *gym*, 2; *sports*, 1; **faire du sport** *to play sports*, 1; **Qu'est-ce que tu fais comme sport?** *What sports do you play?* 4
le sportif (la sportive) *sportsman (sportswoman)*, 4
le stade *stadium*, 6
la stalactite *stalactite*, 11
la station-service *service station, gas station*, 11
la statue *statue*, 12
le steak-frites *steak and French fries*, 5
la stratégie *strategy*, 1
le style *style*; **C'est tout à fait ton style.** *It looks great on you!* 10

le stylo *pen*, 0; un stylo plume *fountain pen*, 3
la subvention *subsidy*, 7
le sucre *sugar*, 8
sucré(e) *sweet*, 8
le sud *South*, 9
suggérer *to suggest*, 11
suis : Qui suis-je? *Who am I?* 0; **Désolé(e), je suis occupé(e).** *Sorry, I'm busy.* 6; **Je suis bien chez . . . ?** *Is this . . . .'s house?* 9
suisse *Swiss* (adj.), 1; la Suisse *Switzerland*, 0
suivant(e) *following*, 2
suivre *to follow*, 9
le sujet *subject*, 10
super *super*, 2; **Super!** *Great!* 1; **pas super** *not so hot*, 2
le supermarché *supermarket*, 8
supplémentaire *supplementary, additional*, 1
supportez (supporter) *to put up with*, 2
sur *on*; sur place *on-site*, 4; sur un total de *out of a total of*, 4
le surligneur *highlighting marker*, 3
surtout *especially*, 1
le sweat-shirt *sweatshirt*, 3
sympa (abbrev. of **sympathique**) *nice*, 7

ta *your*, 7
la table *table*, 7; la table de comparaison de tailles *size conversion chart*, 10
le tableau *blackboard*, 0; *painting*, 8
la tache *spot*, 7
la tâche domestique *household chore*, 9
la taille *size*, 10; taille unique *one size fits all*, 10; **en taille...** *in size. . .* , 10
la taille élastiquée *elastic waist*, 10
le taille-crayon *pencil sharpener*, 3
tant : tant privée que professionelle *private as well as professional*, 9
la tante *aunt*, 7
tard *late*; plus tard *later*, 8
le tarif : tarif réduit *reduced fee*, 6
la tarte *pie*, 8
le tas *pile, heap*; **J'ai des tas de choses à faire.** *I have lots of things to do.* 5
le taux de réussite *rate of success*, 2
le taxi *taxi*, 12; **en taxi** *by taxi*, 12
le Tchad *Chad*, 0
Tchao! *Bye!* 1
la techno *techno music*, 1; La techno me fait délirer. *I'm wild about techno (music)*, 1
le tee-shirt *T-shirt*, 3

la télécarte *phone card*, 9
le télécopieur *fax machine*, 9
le téléphone *telephone*, 0; **parler au téléphone** *to talk on the phone*, 1; le téléphone à pièces *coin-operated telephone*, 9; le téléphone sans fil *cordless telephone*, 9
téléphoné (pp. of téléphoner) *called, phoned*, 9; **Vous pouvez lui dire que j'ai téléphoné?** *Can you tell him/her that I called?* 9
téléphoner *to call, to phone*, 9; **Téléphone-lui/-leur!** *Call him/her/them!* 9
téléphonique : la cabine téléphonique *phone booth*, 9
la télévision *television*, 0; **regarder la télé(vision)** *to watch TV*, 1
tellement *so; so much*; **Pas tellement.** *Not too much.* 4
le temps *time*, 4; *weather*, 4; **de temps en temps** *from time to time*, 4; **Je regrette, mais je n'ai pas le temps.** *I'm sorry, but I don't have time.* 8; Quel temps est-ce qu'il fait à... ? *How's the weather in . . . ?* 4; **Quel temps fait-il?** *What's the weather like?* 4
Tenez. *Here you are. (formal, plural)*, 10
le tennis *tennis*, 4; **jouer au tennis** *to play tennis*, 4
la tenue *outfit*; une tenue de gymnastique *gym uniform*, 3
la terminale *final year of French high school, usually spent preparing for the bac*, 2
termine (terminer) *to finish*, 2
la terrasse *terrace*, 4
terrible *terrible, awful*; **Pas terrible.** *Not so great.* 1
le territoire d'outre-mer *overseas territory*, 12
tes *your*, 7
le test *test*, 10
le théâtre *theater*, 6; **faire du théâtre** *to do drama*, 4
théorique *theoretical*, 12
les thermes (m. pl.) *thermal baths*, 9
le thon *tuna*, 5
Tiens! *Hey!* 3
tient (tenir) *to hold*, 12
le tiers *one third*; un tiers de la population *one third of the population*, 12
le tilleul *lime green*, 10
le timbre *stamp*, 12
timide *shy*, 7
le tissu *cloth, fabric*, 10
toi *you*, 1; **Et toi?** *And you?* 1
le tollé *outcry*, 12
la tomate *tomato*, 8
tomber *to fall*, 10
ton *your*, 7
tondre *to mow*, 7; **tondre le gazon** *to mow the lawn*, 7

le top : le top des radios   *the top radio stations*, 3
le total   *total*, 10
toujours   *still, always*, 9
la tour   *tower*, 5
le tour   *measurement;* tour de poitrine   *chest size*, 10; le tour   *turn;* à ton tour   *Now it's your turn.* 7
tournez : Vous tournez...   *You turn . . .*, 12
le tournoi   *tournament*, 4
tous   *all*, 2
tout(e)   *all*, 2; **A tout à l'heure!** *See you later!* 1; **J'ai pensé à tout.** *I've thought of everything.* 11; pas du tout   *not at all*, 2; **Il/Elle ne va pas du tout avec...**   *It doesn't go at all with . . .*, 10; **C'est tout à fait ton style.**   *It looks great on you!* 10; **tout de suite**   *right away*, 6; **C'est tout de suite à...**   *It's right there on the . . .*, 12; **J'y vais tout de suite.**   *I'll go right away.* 8; **Vous allez tout droit jusqu'à...**   *You go straight ahead until you get to . . .*, 12; **tout(e) seul(e)**   *all alone*, 12
tout le monde (m.s.)   *everyone*, 7
la tradition   *tradition*, 8
traditionnel(le)   *traditional*, 8
le train   *train*, 12; **en train**   *by train*, 12; **un billet de train**   *train ticket*, 11
traité : être traité comme un gosse   *to be treated like a kid*, 2
le trajet   *route*, 12
la tranche   *slice*, 8; **une tranche de** *a slice of*, 8
transparent(e)   *transparent*, 3
le travail   *work*, 3
le travail scolaire   *school work*, 2
travailler   *to work*, 9; travailler la pâte   *to knead the dough*, 8
les **travaux pratiques** (m. pl.)   *lab*, 2
traverser to cross, 12
très   *very*, 1; **Très bien.**   *Very well.* 1; **Très heureux (heureuse).** *Pleased to meet you.* 7
le trésor   *treasure*, 3; chasse au trésor   *treasure hunt*, 3
trois   *three*, 0
troisième   *third*, 9; la troisième étape   *third step*, 1
la trompette   *trumpet*, 0
trop   *too (much)*, 10; **Il/Elle est trop cher/chère.**   *It's too expensive.* 10; **Non, pas trop.**   *No, not too much.* 2
tropical(e)   *tropical*, 8
la trousse   *pencil case*, 3
trouver   *to find*, 9; **Comment tu trouves ça?**   *What do you think of that/it?* 2; **Comment tu trouves...?**   *What do you think of . . . ?* 2; **Je le/la/les trouve...** *I think it's/they're . . .*, 10; Tu trouves?   *Do you think so?* 10

le truc   *thing*, 5; **J'ai des trucs à faire.** *I have some things to do.* 5
tu   *you*, 0; Tu te rappelles?   *Do you remember?*, 7
la Tunisie   *Tunisia*, 0
typique   *typical, characteristic*, 8
typiquement   *typically, characteristically*, 8

un (m.)   *a, an*, 3
une (f.)   *a, an*, 3
l' uniforme (m.)   *uniform*, 0
universel(le)   *universal*, 12
utiliser   *to use*, 10

va : Ça va.   *Fine.* 1; (Comment) ça va?   *How's it going?* 1; Comment est-ce qu'on y va?   *How can we get there?* 12; Il/Elle me va?   *Does it suit me?* 10; Il/Elle ne te/vous va pas du tout.   *It doesn't look good on you at all.* 10; Il/Elle ne va pas du tout avec...   *It doesn't go at all with . . .*, 10
les **vacances** (f. pl.)   *vacation*, 1; **Bonnes vacances!**   *Have a good vacation!* 11; **en colonie de vacances**   *to/at a summer camp*, 11; **en vacances**   *on vacation*, 4
vais : Je vais...   *I'm going . . .*, 6; *I'm going (to) . . .*, 11; **J'y vais tout de suite.**   *I'll go right away.* 8
la vaisselle   *dishes*, 7; **faire la vaisselle** *to do the dishes*, 7
valable   *valid*, 6
la valise   *suitcase*, 11
la vanille   *vanilla*, 8
vas : Qu'est-ce que tu vas faire? *What are you going to do?* 6
la vedette   *celebrity*, 1
végétarien(ne)   *vegetarian*, 5
le vélo   *biking*, 1; **à vélo**   *by bike*, 12; **faire du vélo**   *to bike*, 4
le vendeur   *salesperson*, 3
la vendeuse   *salesperson*, 3
vendre   *to sell*, 9
vendredi   *Friday*, 2; **le vendredi** *on Fridays*, 2
la vente   *sales*, 6
le verbe   *verb*, 7
la verdure   *vegetation*, 11
véritable   *real*, 11; **C'était un véritable cauchemar!**   *It was a real nightmare!* 11

le verre   *glass*, 6
vers   *about*, 6
vert(e)   *green*, 3
la veste   *suit jacket, blazer*, 10
le vêtement   *clothing item*, 10
veux : Je veux bien.   *I'd really like to.* 6; **Tu veux... avec moi?**   *Do you want to . . . with me?* 6
la viande   *meat*, 8
vide   *empty*, 12
la vidéo   *video*, 4; **faire de la vidéo** *to make videos*, 4; **des jeux vidéo** *video games*, 4
la **vidéocassette**   *videotape*, 3
la vie scolaire   *school life*, 2
viennois(e)   *Viennese* (adj.), 5
viens : Tu viens?   *Will you come?* 6
vietnamien(ne)   *Vietnamese* (adj.), 1
vieux (vieille)   *old*, 4
le village   *town*, 4
la ville   *city*, 12
le vinaigre   *vinegar*, 8
la violence   *violence*, 1
violet(te)   *purple*, 3
la virgule   *comma*, 3
la visite   *visit, tour*, 12
visiter   *to visit (a place)*, 9
le visiteur   *visitor*, 9
vite   *fast, quickly*, 2
la vitrine   *window (of a shop);* **faire les vitrines**   *to window-shop*, 6
vivant(e)   *lively, living*, 7
Vive... !   *Hurray for . . . !* 3
vivre   *to live*, 2; l'art de vivre   *the art of living*, 12
le vocabulaire   *vocabulary*, 1
Voici...   *Here's . . .*, 7
Voilà.   *Here.* 3; Voilà... *There's . . .*, 7
la voile   *sailing*, 11; **faire de la planche à voile**   *to go windsurfing*, 11; **faire de la voile** *to go sailing*, 11
voir   *to see*, 6; **voir un film**   *to see a movie*, 6; **aller voir un match** *to go see a game*, 6; **voir une pièce** *to see a play*, 6
le voisin (la voisine)   *neighbor*, 1
la voiture   *car*, 7; **en voiture**   *by car*, 12; **laver la voiture**   *to wash the car*, 7
la voix   *voice*, 3
le volley(-ball)   *volleyball*, 4; **jouer au volley(-ball)** *to play volleyball*, 4
volontiers   *with pleasure, gladly*, 8
vos   *your*, 7
votre   *your*, 7
voudrais : Je voudrais...   *I'd like . . .* 3
vouloir   *to want*, 6; **Je n'en veux plus.**   *I don't want anymore.* 8; **Je veux bien.**   *I'd really like to.* 6; *Gladly.* 8; **Oui, j'en veux bien.**   *Yes, I'd like some.* 8; **Oui, si tu veux.**   *Yes, if you want to.* 7; **Tu veux...?**   *Do you want . . . ?*

6; **voulez : Vous voulez...?** *Do you want . . . ?* 8

vous *you*, 1

le voyage *voyage, trip*, 0

voyager *to travel*, 1; **Bon voyage!** *Have a good trip!* 11

vrai(e) *true*, 2

vraiment *really*, 11; **Non, pas vraiment.** *No, not really.* 11

vu (pp. of voir) *seen, saw*, 9

la vue *view*, 6

le week-end *on weekends*, 4; *weekend*, 6

le western *western (movie)*, 0

le xylophone *xylophone*, 0

y *there*, 12; **Allons-y!** *Let's go!* 4; **Comment est-ce qu'on y va?** *How can we get there?* 12; **J'y vais tout de suite.** *I'll go right away.* 8; **On peut y aller...** *We can go there . . .* , 12

les yaourts (m.) *yogurt*, 8

les yeux (m. pl.) *eyes*, 8

la yole *skiff (a type of boat)*, 12

le yo-yo *yo-yo*, 0

le zèbre *zebra*, 0

zéro *a waste of time*, 2; *zero*, 0

le zoo *zoo*, 6

zoologique *zoological, having to do with animals*, 6

le zouk *zouk (style of music and dance)*, 12

Zut! *Darn!* 3

In this vocabulary, the English definitions of all active French words in the book have been listed, followed by their French equivalent. The number after each entry refers to the chapter in which the entry is introduced. It is important to use a French word in its correct context. The use of a word can be checked easily by referring to the chapter where it appears. French words and phrases are presented in the same way as in the French-English vocabulary.

a *un, une,* 3
able: to be able to *pouvoir,* 8
about *vers,* 6
across from *en face de,* 12
adore *adorer,* 1; **I adore ...** *J'adore... ,* 1
advise *conseiller;* **What do you advise me to do?** *Qu'est-ce que tu me conseilles?* 9
aerobics *l'aérobic* (f.), 4; **to do aerobics** *faire de l'aérobic,* 4
after *après,* 9; **And after that, ...** *Et après ça...,* 9
afternoon *l'après-midi* (m.), 2; **afternoon off** *l'après-midi libre,* 2; **in the afternoon** *l'après-midi,* 2
afterwards *après,* 9; **Afterwards, I went out.** *Après, je suis sorti(e).* 9; **And afterwards?** *Et après?* 9
Agreed. *Entendu.* 6
algebra *l'algèbre* (f.), 2
all *tout(e):* **Not at all.** *Pas du tout.* 4
already *déjà,* 9
also *aussi,* 1
am: I am ... years old. *J'ai... ans.* 1
an *un, une,* 3
and *et,* 1
annoying *embêtant(e),* 7; *pénible,* 7
answer *répondre,* 9; **There's no answer.** *Ça ne répond pas.* 9
any (of it) *en,* 8; **any more: I don't want any more.** *Je n'en veux plus.* 8
anything: I didn't forget anything. *Je n'ai rien oublié.* 11
apple *la pomme,* 8
apple juice *le jus de pomme,* 5
April *avril,* 4
are: These/those are ... *Ce sont... ,* 7; **They're ...** *Ils/Elles sont... ,* 7
art class *les arts plastiques* (m. pl.), 2
at *à la, au, à l', aux,* 6; **at ... fifteen** *à... heure(s) quinze,* 2; **at ... forty-five** *à... heure(s) quarante-cinq,* 2; **at ... thirty** *à... heure(s) trente,* 2; **at ... ('s) house** *chez... ,*

6; **at the record store** *chez le disquaire,* 12; **At what time?** *A quelle heure?* 6
August *août,* 4
autumn *l'automne* (m.), 4
aunt *la tante,* 7
avocado *l'avocat* (m.), 8

backpack *le sac à dos,* 3
bad *mauvais(e),* 5; **Not bad.** *Pas mal.* 1; **Oh, pas mauvais.** *Oh, not bad.* 9; **Very bad.** *Très mauvais.* 9
bag *le sac,* 3
baggy *large,* 10
bakery *la boulangerie,* 12
banana *la banane,* 8
bank *la banque,* 12
baseball *le base-ball,* 4; **to play baseball** *jouer au base-ball,* 4
basketball *le basket(-ball),* 4; **to play basketball** *jouer au basket (-ball),* 4
bathing suit *le maillot de bain,* 10
be *être,* 7
be able to, can *pouvoir,* 8; **Can you ...?** *Tu peux... ?* 12
beach *la plage,* 1
beans *les haricots* (m.), 8; **green beans** *les haricots verts* (m.), 8
because *parce que,* 5
beef *le bœuf,* 8
begin *commencer,* 9
behind *derrière,* 12
belt *la ceinture,* 10
better *mieux,* 9; **It's going to get better!** *Ça va aller mieux!* 9
between *entre,* 12
big *grand(e),* 10
bike *le vélo; faire du vélo,* 4; **by bike** *à vélo,* 12

biking *le vélo,* 1
binder: loose-leaf binder *le classeur,* 3
biology *la biologie,* 2
black *noir(e),* 3
blackboard *le tableau,* 0; **Go to the blackboard!** *Allez au tableau!* 0
blazer *la veste,* 10
blond *blond(e),* 7
blue *bleu(e),* 3
boat *le bateau,* 11; **by boat** *en bateau,* 12; **to go boating** *faire du bateau,* 11
book *le livre,* 0
bookstore *la librairie,* 12
boots *les bottes* (f.), 10
boring *barbant(e),* 2; **It was boring.** *C'était ennuyeux.* 11; *C'était barbant!* 11
borrow *emprunter,* 12
bottle *la bouteille,* 8; **a bottle of** *une bouteille de,* 8
box *le paquet,* 8; **a package/box of** *un paquet de,* 8
boy *le garçon,* 8
bracelet *le bracelet,* 3
bread *le pain,* 8; **long, thin loaf of bread** *la baguette,* 12
break *la récréation,* 2
breakfast *le petit déjeuner,* 8
bring *apporter,* 9; **Bring me back ...** *Rapporte-moi... ,* 8; **Please bring me ...** *Apportez-moi... , s'il vous plaît.* 5; **Will you bring me ...?** *Tu me rapportes... ?* 8
brother *le frère,* 7
brown *marron* (inv.), 3
brunette *brun(e),* 7
bus *le bus,* 12; **by bus** *en bus,* 12; **to miss the bus** *rater le bus,* 9
busy *occupé(e),* 6; **It's busy.** *C'est occupé.* 9; **Sorry, I'm busy.** *Désolé(e), je suis occupé(e).* 6
but *mais,* 1
butter *le beurre,* 8
buy *acheter,* 9; **Buy (me) ...** *Achète(-moi)... ,* 8
Bye! *Tchao!* 1

C

cafeteria *la cantine,* 9; **at the school cafeteria** *à la cantine,* 9

cake *le gâteau,* 8

calculator *la calculatrice,* 3

call *téléphoner,* 9; **Call him/her/them!** *Téléphone-lui/-leur!* 9; **Can you call back later?** *Vous pouvez rappeler plus tard?* 9; **Who's calling?** *Qui est à l'appareil?* 9

camera *l'appareil-photo* (m.), 11

camp *la colonie de vacances,* 11; **to/at a summer camp** *en colonie de vacances,* 11

camping *le camping,* 11; **to go camping** *faire du camping,* 11

can: to be able to, can *pouvoir,* 8; **Can I talk to you?** *Je peux te parler?* 9; **Can you . . . ?** *Est-ce que tu peux... ?* 12; **Can you . . . ?** *Tu peux... ?* 8; **Can I try on . . . ?** *Je peux essayer... ?* 10; **We can . . .** *On peut... ,* 6; **What can I do?** *Qu'est-ce que je peux faire?* 9

can *la boîte,* 8; **a can of** *une boîte de,* 8

can't: I can't right now. *Je ne peux pas maintenant.* 8; **No, I can't.** *Non, je ne peux pas.* 12

canary *le canari,* 7

cap *la casquette,* 10

car *la voiture,* 7; **by car** *en voiture,* 12; **to wash the car** *laver la voiture,* 7

cards *les cartes* (f.), 4; **to play cards** *jouer aux cartes,* 4

carrot *la carotte,* 8

cassette tape *la cassette,* 3

cat *le chat,* 7

CD/compact disc *le disque compact/le CD,* 3

Certainly. *Bien sûr.* 9

chair *la chaise,* 0

check *l'addition* (f.), 5; **The check, please.** *L'addition, s'il vous plaît.* 5

cheese *le fromage,* 5; **toasted ham and cheese sandwich** *le croque-monsieur,* 5

chemistry *la chimie,* 2

chic *chic* (inv.), 10

chicken (animal) *la poule,* 8; **chicken meat** *le poulet,* 8

child *l'enfant* (m./f.), 7; **children** *les enfants,* 7

chocolate *le chocolat,* 1; **hot chocolate** *un chocolat,* 5

choir *la chorale,* 2

choose *choisir,* 10; **Have you chosen?** *Vous avez choisi?* 5

class *le cours,* 2; **What classes do you have . . . ?** *Tu as quels cours... ?* 2

clean: to clean the house *faire le ménage,* 7

clear: to clear the table *débarrasser la table,* 7

close: Close the door! *Fermez la porte!* 0

close to *près de,* 12

clothing *les vêtements,* 10

coast *le bord,* 11; **to/on the coast** *au bord de la mer,* 11

coat *le manteau,* 10

coconut *la noix de coco,* 8

coffee *le café,* 5

cola *le coca,* 5

cold *froid(e)* 4; **It's cold.** *Il fait froid.* 4

color *la couleur,* 3; **What color is . . . ?** *De quelle couleur est... ?* 3

come: Will you come? *Tu viens?* 6

compact disc/CD *le disque compact/le CD,* 3

computer *l'ordinateur* (m.), 3

computer science *l'informatique* (f.), 2

concert *le concert,* 1

continue *continuer,* 12

cool *cool,* 2; **It's cool out.** *Il fait frais.* 4; **Very cool (great).** *Très chouette.* 9

corn *le maïs,* 8

corner *le coin,* 12; **on the corner of** *au coin de,* 12

cotton (adj.) *en coton,* 10

could: Could you do me a favor? *(Est-ce que) tu peux me rendre un petit service?* 12; **Could you go by . . . ?** *Tu pourrais passer à... ?* 12

countryside *la campagne,* 11; **to/in the countryside** *à la campagne,* 11

course *le cours,* 2

course: Of course. *Bien sûr.* 3

cousin *le cousin (la cousine),* 7

cross *traverser,* 12

cute *mignon(ne),* 7

D

dairy products *les produits* (m.) *laitiers,* 8

dance *danser,* 1

dance *la danse,* 2

Darn! *Zut!* 3

daughter *la fille,* 7

day *le jour,* 2

December *décembre,* 4; **in December** *en décembre,* 4

decided: Have you decided? *Vous avez choisi?* 5; **Have you decided to take . . . ?** *Vous avez décidé de prendre... ?* 10

delicious *délicieux(-euse),* 5

denim *le jean,* 10; **in denim** *en jean,* 10

deposit *déposer,* 12; **to deposit money** *déposer de l'argent,* 12

dictionary *le dictionnaire,* 3

difficult *difficile,* 2

dinner *le dîner,* 8; **to have dinner** *dîner,* 9

dishes *la vaisselle,* 7; **to do the dishes** *faire la vaisselle,* 7

dismissal (when school gets out) *la sortie,* 2

do *faire,* 4; **Do you play/do . . . ?** *Est-ce que tu fais... ?* 4; **I do.** *Moi, si.* 2; **to do homework** *faire les devoirs,* 7; **to do the dishes** *faire la vaisselle,* 7; **I don't play/do . . .** *Je ne fais pas de... ,* 4; **I have errands to do.** *J'ai des courses à faire.* 5; **I play/do . . .** *Je fais... ,* 4; **In your opinion, what do I do?** *A ton avis, qu'est-ce que je fais?* 9; **Sorry. I have homework to do.** *Désolé(e). J'ai des devoirs à faire.* 5; **What are you going to do . . . ?** *Qu'est-ce que tu vas faire... ?* 6; *Tu vas faire quoi... ?* 6; **What can I do?** *Qu'est-ce que je peux faire?* 9; **What did you do . . . ?** *Qu'est-ce que tu as fait... ?* 9; **What do you advise me to do?** *Qu'est-ce que tu me conseilles?* 9; **What do you do . . . ?** *Qu'est-ce que tu fais... ?* 4; **What do you do when . . . ?** *Qu'est-ce que tu fais quand... ?* 4

dog *le chien,* 7; **to walk the dog** *promener le chien,* 7

done, made *fait* (pp. of faire), 9

door *la porte,* 0

down: You go down this street to the next light. *Vous continuez jusqu'au prochain feu rouge.* 12

dozen *la douzaine,* 8; **a dozen** *une douzaine de,* 8

drama *le théâtre,* 4; **to do drama** *faire du théâtre,* 4

dress *la robe,* 10

drink *la boisson,* 5; **What do you have to drink?** *Qu'est-ce que vous avez comme boissons?* 5; **What is there to drink?** *Qu'est-ce qu'il y a à boire?* 5

drugstore *la pharmacie,* 12

E

earn *gagner,* 9

earrings *les boucles d'oreilles* (f.), 10

easy *facile,* 2

eat *manger,* 6

egg *l'œuf* (m.), 8

English (language) *l'anglais* (m.), 1

envelope *l'enveloppe* (f.), 12

eraser *la gomme,* 3
errands *les courses* (f.), 7; **I have errands to do.** *J'ai des courses à faire.* 5
especially *surtout,* 1
euro (European Community monetary unit) *l'euro* (m.); *Ça fait... euros./ C'est... euros.* It's . . . euros. 5
evening *le soir,* 4; **in the evening** *le soir,* 4
everything *tout,* 11; **I've thought of everything.** *J'ai pensé à tout.* 11
exam *l'examen* (m.), 1
excellent *excellent(e),* 5; **Yes, excellent.** *Oui, excellent.* 9
excuse: Excuse me. *Excusez-moi.* 3; **Excuse me, . . . , please?** *Pardon, . . . , s'il vous plaît?* 12; **Excuse me. Where is . . . , please?** *Pardon. Où est... , s'il vous plaît?* 12; **Excuse me. I'm looking for . . . , please.** *Pardon. Je cherche... , s'il vous plaît.* 12
expensive *cher (chère),* 10; **It's too expensive.** *C'est trop cher.* 10

F

fail *rater,* 9; **to fail a test** *rater un examen,* 9; **to fail a quiz** *rater une interro,* 9
fall *l'automne* (m.), 4; **in the fall** *en automne,* 4
fantastic *sensass (sensationnel),* 10
far from *loin de,* 12
fascinating *passionnant(e),* 2
fat *gros (se),* 7
father *le père,* 7
February *février,* 4; **in February** *en février,* 4
feel: I feel like . . . *J'ai envie de... ,* 11; **I don't feel like it.** *Ça ne me dit rien.* 6
finally *enfin,* 9; *finalement,* 9
find *trouver,* 9
Fine. *Ça va.* 1; **Yes, it was fine.** *Oui, ça a été.* 9
first *d'abord,* 7; **OK, if you . . . first.** *D'accord, si tu... d'abord.* 7
fish *le poisson,* 7
flour *la farine,* 8
foot *le pied,* 12; **on foot** *à pied,* 12
football *le football américain,* 4; **to play football** *jouer au football américain,* 4
for *pour,* 3; **What do you need for . . . ?** (informal) *Qu'est qu'il te faut pour... ?* 3
forest *la forêt,* 11; **to/in the forest** *en forêt,* 11
forget *oublier,* 9; **Don't forget . . .** *N'oublie pas de... ,* 8; **Forget him/**

her/them! *Oublie-le/-la/-les!* 9; **I didn't forget anything.** *Je n'ai rien oublié.* 11; **You didn't forget . . . ?** *Tu n'as pas oublié... ?* 11
franc (former monetary unit of France) *le franc,* 3
French (language) *le français,* 1; **French fries** *les frites* (f.), 1
Friday *vendredi,* 2; **on Fridays** *le vendredi,* 2
friend *l'ami(e)* (m./f.), 1; **to go out with friends** *sortir avec les copains,* 1
from *de,* 0
front: in front of *devant,* 6
fruit *le fruit,* 8
fun: Did you have fun? *Tu t'es bien amusé(e)?* 11; **Have fun!** *Amuse-toi bien!* 11; **What do you do to have fun?** *Qu'est-ce que tu fais pour t'amuser?* 4
funny *amusant(e),* 7

G

gain: to gain weight *grossir,* 10
game *le match,* 6; **to play video games** *jouer à des jeux vidéo,* 4; **to watch a game (on TV)** *regarder un match,* 6; **to go see a game** *aller voir un match,* 6
geography *la géographie,* 2
geometry *la géométrie,* 2
German (language) *l'allemand* (m.), 2
get: Get . . . *Prends... ,* 8; **How can we get there?** *Comment est-ce qu'on y va?* 12
gift *le cadeau,* 11
girl *la fille,* 0
give *donner,* 5; **Please give me . . .** *Donnez-moi... , s'il vous plaît.* 5
Gladly. *Je veux bien.* 8
go *aller,* 6; **Go to the blackboard!** *Allez au tableau!* 0; **I'm going . . .** *Je vais... ,* 6; **What are you going to do . . . ?** *Tu vas faire quoi... ?* 6; **It doesn't go at all with . . .** *Il/Elle ne va pas du tout avec... ,* 10; **It goes very well with . . .** *Il/Elle va très bien avec... ,* 10; **to go out with friends** *sortir avec les copains,* 1; **I'd like . . . to go with . . .** *J'aimerais... pour aller avec... ,* 10; **Afterwards, I went out.** *Après, je suis sorti(e).* 9; **Could you go by . . . ?** *Tu pourrais passer à... ?* 12; **Did it go well?** *Ça s'est bien passé?* 11; **I'm going to have . . . , please.** *Je vais prendre... , s'il vous plaît.* 5; **What are you going to do . . . ?** *Qu'est-ce que tu vas faire... ?* 6; **I went . . .** *Je suis*

allé(e)... , 9; **I'm going to . . .** *Je vais... ,* 11; **Let's go . . .** *Allons... ,* 6; **to go for a walk** *faire une promenade,* 6; **We can go there . . .** *On peut y aller... ,* 12; **Where are you going to go . . . ?** *Où est-ce que tu vas aller... ?* 11; **Where did you go?** *Tu es allé(e) où?* 9; **You keep going until the next light.** *Vous continuez jusqu'au prochain feu rouge.* 12; **How's it going?** *(Comment) ça va?* 1
golf *le golf,* 4; **to play golf** *jouer au golf,* 4
good *bon(ne),* 5; **Have a good trip!** *Bon voyage!* 11; **Did you have a good . . . ?** *Tu as passé un bon... ?* 11; **It doesn't look good on you at all.** *Il/Elle ne te/vous va pas du tout.* 10; **It's pretty good!** *C'est pas mauvais!* 5; **not good** *pas bon,* 5; **Yes, very good.** *Oui, très bon.* 9
Goodbye! *Au revoir!* 1; *Salut!* 1
got: No, you've got to . . . *Non, tu dois... ,* 7
grammar *la grammaire,* 1
grandfather *le grand-père,* 7
grandmother *la grand-mère,* 7
grapes *le raisin,* 8
great *génial(e),* 2; **Great!** *Super!* 1; **It looks great on you!** *C'est tout à fait ton style!* 10; **It was great!** *C'était formidable!* 11; **Not so great.** *Pas terrible,* 1
green *vert(e),* 3
green beans *les *haricots verts* (m.), 8
grey *gris(e),* 3
grocery store (small) *l'épicerie* (f.), 12
gross *dégoûtant(e),* 5
grow *grandir,* 10
guava *la goyave,* 8
gym *le sport,* 2

H

half *demi(e),* 6; **half past** *et demie,* 6; **half past** (after *midi* and *minuit*) *et demi,* 6
ham *le jambon,* 5; **toasted ham and cheese sandwich** *le croque-monsieur,* 5
hamburger *le hamburger,* 1
hand *la main,* 0
happened: What happened? *Qu'est-ce qui s'est passé?* 9
happy *content(e),* 7
hard *difficile,* 2
hat *le chapeau,* 10
have *avoir,* 2; **At what time do you have . . . ?** *Tu as... à quelle heure?* 2; **Did you have a good**

weekend? *Tu as passé un bon week-end?* 9; **Do you have...?** *Vous avez... ? 2; Tu as... ? 3;* **Do you have that in...?** (size, fabric, color) *Vous avez ça en... ? 10;* **Have...** *Prends/Prenez...,* 5; **What are you having?** *Vous prenez?* 5; **I don't have...** *Je n'ai pas de...,* 3; **I have some things to do.** *J'ai des trucs à faire.* 5; **I have...** *J'ai...,* 2; **I'll have..., please.** *Je vais prendre..., s'il vous plaît.* 5; **to take or to have (food or drink)** *prendre,* 5; **We have...** *Nous avons...,* 2; **What classes do you have...?** *Tu as quels cours... ? 2;* **What do you have...?** *Tu as quoi... ? 2;* **What kind of...do you have?** *Qu'est-ce que vous avez comme...* 5; **Will you have...?** *Tu prends/Vous prenez... ? 8*

health *le cours de développement personnel et social (DPS),* 2
Hello. *Bonjour.* 1; **Hello? (on the phone)** *Allô?* 9
help: **May I help you?** *(Est-ce que) je peux vous aider?* 10
her *la,* 9; *son/sa/ses,* 7; **to her** *lui,* 9
Here. *Voilà.* 3; **Here's...** *Voici...,* 7
Hi! *Salut!* 1
hiking *la randonnée,* 11; **to go hiking** *faire de la randonnée,* 11
him *le,* 9; **to him** *lui,* 9
his *son/sa/ses,* 7
history *l'histoire (f.),* 2
hockey *le *hockey,* 4; **to play hockey** *jouer au hockey,* 4
Hold on. *Ne quittez pas.* 9
homework *les devoirs (m.),* 2; **I've got homework to do.** *J'ai des devoirs à faire.* 5; **to do homework** *faire les devoirs,* 7
horrible *épouvantable,* 9; **It was horrible.** *C'était épouvantable.* 9
horseback riding *l'équitation (f.),* 1; **to go horseback riding** *faire de l'équitation,* 1
hose (clothing) *le collant,* 10
hot *chaud,* 4; **It's hot.** *Il fait chaud.* 4; **not so hot** *pas super,* 2
hot chocolate *le chocolat,* 5
hot dog *le *hot-dog,* 5
house: **at my house** *chez moi,* 6; **Is this...'s house?** *Je suis bien chez...?* 9; **to/at...'s house** *chez...,* 6
housework *le ménage,* 1; **to do housework** *faire le ménage,* 1
how: **How old are you?** *Tu as quel âge?* 1; **How about...?** *On...?* 4; **How do you like it?** *Comment tu trouves ça?* 5; **How much is...?** *C'est combien...?*

5; **How much is it?** *C'est combien?* 3; **How much is it, please?** (total) *Ça fait combien, s'il vous plaît?* 5; **How's it going?** *(Comment) ça va?* 1
how much *combien,* 3; **How much is...?** *C'est combien,... ? 3;* **How much is it?** (total) *Ça fait combien, s'il vous plaît?* 5
hundred *cent,* 3; **two hundred** *deux cents,* 3
hungry: **to be hungry** *avoir faim,* 5; **No thanks. I'm not hungry anymore.** *Non, merci. Je n'ai plus faim.* 8
husband *le mari,* 7

I *je,* 1; **I do.** *Moi, si.* 2; **I don't.** *Moi, non.* 2
ice cream *la glace,* 1
ice-skate *faire du patin à glace,* 4
idea *l'idée (f.),* 4; **Good idea.** *Bonne idée.* 4; **I have no idea.** *Je n'en sais rien.* 11
if *si,* 7; **OK, if you...first.** *D'accord, si tu... d'abord.* 7
impossible *impossible,* 7; **No, that's impossible.** *Non, c'est impossible.* 7
in *dans,* 6; **in (a city or place)** *à,* 11; **in (before a feminine country)** *en,* 11; **in (before a masculine noun)** *au,* 11; **in (before a plural country)** *aux,* 11; **in front of** *devant,* 6; **in the afternoon** *l'après-midi,* 2; **in the evening** *le soir,* 4; **in the morning** *le matin,* 2
in-line skate *le roller en ligne,* 4; **to in-line skate** *faire du roller en ligne,* 4
indifference: **(expression of indifference)** *Bof!* 1
intend: **I intend to...** *J'ai l'intention de...,* 11
interest: **That doesn't interest me.** *Ça ne me dit rien.* 4
interesting *intéressant(e),* 2
is: **He is...** *Il est...,* 7; **It's...** *C'est...,* 2; **She is...** *Elle est...,* 7; **There's...** *Voilà...,* 7; **This is...** *C'est...; Voici...,* 7
it *le, la,* 9
It's... *C'est...,* 2; **It's...** *Il est...* (time), 6; **It's...euros.** *C'est... euros.* 5; *Ça fait... euros.* 5; **No, it's...** *Non, c'est...,* 4; **Yes, it's...** *Oui, c'est...,* 4

jacket *le blouson,* 10; **suit jacket** *la veste,* 10
jam *la confiture,* 8
January *janvier,* 4; **in January** *en janvier,* 4
jeans *le jean,* 3
jog *faire du jogging,* 4
jogging *le jogging,* 4
juice *le jus,* 5; **orange juice** *le jus d'orange,* 5; **apple juice** *le jus de pomme,* 5
July *juillet,* 4; **in July** *en juillet,* 4
June *juin,* 4; **in june** *en juin,* 4

K

kilogram *le kilo(kilogramme),* 8; **a kilogram of** *un kilo de,* 8
kind: **What kind of...do you have?** *Qu'est-ce que vous avez comme... ?* 5
know: **I don't know.** *Je ne sais pas.* 10

L

lab *les travaux pratiques (m. pl.),* 2
later: **Can you call back later?** *Vous pouvez rappeler plus tard?* 9; **See you later!** *A tout à l'heure!* 1
Latin (language) *le latin,* 2
lawn *le gazon,* 7; **to mow the lawn** *tondre le gazon,* 7
learn *apprendre,* 0
leather *le cuir,* 10; **in leather** *en cuir,* 10
leave *partir,* 11; **Can I leave a message?** *Je peux laisser un message?* 9; **You can't leave without...** *Tu ne peux pas partir sans...,* 11
left *la gauche,* 12; **to the left** *à gauche (de),* 12
lemon *le citron,* 8
lemon soda *la limonade,* 5
lemonade *le citron pressé,* 5
let's: **Let's go...** *Allons...,* 6; **Let's go!** *Allons-y!* 4
letter *la lettre,* 12; **to send letters** *envoyer des lettres,* 12
lettuce *la salade (f.),* 8
library *la bibliothèque,* 6
like *aimer,* 1; **I'd really like...** *Je voudrais bien...,* 11; **Do you**

like ...? *Tu aimes... ?* 1; **Do you like it?** *Il/Elle te (vous) plaît?* 10; **How do you like ...?** *Comment tu trouves... ?* 10; **How do you like it?** *Comment tu trouves ça?* 5; **I (really) like ...** *Moi, j'aime (bien)...,* 1; **I don't like ...** *Je n'aime pas...,* 1; **I like it, but it's expensive.** *Il/Elle me plaît, mais il/elle est cher (chère).* 10; **I'd like ...** *Je voudrais...,* 3; **I'd like ... to go with ...** *J'aimerais... pour aller avec...,* 10; **I'd really like to.** *Je veux bien.* 6; **I'd like to buy ...** *Je voudrais acheter...,* 3; **What would you like?** *Vous désirez?* 10

like: What are they like? *Ils/Elles sont comment?* 7; **What is he like?** *Il est comment?* 7; **What is she like?** *Elle est comment?* 7

listen *écouter,* 1; **Listen!** *Ecoutez!* 0; **I'm listening.** *Je t'écoute.* 9; **to listen to music** *écouter de la musique,* 1

liter *le litre,* 8; **a liter of** *un litre de,* 8

long *long (ue),* 10

look: Look at the map! *Regardez la carte!* 0; **It doesn't look good on you at all.** *Il/Elle ne te/vous va pas du tout.* 10; **I'm looking for something for ...** *Je cherche quelque chose pour...,* 10; **It looks great on you!** *C'est tout à fait ton style!* 10; **Look, here's/there's/it's ...** *Regarde, voilà...,* 12; **No, thanks, I'm just looking.** *Non, merci, je regarde.* 10; **to look for** *chercher,* 9

look after: to look after ... *garder...,* 7

looks: It looks great on you! *C'est tout à fait ton style!* 10

loose-leaf binder *le classeur,* 3

lose *perdre,* 9; **to lose weight** *maigrir,* 10

lot: A lot. *Beaucoup.* 4

lots: I have lots of things to do. *J'ai des tas de choses à faire.* 5

lower (number) *moins,* 0

luck *la chance,* 11; **Good luck!** *Bon courage!* 2; *Bonne chance!* 11

lunch *le déjeuner,* 2; **to have lunch** *déjeuner,* 9

ma'am *madame (Mme),* 1

made *fait (pp of faire),* 9

magazine *le magazine,* 3

make *faire,* 4

mall *le centre commercial,* 6

mango *la mangue,* 8

map *la carte,* 0

March *mars,* 4; **in March** *en mars,* 4

market *le marché,* 8

math *les maths (f. pl.), les mathématiques,* 1

May *mai,* 4; **in May** *en mai,* 4

may: May I ...? *(Est-ce que) je peux... ?* 7; **May I help you?** *(Est-ce que) je peux vous aider?* 10

me *moi,* 2; **Me, too.** *Moi aussi.* 2; **Not me.** *Pas moi.* 2

mean *méchant(e),* 7

meat *la viande,* 8

medicine *les médicaments (m.),* 12

meet *retrouver,* 6; *rencontrer,* 9; **I'd like you to meet ...** *Je te (vous) présente...,* 7; **Pleased to meet you.** *Très heureux (heureuse).* 7; **O.K., we'll meet ...** *Bon, on se retrouve...,* 6; **We'll meet...** *Rendez-vous...,* 6

menu *la carte,* 5; **The menu, please.** *La carte, s'il vous plaît.* 5

message *le message,* 9; **Can I leave a message?** *Je peux laisser un message?* 9

metro *le métro,* 12; **at the ... metro stop** *au métro...,* 6

midnight *minuit,* 6; **It's midnight.** *Il est minuit.* 6; **It's half past midnight.** *Il est minuit et demi.* 6

milk *le lait,* 8

mineral water *l'eau minérale (f.),* 5

minute *la minute,* 9; **Do you have a minute?** *Tu as une minute?* 9

miss, Miss *mademoiselle (Mlle),* 1

miss *rater,* 9; **to miss the bus** *rater le bus,* 9

moment *le moment,* 5; **One moment, please.** *Un moment, s'il vous plaît.* 5

Monday *lundi,* 2; **on Mondays** *le lundi,* 2

money *l'argent (m.),* 11

More ...? *Encore de... ?* 8; **I don't want any more.** *Je n'en veux plus.* 8

morning *le matin,* 2; **in the morning** *le matin,* 2

mother *la mère,* 7

mountain *la montagne,* 11; **to/in the mountains** *à la montagne,* 11

movie *le film,* 6; **to see a movie** *voir un film,* 6

movie theater *le cinéma,* 6; **the movies** *le cinéma,* 1

mow: to mow the lawn *tondre le gazon,* 7

Mr. *monsieur (M.),* 1

Mrs. *madame (Mme),* 1

much: How much is ...? *C'est combien,... ?* 5; **How much is it, please?** *Ça fait combien, s'il vous plaît?* 5; **How much is it?** *C'est combien?* 3; **No, not too much.** *Non, pas trop.* 2; **Not much.** *Pas grand-chose.* 6; **Not too much.** *Pas tellement.* 4; **Not very much.** *Pas beaucoup.* 4; **Yes, very much.** *Oui, beaucoup.* 2

museum *le musée,* 6

mushroom *le champignon,* 8

music *la musique,* 2

my *mon/ma/mes,* 7

name: His/Her name is ... *Il/Elle s'appelle...,* 1; **My name is ...** *Je m'appelle...,* 0; **What is your name?** *Tu t'appelles comment?* 0

natural science *les sciences naturelles (f.),* 2

need: I need ... *Il me faut...,* 3; **I need ...** *J'ai besoin de...,* 8; **What do you need for ...?** (formal) *Qu'est-ce qu'il vous faut pour... ?* 3; **What do you need for ...?** (informal) *Qu'est-ce qu'il te faut pour... ?* 3; **What do you need?** *De quoi est-ce que tu as besoin?* 8

neither: Neither do I. *Moi non plus.* 2; **neither tall nor short** *ne... ni grand(e) ni petit(e),* 7

never *ne... jamais,* 4

next *prochain(e),* 12; **You go down this street to the next light.** *Vous continuez jusqu'au prochain feu.* 12

next to *à côté de,* 12

nice *gentil (gentille),* 7; *sympa (sympathique),* 7; **It's nice weather.** *Il fait beau.* 4

nightmare *le cauchemar,* 11; **It was a real nightmare!** *C'était un véritable cauchemar!* 11

no *non,* 1

noon *midi,* 6; **It's noon.** *Il est midi.* 6; **It's half past noon.** *Il est midi et demi.* 6

not: Oh, not bad. *Oh, pas mal/ mauvais.* 9; **not yet** *ne... pas encore,* 9; **Not at all.** *Pas du tout.* 4; **Not me.** *Pas moi.* 2; **Not so great.** *Pas terrible.* 1; **not very good** *pas bon,* 5; **No, not really.** *Non, pas vraiment.* 11; **No, not too much.** *Non, pas trop.* 2

notebook *le cahier,* 0, 3

nothing *rien,* 6; **Nothing special.** *Rien de spécial.* 6

novel *le roman,* 3

November *novembre,* 4; **in November** *en novembre,* 4

now *maintenant,* 2; **I can't right now.** *Je ne peux pas maintenant.* 8

O

o'clock *...heures,* 2; **at . . . o'clock** *à... heure(s),* 2
October *octobre,* 4; **in October** *en octobre,* 4
of *de,* 0; **of course** *bien sûr,* 3; **of it** *en,* 8; **of them** *en,* 8
often *souvent,* 4
O.K. *D'accord.* 4; **Is that O.K. with you?** *Tu es d'accord?* 7; **Well, O.K.** *Bon, d'accord.* 8; **Yes, it was O.K.** *Oui, ça a été.*
okra *les gombos* (m.), 8
old: How old are you? *Tu as quel âge?* 1; **I am . . . years old.** *J'ai... ans.* 1; **older** *âgé(e),* 7
omelet *l'omelette* (f.), 5
on: Can I try on . . . ? *Je peux essayer le/la/les... ?* 10; **on foot** *à pied,* 12; **on Fridays** *le vendredi,* 2; **on Mondays** *le lundi,* 2; **on Saturdays** *le samedi,* 2; **on Sundays** *le dimanche,* 2; **on Thursdays** *le jeudi,* 2; **on Tuesdays** *le mardi,* 2; **on Wednesdays** *le mercredi,* 2
once: once a week *une fois par semaine,* 4
onion *l'oignon* (m.), 8
open: Open your books to page . . . *Ouvrez vos livres à la page... ,* 0
opinion *l'avis* (m.), 9; **In your opinion, what do I do?** *A ton avis, qu'est-ce que je fais?* 9
or *ou,* 1
orange (color) *orange* (inv.), 3
orange *l'orange* (f.), 8
orange juice *le jus d'orange,* 5;
our *notre/nos,* 7
out: Out of the question! *Pas question!* 7; **out of style,** *démodé(e),* 10

P

package *le paquet,* 8; **a package/box of** *un paquet de,* 8
page *la page,* 0
pancake: a very thin pancake *la crêpe,* 5
pants *le pantalon,* 10
papaya *la papaye,* 8
paper *le papier,* 0; **sheets of paper** *les feuilles de papier* (f.), 3
pardon: Pardon me. *Pardon.* 3
parent *le parent,* 7
park *le parc,* 6

party *la boum,* 6; **to go to a party** *aller à une boum,* 6
pass: You'll pass . . . *Vous passez...,* 12
passport *le passeport,* 11
pastry *la pâtisserie,* 12; **pastry shop** *la pâtisserie,* 12
peach *la pêche,* 8
pear *la poire,* 8
peas *les petits pois* (m.), 8
pen *le stylo,* 0
pencil *le crayon,* 3; **pencil case** *la trousse,* 3; **pencil sharpener** *le taille-crayon,* 3
perfect *parfait(e),* 10; **It's perfect.** *C'est parfait.* 10
phone *le téléphone,* 1; **to talk on the phone** *parler au téléphone,* 1
photography: to do photography *faire de la photo,* 4
physical education *l'éducation physique et sportive (EPS)* (f.), 2
physics *la physique,* 2
pick *choisir,* 10; **to pick up your room** *ranger ta chambre,* 7
picnic *le pique-nique,* 6; **to have a picnic** *faire un pique-nique,* 6
picture *la photo,* 4; **to take pictures** *faire des photos,* 4
pie *la tarte,* 8
piece *le morceau,* 8; **a piece of** *un morceau de,* 8
pineapple *l'ananas* (m.), 8
pink *rose,* 3
pizza *la pizza,* 1
place *l'endroit* (m.), 12
plane *l'avion* (m.), 12; **by plane** *en avion,* 12
plane ticket *le billet d'avion,* 11
plans: I don't have any plans. *Je n'ai rien de prévu.* 11
plate *l'assiette* (f.), 5
play *la pièce,* 6; **to see a play** *voir une pièce,* 6
play *jouer,* 4; *faire,* 4; **I don't play/ do . . .** *Je ne fais pas de... ,* 4; **I play . . .** *Je joue... ,* 4; **I play/ do . . .** *Je fais... ,* 4; **to play baseball** *jouer au base-ball,* 4; **to play basketball** *jouer au basket (-ball),* 4; **to play football** *jouer au football américain,* 4; **to play golf** *jouer au golf,* 4; **to play hockey** *jouer au hockey,* 4; **to play soccer** *jouer au foot(ball),* 4; **to play sports** *faire du sport,* 1; **to play tennis** *jouer au tennis,* 4; **to play video games** *jouer à des jeux vidéo,* 4; **to play volleyball** *jouer au volley(-ball),* 4; **What sports do you play?** *Qu'est-ce que tu fais comme sport?* 4
please *s'il te/vous plaît,* 3; **Yes, please.** *Oui, s'il te/vous plaît.* 8
pleased: Pleased to meet you. *Très heureux (-euse).* 7

pleasure *le plaisir,* 8; **Yes, with pleasure.** *Oui, avec plaisir.* 8
pork *le porc,* 8
post office *la poste,* 12
poster *le poster,* 0
potato *la pomme de terre,* 8
pound *la livre,* 8; **a pound of** *une livre de,* 8
practice *répéter,* 9
prefer *préférer,* 1; **I prefer . . .** *Je préfère... ,* 1; *J'aime mieux... ,* 1
problem *le problème,* 9; **I've got a little problem.** *J'ai un petit problème.* 9
pullover (sweater) *le pull-over,* 3
purple *violet(te),* 3
put *mettre,* 10; **to put on** *mettre,* 10

Q

quarter *le quart,* 6; **quarter past** *et quart,* 6; **quarter to** *moins le quart,* 6
question: Out of the question! *Pas question!* 7
quiche *la quiche,* 5
quiz *l'interro(gation)* (f.), 9

R

radio *la radio,* 3
rain: It's raining. *Il pleut.* 4
raise: Raise your hand! *Levez la main!* 0
rarely *rarement,* 4
read *lire,* 1; **read** *lu* (pp. of lire), 9
really *vraiment,* 11; **I (really) like . . .** *Moi, j'aime (bien)... ,* 1; **I'd really like . . .** *Je voudrais bien... ,* 11; **I'd really like to.** *Je veux bien.* 6; **No, not really.** *Non, pas vraiment.* 11
record store *le disquaire,* 12; **at the record store** *chez le disquaire,* 12
recreation center *la Maison des jeunes et de la culture (MJC),* 6
red *rouge,* 3; **redheaded** *roux (rousse),* 7
rehearse *répéter,* 9
relative *le parent,* 7
Repeat! *Répétez!* 0
restaurant *le restaurant,* 6
retro (style) *rétro* (inv.), 10
return: to return something *rendre,* 12
rice *le riz,* 8
ride: to go horseback riding *faire de l'équitation,* 1

right *la droite,* 12; **to the right** *à droite (de),* 12

right away *tout de suite,* 6; **Yes, right away.** *Oui, tout de suite.* 5; **I'll go right away.** *J'y vais tout de suite.* 8

right now *maintenant,* 8; **I can't right now.** *Je ne peux pas maintenant.* 8

right there: It's right there on the . . . *C'est tout de suite à . . . ,* 12

room *la chambre,* 7; **to pick up your room** *ranger ta chambre,* 7

ruler *la règle,* 3

S

sailing *la voile,* 11; **to go sailing** *faire de la voile,* 11; *faire du bateau,* 11

salad *la salade,* 8

salami *le saucisson,* 5

sandals *les sandales* (f.), 10

sandwich *un sandwich,* 5; **cheese sandwich** *un sandwich au fromage,* 5; **ham sandwich** *un sandwich au jambon,* 5; **salami sandwich** *un sandwich au saucisson,* 5; **toasted ham and cheese sandwich** *le croque-monsieur,* 5

Saturday *samedi,* 2; **on Saturdays** *le samedi,* 2

saw *vu* (pp. of *voir*), 9

scarf *l'écharpe* (f.), 10

school *l'école* (f.), 1

science class *les sciences naturelles,* 2

scuba diving *la plongée,* 11; **to go scuba diving** *faire de la plongée,* 11

sea *la mer,* 11

second *la seconde,* 9; **One second, please.** *Une seconde, s'il vous plaît.* 9

see *voir,* 6; **See you later!** *A tout à l'heure!* 1; **See you soon.** *A bientôt.* 1; **See you tomorrow.** *A demain.* 1; **to go see a game** *aller voir un match,* 6; **to see a movie** *voir un film,* 6; **to see a play** *voir une pièce,* 6

seen *vu* (pp. of *voir*), 9

sell *vendre,* 9

send *envoyer,* 12; **to send letters** *envoyer des lettres,* 12

sensational *sensass,* 10

September *septembre,* 4; **in September** *en septembre,* 4

service: At your service; You're welcome. *A votre service.* 3

shall: Shall we go to the café? *On va au café?* 5

sheet *la feuille,* 0; **a sheet of paper** *une feuille de papier,* 0

shirt (man's) *la chemise,* 10; **(woman's)** *le chemisier,* 10

shoes *les chaussures* (f.), 10

shop: to go shopping *faire les magasins,* 1; **to window-shop** *faire les vitrines,* 6; **Can you do the shopping?** *Tu peux aller faire les courses?* 8

shopping *les courses* (f.), 7; **to do the shopping** *faire les courses,* 7

short (height) *petit(e),* 7; **(length)** *court(e),* 10

shorts: (pair of) shorts *le short,* 3

should: You should . . . *Tu devrais . . . ,* 9; **You should talk to him/her/them.** *Tu devrais lui/leur parler.* 9

show *montrer,* 9

shy *timide,* 7

sing *chanter,* 9

sir *monsieur* (M.), 1

sister *la sœur,* 7

Sit down! *Asseyez-vous!* 0

size *la taille,* 10

skate: to ice-skate *faire du patin à glace,* 4; **to in-line skate** *faire du roller en ligne,* 4

ski *faire du ski,* 4; **How about skiing?** *On fait du ski?* 5; **to water-ski** *faire du ski nautique,* 4; **skiing** *le ski,* 1

skirt *la jupe,* 10

sleep *dormir,* 1

slender *mince,* 7

slice *la tranche,* 8; **a slice of** *une tranche de,* 8

small *petit(e),* 10

smart *intelligent(e),* 7

snack: afternoon snack *le goûter,* 8

snails *les escargots* (m.), 1

sneakers *les baskets* (f. pl.), 3

snow: It's snowing. *Il neige.* 4

so: not so great *pas terrible,* 5

So-so. *Comme ci comme ça.* 5

soccer *le football,* 1; *le foot,* 4; **to play soccer** *jouer au foot(ball),* 4

socks *les chaussettes* (f.), 10

soda: lemon soda *la limonade,* 5

some *des,* 3; **some** *du, de la, de l', des,* 8; **some (of it)** *en,* 8; **Yes, I'd like some.** *Oui, j'en veux bien.* 8

something *quelque chose,* 6; **I'm looking for something for . . . ,** *Je cherche quelque chose pour . . . ,* 10

sometimes *quelquefois,* 4

son *le fils,* 7

soon: See you soon. *A bientôt.* 1

Sorry. *Je regrette.* 3; *Désolé(e).* 5; **Sorry, but I can't.** *Désolé(e), mais je ne peux pas.* 4; **I'm sorry, but I don't have time.** *Je regrette, mais je n'ai pas le temps.* 8; **Sorry, I'm busy.** *Désolé(e), je suis occupé(e).* 6

Spanish (language) *l'espagnol* (m.), 2

speak *parler,* 9; **Could I speak to . . . ?** *(Est-ce que) je peux parler à . . . ?* 9

special *spécial(e),* 6; **Nothing special.** *Rien de spécial.* 6

sports *le sport,* 1; **to play sports** *faire du sport,* 1; **What sports do you play?** *Qu'est-ce que tu fais comme sport?* 4

spring *le printemps,* 4; **in the spring** *au printemps,* 4

stadium *le stade,* 6

stamp *le timbre,* 12

stand: Stand up! *Levez-vous!* 0

start *commencer,* 9

stationery store *la papeterie,* 12

steak *le bifteck,* 8; **steak and French fries** *le steak-frites,* 5

stop: at the . . . metro stop *au métro . . . ,* 6

store *le magasin,* 1

straight ahead *tout droit,* 12; **You go straight ahead until you get to . . .** *Vous allez tout droit jusqu'à . . . ,* 12

strawberry *la fraise,* 8; **water with strawberry syrup** *le sirop de fraise (à l'eau),* 5

street *la rue,* 12; **Take . . . Street, then cross . . . Street.** *Prenez la rue . . . , puis traversez la rue . . . ,* 12

strong *fort(e),* 7

student *l'élève* (m./f.), 2

study *étudier,* 1

study hall *l'étude* (f.), 2

style *la mode,* 10; **in style** *à la mode,* 10; **out of style** *démodé(e),* 10

subway *le métro,* 12; **by subway** *en métro,* 12

sugar *le sucre,* 7

suit: Does it suit me? *Il/Elle me va?* 10; **It suits you really well.** *Il/Elle te/vous va très bien.* 10

suit jacket *la veste,* 10

suitcase *la valise,* 11

summer *l'été* (m.), 4; **in the summer** *en été,* 4

summer camp *la colonie de vacances,* 11; **to/at a summer camp** *en colonie de vacances,* 11

Sunday *dimanche,* 2; **on Sundays** *le dimanche,* 2

sunglasses *les lunettes de soleil* (f. pl.), 10

super *super,* 2

supermarket *le supermarché,* 8

sure: I'm not sure. *J'hésite.* 10

sweater *le cardigan,* 10

sweatshirt *le sweat-shirt,* 3

swim *nager,* 1; *faire de la natation,* 4

swimming *la natation,* 4

swimming pool *la piscine,* 6

syrup: water with strawberry syrup *le sirop de fraise (à l'eau),* 5

T

T-shirt *le tee-shirt*, 3
table *la table*, 7; **to clear the table** *débarrasser la table*, 7
tacky *moche*, 10; **I think it's (they're) really tacky.** *Je le/la/les trouve moche(s)*. 10
take or **have (food or drink)** *prendre*, 5; **Are you taking it/them?** *Vous le/la/les prenez?* 10; **Are you taking ...?** *Tu prends... ?* 11; **Have you decided to take ...?** *Vous avez décidé de prendre... ?* 10; **I'll take it/them.** *Je le/la/les prends*. 10; **to take a test** *passer un examen*, 9; **to take pictures** *faire des photos*, 4; **We can take ...** *On peut prendre... ,* 12; **Take ... Street, then ... Street.** *Prenez la rue... , puis la rue... ,* 12
take out: Take out a sheet of paper. *Prenez une feuille de papier*. 0; **to take out the trash** *sortir la poubelle*, 7
taken *pris* (pp. of *prendre*), 9
talk *parler*, 1; **Can I talk to you?** *Je peux te parler?* 9; **to talk on the phone** *parler au téléphone*, 1; **We talked.** *Nous avons parlé*. 9
tall *grand(e)*, 7
taxi *le taxi*, 12; **by taxi** *en taxi*, 12
teacher *le professeur*, 0
telephone *le téléphone*, 0
television *la télévision*, 0
tell *dire*, 9; **Can you tell her/him that I called?** *Vous pouvez lui dire que j'ai téléphoné?* 9
tennis *le tennis*, 4; **to play tennis** *jouer au tennis*, 4
terrible *horrible*, 10
test *l'examen* (m.), 1
Thank you. *Merci*. 3; **No thanks. I'm not hungry anymore.** *Non, merci. Je n'ai plus faim*. 8
that *ce, cet, cette*, 3; **This/That is ...** *Ça, c'est... ,* 12
theater *le théâtre*, 6
their *leur/leurs*, 7
them *les*, 9; **to them** *leur*, 9
then *ensuite*, 9
there *-là* (noun suffix), 3; **there** *il y a*, 5; **there** *y, là*, 12; **Is ... there, please?** *(Est-ce que)... est là, s'il vous plaît?* 9; **There's ...** *Voilà... ,* 7; **There is/There are ...** *Il y a... ,* 5; **What is there to drink?** *Qu'est-ce qu'il y a à boire?* 5
these *ces*, 3; **These/those are ...** *Ce sont... ,* 7
thing *la chose*, 5; *le truc*, 5; **I have lots of things to do.** *J'ai des tas de choses à faire*. 5; **I have some things to do.** *J'ai des trucs à faire*. 5
think *penser*, 11; **I think it's/they're ...** *Je le/la/les trouve... ,* 10; **I've thought of everything.** *J'ai pensé à tout*. 11; **What do you think of ...?** *Comment tu trouves... ?* 2; **What do you think of that/it?** *Comment tu trouves ça?* 2
thirsty: to be thirsty *avoir soif*, 5
this *ce, cet, cette*, 3; **This is ...** *C'est... ,* 7; **This is ...** *Voilà/Voici... ,* 7; **This/That is ...** *Ça, c'est... ,* 12
those *ces*, 3; **These/Those are ...** *Ce sont... ,* 7
Thursday *jeudi*, 4; **on Thursdays** *le jeudi*, 2
ticket *le billet*, 11; **plane ticket** *le billet d'avion*, 11; **train ticket** *le billet de train*, 11
tie *la cravate*, 10
tight *serré(e)*, 10
time *le temps*, 8; **a waste of time** *zéro*, 2; **at the time of** *à l'heure de*, 1; **At what time do you have ...?** *Tu as... à quelle heure?* 2; **At what time?** *A quelle heure?* 6; **from time to time** *de temps en temps*, 4; **I'm sorry, but I don't have time.** *Je regrette, mais je n'ai pas le temps*. 8; *Je suis désolé(e), mais je n'ai pas le temps*. 12; **What time is it?** *Quelle heure est-il?* 6
to *à la, au, à l', aux*, 6; **to (a city or place)** *à*, 11; **to (before a feminine country)** *en*, 11; **to (before a masculine noun)** *au*, 11; **to (before a plural noun)** *aux*, 11; **to her** *lui*, 9; **to him** *lui*, 9; **to them** *leur*, 9; **five to ...** *moins cinq*, 6
today *aujourd'hui*, 2
tomato *la tomate*, 8
tomorrow *demain*, 2; **See you tomorrow.** *A demain*. 1
tonight *ce soir*, 7; **Not tonight.** *Pas ce soir*. 7
too (much) *trop*, 10; **It's/They're too ...** *Il/Elle est (Ils/Elles sont) trop... ,* 10; **Me too.** *Moi aussi*. 2; **No, it's too expensive.** *Non, c'est trop cher*. 10; **No, not too much.** *Non, pas trop*. 2; **Not too much.** *Pas tellement*. 4
track *l'athlétisme* (m.), 4; **to do track and field** *faire de l'athlétisme*, 4
train *le train*, 12; **by train** *en train*, 12; **train ticket** *le billet de train*, 11
trash(can) *la poubelle*, 7; **to take out the trash** *sortir la poubelle*, 7
travel *voyager*, 1

trip *le voyage*, 11; **Have a good trip!** *Bon voyage!* 11
true *vrai*, 2
try: Can I try on ...? *Je peux essayer... ?* 10; **Can I try it (them) on ?** *Je peux l'/les essayer?* 10
Tuesday *mardi*, 2; **on Tuesdays** *le mardi*, 2
turn *tourner*, 12; **You turn ...** *Vous tournez... ,* 12
TV *la télé(vision)*, 1; **to watch TV** *regarder la télé(vision)*, 1

U

umbrella *le parapluie*, 11
uncle *l'oncle* (m.), 7
uncooked *cru(e)*, 5
until *jusqu'à*, 12; **You go straight ahead until you get to ...** *Vous allez tout droit jusqu'à... ,* 12
useless *nul(le)*, 2
usually *d'habitude*, 4

V

vacation *les vacances* (f. pl.), 1; **Have a good vacation!** *Bonnes vacances!* 11; **on vacation** *en vacances*, 4
vacuum (verb) *passer l'aspirateur*, 7
VCR (videocassette recorder) *le magnétoscope*, 0
vegetables *les légumes* (m.), 8
very *très*, 1; **Very well.** *Très bien*. 1; **Yes, very much.** *Oui, beaucoup*. 2
video *la vidéo*, 4; **to make videos** *faire de la vidéo*, 4; **video games** *des jeux vidéo*, 4
videocassette recorder (VCR) *le magnétoscope*, 0
videotape *la vidéocassette*, 3
visit (a place) *visiter*, 9
volleyball *le volley(-ball)*, 4; **to play volleyball** *jouer au volley(-ball)*, 4

W

wait for *attendre*, 9
Waiter! *Monsieur!* 5
Waitress! *Madame!* 5; *Mademoiselle!* 5

walk: to go for a walk *faire une promenade,* 6; **to walk the dog** *promener le chien,* 7

wallet *le portefeuille,* 3

want *vouloir,* 6; **Do you want . . . ?** *Tu veux... ?* 6; **Do you want . . . ?** *Vous voulez... ?* 8; **I don't want any more.** *Je n'en veux plus.* 8; **Yes, if you want to.** *Oui, si tu veux.* 7

wash *laver,* 7; **to wash the car** *laver la voiture,* 7

waste: a waste of time *zéro,* 2

watch *la montre,* 3

watch *regarder,* 1; **to watch a game (on TV)** *regarder un match,* 6; **to watch TV** *regarder la télé(vision),* 1

water *l'eau* (f.), 5; **mineral water** *l'eau minérale,* 5; **water with strawberry syrup** *le sirop de fraise (à l'eau),* 5

water ski *le ski nautique,* 4; **to water-ski** *faire du ski nautique,* 4

wear *mettre, porter,* 10; **I don't know what to wear for . . .** *Je ne sais pas quoi mettre pour... ,* 10; **Wear . . .** *Mets... ,* 10; **What shall I wear?** *Qu'est-ce que je mets?* 10; **Why don't you wear . . . ?** *Pourquoi est-ce que tu ne mets pas... ?* 10

weather *le temps,* 4; **What's the weather like?** *Quel temps fait-il?* 4

Wednesday *mercredi,* 2; **on Wednesdays** *le mercredi,* 2

week *la semaine,* 4; **once a week** *une fois par semaine,* 4

weekend *le week-end,* 6; **Did you have a good weekend?** *Tu as passé un bon week-end?* 9; **on weekends** *le week-end,* 4; **this weekend** *ce week-end,* 6

welcome: At your service; You're welcome. *A votre service.* 3

well *bien,* 1; **Did it go well?** *Ça s'est bien passé?* 11; **Very well.** *Très bien.* 1

went: Afterwards, I went out. *Après, je suis sorti(e).* 9; **I went . . .** *Je suis allé(e)... ,* 9

what *comment,* 0; **What is your name?** *Tu t'appelles comment?* 0; **What do you think of . . . ?** *Comment tu trouves... ?* 2; **What do you think of that/it?** *Comment tu trouves ça?* 2; **What's his/her name?** *Il/Elle s'appelle comment?* 1

what *qu'est-ce que,* 1; **What are you going to do . . . ?** *Qu'est-ce que tu vas faire... ?* 6; **What do you do to have fun?** *Qu'est-ce que tu fais pour t'amuser?* 4; **What do you have to drink?** *Qu'est-ce que vous avez comme boissons?* 5; **What do you need for . . . ?** (formal) *Qu'est-ce qu'il vous faut pour... ?* 3; **What happened?** *Qu'est-ce qui s'est passé?* 9; **What kind of . . . do you have?** *Qu'est-ce que vous avez comme... ?* 5

what *quoi,* 2; **I don't know what to wear for . . .** *Je ne sais pas quoi mettre pour... ,* 10; **What are you going to do . . . ?** *Tu vas faire quoi... ?* 6; **What do you have . . . ?** *Tu as quoi... ?* 2; **What do you need?** *De quoi est-ce que tu as besoin?* 5

When? *Quand (ça)?* 6

where *où,* 6; **Where?** *Où (ça)?* 6; **Where are you going to go . . . ?** *Où est-ce que tu vas aller... ?* 11; **Where did you go?** *Tu es allé(e) où?* 9

which *quel(le),* 1

white *blanc(he),* 3

who *qui,* 0; **Who's calling?** *Qui est à l'appareil?* 9

whom *qui,* 6; **With whom?** *Avec qui?* 6

why *pourquoi,* 0; **Why don't you . . . ?** *Pourquoi tu ne... pas?* 9; **Why not?** *Pourquoi pas?* 6

wife *la femme,* 7

win *gagner,* 9

window *la fenêtre,* 0; **to window-shop** *faire les vitrines,* 6

windsurfing *la planche à voile,* 11; **to go windsurfing** *faire de la planche à voile,* 11

winter *l'hiver* (m.), 4; **in the winter** *en hiver,* 4

with *avec,* 6; **with me** *avec moi,* 6; **With whom?** *Avec qui?* 6

withdraw *retirer,* 12; **withdraw money** *retirer de l'argent,* 12

without *sans,* 11; **You can't leave without . . .** *Tu ne peux pas partir sans... ,* 11

work *travailler,* 9

worry: Don't worry! *Ne t'en fais pas!* 9

would like: I'd like to buy . . . *Je voudrais acheter... ,* 3

year *l'an* (m.); **I am . . . years old.** *J'ai... ans.* 1

yellow *jaune,* 3

yes *oui,* 1; **Yes, please.** *Oui, s'il te/vous plaît.* 8

yesterday *hier,* 9

yet: not yet *ne... pas encore,* 9

yogurt *les yaourts* (m.), 8

you *tu, vous,* 0; **And you?** *Et toi?* 1

young *jeune,* 7

your *ton/ta/tes,* 7; *votre/vos,* 7

zoo *le zoo,* 6

Grammar Index

Grammar Index

Page numbers in boldface type refer to the **Grammaire** and **Note de grammaire** presentations. Other page numbers refer to grammar structures presented in the **Comment dit-on... ?, Tu te rappelles?, Vocabulaire,** and **A la française** sections. Page numbers beginning with **R** refer to the Grammar Summary in this Reference Section.

à: expressions with **jouer 113;** contractions with **le, la, l',** and **les 113,** 177, 360, R21; with cities and countries **330,** R21

adjectives: demonstrative adjectives **85,** R17; adjective agreement and placement 86, **87, 210,** R15–R18; possessive adjectives 203, **205,** R18; adjectives as nouns **301,** R18

à quelle heure: 58, 183, **185,** R20

adverbs: adverbs of frequency **122;** adverb placement with the **passé composé 272,** R18

agreement of adjectives: **87, 210,** R15–R18

aller: 151, 173, **174,** 328, 329, R26; **aller** in the **passé composé** 270, 338, R28

articles: definite articles **le, la, l',** and **les 28,** R19; definite articles with days of the week **173;** indefinite articles **un, une,** and **des** 79, **81,** R19; partitive articles **du, de la,** and **de l'** 235, **236,** 364, R19

avec qui: 183, **185,** R20

avoir: 55, R26; **avoir besoin de 238; avoir envie de** 329; with **passé composé** 269, **271,** 273, **277,** 303, 338, R28

ce, cet, cette, and **ces: 85,** R17

c'est: versus **il/elle est** + adjective **310**

cognates: 6–7, 27, 84, 112

commands: 11, 148, 151, **152,** 240, 333, R28; commands with object pronouns 151, 240, **279,** 336, R22–R23

contractions: See **à** or **de.**

countries: prepositions with countries **330,** R21

de: expressions with **faire 113;** contractions **116, 369,** R21; indefinite articles (negative) **81;** indicating relationship or ownership **204;** partitive article **236,** R19; with expressions of quantity **242**

definite articles: **28,** R19

demonstrative adjectives: **85,** R17

devoir: 213, R27; **devrais** 279, 330

dire: 276, R27

direct object pronouns: **279, 309,** 336, R22

dormir: 334, R26

elle(s): See pronouns.

en: pronoun 242, 247, **248,** 333, R23; preposition before geographic names **330,** R21

-er verbs: 26, 31, 32, **33,** 119, R24; with **passé composé 271,** 273, 338, R28

est-ce que: 115, 185, R20

être: 61, 179, 183, 203, 209, 210, **211,** R26; with **passé composé** 270, 337, 338, R28

faire: with **de** + activity **113, 116;** weather 118, R22, R26

falloir: il me/te faut 82, 238, 301, 365, R22

future (near): **aller** + infinitive 84, 151, 173, 328, 329, R27; with the present tense 175, 334

il(s): See pronouns.

il est/ils sont: + adjective: 209; versus **c'est** + adjective **310**

imperatives: 11, 148, 151, **152,** 240, 333, R28

indefinite articles: 79, **81,** R19

indirect object pronouns: 276, **279,** 336, R23

interrogatives: 58, 183, **185,** 329, R20; **quel** 25; **quels** 55; **pourquoi** 179, 240, 279, 300, 330

-ir verbs: **303,** R24; with **passé composé 303,** R28

je: See pronouns.

lui: See pronouns.

leur: See pronouns.

mettre: 299, R27

ne... jamais: 122, R18
ne... ni... ni...: 208, 209
ne... pas: 26, 61; with indefinite articles 80, 81, 338, R19
ne... rien: 122, 146, 179, 329, 330; with the **passé composé 333**
negation: **26,** 61; indefinite articles (**ne... pas de**) 80, **81,** 116, R19; with **rien** 122, 146, 179, 329, 330, 333; with the **passé composé** 338
negative statements or questions and **si: 54,** R20
nous: See pronouns.

object pronouns: See pronouns.
on: with suggestions 122, 145
où: 183, **185,** 329, R20

partir: 334, R26
partitive articles: 235, **236,** 364, R19
passé composé: with **avoir** 269, **271,** 273, 277, 338, R28; with **être** 270, 337, 338, R28
placement of adjectives: **87,** R17
placement of adverbs: **122, 272,** R18
possessive adjectives: **205,** R18
pourquoi 179, 240, 279, 300, 330
pouvoir: 122, 146, 179, 213, 240, **241,** R27; **pourrais** 364
prendre: 148, **149,** R27
prepositions: **369,** R21; expressions with **faire** and **jouer 113;** prepositions **à** and **en 330,** R21; preposition **de 204, 242,** R21; preposition **chez** 183
pronouns: subject pronouns 24, 26, **33, 116,** R22; direct object pronouns **279, 309,** 336, R22; indirect object pronouns 276, **279,** 336, R23; pronouns and infinitives 279, 301; pronoun **en** 242, 247, **248,** 333, R23; pronoun **y** 151, 240, 327, 364, 366, **367,** R23

quand: 118, 183, **185,** R20
quantities: **242**
quel(s), quelle(s): See question words.
qu'est-ce que: 185, 329, 330, 337

question formation: **115,** R20
question words: 58, 183, **185,** 329, R20; **quel** 25; **quels** 55; **pourquoi** 179, 240, 279, 300, 330
qui: 183, **185,** R20
quoi: 55, **185,** 300

re-: prefix 241
-re verbs: **277,** R24; with **passé composé 277,** 338, R28
rien: See **ne... rien.**

si: 54, R20; indicating condition 213, 364
sortir: 334, R26
subject pronouns: 24, 26, **33, 116,** R22

time: 58, 183, **185**
tu: See pronouns.

un, une, des: 79, **81,** R19

venir: 179
verbs: commands 10, 148, 151, **152,** 240, 333, R28; **-er** 26, 31, 32, **33,** 119, R24; **-ir** verbs **303,** R24; passé composé with **avoir** 269, **271,** 273, **277, 303,** 338, R28; passé composé with **être** 270, 337, 338, R28; **-re** verbs **277,** R24
vouloir: 179, **180,** R27
vous: See pronouns.

y: 151, 240, 327, 364, 366, **367,** R23

Credits

ACKNOWLEDGMENTS

For permission to reprint copyrighted material, grateful acknowledgment is made to the following sources:

Agence Vu: Two photographs from "Je passe ma vie au téléphone" by Anne Vaisman, photographs by Claudine Doury, from *Phosphore*, no. 190, February 1997. Copyright © 1997 by Agence Vu.

Air France: Front of Air France boarding pass, "Carte d'accès à bord."

Bayard Presse International: From "Allez, c'est à vous de choisir," text by Florence Farcouli, illustrations by Olivier Tossan, from *Okapi*, no. 568-9, September 1995. Copyright © 1995 by Bayard Presse International. Text and illustrations from "Sondage: les lycéens ont-ils le moral?" from *Phosphore*, no. 160, September 1989. Copyright © 1989 by Bayard Presse International. From "Je passe ma vie au téléphone" by Anne Vaisman from *Phosphore*, no. 190, February 1997. Copyright © 1997 by Bayard Presse International.

C'Rock Radio, Vienne: Logo for C'Rock Radio, 89.5 MHz.

Cacharel: Four adapted photographs with captions of Cacharel products from *Rentrée très classe à prix petits : Nouvelles Galeries Lafayette.*

Canal B, Bruz: Logo for Canal B Radio, 94 MHz.

Cathédrale d'images: Advertisement, "Cathédrale d'images," from *Évasion Plus.*

Comité Français d'Education pour la Santé, 2, rue Auguste Comte-92170 Vanves: From "Les groupes d'aliments" from the brochure *Comment équilibrer votre alimentation,* published and edited by the Comité Français d'Education pour la Santé.

Editions S.A.E.P.: Recipe and photograph for "Croissants au coco et au sésame," recipe and photograph for "Mousseline africaine de petits légumes," "Signification des symboles accompagnant les recettes," and jacket cover from *La Cuisine Africaine* by Pierrette Chalendar. Copyright © 1993 by S.A.E.P.

EF Foundation: From "Le rêve américain devient réalité, en séjour Immersion avec EF: Vivre à l'américaine," photograph, and "Vacances de Printemps" from "Les U.S.A. en cours Principal: le séjour EF idéal" from *EF Voyages Linguistiques: Hiver, Printemps et Eté 1993.*

Femme Actuelle: Text from "En direct des refuges: Poupette, 3 ans" by Nicole Lauroy from *Femme Actuelle,* no. 414, August 31–September 6, 1992. Copyright © 1992 by Femme Actuelle. Text from "En direct des refuges: Jupiter, 7 mois" by Nicole Lauroy from *Femme Actuelle,* no. 436, February 1993. Copyright © 1993 by Femme Actuelle. Text from "En direct des refuges: Flora, 3 ans" by Nicole Lauroy from *Femme Actuelle,* no. 457, July 1993. Copyright © 1993 by Femme Actuelle. Text from "En direct des refuges: Dady, 2 ans" and from "Mayo a trouvé une famille" by Nicole Lauroy from *Femme Actuelle,* no. 466, August 30–September 5, 1993. Copyright © 1993 by Femme Actuelle. Text from "En direct des refuges: Camel, 5 ans" by Nicole Lauroy from *Femme Actuelle,* no. 472, October 11–17, 1993. Copyright © 1993 by Femme Actuelle.

France Miniature: Cover, illustration and adapted text from brochure, *Le Pays France Miniature.*

France Télécom: Front and back of the Télécarte.

Galeries Lafayette: Four adapted photographs with captions of Cacharel products and two photographs with captions of NAF NAF products from *Rentrée très classe à prix petits: Nouvelles Galeries Lafayette.*

Grands Bateaux de Provence: Advertisement, "Bateaux 'Mireio,'" from *Evasion Plus.*

Grottes de Thouzon: Advertisement, "Grottes de Thouzon," photograph by M. Crotet, from *Evasion Plus,* Provence, Imprimerie Vincent, 1994.

Groupe Filipacchi: Advertisement, "Casablanca," from *7 à Paris,* no. 534, February 2–18, 1992, p. 43.

Hachette Livre: From "Où dormir?" and "Où manger?" from "Arles (13200)" from *Le Guide du Routard : Provence-Côte d'Azur, 2000/2001.* Copyright by Hachette Livre (Hachette Tourisme).

L'Harmattan: Excerpts from French text and six illustrations from *Cheval de bois/Chouval bwa* by Isabelle and Henri Cadoré, illustrated by Bernadette Coléno. Copyright © 1993 by L'Harmattan.

Loca Center: Advertisement, "Loca Center," from *Guide des Services: La Martinique à domicile.*

Ministère de la Culture: From "Les jeunes aiment sortir" (Retitled: "Les loisirs préférés") from *Francoscopie: Comment vivent les Français, 1997* by Gérard Mermet.

Le Monde: From "Baccalauréat 1996. Les hauts et les bas: Taux de réussite par série" from *Le Monde de l'Education,* no. 240, September 1996. Copyright © 1996 by Le Monde.

Musée de l'Empéri: Adapted advertisement, "Château-Musée de l'Empéri," from *Evasion Plus.*

NAF NAF: Two photographs with captions of NAF NAF products from *Rentrée très classe à prix petits : Nouvelles Galeries Lafayette.*

NRJ, Paris: Adaptation of logo for NRJ Radio, 100.3 MHz.

OUÏ FM, Paris: Logo for OUÏ FM Radio, 102.3 MHz.

Parc Astérix S.A.: Cover of brochure, *Parc Astérix,* 1992. Advertisement for Parc Astérix from *Paris Vision,* 1993, p. 29.

Parc Zoologique de Paris: Cover and map from brochure, *Parc Zoologique de Paris.*

RCV: La Radio Rock, Lille: Logo for RCV: La Radio Rock, 99 MHz.

Village des Sports: Advertisement, "Village des Sports: c'est l'fun, fun, fun!," from *Région de Québec.*

PHOTOGRAPHY CREDITS

Abbreviations used: (t) top, (b) bottom, (l) left, (r) right, (c) center.

Rencontre culturelle students, HRW Photo/John Langford

Panorama fabric, Copyright © 1992 by Dover Publications, Inc.

All other fabric: HRW Photo.

All globes: Mountain High Maps® Copyright ©1997 Digital Wisdom, Inc.

TABLE OF CONTENTS: vii, HRW Photo/Sam Dudgeon; viii (both), HRW Photo/Marty Granger/Edge Productions; ix (t), © Owen Franken/Stock Boston; ix (b), HRW Photo/Marty Granger/Edge Productions; x, HRW Photo/Marty Granger/Edge Productions; xi (both), HRW Photo/Marty Granger/Edge Productions; xii (t), HRW Photo/Edge Productions; xii (b), © Hilary Wilkes/International Stock Photography; xiii, © Owen Franken/CORBIS; xiv, © Julio Donoso/Woodfin Camp & Associates; xv (both), HRW Photo/Edge Productions; xvi, © Owen Franken/CORBIS; xvii (both), HRW Photo/Marty Granger/Edge Productions; xviii, © Benelux Press/Leo de Wys; xix, HRW Photo/Marty Granger/Edge Productions; xx, Corbis Images; xxi, HRW Photo/Marty Granger/Edge Productions; xxii, HRW Photo/Marty Granger/Edge Productions.

PRELIMINARY CHAPTER: xxvi (t, c), © Joe Viesti/Viesti Collection, Inc.; xxvi (b), © Robert Fried/Stock Boston; 1 (tl), D&P Valenti/H. Armstrong Roberts; 1 (tr), Stone/Tim MacPherson; 1 (c), ©Michael Dwyer/Stock Boston; 1 (bl), © Owen Franken/Stock Boston; 1 (br), Viesti Collection, Inc.; 2 (t, c), Archive Photos; 2 (bl), Aslan/Barthelémy/Nivier/Roussière/SIPA Press; 2 (br), AP/Wide World Photos; 3 (t), Vedat Acickalin/SIPA PRESS; 3 (c), Gastaud/SIPA Press; 3 (bl), Sean Roberts/Everett Collection; 3 (br), Shawn Botterill/Allsport; 4 (tl), Arianespace/SIPA Press; 4 (tc), Nabil Zorkot; 4 (tr), Boisière/SIPA Press; 4 (cl), © Robert Frerck/Odyssey/Chicago; 4 (cr), K. Scholz/H. Armstrong Roberts; 4 (bl), HRW Photo/May Polycarpe; 4 (br), © Telegraph Colour Library/FPG International; 5 (l), Pictor Uniphoto; 5 (r), HRW Photo/John Langford; 6 (row 1, l), Digital imagery® © 2003 PhotoDisc, Inc.; 6 (row 1, cl), © Stockbyte; 6 (row 1, c), Digital imagery® © 2003 PhotoDisc, Inc.; 6 (row 1, cr), HRW Photo/Victoria Smith; 6 (row 1, r), Mountain High Maps® Copyright©1997 Digital Wisdom, Inc.; 6 (row 2, l), David Simson/Stock Boston; 6 (row 2, cl, c), Corbis Images; 6 (row 2, cr), CORBIS/Stuart Westmorland; 6 (row 2, r), Digital imagery® © 2003 PhotoDisc, Inc.; 6 (row 3, l, cl), Digital imagery® © 2003 PhotoDisc, Inc.; 6 (row 3, c), ©1998 Artville, LLC; 6 (row 3, cr), EyeWire, Inc.; 6 (row 3, r), © Stockbyte; 6 (row 4, l), CORBIS/Gunter Marx; 6 (row 4, cl), HRW Photo/Victoria Smith; 6 (row 4, c, cr, r), Digital imagery® © 2003 PhotoDisc, Inc.; 6 (row 5, all), Digital imagery® © 2003 PhotoDisc, Inc.; 6 (row 6), Digital imagery® ©2003 PhotoDisc, Inc.; 7 (tl), Clay Myers/The Wildlife Collection; 7 (tc), Leonard Lee Rue/FPG International; 7 (tr), Tim Laman/The Wildlife Collection; 7 (bl), Jack Swenson/The Wildlife Collection; 7 (bc), Tim Laman/The Wildlife Collection; 7 (br), Martin Harvey/The Wildlife Collection; 9 (tl, tc, tr), HRW Photo/Victoria Smith; 9 (c, cl, bl, bc), HRW Photo/Marty Granger/Edge Productions; 9 (cr), David Frazier Photolibrary; 9 (br), HRW Photo/Louis Boireau; 10, ©David Stover/Pictor; 11 (both), HRW Photo/Victoria Smith.

LOCATION: POITIERS: 12-13 (all), HRW Photo/Marty Granger/Edge Productions; 14 (both), Tom Craig/FPG International; 15 (t, c, bl), HRW Photo/Marty Granger/Edge Productions; 15 (br), HRW Photo.

CHAPTER 1 16-17, HRW Photo/Marty Granger/Edge Productions; 18 (tr inset), HRW Photo/Louis Boireau/Edge Productions; 18 (remaining), HRW Photo/Marty Granger/Edge Productions; 19 (all), HRW Photo/Marty Granger/Edge Productions; 20 (all), HRW Photo/Marty Granger/Edge Productions; 21 (tc), HRW Photo/Sam Dudgeon; 21 (br), HRW Photo/Alan Oddie; 21 (remaining), HRW Photo/Marty Granger/Edge Productions; 22 (cl), HBJ Photo/Mark Antman; 22 (c), HRW photo; 22 (cr), HRW photo/John Langford 22; (l), HRW Photo/Marty Granger/Edge Productions; 22 (r), IPA/The Image Works; 23 (all), HRW Photo/Marty Granger/Edge Productions; 24, HRW Photo/Marty Granger/Edge Productions; 25, Toussaint/Sipa Press; 30 (all), HRW Photo/Marty Granger/Edge Productions; 34 (tl), HRW Photo/Sam Dudgeon; 34 (tc), HRW Photo/Marty Granger/Edge Productions; 34 (tr), Robert Brenner/PhotoEdit; 34 (cl), HRW Photo/David Frazier; 34 (c), HBJ Photo/Pierre Capretz; 34 (cr), Marc Antman/The Image Works; 34 (bl), Christine Galida/HRW Photo; 34 (bc), © Stephen Frisch/Stock Boston; 34 (br), © TRIP/ASK Images; 36 (t), Frank Siteman/The Picture Cube; 36 (tc), Richard Hutchings/PhotoEdit; 36 (bc), David C. Bitters/The Picture Cube; 36 (b), R. Lucas/The Image Works; 37 (t), HRW Photo/Russell Dian; 37 (tc), HRW Photo/May Polycarpe; 37 (bc), R. Lucas/The Image Works; 37 (b), © Arthur Tilley/FPG International; 41 (l), HRW Photo/Sam Dudgeon; 41 (r), HRW Photo/David Frazier; 42 (tr), © Telegraph Colour Library/FPG International; 42 (tl, tc, br), HRW Photo/Marty Granger/Edge Productions; 42 (bl), David Young-Wolff/PhotoEdit.

CHAPTER 2 46-47, © Owen Franken/Stock Boston; 48 (all), HRW Photo/Marty Granger/Edge Productions; 49 (br inset), ©1997 Radlund & Associates for Artville; 49 (remaining), HRW Photo/Marty Granger/Edge Productions; 56 (l), HRW Photo/Louis Boireau/Edge

Productions; 56 (remaining), HRW Photo/Marty Granger/Edge Productions.

CHAPTER 3 74-75, HRW Photo/Marty Granger/ Edge Productions; 76 (all), HRW Photo/Edge Productions; 77 (all), HRW Photo/Edge Productions; 79 (all), HRW Photo/Sam Dudgeon; 80, HRW Photo/Sam Dudgeon; 81 (r), HRW Photo/Eric Beggs; 81 (remaining), HRW Photo/Sam Dudgeon; 83 (l,c), HRW Photo/Marty Granger/ Edge Productions; 83 (r), HRW photo/Louis Boireau/Edge Productions; 86 (all), HRW Photo/Sam Dudgeon; 88, © European Communities; 89 (both), © European Communities; 92 (t), Digital imagery® © 2003 PhotoDisc, Inc.; (92 t inset), Sam Dudgeon; 92 (ctr), HRW Photo; 92 (ctl), Digital imagery® © 2003 PhotoDisc, Inc.; 92 (cbr), Digital imagery® © 2003 PhotoDisc, Inc.; 92 (b), Artville, LLC; 92 (cbl), HRW Photo; 93 (bc), Digital imagery® © 2003 PhotoDisc, Inc.; 93 (remaining), HRW Photo; 95 (both), HRW Photo/Sam Dudgeon; 100 (all), HRW Photo/Sam Dudgeon.

LOCATION: QUEBEC 102-103, J. A. Kraulis/Masterfile; 104 (t, c, bl), HRW Photo/Marty Granger/Edge Productions; 104 (br), Wolfgang Kaehler; 105 (t), HRW Photo/ Marty Granger/Edge Productions; 105 (bl), HRW Photo/Marty Granger/Edge Productions; 105 (br), HRW Photo/Marty Granger/Edge Productions; 105 (cl), Hervey Smyth, Vue de la Prise de Québec, le 13 septembre 1759, Engraving, 35.9 x 47.8 cm, Musée du Québec, 78.375, Photo by Jean-Guy Kérouac.; 105 (cr), HRW Photo/Marty Granger/Edge Productions.

CHAPTER 4 106-107, HRW Photo/Marty Granger/ Edge Productions; 108 (c), HRW Photo/Marty Granger/ Edge Productions; 109 (all), HRW Photo/Marty Granger/Edge Productions; 111 (all), HRW Photo/Marty Granger/Edge Productions; 112 (tl), HRW Photo/ Marty Granger/Edge Productions; 112 (tc), David Young-Wolff/PhotoEdit; 112 (tr), HRW Photo/Sam Dudgeon; 112 (cl), Bill Bachmann/PhotoEdit; 112 (c, cr, bc, HRW Photo/Marty Granger/Edge Productions; 112 (bl), David Lissy/Leo de Wys; 112 (br), HRW Photo; 114 (tl, tc), HRW Photo/Victoria Smith; 114 (tr), © 2000 Robert Fried; 117 (l), Robert Fried Photography; 117 (cl, r), HRW Photo/ Sam Dudgeon; 117 (c), HBJ Photo/May Polycarpe; 117 (cr), HRW Photo/Marty Granger/Edge Productions; 120 (tl), © Telegraph Colour Library/FPG International; 120 (tc), Dean Abramson/Stock Boston; 120 (tr), Corbis Images; 120 (remaining), © Bill Stanton/International Stock Photography; 121 (l), HRW photo/Louis Boireau/ Edge Productions; 121 (c, r), HRW Photo/Marty Granger/ Edge Productions; 128, HRW Photo; 129, HRW Photo/ Marty Granger/Edge Productions; 131, HRW Photo/ Marty Granger/Edge Productions.

LOCATION: PARIS 136-137, Paul Steel/The Stock Market; 138 (all), HRW Photo/Marty Granger/Edge Productions;

139 (tr), Bob Handelman/ STONE; 139 (tl, br), HRW Photo/Marty Granger/Edge Productions; 139 (bl), Peter Menzel/Stock Boston.

CHAPTER 5 140-141, © Hilary Wilkes/International Stock Photography; 142 (all), HRW Photo/Edge Productions; 143 (all), HRW Photo/Edge Productions; 147 (drinks br), Digital imagery® ©2003 PhotoDisc, Inc.; 147 (remaining), HRW Photo/Victoria Smith; 150 (l, c), HRW Photo/Marty Granger/Edge Productions; 150 (r), HRW Photo/Louis Boireau/Edge Productions; 152 (both), HRW Photo/Sam Dudgeon; 154 (cr), HRW Photo/Michelle Bridwell; 154 (remaining), HRW Photo/Sam Dudgeon; 159 (t, b), Pomme de Pain; 159 (c), Steven Mark Needham/ Envision; 160, © Telegraph Colour Library/FPG International.

CHAPTER 6 168-169, © Owen Franken/CORBIS; 170 (cr), Sebastien Raymond/Sipa Press; 170 (remaining), HRW Photo/Marty Granger/Edge Productions; 171 (cr), Corbis Images; 171 (remaining), HRW Photo/Marty Granger/ Edge Productions; 172, Corbis Images; 172 (inset), HRW Photo/Marty Granger/Edge Productions; 175 (tl, tc, tr, br), HRW Photo/Marty Granger/Edge Productions; 175 (bc), David R. Frazier Photolibrary; 175 (bl), HRW Photo/Sam Dudgeon; 176 (tr), Tabuteau/The Image Works; 176 (cl), Maratea/International Stock Photography; 176 (ccl), Greg Meadors/Stock Boston; 176 (bl), Robert Fried/Stock Boston; 176 (bcl), Courtesy Marion Bermondy; 176 (bcr), HBJ Photo/Mark Antman; 176 (br), R. Lucas/The Image Works; 176 (remaining), HRW Photo/Marty Granger/ Edge Productions; 178 (l), HRW Photo/Louis Boireau/ Edge Productions; 178 (c, r), HRW Photo/Marty Granger/ Edge Productions; 182 (tl), HBJ Photo/Mark Antman; 182 (tr), HRW Photo/Marty Granger/Edge Productions; 182 (b), Ulrike Welsch/PhotoEdit; 185, HRW Photo/Marty Granger/Edge Productions; 191 (all), HRW Photo/Marty Granger/Edge Productions; 192, HRW Photo/Dianne Schrader; 194 (tl), HRW Photo/Pierre Capretz; 194 (tr), SuperStock; 194 (b), HRW Photo/Dianne Schrader.

CHAPTER 7 198-199, © Julio Donoso/Woodfin Camp & Associates; 200 (tl, tc, cl), HRW Photo/Marty Granger/ Edge Productions; 200 (tr), HRW Photo/Marty Granger/ Edge Productions; 200 (cr), HRW Photo/Russell Dian; 200 (b), HRW Photo; 200 (b inset), Digital imagery® ©2003 PhotoDisc, Inc.; 201 (tl, tr, c), HRW Photo; 201 (b), HRW Photo/Marty Granger/Edge Productions; 202 (l, cl), HRW Photo/Russell Dian; 202 (cr, r), HRW Photo; 203, HRW Photo/Russell Dian; 204 (Row 3 cl), HRW Photo/Marty Granger/Edge Productions; 204 (Row 4 cl), Courtesy Marion Bermondy; 204 (Row 4 cr), David Austen/Stock Boston; 204 (Row 4 r), John Lei/Stock Boston; 204 (remaining), HRW Photo; 205 (l), HRW Photo/Daniel Aubry; 205 (cl), David Young-Wolff/PhotoEdit; 205 (c), HRW Photo/May Polycarpe; 205 (cr), Tony Freeman/ PhotoEdit; 205 (r), HRW Photo/Sam Dudgeon; 209 (l), Firooz Zahedi/The Kobal Collection/Paramount Studios;

209 (r), TM © 20th Century Fox Film Corp., 1992; 212 (all), HRW Photo/Marty Granger/Edge Productions; 216 (t, b), Walter Chandoha; 216 (c), HRW Photo; 217 (t, c), Walter Chandoha; 217 (b), Gerard Lacz/Peter Arnold, Inc.; 220, ©1999 Image Farm Inc.; 220 (inset), HRW Photo/Russell Dian; 221, ©1999 Image Farm Inc.; 221 (inset), HRW Photo/Russell Dian.

LOCATION: ABIDJAN 226-227, Betty Press/Panos Pictures; 228 (t, br), Nabil Zorkot; 228 (b), John Elk III/Bruce Coleman, Inc.; 229 (t), Nabil Zorkot; 229 (bl), M. & E. Bernheim/Woodfin Camp & Associates; 229 (br), Nabil Zorkot.

CHAPTER 8 230-231, HRW Photo/Edge Productions; 232 (all), HRW Photo/Edge Productions; 233 (all), HRW Photo/Edge Productions; 234 (c), HRW Photo/Sam Dudgeon ; 234 (remaining), HRW Photo; 237, Etienne Nangbo/Les images de chez nous; 239 (l, r), HRW Photo/Marty Granger/Edge Productions; 239 (c), HRW photo/Edge Productions; 244 (all), HRW Photo; 245 (tl), HRW Photo/Lance Shriner; 245 (tr), HRW Photo; 245 (bl), HRW Photo/Sam Dudgeon; 245 (br), HRW Photo/Eric Beggs;. 252, HRW Photo.

LOCATION: ARLES 260-261, HRW Photo/Marty Granger/Edge Productions; 262 (tl), HRW Photo; 262 (tr), Erich Lessing/Art Resource; 262 (b), © Ruggero Vanni/CORBIS; 263 (br), HRW Photo/Marty Granger/Edge Productions; 263 (bl), G. Carde/SuperStock; 263 (t), W. Gontscharoff/SuperStock.

CHAPTER 9 264-265, © Owen Franken/CORBIS; 266 (all), HRW Photo/Marty Grange/Edge Productions; 267 (all), HRW Photo/Marty Granger/Edge Productions; 268 (r), Ermakoff/The Image Works; 268 (remaining), HRW Photo/Marty Granger/Edge Productions; 269 (r), © Digital Vision; 269 (l), HRW Photo/John Langford; 270 (l), HRW Photo/Michael Young; 270 (r), HRW Photo/Victoria Smith; 275 (tl), © Telegraph Colour Library/FPG International; 275 (tcl), HRW Photo/John Langford; 275 (tcr), © Digital Vision; 275 (tr), ©Esbin-Anderson/The Image Works; 275 (bl), Robert Fried; 275 (br), Anthony Redpath/The Stock Market; 278 (all), HRW Photo/Marty Granger/ Edge Productions; 284, © Marcel Scholing/Zefa; 287, HRW Photo/Marty Granger/Edge Productions.

CHAPTER 10 292-293, HRW Photo/Marty Granger/Edge Productions; 294 (all), HRW Photo/Marty Granger/ Edge Productions; 295 (all), HRW Photo/Marty Granger/Edge Productions; 296 (all), HRW Photo/ Marty Granger/Edge Productions; 302, HRW Photo/Michelle Bridwell; 305 (all), HRW Photo/Marty Granger/Edge Productions; 312 (all), HRW Photo/Sam Dudgeon; 313 (all), HRW Photo/Sam Dudgeon; 316, HRW Photo/Marty Granger/Edge Productions; 318, HRW Photo; 320 (both), HRW Photo/Sam Dudgeon.

CHAPTER 11 322-323, © Benelux Press/Leo de Wys; 324 (cl inset), HRW Photo/May Polycarpe; 324 (cr inset), HRW photo/Edge Productions; 324 (bl inset), David Florenz/Option Photo; 324 (remaining), HRW Photo/ Marty Granger/Edge Productions; 325 (all), HRW Photo/Marty Granger/Edge Productions; 326 (all), HRW Photo/Marty Granger/Edge Productions; 329, © Telegraph Colour Library/FPG International; 331 (tl), © Robert Frerck/Woodfin Camp & Associates; 331 (tc), Digital imagery® © 2003 PhotoDisc, Inc.; 331 (tr), CORBIS Images; 331 (bl), © E. Bordis/Leo de Wys, Inc.; 331 (bc), © IFA Bilderteam/Leo de Wys, Inc.; 331 (br), Digital imagery® © 2003 PhotoDisc, Inc.; 332 (l), HRW Photo/Edge Productions; 332 (c, r), HRW Photo/Marty Granger/Edge Productions; 333, © European Communities; 335, Pierre Jaques/FOC photo; 337 (l), HRW Photo/May Polycarpe; 337 (r), HRW Photo/Sam Dudgeon; 337 (bkgd), Digital imagery® © 2003 PhotoDisc, Inc.; 338 (tl), HRW Photo/Marty Granger/ Edge Productions; 338 (tr), Robert Fried/Stock Boston; 338 (bl), Francis De Richem/The Image Works; 338 (bc), Joachim Messer/Leo de Wys; 338 (br), J. Messerschmidt/ Leo de Wys; 342, J. Messerschmidt/Leo de Wys; 345 (l), HRW Photo/Marty Granger/Edge Productions; 345 (r), Corbis Images.

LOCATION: FORT-DE-FRANCE 350-353 (all), HRW Photo/Marty Granger/Edge Productions.

CHAPTER 12 354-355, HRW Photo/Marty Granger/Edge Productions; 354 (l inset), HRW Photo/Victoria Smith; 356 (all), HRW Photo/Marty Granger/Edge Productions; 357 (all), HRW Photo/Marty Granger/ Edge Productions; 358 (all), HRW Photo/Marty Granger/Edge Productions; 359 (tl), HRW Photo; 359 (tc, tr, bl, br), HRW Photo/Marty Granger/ Edge Productions; 359 (cl), HBJ Photo/Patrick Courtault; 359 (c), HBJ Photo/Pierre Capretz; 359 (cr), IPA/The Image Works; 359 (bc), Robert Fried/Stock Boston; 362 (tl, bc), Chris Huxley/Leo de Wys; 362 (tc, tr, bl), HRW Photo/ Marty Granger/Edge Productions; 362 (br), HRW Photo; 365 (tl), HRW Photo/Helen Kolda; 365 (tc), © AFP/ CORBIS; 365 (tr), HRW Photo/Sam Dudgeon (by F. Johan and N. Vogel ©Casterman); 365 (bl, br), HRW Photo/Sam Dudgeon; 365 (bc),HRW Photo/Russell Dian; 366 (tl), Elizabeth Zuckerman/PhotoEdit; 366 (tc, cl, cr), HRW Photo/Marty Granger/Edge Productions; 366 (tr), Amy Etra/PhotoEdit; 366 (c), HRW Photo/Louis Boireau; 366 (bl), Robert Rathe/Stock Boston; 366 (bc), Dean Abramson/Stock Boston; 366 (br), Marc Antman/The Image Works; 368 (all), HRW Photo/Marty Granger/Edge Productions; 372 (l), HRW Photo/Marty Granger/Edge Productions;372 (r), Chris Huxley/Leo de Wys; 376 (bl), David R. Frazier Photolibrary; 376 (remaining), HRW Photo/Marty Granger/Edge Productions; 380 (cr), Chris

Huxley/Leo de Wys; 380 (remaining), HRW Photo/Marty Granger/Edge Productions.

REVISIONS All photos HRW Photo/Marty Granger Edge Productions except: xx, HRW Photo/Sam Dudgeon; REVISIONS 3 (br), HRW Photo/Alan Oddie; REVISIONS 6 (tl), HRW Photo; (cr), ©Brooklyn Production/CORBIS Images/HRW; (bcr), HBJ Photo/May Polycarpe; (br), Robert Brenner/PhotoEdit; REVISIONS 8, HRW Photo/Sam Dudgeon; REVISIONS 9 (b), HRW Photo/Louis Boireau; REVISIONS 16, HRW Photo/Victoria Smith; REVISIONS 17 (b), Owen Franken/Stock Boston; REVISIONS 18 (all), HRW Photo/Victoria Smith; REVISIONS 21 (cl), Greg Meadors/Stock Boston; (cr), HBJ Photo/Mark Antman; (r), Tabuteau/The Image Works; REVISIONS 22 (tr), Tabuteau/The Image Works; (bcr), Robert Fried/Stock Boston; (br), Maratea/International Stock Photography; REVISIONS 24 (tl), HRW Photo/Columbia Photo; (tc), HRW Photo/Sam Dudgeon; (tr), HRW Photo; (bc, br), Digital Image copyright © 2004 PhotoDisc; REVISIONS 25 (tc, tr), Digital Image copyright © 2004 Artville; (br), HRW Photo/Victoria Smith; (bc), HRW Photo; REVISIONS 26 (all), HRW Photo/Sam Dudgeon; REVISIONS 27 (t), HRW Photo/Sam Dudgeon; (b,c), HRW Photo/Victoria Smith.

ADDITIONAL VOCABULARY R9 (tl, bl), HRW Photo/Sam Dudgeon; R9 (br, br inset), Digital imagery® ©2003 PhotoDisc, Inc.; R9 (tr 1 and 2), Digital imagery® © 2003 PhotoDisc, Inc.; R9 (tr 3 and 4), HRW Photo/Sam Dudgeon; R10 (cr), HRW Photo/Russell Dian; R10 (remaining), Digital imagery® © 2003 PhotoDisc, Inc.; R11 (tl, bl), Corbis Images; R11 (tr), HRW Photo/Michelle Bridwell; R11 (cl), HRW Photo/Sam Dudgeon; R11 (cr, bc, br), Digital imagery® © 2003 PhotoDisc, Inc.; R12 (t), Corbis Images; R12 (bl, br), Digital imagery® © 2003 PhotoDisc, Inc.; R13 (cr), © Digital Vision; R13 (remaining), Digital imagery® © 2003 PhotoDisc, Inc.; R14 (tl, bl, bc), Digital imagery® © 2003 PhotoDisc, Inc.; R14 (tr), Corbis Images; R14 (br), EyeWire, Inc. Image Club Graphics ©1997 Adobe Systems, Inc.

ILLUSTRATION AND CARTOGRAPHY CREDITS

Abbreviations used: (t) top, (b) bottom, (l) left, (r) right, (c) center.

All art, unless otherwise noted, by Holt, Rinehart & Winston.

PRELIMINARY CHAPTER: Page xxiii, GeoSystems; xxiv, GeoSystems; xxv, GeoSystems; 6, Bruce Roberts; 9, Ellen Beier; 11, Jocelyne Bouchard.

LOCATION: POITIERS
Chapter One: Page 12, MapQuest.com; 22, Vincent Rio; 23, Jocelyne Bouchard; 26, Jocelyne Bouchard; 27, Yves Larvor; 28, Camille Meyer; 29, Yves Larvor; 30, MapQuest.com; 31, Yves Larvor; 33, Vincent Rio; 49, Yves Larvor. **Chapter Two:** Page 51, Yves Larvor; 52 (t), Bruce Roberts; 52 (b), Brian Stevens; 54, Bruce Roberts; 56, Pascal Garnier; 58, Keith Petrus; 59, Guy Maestracci; 60, MapQuest.com; 62, Brian Stevens; 72, Bruce Roberts. **Chapter Three:** Page 79, Yves Larvor; 80, Vincent Rio; 81, Michel Loppé; 82, Brian Stevens; 83, MapQuest.com; 84, Brian Stevens; 87, Vincent Rio; 89, Michel Loppé; 90, Jean-Pierre Foissy; 91, Michel Loppé; 94, Brian Stevens; 100, Bruce Roberts.

LOCATION: QUEBEC
Chapter Four: Page 102, MapQuest.com; 113, Michel Loppé; 115, Yves Larvor; 117, Jocelyne Bouchard; 118, Brian Stevens; 119, Jocelyne Bouchard; 120, MapQuest.com; 134, Jocelyne Bouchard.

LOCATION: PARIS
Chapter Five: Page 136, MapQuest.com; 145, Andrew Bylo; 146, Vincent Rio; 147, Jocelyne Bouchard; 148, Vincent Rio; 149, Camille Meyer; 150, MapQuest.com; 155, Guy Maestracci; 156, Jean-Pierre Foissy; 161, Vincent Rio; 166, Yves Larvor. **Chapter Six:** Page 174, Jocelyne Bouchard; 177 (t), Yves Larvor; 177 (c), Guy Maestracci; 178, MapQuest.com; 179, Jean-Pierre Foissy; 180, Brian Stevens; 181, Jean-Pierre Foissy; 183, Jean-Pierre Foissy; 184, Jocelyne Bouchard; 193, Guy Maestracci; 196 (t), Jocelyne Bouchard, 196 (b), Guy Maestracci. **Chapter Seven:** Page 203, Vincent Rio; 206 (cr), Guy Maestracci; 206 (b), Jocelyne Bouchard; 207, Vincent Rio; 208, Pascal Garnier; 209, Brian Stevens; 210, Jean-Pierre Foissy; 211, Vincent Rio; 212, MapQuest.com; 213 (tr), Pascal Garnier; 213 (br), Guy Maestracci; 214 (t), Vincent Rio; 214 (b), Pascal Garnier; 218, Jocelyn Bouchard; 223, Guy Maestracci; 224, Pascal Garnier.

LOCATION: ABIDJAN
Chapter Eight: Page 226, MapQuest.com; 235, Yves Larvor; 236, Camille Meyer; 237, George Kimani; 239, MapQuest.com; 240, Andrew Bylo; 242, Yves Larvor; 246 (t), Michel Loppé; 246 (b), Jocelyne Bouchard; 247, Michel Loppé; 248 (bl), George Kimani; 248 (tr), Jocelyne Bouchard; 254, George Kimani; 255, Yves Larvor; 258, Yves Larvor.

LOCATION: ARLES
Chapter Nine: Page 260, MapQuest.com; 269, Jean-Pierre Foissy; 271, Camille Meyer; 273, Guy Maestracci; 272, Jocelyne Bouchard; 278, MapQuest.com; 280, Brian Stevens; 285, Vincent Rio; 290, Jocelyne Bouchard. **Chapter Ten:** Page 297, Jocelyne Bouchard; 298 (c), Michel Loppé; 298 (t), Yves Larvor; 299, Vincent Rio; 300, Jean-Pierre Foissy; 305, MapQuest.com; 306, Jean-Pierre Foissy; 268 (t), Brian Stevens; 268 (c), Jocelyne Bouchard; 270, Jean-Pierre Foissy; 307, Michel Loppé; 308, Guy Maestracci; 310, Jean-Pierre Foissy; 320, Yves Larvor. **Chapter Eleven:** Page 327 (c), Brian Stevens; 327 (b), Russell Moore; 328, Guy Maestracci; 332, MapQuest.com; 333, Michel Loppé; 334, Yves Larvor; 336, Jean-Pierre Foissy; 343, Bruce Roberts; 344, Yves Larvor; 354, Yves Larvor.

LOCATION: FORT-DE-FRANCE
Chapter Twelve: Page 350, MapQuest.com; 361, Anne de Masson; 363, Anne de Masson; 364, Jean-Pierre Foissy; 366, Brian Stevens; 367, MapQuest.com; 369, Anne Stanley; 370, Anne de Masson; 371, Anne de Masson; 372, Anne Stanley; 377, Yves Larvor; 379, Anne Stanley; 380, Anne de Masson; 381, Anne de Masson; 382, Anne de Masson.

REVISIONS: REVISIONS 2, Ellen Beier; REVISIONS 3 (c), Yves Larvor; REVISIONS 3 (br), Guy Maestracci; REVISIONS 12, Yves Larvor; REVISIONS 14, Brian Stevens; REVISIONS 23, Jean-Pierre Foissy.